Great Expectations

In *Great Expectations: The Sociology of Survival and Success in Organized Team Sports*, sociological analysis proves to be a powerful ally for grasping how the sports world unfolds for team players, providing a range of sociological ideas and concepts that extend throughout the book. The text boxes and class discussion sections help summarize key issues, linking important sociological concepts to the topics at hand. The eight chapters begin with an introduction and then detail athletes' activities at different stages in their development.

Christopher B. Doob is professor emeritus of sociology at Southern Connecticut State University. His published works include *Sociology: An Introduction, 6th Edition* (1999); *Social Inequality and Social Stratification in U.S. Society* (2012); *Race, Ethnicity, and the Urban American Mainstream* (2004); and *Racism: An American Cauldron, 3rd Edition* (1998), the second edition of which received a Myers Center Award for the Study of Human Rights. In addition, Doob has been active in his community, serving as coordinator for the Southern Connecticut State University's Urban Initiatives, which established math tutoring classes for inner-city children. He has also participated in the struggle for welfare rights and been a long-time volunteer in two local adult education programs.

Great Expectations
The Sociology of Survival and Success in Organized Team Sports

Christopher B. Doob

NEW YORK AND LONDON

First published 2018
by Routledge
711 Third Avenue, New York, NY 10017

and by Routledge
2 Park Square, Milton Park, Abingdon, Oxon, OX144RN

Routledge is an imprint of the Taylor & Francis Group, an informa business

© 2018 Taylor & Francis

The right of Christopher B. Doob to be identified as author of this work has been asserted by him in accordance with sections 77 and 78 of the Copyright, Designs and Patents Act 1988.

All rights reserved. No part of this book may be reprinted or reproduced or utilised in any form or by any electronic, mechanical, or other means, now known or hereafter invented, including photocopying and recording, or in any information storage or retrieval system, without permission in writing from the publishers.

Trademark notice: Product or corporate names may be trademarks or registered trademarks, and are used only for identification and explanation without intent to infringe.

Library of Congress Cataloging-in-Publication Data
A catalog record for this book has been requested

ISBN: 978-1-138-48892-2 (hbk)
ISBN: 978-1-138-48896-0 (pbk)
ISBN: 978-1-351-03902-4 (ebk)

Typeset in Adobe Caslon by
Servis Filmsetting Ltd, Stockport, Cheshire

Contents

Preface	VIII
Acknowledgements	XI
Introduction: Athletes' Journey in Organized Sports	**1**
Historical Events in the Development of Organized Sports	4
The Structure of Organized Sports Programs	11
Conclusion	24
Summary	26
Class Discussion Issues	28
1 In the Beginning: Is It Enough Just to Have Fun?	**34**
The Growth of Young Children's Sports Programs	35
The Terrain for Children's Organized Sports	40
Young Athletes' Sports-related Struggles	46
Conclusion	56
Summary	57
Class Discussion Issues	59

2 Teens in Triumph and Turmoil: Adolescents' Organized Sports — 65
Teen Sports: Historical Growth of High-school Play — 67
Adolescents' Efforts to Advance in Organized Sports — 75
Conclusion — 94
Summary — 95
Class Discussion Issues — 97

3 One Level Down: College and Minor-league Sports Programs — 104
The Organizational Growth of College Sports and the Minor Leagues — 106
The Kingpins: Big-time Football and Basketball — 114
Other Elite Programs in College Sports — 124
College or the Minor Leagues? — 128
A Special Case — 138
Conclusion: A Pair of Issues about College Athletes' Just Treatment — 142
Summary — 143
Class Discussion Issues — 145

4 Scaling the Heights: Players in the Four Major Leagues — 154
The Historical Growth of the Top Professional Leagues — 156
Distinctive Careers by the Numbers — 164
The Big Leagues: Taking on the Challenge — 167
Conclusion: What Happens in Pro Sports Seldom Stays in Pro Sports — 195
Summary — 197
Class Discussion Issues — 199

5 WITHOUT FAME AND FORTUNE: PRO TEAM SPORTS AT THE MARGINS — 210
- THE HISTORY OF THE NICHE LEAGUES — 212
- GROWING PAINS FOR THE NICHE SPORTS — 220
- CONCLUSION — 231
- SUMMARY — 233
- CLASS DISCUSSION ISSUES — 234

6 STARS WHO WEREN'T SUPPOSED TO MAKE IT — 242
- REASONS WHY SOME PROSPECTS ARE EXCLUDED, AT LEAST TEMPORARILY — 244
- COACHES' TACTICS IN SINGLING OUT SOME PROSPECTS WHO WERE INITIALLY OVERLOOKED OR NEARLY SO — 253
- CONCLUSION — 262
- SUMMARY — 263
- CLASS DISCUSSION ISSUES — 263

7 A NEW PLAYBOOK: THE CHALLENGE OF RETIREMENT FROM PROFESSIONAL SPORTS — 267
- PLAYERS' ADJUSTMENT TO POST-RETIREMENT CHALLENGES — 270
- SUCCESSFUL POST-CAREER EMPLOYMENT — 275
- EX-PROS STILL LINKED DIRECTLY TO THE GAME — 279
- CONCLUSION: A PRELIMINARY LOOK AT COLLEGE ATHLETES' RETIREMENT — 285
- SUMMARY — 287
- CLASS DISCUSSION ISSUES — 288

SOCIOLOGICAL CONCEPTS AND IDEAS — 294
INDEX — 299

Preface

This book examines the modern American sports world and its team programs for different levels of players. Elite participants involved in team sports are the primary focus, beginning with organized activities for young children and continuing to the professional ranks. These athletes undertake a journey, varying in length from short, even abruptly so, to sometimes as much as several decades in length.

At each level of advancement, the necessity of survival forces athletes to face more formidable competition along with the frequent risk of injury, burnout, or disruptive relations with coaches, teammates, and (at the youth level) parents.

Organized sports often develop in a pressure-laden context, with about 70 percent of young athletes leaving programs by the age of 13, primarily because of burnout. Survivors face an intimidating numbers game—four or fewer chances in 100 of high-school athletes joining a Division I program in a popular sport and a miniscule one chance in 1,000 of reaching the majors. The few who attain the big leagues in the most popular sports have short careers, about three to five years. The overall prospects are forbidding, and yet large numbers of parents, coaches, and the young athletes themselves commit to the demanding prospect of school sports, local programs, travel teams, and tournaments, fervently striving for big-time success.

Once I discussed the quest for fame and fortune in sports with an experienced pediatrician who had witnessed numerous parents encouraging or pressuring their children to succeed at the Division I or pro levels. I asked him if the parents realized what a long shot they are promoting. "The numbers are so daunting," he said, "that they simply avoid a realistic look." In the upcoming chapters, ample evidence bolsters that conclusion.

Sociological analysis proves helpful in understanding such responses to sports programs. The renowned sociologist C. Wright Mills asserted that the field of sociology "enables us to grasp history and biography and the relations between the two within society" (Mills 1959, 6). Mills's reference to history was a broad one, including in the upcoming volume history in the conventional sense but also incorporating other contextual influences like community, family, coaches, teachers, and teammates along with such individual traits as athletes' age, gender, race, ethnicity, and social class. The historical dimension recognizes that since the middle of the 20th century national and local political and economic leadership has often promoted an expanded role for organized sports, with an enlarged emphasis on winning and the development of elite programs often linked to such commercial enterprises as shoe and apparel companies, travel teams, and out-of-school tournaments and, of course, revenue-expanding college and professional teams.

Since entering sociology I have found Mills's perspective useful, and as a result the introduction and the following five chapters begin with an historical section that provides some background for and insight into contemporary sports programming and then in each case follows up with what Mills considered biographical material examining the factors influencing modern athletes' involvement in organized sports programs.

The introduction contains a general framework for athletes in organized team sports, featuring three stages players encounter within a given sports program. Succinct references to these stages sometimes appear in the subsequent five chapters, which cover different levels of organized sports. In addition, individual chapters mostly introduce a concept or idea that proves useful in guiding the analysis of the subject at hand.

The 11 sports included in the book are for males' football, baseball, basketball, hockey, soccer, and lacrosse and for females' basketball, fast-pitch softball, volleyball, soccer, and lacrosse. From youth programs to the pro level, these are arguably the most popular sports. For instance, all five of the female sports are included in the top ten most frequently played in high school, and five of the six male sports possess established pro leagues that are two decades or older in duration.

Besides the number and level of sports covered, the text supplies extensive coverage of research from several disciplines, case-study material, survey data, photos, and detailed references to players that should make reading it both enjoyable and stimulating, promoting retention of the material as well as a grasp of the relationship between sociological concepts and ideas and players' experiences. The tables, boxes, and suggestions for class discussion pinpoint key issues, sometimes linking important sociological concepts to the topics at hand.

There are eight chapters, beginning with an introduction and then detailing athletes' activities at different stages in their development. In addition, one chapter focuses on athletes who unexpectedly became stars and another on retired pros' lives. The book offers a distinctive perspective on players' thoughts and actions as they strive to survive and succeed in organized sports.

Reference

Mills, C. Wright. 1959. *The Sociological Imagination*. New York: Oxford University Press.

ACKNOWLEDGEMENTS

The following individuals have contributed insights or information that have distinctly enriched this project: Jim DeLucia, Dick DeNicola, Pete Low, Brian Molloy, Pete Spadora, and Enrique Tello. Four talented members of the Taylor & Francis team—Samantha Barbaro, Alaina Christensen, James Darley, and Erik Zimmerman—have significantly contributed to the book's quality. As always Teresa Carballal has been a deft reader and commenter, making an understated contribution that has been incalculable.

The author would like to thank the reviewers for their valuable insights on the text:

Eric Wright, Indiana University Bloomington
Rachel Allison, Mississippi University
Ruben Buford May, Texas A&M University
Richard King, Washington State University
Jeff Montez de Oca, University of Colorado, Colorado Springs
Kyle Green, Utica College
Barry Truchil, Rider University

INTRODUCTION
ATHLETES' JOURNEY IN ORGANIZED SPORTS

In the case of *NCAA v. Board of Regents of the University of Oklahoma*, the University of Oklahoma and the University of Georgia sued the National Collegiate Athletic Association for the right to negotiate their own television contracts for college football, avoiding NCAA control. Associate Justice Byron Raymond "Whizzer" White, an all-American halfback and Heisman Trophy runner-up, dissented, indicating that the NCAA was a nonprofit educational association composed of nearly 800 nonprofit colleges and universities and involved over 100 nonprofit athletic conferences. White wrote, "Although some of the NCAA's activities, viewed in isolation, bear a resemblance to those undertaken by professional sports leagues and associations, the Court errs in treating intercollegiate athletics under the NCAA's control as a purely commercial venture in which colleges and universities participate solely, or even primarily, in the pursuit of profits. Accordingly, I dissent" (JUSTIA: US Supreme Court 1984).

White's position would have prevailed in earlier times, but organizations often change their approaches and goals. Because of the ruling in this case, big-time universities have developed football and basketball programs that have become huge moneymakers, bringing in unprecedented revenues, enriching many prominent coaches, and also encouraging a host of rule infractions as officials on some of the high-profile teams cut corners to maintain or increase their winning ways. Smaller organizations, such as local youth sports programs, can also change significantly, sometimes quickly.

The case just cited illustrates what writer George Packer has called "the unwinding"—a society-wide process starting to reveal itself in mid-20th century America where many of the structures that bound people together—communities, businesses, farms, political organizations, religious groups, colleges, schools, and more—began to decline and sometimes collapse, losing vitality for and control over their members. While many people might find themselves without support they previously experienced, the unwinding process can prove beneficial as in the case of big-time college football and basketball programs in *NCAA v. Board of Regents of the University of Oklahoma*. Packer wrote,

> The unwinding brings freedom, more than the world has ever granted, and to more kinds of people than ever before ... And with freedom the unwinding brings its illusions ... Winning and losing are all-American games, and in the unwinding winners win bigger than ever, floating away like bloated dirigibles, and losers have a long way to fall before they hit bottom, and sometimes they never do.
>
> (Packer 2013, 3–4)

Ample evidence in these chapters supports these conclusions, which are consistent with Mills's ideas about locating events in the context of history and biography mentioned in the preface. As far as organized sports are concerned, the unwinding process has been a steadily evolving historical condition, with teams and athletes relentlessly competing to win, often involving very young players. Yet as ample material included in these chapters indicates, many researchers, parents, and coaches are often concerned about and resistant to such win-at-all-cost tendencies, making sustained, thoughtful efforts to develop sports programs that are an enjoyable, fairly relaxed experience for young people of varied talent levels. Differences of opinion, even conflict on these issues is apparent throughout youth sports.

Sports programs involve different levels of formal organizations. A *formal organization* is a group possessing clearly stated rules, well defined members' roles, and distinct objectives. Organized sports include regulatory bodies like the NCAA, athletic associations, conferences, and also teams. Sports teams are formal organizations that provide the setting for the activities in which the athletes discussed in these chapters are engaged. This introduction focuses on sports programs generally, briefly discussing stages within programs where players of all ages and skills, from five- and six-year-olds to professionals, must compete well in order to be successful.

It is important to consider a couple of points about organized sports that will remain relevant throughout these chapters. First, while the formal structure is a fundamental reality in sports teams' activities, informal elements can also shape them. For instance, on a particular high-school or college team the head coach on paper might be the chief authority, but in practices and during games an assistant coach is much better liked and respected, and so when players seek advice on most team-related matters they are much more likely to turn to that individual than the head coach (Bruce 2013, 104–05; Doob 2000, 115).

Second, as formal organizations, teams involve a power dimension, which affects such issues as how team leaders relate to players. Whether administrators or coaches, those in charge are committed to getting participants to abide by their wishes. As sports programs have matured, the number of organizations competing for teams' or leagues' interests or their regulation tends to expand. Inevitably these structures possess unequal power (Eitzen and Sage 2009, 196), and often, as in the case of the University of Oklahoma football team, certain organizations find it useful to challenge the current system and seek greater power and the rewards that go with it.

Another basic concept, which links to organized sports, is *role*—the expected behaviors associated with a particular social position (Doob 2000, 129–30; Merton 1968, 41). In this book the roles involve players in primarily elite organized team sports. Survival and success are basic demands of the game—the emphasis on remaining active participants by moving up through advancing levels and improving in increasingly competitive settings. Besides the athletes themselves, parents are heavily invested in their children's sports programs, and coaches are an essential element. While learning roles entails developing skills and understanding and complying with certain significant individuals' expectations, it also can include such emotional challenges as becoming comfortable playing a new position.

This introduction examines the common stages within all organized sports programs while the following five chapters focus on athletes' performance at different levels, beginning with young children. Looking back at early American sports activity, it is clear that it has become considerably more organized and complex, and yet some continuity is apparent, involving, for instance, teens' frequent enthusiastic participation and also pressures from various sources to change and improve programs.

Historical Events in the Development of Organized Sports

In 2015 the nation spent an estimated $5 billion on athletes' programs, sports tutoring, travel teams, and uniforms and equipment for youths of high-school age and younger (Hyman 2015; University of Florida 2015), underscoring the significance that sports currently possess in Americans' lives. Such an emphasis on youth sports programs contrasts sharply with the distant beginnings of sports activity in what became American society—in particular, the early Puritan settlements where religion was a dominant force, and leaders were often concerned that play could represent "idleness," failing to serve the family, community, or God. A pair of psychologists noted, "[A]s late as 1792, the Methodist Church of America, worried that the serious mission of life was threatened, warned that children 'shall be indulged with nothing which the world calls play. Let this rule be observed with the strictest nicety; for those who play when they are young, will play when they are old'" (Lehman and Witty 1927, 2).

Among the Puritans, however, this position was not always dominant. Many enjoyed a good time, celebrating and attending festivals where they sang songs and entertained with stories. With parental permission children even played games (*USHistory.org* 2016).

Throughout the colonial era, children were more likely to occupy themselves with improvised playthings than to play games. Whether made by parents or more likely the children themselves, these items were whittled from wood or fashioned from cloth to produce objects for fantasy skits (Chudacoff 2007, 32). Frequently in their rigidly structured world, children's play replicated gender roles, with boys often carving weapons, tools, and horses, prominent elements in the male world, while girls at play tended to engage in activities that mimicked women's domestic work. A minister, for example, observed a friend's young daughter "tying strings to a chair and walking back and forth with them in order to simulate the spinning of yarn ... [and] getting rags and washing them without water to imitate the washing of clothes" (Chudacoff 2007, 33).

During the 19th century, a vigorous religious support for sports developed. Ministers and their male allies—so-called "muscular Christians"—endorsed a balanced development involving body, mind, and spirit and emphasized outdoor competitive and recreational activities. The Young Men's Christian Association (YMCA) was one of the first organizations to produce competitive youth sports programming, underscoring the importance of drawing young males into healthy activities and away from alcoholism and other destructive activities that they might find tempting when leaving farms for the alleged dangers of urban life (Albrecht and Strand 2010, 16). In short, the muscular Christians initiated influential practices in mainstream America, emphasizing that sports could play a significant part in young people's lives.

College football with its highly violent game represented the epitome of this sporting manliness. Were the country's leaders concerned about the growing number of serious injuries and deaths? Not in the late 1890s. They felt that the violence of football was essential in a highly urbanized society that seemed to be making men increasingly effeminate.

In 1885 Theodore Roosevelt, who eventually supported the reform of college football, wrote, "I would a hundred fold rather keep the game as it is now, with the brutality, than give it up." The future president asserted that a leader "can't be efficient unless he is manly," and he suggested the game's rough play promoted that essential quality (McQuilkin and Smith 1993, 59). Roughness was an understatement. Coaches encouraged "on-field savagery includ[ing] late hits, punching, kneeing, eye-gouging and vicious blows to the windpipe – often proved fatal" (Davis 2010). A reassessment was in the offing.

Two decades later 18 men died in college and semipro games, and opposition to the vicious play increased. In an article published in the June and July 1905 issues of *McClure's Magazine* entitled "The College

Athlete," Henry Beech Needham, a crusading journalist, brought the brutal, scandalous condition of the college game to public attention. Needham was a friend of President Roosevelt who became involved in promoting reform as he appreciated the game's growing brutality. Roosevelt was blunt, reversing his earlier support for rough, even violent play. "I demand that football change its rules or be abolished," Roosevelt said. "Change the game or forsake it!" (Davis 2010).

Several weeks after the football season, representatives from 60 eastern and midwestern colleges convened, creating a rules committee which increased the number of yards for a first down from five to ten, expanded the number of attempts to achieve a first down from three to four, and legalized the forward pass, which would spread players and mitigate the use of brute force. While violence was frequent, the motivation for the reforms was difficult to determine. Assessing the reformers, one historian suggested that they were less concerned about carnage on the field, which he concluded was exaggerated and sensationalized, than the state of the game, which they believed was becoming too commercial and corrupted, with recruitment violations and illicit subsidies for supposed amateur athletes (Smith 2011, 50; Watterson 2000). Regardless of the reformers' motives, one important outcome was clear: That the year after the reforms the number of deaths did not decline. In fact, what the reforms appeared to accomplish was to placate the college and university officials thinking about shutting down their football programs, and as a result the public uproar produced by that threat calmed down (Gordon 2014), creating, in fact, a more tranquil atmosphere in which the game over time became gradually less violent. Clearly the college football situation in the early 20th century illustrates the previous point about formal organizations, indicating that as sports programs develop, different groups with conflicting points of view will clash over various issues involving them.

Certainly that can also be the case with children's programs. At the turn of the 20th century, organized sports for children were starting to develop. New York City's Public School Athletic League provided boys' programs involving three levels of proficiency along with options to engage in sports within the school or outside of it. Programs also developed for girls, but they only involved activities within their own schools.

By 1910 various American cities started recreation programs which provided not only playgrounds but facilities for such games as soccer, hockey, football, and swimming. A popular theory of play indicated that in team sports young men "develop their self-perceptions of self-sacrifice, obedience, self-control, and loyalty," prized traditional outlooks which program advocates feared could readily be lost in the industrial era (Albrecht and Strand 2010, 16–17).

As the 20th century progressed, a number of volunteer organizations, some of which were backed by successful businesses, became involved in children's organized sports. Independent from the public-school system, the leaders of these programs wanted to establish themselves as major players in the future of youth sports. Two influential organizations have been Pop Warner football, founded in 1929, and Little League baseball, started in 1939 (Albrecht and Strand 2010, 17). Little League involved not only playing baseball but like public programs also emphasized such important values as "citizenship, sportsmanship, and manhood" (Albrecht and Strand 2010, 18).

By the 1950s youth sports programs started to proliferate, changing the early athletic activity for millions of children, who in previous decades had little or no exposure to organized play. Parents' reasons for favoring organized youth sports have included the necessity to find programs for their children during working hours, the longtime conviction that athletics are a positive developmental experience, the sometimes fervent hope of having one's offspring join the ranks of celebrated and wealthy athletes, and the concern that without supervised play children, particularly boys, can readily either encounter dangers or get into trouble (Coakley 2006, 154). With the possibility of college scholarships and even a professional career, a growing number of parents have provided their children a variety of often costly sports programs, including sports-oriented schools, tutoring sessions, or travel teams, all of which can help develop elite athletes, who often visualize themselves as youths headed for the pros (Bowers, Chalip, and Green 2010, 175). As unwinding was expanding throughout society, it has become increasingly apparent in youth sports where high-level programs often separate talented youths from their mainstream peers.

For instance, IMG Academy contains some of the most successful high-school sports programs. It's a boarding school where students attend courses in the morning and then spend the rest of the day engaged in their sport. The facility is located in Bradenton, Florida, and enrolls athletes playing baseball, basketball, football, golf, lacrosse, soccer, tennis, track & field, and cross country (Bowers, Chalip, and Green 2010, 176). A notification from the school makes the somewhat confusing claim that while there are no scholarships, IMG provides some financial aid "based on an academic, athletic, character and financial review" (IMG Academy 2017). IMG and private schools of its ilk have the reputations, funds, and know-how to remain at the top of the high-school athletic heap. In 2017 the IMG football team had 22 seniors who would win full scholarships to Football Bowl Subdivision schools, which possess the nation's 130 most elite college football teams (Staples 2017).

While elite private schools recruit many top athletic prospects, public high schools can develop successful programs in such sports as baseball, fastpitch softball, basketball, and football. These teams are often well funded in part because of the public attention the best participants can create, winning college scholarships and bringing extensive media attention both to themselves and their communities (Bowers, Chalip, and Green 2010, 177).

To this point the focus has been on the history of amateur sports. In addition, the pro leagues possess their own histories. During the years directly following the Civil War, the only standard for athletes was amateurism. However, industry was flourishing, giving many Americans the money and time for entertainment, including professional baseball. The Cincinnati Red Stockings of 1869 were probably the most popular entry, traveling around the country winning 65 games and tying one and receiving an invitation to the White House where President Grant praised "the western Cinderella club" (Vecsey 2006, 24–25).

During that era there were professional teams but not yet any leagues. Then in 1871 the National Association of Professional Base Ball Players made the first effort to establish a pro league, but it failed, particularly in developing a sound economic plan and providing schedules that made it possible for teams to compete in an organized fashion. Intelligent organizational development, however, was about to materialize. Five years later following the *Chicago Tribune*'s emphatic request to reorganize the league, the leaders of what became the National League gathered, selecting affluent clubs located in prosperous midwestern and eastern cities, establishing a centrally imposed schedule, and creating the world's first financially successful sports league, one that has survived to modern times (Cain and Haddock 2005, 1120–21).

It was a beginning but a distinctly modest venture by modern standards. In 1900 during the league's 25th year, the eight National League teams had a mean per game attendance of 3,214 spectators (*Baseball. Reference.com* 2016). Three years later an agreement stated that representatives of the National League and the newly formed American League along with a permanent chairman would form a governing body of what is now Major League Baseball (MLB). This arrangement, however, proved unworkable, even corrupted, and it was not until 1921 when Judge Kenesaw Mountain Landis became the league's first commissioner that MLB became a stable operation (*MLB.com* 2017).

Eventually the other three major pro leagues followed—the National Football League (NFL), the National Basketball Association (NBA), and the National Hockey League (NHL). All had their early struggles, but as Chapter 4 indicates, those four professional team sports have been highly successful in gaining spectators and viewers and in making money for both owners and players. Success has been more modest for other professional team sports.

Among the remaining pro leagues examined in these chapters, the Women's National Basketball Association (WNBA) and Major League Soccer (MLS) have been the most successful, lasting over two decades and appearing likely to survive into the indefinite future. Chapter 5 focuses on these "niche" pro leagues—the WNBA, MLS, and leagues in three other sports.

Admittedly participation in a professional sports program versus one for young children involves vastly different experiences, and yet it becomes apparent that in both cases athletes who remain active in a specific program must deal with certain broadly similar issues in order to survive and succeed within it. Whether teens or pros, selected athletes historically, notably African Americans and women, have needed to confront certain challenges. In upcoming chapters there is discussion about major-league sports and discriminatory conditions black athletes have faced at various program levels. Now, however, the focus is on female sports.

Through the 1960s athletic programs for girls and women had much less funding and support than those for their male counterparts. Then in 1972 Congress passed Title IX, a law declaring that females of all ages in educational organizations receiving federal aid for any programs including sports programs would not encounter discriminatory treatment (Albrecht and Strand 2010, 18). Since the advent of Title IX, girls' and women's sports programs have enlarged and improved significantly. Despite the gains, however, research has found that sports participation rates for girls have remained 2 to 6 percent lower than for boys, with girls tending to start sports about a half-year later (The Aspen Institute: Project Play 2015).

Similar challenges for women are also apparent on the professional level. The WNBA, for instance, is a league that has produced mixed results. On the one hand, it is clearly the most successful women's professional league in US sports history, surviving for over two decades with 12 current franchises, but financially it is much less profitable than the men's major pro leagues in attendance and media coverage (DeMause 2014). Summary I.1 lists the principal issues covered in the historical section.

SUMMARY I.1

Some Historical Highlights in American Sports History

- The dominant belief in Puritan settlements that play and sports represented idleness that failed to serve God, the family, and the community; on the other hand, Puritan parents sometimes provided children permission to play games.
- In the 19th century, the so-called "muscular Christians" promoted a balanced development of mind, body, and spirit and emphasized outdoor competitive and recreational play.
- College football the epitome of a new flowering of sports, with the game representing an avenue for late-19th-century men to escape the supposed effeminate impact of an increasingly urbanized world. However, as the game became increasingly more violent and players' deaths mounted, representatives from 60 colleges met to reform it, with limited short-term effects.
- Early in the 20th century, various cities began developing organized sports for both boys and girls, supported by the underlying idea that such activities encouraged young men to develop a set of highly desirable traits. In addition,

- volunteer programs, sometimes with substantial financial backing, formed, and two of those organizations remain active today—Pop Warner football and Little League baseball.
- Modern young people's organized programming represents a combination of private and public programs: IMG Academy, one of the most successful private schools recruiting top athletes. On the other hand, public-school entries in sports like fastpitch softball and football can win top athletes college scholarships, and the accompanying acclaim can produce enthusiastic support in local communities.
- The passage of Title IX has promoted girls' and women's programs in sports and other areas, and yet girls' participation in organized sports still lags behind boys'.
- The National League founded in 1876 has been the first lasting professional league, and eventually highly successful pro leagues in football, basketball, and hockey followed. Outside of those four, no other pro leagues have had substantial economic success although the WNBA and MLS have remained for over two decades.

Whether the focus is on female or male athletes, an element in the organized sports world is the role of competition, which becomes more intense as young athletes join progressively more elite units in their adolescent squads, college teams, and for a select few the professional ranks. As players move into more advanced programs, the chances of survival decline. A miniscule number—for men's football, basketball, hockey, and soccer and women's basketball fewer than one in a thousand high-school prospects—reach the top league in their sport (NCAA 2013). Yet as we will see many commit themselves to advancing as far as possible in their game, carrying on against increasingly formidable odds.

The Structure of Organized Sports Programs

Whether players are children aged five or six, professionals, or at some level in between, competent coaches seek to improve their skills, understanding of their sport, and overall performance (Green 2005, 234). The fact that the teams in question are formal organizations means that they usually require fairly structured roles, practices that can be repetitious and tedious, playing time adjusted to athletes' level of competence, and the game under officials' control. The challenges to the players discussed in the upcoming pages will appear many times in subsequent chapters.

The first stage in an organized program involves enrollment—a condition that becomes harder to achieve as players confront recruitment at increasingly higher levels. The second stage is retention by a team, an outcome that requires a combination of personal investment and assistance from key individuals. The third stage is advancement from the program at hand (American Psychological Association 2017; Ericsson, Krampe, and Tesch-Römer 1993; Green 2005).

The Enrollment/Recruitment Stage in Sports Organizations

"Enrollment" seems the appropriate general term, including, for instance, youthful participants who join a largely open program. However, in referring to players who advance to elite status, the word "recruitment" appears preferable, involving selection from among a set of candidates, with some, perhaps many failing to qualify.

Significant individuals such as parents and friends can encourage young people to join sports programs. Once involved in a particular game, participants often find that their new teammates can help solidify their sense of involvement. Sometimes, however, developing relationships and role identities are insufficient to recruit athletes to a sport because of such distractions as a different sport, work, social life, or another activity. Studies have indicated that such alternative attractions can become more powerful during the teen years. A well-documented means of countering such distractions is to introduce children to sports at youthful ages, starting to develop their commitment at that time (Green 2005, 237).

That strategy, however, can also contain a downside. The Mayo Clinic has cautioned that very young children, say four- and five-year-olds, often have not developed abilities for organized sports, and as a result they are unlikely to be strongly motivated. When they are between six and nine, their vision, attention span, and ability to follow directions markedly improve, making them better candidates for participating in such games as softball, baseball, or soccer (Mayo Clinic 2017).

Enrollment in preteen organized sports can be relatively relaxed, generally less competitive than it is for college teams. To observers it might seem likely that in Division I the competitive desire to recruit the best team possible would involve a focus on players' skills, but that is not necessarily team officials' priority. "We look for character first when we look

These children, perhaps aged nine or ten, are likely to possess the attention span and the ability to follow directions that make them good candidates for team play. (Source: Monkey Business Images / Shutterstock.com)

at an athlete," director of player personnel Geoff Martzen at Brigham Young University said. "They have to have the character to make it in the program, then the athletics" (Magre 2013).

Once enrolled in a program, an athlete faces the prospect of joining it as an active member.

The Retention Stage in Sports Programs

This phase has three components—motivation, commitment, and the influence of agents of socialization (Ericsson, Krampe, and Tesch-Römer 1993, 370–72; Green 2005, 238–43). Participants who effectively deal with these three issues are well positioned to develop both the athletic and interpersonal skills that allow them to be successful in their current level of organized sports.

— *Motivation*

Athletes join sports programs only if they value them. Effective motives include excitement resulting from participating in the sport, interaction and friendship with teammates, skill development, and improved conditioning. For most participants, particularly young children, such outcomes as winning games and procuring prizes prove less compelling.

While clearly people involved in sports perceive the benefit of participation, there is limited knowledge about the specifics producing such positive outcomes—for instance, the idea of having fun playing games. It's a frequently used phrase applied to sports programs, but its meaning appears to vary widely from one setting to another (Green 2005, 238–39).

What is readily apparent, however, is that not having fun can dishearten youthful participants and devastate programs. The National Alliance for Youth Sports, which is a nonprofit organization that provides various programs and services for parents, coaches, and administrators involved in childhood athletics, has indicated that about 70 percent of children in sports programs quit by the age of 13 (Miner 2016; O'Sullivan 2013). An official of the organization suggested that a number of specific reasons appear to contribute to the outcome, but that "[M]ost of the reasons boil down to one thing--that the child does not find the sport fun anymore" (Dilworth 2015). It's an exposure to unraveling that young participants tend to find intolerable.

A professor of marketing indicated that if 70 percent of Walmart customers left the company's stores and vowed never to return, the leadership would quickly adjust, producing a more productive approach. Nothing comparable, however, has materialized with youth sports (Wallace 2016). An implication of the professor's observation seems to be that greater tolerance for organizations' ineffectiveness exists when the financial stakes are fairly low than when they are high. Yet beyond the financial consideration, supporters of sports' potential contribution to young people's lives can readily argue the importance of improved programming.

One researcher has suggested a reorganization to improve children's sports programs might begin by listening to children participating in them. Amanda J. Visek, an associate professor at the School of Public Health at George Washington University, asked 142 female and male soccer players, three-quarters of whom also played other sports, what were the most prominent factors making organized sports fun. It turned out that at the top of the list were "being a good sport," "trying hard," and "positive coaching" while winning, often believed to be the dominant condition making sports fun and many parents' top choice, came near the bottom of the 81 determinants of fun included in the study (Milken Institute School of Public Health, George Washington University 2014). Organized programs have formal objectives, and this study brings out the significant but often overlooked point that those objectives are often distinctly at odds with those the youthful clients have in mind.

Young dropouts from various sports programs often validate Visek's findings. After several years of youth sports, Kate, a talented but underperforming athlete, indicated that she was quitting. "I just can't take it anymore, coach," she said. "I think I am done playing." The coach considered possible reasons the girl might have for her decision—burnout, teammate relations, or perhaps even something about his coaching style. But then the girl explained. "It's my dad. He loves me and I know he only wants the best for me, but he just can't stop coaching me, in the car, and from the sideline each and every game. I can't play when he is around, and he insists on coming to every game, every road trip, you name it. It's like it's more important to him than to me." The coach indicated that clearly children like Kate are not having fun and that a major reason they no longer enjoy the experience is that they have lost ownership of it. Kate was convinced that it was her father and no longer she who was the chief beneficiary of the program. Like Kate sometimes the dropouts are talented athletes (O'Sullivan 2015).

While dropouts are common, especially in youth programs, many participants stay committed and, in fact, some who leave early return to organized sports at more advanced ages. These athletes generally display the second attribute of the retention stage.

— *Commitment*

Successful athletes make a commitment to programs when they value them sufficiently to decide that they deserve the investment of time and energy. Athletes are particularly likely to commit themselves if they feel that coaches and teammates appreciate their participation, making them feel like worthy contributors. In seeking to commit themselves to a sport in which they will specialize, young athletes are likely to consult with such influential sources as parents, siblings, coaches, teachers, or friends and end up choosing a sport which motivates them because they feel they can be successful, proving to be assets for the team (Petitpas, Cornelius, Raalte, and Jones 2005, 67–68; Scanlan, Russell, Wilson, and Scanlan, 2003; Stevenson 1990).

Gloria Balague, a sports psychologist, has worked with world-class athletes, primarily in rhythmic gymnastics and track & field. She has supported the idea that athletes can enhance their commitment by planning their program—in detail.

An essential preliminary step, Balague contended, involves the athletes themselves determining what are their specific values—those which they want to maintain, whether or not they are in line with what coaches, teammates, or others associated with the sport might choose.

Then keeping their values in mind, the athletes need to specify their goals, which "for the elite athlete should be specific, flexible, written down, and imagined" (Balague 1999, 90). The approach is distinctly concrete, emphasizing a "a step-by-step pathway" to attaining goals. Too often, the sports psychologist indicated, coaches and players set broad goals, perhaps involving an entire year. Instead Balague suggested that projected goals should represent "a clear, concrete knowledge of what to do at each practice" (Balague 1999, 91). Balague's approach has been developed with athletes in individual sports, but participants should also be able to use it as a productive exercise in team programs.

While elite athletes are bound to be involved in their sport, a select number of them are particularly committed. A study involving 33 research subjects in 22 international sports and including 15 Olympic or world champions focused on athletes displaying "mental toughness" as a key factor in the performance of their role—unyielding pursuit of a goal in spite of persistent problems along the way. The types of adversity these athletes needed to face included pain from high-level exertion or injury, distraction caused by recent personal tragedy, or some mishap in the course of competition.

The researchers referred to one athlete who epitomized mental toughness. The individual describing her was an elite respondent in the study. He said,

> She just had this ability to overcome adversity, she always did … and she would just find ways to push herself through whatever

she needs to push through ... I think her mother had died of cancer five or six years ago, and her brother got killed this year and she's somebody who always seems to emerge from beyond whatever she's dealing with, to get through it and surpass what anybody would think you could do. She's tough, she'll go that extra yard, that extra hard yard that most people won't.
(Middleton, Marsh, Martin, Richards, and Perry 2004)

Elite athletes are normally expected to possess a deep commitment to their sport, but whether professional or amateur, they sometimes find it hard to maintain it. Sports psychologists, however, can assist them by:

- using such mental techniques as visualization or relaxation procedures that can overcome various difficulties and improve their potential performance.
- helping athletes develop strategies to alleviate pressure from coaches, parents, and even from themselves.
- assisting individuals in making such adjustments to injury as developing more tolerance for pain, committing to physical-therapy regimens, or learning to live with being temporarily forced to be inactive.
- providing coaches for children's teams with tips for having fun in their programs and developing positive self-images during them (American Psychological Association 2017).

Sports psychologists are one of several influential groups that can affect players' participation in organized programs during the retention stage.

— *The Influence of Agents of Socialization*
A key concept related to this topic is *socialization*, which is a lifelong process of becoming a social being, learning the necessary culture content and behavior in the course of relations with people who supply influential guidance about established societal standards (Delaney and Madigan 2009, 82–83; Doob 2000, 145; Eitzen and Sage 2009, 64). For instance, in their ongoing involvement with organized sports, highly committed athletes are likely to seek advice from such agents of socialization as parents, coaches, teammates, or siblings (Green 2005, 242–43).

Sometimes siblings can play a particularly significant role in their sisters' and brothers' involvement in sports. A questionnaire given to 229 athletes aged 15 to 35 who participated in 34 sports and contained a segment of elite performers suggested that older siblings had a distinct effect on their younger sisters and brothers. Specifically, compared to non-elite athletes' younger siblings, elite athletes' younger sisters and brothers were four times more likely to engage in competitive sports and, in particular, more inclined to do so at an elite level (*Pathways to the Podium Research Project* 2012).

While siblings can be agents of socialization, parents and coaches are likely to be the most influential sources in children's sports programs. A research team specializing in sport management suggested that youthful athletes' parents should consider themselves as belonging to one of three components of a "sports triangle" featuring players, parents, and coaches who need "to work with each other to promote upbeat, productive programs" (Holden, Forester, Keshock, and Pugh 2015). In short, each individual within the sports triangle should make an effort to understand the other participants' role and to establish productive relations with them. Certainly parents' contribution is significant.

Parents tend to consider it their responsibility to locate effective, well-run sports programs for their children (Coakley 2006, 154–55). The cost of these programs along with other eventual expenses can mount up. Families of some elite athletes spend over $20,000 a year on local programs, camps, travel teams, transportation, hotels, equipment, and individual coaching. Not surprisingly a Sports & Fitness Industry survey indicated parents' income level has significantly affected their ability to support their children in organized-sports programs. While just 38 percent of children from households earning $25,000 a year or less participated in these activities, the figure rose sharply to 67 percent for families making $100,000 or more (The Aspen Institute: Project Play 2015).

Beyond their financial contribution, parents also affect their children's socialization to their sports programs, displaying a greater early influence than coaches, teachers, and peers. As new arrivals enter programs, they tend to be sensitive to their fathers' and mothers' assessment of their performance.

In spite of many parents' distinct contribution to their children's sports programs, some have been the objects of criticism. A survey of 250 youth coaches indicated that the distinct majority felt that a substantial number of parents were overbearing, focused above all else on winning. Seventy-five percent of the coaches felt that parents overemphasized the importance of winning, and 74 percent felt that this misplaced emphasis undermined the parent-child relationship. Commenting on the research, Dr. Amy Kaltzell, a sports psychologist, said, "The pressure on young athletes to play well has never been greater and parents often unwittingly make choices that value winning over the child's well-being" (Nadeau 2015).

In pressuring their children to win, parents can become boisterous and obnoxious. To mitigate the impact, some coaches have taken such measures as imposing standards of conduct and locating spectator sections as far as possible from the playing area. A team of researchers has suggested that if coaches require parents to hear about the destructive impact their actions can have as well as a detailed description of the kind of behavior their children distinctly prefer, it might give them valuable insight (Omli, LaVoi, and Wiese-Bjornstal 2008, 32).

While in the early years of sports programs parents often play a major role as agents of socialization, one frequent reality is that coaches and teammates become increasingly important during the adolescent phase (Fredericks and Eccles 2004; Taylor, Schweichler, Jorgensen, McKown, and Teresak 2014). Like parents, coaches have also been subjects of research. A team of sports psychologists indicated that coaches' abilities develop gradually and are situational—that someone who has worked with young children in a noncompetitive setting will have limited knowledge about training elite adolescent athletes. In addition, competent coaches approach their main tasks, namely organization, training, and competition, distinctly aware of their own strengths and weaknesses. Effective members of the profession are flexible, readily trying new and different ways of addressing players' needs (Côté, Young, North, and Duffy 2007, 5–6).

A particular challenge coaches often must face is that at about the age of 13, some athletes become more inclined to specialize in a single sport, developing its required skills and emphasizing competition and performance. Effective coaches engage in thorough needs assessment for these athletes, carefully picking drills and practices that will improve them (Côté, Young, North, and Duffy 2007, 11–12).

Some coaches, however, are ineffective, with a contributing factor being that about 90 percent of the 2.5 million volunteer coaches have received little or no training. It is a significant statistic because trained youth coaches display higher retention rates than their untrained counterparts (Beatty and Fawver 2013; Bornstein 2011). Parents are often worried about their children's coaching. In an *ESPN* survey, a nationally representative sample of 322 parents or guardians indicated that 82 percent of the respondents were doubtful about coaches' "quality or behavior" and 61 percent considered that factor "a big concern" (Farrey 2014).

Besides the assessment of coaches' individual performances, some analysts have considered national differences in coaching—for instance, Americans' versus Europeans' style of developing soccer players. Many coaches, both Europeans and Americans, contend that Americans can benefit from exposure to foreign experts, who generally play the game at a much more advanced level (Sokolove 2010).

The definition of formal organization indicated that the structures in question have distinct objectives, which with sports can vary sharply from one nation to another. American coaches are strongly inclined to emphasize winning games while their foreign counterparts tend to focus on a different pair of priorities—practice and individual instruction. José Ramón Alexanco, the director of the youth-training program for FC Barcelona, one of the top professional clubs in the world, addressed the issue of winning. "We don't demand that the youth teams win," said Alexanco. "We demand that they play good soccer. We don't use the word, 'winning'" (Woitalla 2009). A focus on winning, he concluded, is distinctly not the best way to improve players.

Whether it's a major-league career or an activity for 6-year-olds, organized-sports programs eventually end for players, and they either quit the sport or move on to a higher level.

The Advancement Stage

The end of a program does not assure players' advancement. Even if an athlete's performance seems to promise promotion to the next level, it is not inevitable (Green 2005, 244). He or she might be unable to get along with teammates or might flagrantly break team rules, and such conditions can block even an elite athlete's progress.

The advancement stage contains two major challenges. First, there are few sports-development organizations to assist players in making an effective adjustment to the new level. Candidates moving into more elevated programs often can benefit from help in playing at a more advanced level of athletic competition and meeting new role requirements. One challenge new recruits face is that they sometimes must engage in resocialization, relearning in the new setting the physical skills or social relationships they had previously performed. Without assistance from coaches or teammates, they can experience such painful reactions as a sense of stress or feelings of disorientation about the expectations they face in the new program (Green 2005, 247–48). This is a reality at all levels of organized sport, including athletes' advancement to top pro leagues.

Second, the advancement process might run more smoothly with supervision from government or such organizations as the NCAA. Unlike a number of other countries, American policymakers have tended to avoid government supervision of sports (Green 2005, 246–47), opening the door to the prospect of disorganized, even chaotic recruitment at the advancement stage of some programs. Such issues arise when youthful athletes are offered scholarships and enrollment in Division I programs, epitomizing the reality cited earlier that as sports programs develop, organizations', in this case teams', competition to promote their interests expands.

In 2014 after unofficial college visits, 100 freshmen and 12 eighth-graders had made nonbinding verbal commitments to Division I softball programs (Toppmeyer 2014). "It's going to get crazier before it gets much better if the NCAA does not step in," Texas coach Connie Clark said (Riddle 2014). Another veteran coach expressed a similar view about the need for NCAA regulation. "It's gotten crazy," said Bill Conroy, who had organized travel fastpitch teams for 15 years.

At a game in October, Lauren Rice, a seventh grader, who pitched 70 mph (the equivalent of 98 mph in baseball) in a high-school game, had coaches from the University of Missouri among the spectators. When

The college recruitment of fastpitch softball players can be frantic, with scouts and coaches converging on top high-school prospects and sometimes even promising middle schoolers. (Source: Glen Jones / Shutterstock.com)

the head coach offered her a full scholarship, she took it. Later her father said that for parents such early offers were nerve-racking. He added, "If they don't take those opportunities when they're presented, I think a lot of parents, along with some of the kids, feel that they're going to lose out" (Toppmeyer 2014).

It's difficult for college coaches too. Feeling forced to recruit girls that they are reluctant to overlook because the competition will grab them, they are painfully aware that seemingly promising prospects at 14 or 15 might not contribute to their programs in three or four years (Krause 2011).

Whether it's fastpitch softball or another sport like girls' soccer, the dangers of early college recruitment have become increasingly apparent. At a Florida soccer tournament, a game between 14-year-olds from Texas and Ohio drew a distinguished group of coaches, including Anson Dorrance, the women's soccer head coach from the University of North

Carolina, who has won 21 NCAA championships. While Dorrance was one of the first coaches to recruit middle schoolers, he now has distinct second thoughts about the wisdom of the practice. "It's killing all of us," he said. Dorrance cited a danger previously mentioned. "It's killing the schools that have all the scholarships tied up in kids who can't play at their level. It's just, well, it's actually rather destructive" (Popper 2014).

Earlier it was suggested that over time organized sports programs can become more complex and competitive, and also, this material about adolescent girls' recruitment suggests, potentially destructive for both the athletes and even the coaches doing the recruiting.

One more thought about organized sports programs in general, quite possibly a factor that well might promote pro athletes' or prominent college athletes' communication with younger peers in their sport: As this introductory material suggests, the experience has been roughly similar—similar challenges and rewards as both the youngsters and their distinguished elders progress through the various established stages of development sports programs provide. Summary I.2 provides the principal points discussed involving the stages for organized sports programs.

SUMMARY I.2

The Stages for Organized Sports Programs

Three stages are involved:

- The enrollment/recruitment stage

Such significant others as parents and friends can be influential in encouraging young people to join programs. While recruiters value athletes' skills, their character and fit for the program can also be considerations.

- The retention stage

Three phases of retention involve motivation, commitment, and agents of socialization.

— *Motivation*

Athletes participate in sports programs because they value them, with motives including excitement and exhilaration, interaction and friendship with teammates, skill development, and increased fitness. Clearly youthful athletes value having fun, and the failure to do so has been a major reason why large numbers quit their programs.

— *Commitment*

It represents a willingness to invest considerable time and energy in an outcome, including organized-sports programs successful athletes value. A distinct commitment can be one reason why teenage players can be willing to not only set goals but to plan them out, discussing them with such significant others as parents, coaches, or teachers. Even elite athletes can face conditions challenging their commitment, and to confront such situations, the American Psychological Association had offered several strategies that can prove useful.

— *Agents of socialization*

Various sets of people, especially parents and coaches, influence athletes' interest and involvement in organized programs. Three sets of individuals—athletes, their parents, and their coaches—represent a "sports triangle," with coaches often critical of parents and, in turn, many parents having distinct reservations about coaches. A provocative reality is that compared to their American counterparts, top foreign soccer coaches approach their craft very differently with young athletes.

- The advancement stage

The end of an organized program can be an unstable time for athletes, with uncertainty about what follows next. Little support exists for athletes as they encounter the challenges of advancement, nor is there supervision of the advancement process. The college recruitment of top fastpitch softball and women's soccer players is particularly problematic, with a much debated pursuit of youthful prospects, including an elite number in middle school.

Making the team in an elite sport is invariably competitive, but the process can be particularly complicated for candidates who are hard to assess—diamonds in the rough so to speak.

Conclusion

The identification of elite players can be elusive. A team of sports-medicine specialists indicated that in such sports as football, basketball, ice hockey, lacrosse, and soccer, top performers produce superior power and explosiveness in various tests, but less easily measured qualities like ambition, commitment, and mental toughness also contribute to their quality as players (Lorenz, Reiman, Lehecka, and Naylor 2013). Various other sources emphasize that elite athletes display a distinct combination of physical and mental assets (Trninic, Trninic, and Papic 2009; Williams 2014).

Besides those drafted, some undrafted prospects reach the majors and have fine careers. Bruce Bowen is an interesting case in point—a player whose physical skills were marginal for the NBA, but one whose response to the formidable odds against him at the recruitment stage for both college and the NBA featured a role commitment that was carefully planned and tirelessly executed in order to contribute most effectively to the team.

In 2014 Bowen's jersey was hung in the rafters of the San Antonio Spurs' AT&T Center alongside those belonging to two Hall of Famers. This was a player who spent years struggling to survive in the elite game—first, to get into a college with a decent basketball team and then to enter the NBA. As a teenager, Bowen phoned Donny Daniels, the coach at Cal-State Fullerton, lowering his voice and saying he was a high-school coach who had a kid about to play in a tournament close to the college and that it was a sensible move to go see him. Daniels went, Bowen scored 38 points, and won MVP honors, soon receiving a scholarship to the college of his choice.

Four years later, however, no NBA teams drafted Bowen or recruited him afterwards. In 1993 Bowen went to Europe, and in the following four years, he played for five teams, three of which were French and the other two in the minor leagues—the Continental Basketball Association (CBA), with one of the latter organizations cutting him. At that juncture he was an undrafted player four years out of college who most recently had been dismissed by a CBA team—hardly someone bursting with potential for the NBA.

But Bowen persisted, and in 1997 the Miami Heat took him from the Rockford Lightning's (CBA) roster, offering him a 10-day contract. His stat line for the Heat was hardly overwhelming—one minute played in a single game along with one blocked shot. During the next four years, Bowen went from the Heat to the Boston Celtics, then to the Philadelphia

76ers, and back to the Heat. A DraftExpress scouting report concluded, "Below average athlete and all-around talent. Learned how to become a good enough spot-up shooter from the corners to not be a complete offensive liability" (Rodriguez 2014).

In spite of the less-than-glowing evaluation, the third time with the Heat in 2000–01 was the charm, starting to reveal qualities the scouts had missed. In one game Heat coach Pat Riley said that in just one half, Bowen made five of the top defensive plays he'd ever seen. Soon afterwards he controlled Allan Houston of the Knicks and Paul Pierce of the Celtics, two of the leading offensive threats in the league and only improved when joining the San Antonio Spurs.

In the 2007 NBA finals, Bowen held the rising star LeBron James to 36 percent shooting as the Spurs swept the Heat in the championship. At age 30 he started as the team's small forward and became a defensive star, gaining five consecutive appearances on the all-league first defensive team and three NBA championships in a league that for years he couldn't even enter (Friel 2012; *Land of Basketball.com 2017*; Rodriguez 2014).

During those years Bowen became relentless about preparation. Staying after practice he would engage in defending teammates one-on-one. Then he'd study videotapes to learn the moves of stars he had to defend—Kobe Bryant, Steve Nash, and Ray Allen. He also worked hard on his three-point shooting. "I would come in before everyone else at practice and work on my shooting," Bowen recalled. "A lot of times [assistant coach] Brett Brown and I would go in at 10 o'clock at night and leave at midnight" (Rodriguez 2014).

Clearly Bowen wasn't as talented as many other players, but since high school his role development had been meticulous, eventually making him a significant contributor to his team. As previously cited studies indicated, success in elite sports requires a combination of physical and mental traits. Bowen lacked the physical attributes of a top player, but he possessed a large portion of the less easily measured mental qualities—intangibles that made him a prized possession for the Spurs.

Summary

This book examines athletes' involvement in organized sports, starting at perhaps five or six and continuing to the professional level. Survival is a critical reality, with the participants seeking to advance through successively more advanced levels.

The opening section is historical, indicating that while early Puritans tended to view sports negatively, the muscular Christians of the 19th century recognized its contribution to the balanced development of mind, body, and spirit. At the end of that century, college football received widespread support for its production of hearty males at a supposedly precarious time when the increasingly urbanized society appeared to undercut their manhood. Eventually, though, leaders of the college game mobilized to reduce its violence.

Early in the 20th century, city-wide recreation activities became increasingly common. During this era a number of private sports organizations including Pop Warner football and Little League baseball began to establish themselves. Until the 1970s girls and women were highly disadvantaged athletically. With the passage of Title IX opposing gender discrimination, females' organized sports have increased, but participation rates have remained lower than males'.

A final historical issue involves the development of professional team sports. The first sport to professionalize was baseball, and eventually pro leagues in football, basketball, and hockey followed. The WNBA is the most successful of several women's professional leagues, and while it has survived for two decades its limited financial success has kept players' salaries low.

The structure of organized sports programs involves three stages players encounter. Whether it's the WNBA or a children's program, all organized sports involve an enrollment/recruitment stage. Before the age of 6, children often lack the mental and physical abilities to function in sports programs. Recruitment can be a challenging task for programs. Notably at both the Division I and professional levels, coaches and administrative personnel are likely to indicate that character rivals skill as a basic requisite.

At any level of organized sports, dedicated athletes must be able to stick it out—achieve retention in the program. Three factors come into play, namely motivation, commitment, and the influence of agents of socialization. Capable athletes are motivated, generally participating in sports programs only when they value them. Research has shown that winning, which is often valued by parents, tends to be unimportant to many young children, falling near the bottom of a lengthy list of reasons to participate in such programs.

Commitment, with participants investing time and energy in their sports activity, is also necessary for athletes seeking retention. They are more likely to commit themselves to a team if they believe their coaches and teammates value their contribution. A study indicated that world-class, deeply committed athletes often display extreme mental toughness.

Finally, to promote their retention in programs, athletes often obtain the advice and support of agents of socialization. Parents can serve in this capacity, but they sometimes unduly pressure their children to win. While parents are major influences on their young children, coaches and teammates become increasingly influential in the teen years. Important as coaches are, parents often express concern about their effectiveness. In many instances they have received little or no training.

When athletes reach the end of a period of retention, they leave a program—sometimes to drop out of the sport and other times to move onto a higher level. This advancement stage can be stressful, confronting players with a situation where the presence of a large number of candidates makes it unlikely that they will move into a higher-level program. In some instances, such as fastpitch softball or girls' soccer, the pursuit of top candidates for Division I has become frenetic, even involving efforts to recruit candidates still in middle schools.

The chapter ends with Bruce Bowen's unusual, provocative story, showing that athletes' endeavors in organized sports can sometimes produce unexpected outcomes.

Class Discussion Issues

1. What is a distinct example of the unwinding process applying to organized sports? How was this particular situation different in the past?
2. Do you know elite athletes who expect to play in the pros? Are they aware that in most sports less than one in a thousand athletes ever play in a professional league? Do they feel they can beat those odds?

3. Referring to the 18th and 19th centuries, comment on how religion affected the practice of sport. Does it play a role in sports today?
4. How much of a disadvantage does a child from a low-income family face if he or she wants to become an elite athlete? Provide details.
5. Has Title IX been successful for girls and women in sports? What criticisms if any do you have of its implementation?
6. Information in the chapter makes it readily apparent that the four most affluent pro leagues are in an elevated world of their own while the other pro leagues discussed in the book are much more vulnerable. Which of those less prominent leagues, if any, are likely to persist two or more decades from now? Why are they likely to survive?
7. Comment on the large number of young athletes leaving sports programs. If there were one change in those programs you could make to counter that trend, what would it be? Discuss.
8. Are coaches, parents, or even teammates crucial agents of socialization for athletes? Does it matter if the athletes in question are elite or average?
9. Which group provides athletes more headaches—parents or coaches? Supply specific references.
10. As elite athletes advance in their careers, what is the greatest challenge?

References

Albrecht, Jay, and Bradford Strand. 2010. "A Review of Organized Youth Sport in the United States." *YouthFirst: The Journal of Youth Sports* 5 (Spring): 16–20.

American Psychological Association. 2017. "Sport Psychologists Help Professional and Amateur Athletes." www.apa.org/helpcenter/sport-psychologists.aspx.

Balague, Gloria. 1999. "Understanding Identity, Value, and Meaning When Working with Elite Athletes." *Sport Psychologist* 13 (March): 89–98.

Baseball.Reference.com. 2016. "1900 Major League Baseball Attendance & Miscellaneous." www.baseball-reference.com/leagues/MLB/1900-misc.shtml.

Beatty, Garrett, and Bradley Fawver. 2013. "What Is the Status of Youth Coach Training in the U.S.?" The Aspen Institute's Project Play. https://assets.aspeninstitute.org/content/uploads/files/content/upload/Project%20Play%20Research%20Brief%20Coaching%20Education%20--%20FINAL.pdf.

Bornstein, David. 2011. "The Power of Positive Coaching." *The New York Times* (October 20). http://opinionator.blogs.nytimes.com/2011/10/20/the-power-of-positive-coaching/?_r=0.

Bowers, Matthew T., Laurence Chalip, and B. Christine Green. 2010. "Beyond the Façade: Youth Sport Development and the Illusion of Synergy," pp. 173–183 in Matthew T. Bowers, Laurence Chalip and B. Christine Green (eds.), Routledge *Handbook of Sports Development*. New York: Taylor & Francis.

Bruce, Kyle. 2013. "Mayo, the Man and His Work," pp. 94–112 in Morgen Witzel and Malcolm Warner (eds.), *The Oxford Handbook of Management Theorists*. Oxford, UK: Oxford University Press.

Cain, Louis P., and David D. Haddock. 2005. "Similar Economic Histories, Different Industrial Structures: Transatlantic Contrast in the Evolution of Professional Sports Leagues." *The Journal of Economic History* 65 (December): 1117–1120.

Chudacoff, Howard P. 2007. *Children at Play: An American History*. New York: New York University.

Coakley, Jay. 2006. "The Good Father: Parental Expectations and Youth Sports." *Leisure Studies* 25 (April): 153–163.

Côté, Jean, Bradley Young, Julian North, and Patrick Duffy. 2007. "Towards a Definition of Excellence in Sports Coaching." *International Journal of Coaching Science* 1 (January): 3–17.

Davis, Kenneth C. 2010. "School of Hard Knocks." *The New York Times* (December 26). www.nytimes.com/2010/12/26/opinion/26davis.html?_r=0.

Delaney, Tim, and Tim Madigan. 2009. *The Sociology of Sports: An Introduction*. Jefferson, NC: McFarland & Company.

DeMause, Neil. 2014. "WNBA: Hoop Skills Not Enough for Women's Teams." *Aljazeera America* (August 29). http://america.aljazeera.com/articles/2014/8/29/wnba-hoop-skillsnotenoughforwomenasteams.html.

Dilworth, Kate. 2015. "Would You Let Your Kid Quit a Sport Mid-Season?" National Alliance for Youth Sports (February 11). http://www.nays.org/blog/would-you-let-your-child-quit-a-sport-mid-season/.

Doob, Christopher Bates. 2000. *Sociology: An Introduction*, 6th ed. Fort Worth, TX: The Harcourt Press.

Eitzen, D. Stanley, and George H. Sage. 2009. *Sociology of North American Sport*, 8th ed. Boulder, CO: Paradigm Publishers.

Ericsson, K. Anders, Ralf Th. Krampe, and Clemens Tesch-Römer. 1993. "The Role of Deliberate Practice in the Acquisition of Expert Performance." *Psychological Review* 3: 363–406.

Farrey, Tom. 2014. "Concerns about State of Youth Sports." *ESPNW* (October 13). www.espn.com/espnw/w-in-action/article/11675649/parents-concern-grows-kids-participation-sports.

Fredericks, Jennifer A., and Jacquelynne S. Eccles. 2004. "Parental Influences on Youth Involvement in Sports," pp. 145–164 in Maureen R. Weiss (ed.), *Developmental Sport and Exercise Psychology: A Lifespan Perspective*. Morgantown, WV: Fitness Information Technology.

Friel, John. 2012. "Best Undrafted Players in NBA History." *Bleacher Report* (June 28). http://bleacherreport.com/articles/1239700-best-undrafted-players-in-nba-history.

Gordon, Aaron. 2014. "Did Football Cause 20 Deaths in 1905? Reinvestigating a Serial Killer." *Deadspin* (January 22). https://deadspin.com/did-football-cause-20-deaths-in-1905-re-investigating-1506758181.

Green, Christine. 2005. "Building Sport Programs to Optimize Athlete Recruitment, Retention, and Transition: Toward a Normative Theory of Sport Development." *Sport Management* 19 (July): 233–253.

Holden, Shelley L., Brooke E. Forester, Christopher M. Keshock, and Steven F. Pugh. 2015. "How to Effectively Manage Coach, Parent, and Player Relationships." *Contemporary Sports Issues* (June 29). www.thesportjournal.org/article/how-to-effectively-manage-coach-parent-and-player-relationships/.

Hyman, Mark. 2015. "The Troubling Price of Playing Youth Sports." *The Conversation* (June 3). http://theconversation.com/the-troubling-price-of-playing-youth-sports-38191.

IMG Academy. 2017. "I'd Like to Search for ..." www.imgacademy.com/tuition.

JUSTIA: US Supreme Court. 1984. "NCAA v. Board of Regents 468 U.S. 85 (1984)." https://supreme.justia.com/cases/federal/us/468/85/case.html.

Krause, Ken. 2011. "Is Softball College Recruiting Getting Out of Hand?" *Softballperformance.com.* www.softballperformance.com/softball-college-recruiting-hand/.

Land of Basketball.com. 2017. "Bruce Bowen." www.landofbasketball.com/nba_players/b/bruce_bowen.htm.

Lehman, Harvey C., and Paul A. Witty, 1927. *The Psychology of Play Activities.* New York: A.S. Barnes.

Lorenz, Daniel S., Michael P. Reiman, B.J. Lehecka, and Andrew Naylor. 2013. "What Performance Characteristics Determine Elite Versus Nonelite Athletes in the Same Sport?" *Sports Health* 5 (November): 542–547.

Magre, Raphael. 2013. "The Science behind Recruiting." *The Daily Universe* (April 17). http://universe.byu.edu/2013/04/17/1the-science-behind-recruiting/.

Mayo Clinic. 2017. "Children and Sports: Choices for All Ages." www.mayoclinic.org/healthy-lifestyle/childrens-health/in-depth/fitness/art-20048027.

McQuilkin, Scott A., and Ronald A. Smith. 1993. "The Rise and Fall of the Flying Wedge: Football's Most Controversial Play." *Journal of Sport History* 20 (Spring): 57–64.

Merton, Robert K. 1968. *Social Theory and Social Structure*, 3rd ed. New York: The Free Press.

Middleton, Simon C., Herb W. Marsh, Andrew J. Martin, Garry E. Richards, and Clark Perry. 2004. "Discovering Mental Toughness: A Qualitative Study of Mental Toughness in Elite Athletes." *CiteSeer.* http://citeseerx.ist.psu.edu/viewdoc/summary?doi=10.1.1.134.2103.

Milken Institute School of Public Health, George Washington University. 2014. "Being a Good Sport Ranks as the Top 'Fun' Factor in the Study of Youth Sports" (July 10). http://publichealth.gwu.edu/content/being-good-sport-ranks-top-%E2%80%9Cfun%E2%80%9D-factor-study-youth-sports.

Miner, Juliana W. 2016. "Why 70 Percent of Kids Quit Sports by Age 13." *The Washington Post* (June 1). www.washingtonpost.com/news/parenting/wp/2016/06/01/why-70-percent-of-kids-quit-sports-by-age-13/?utm_term=.a341b9429732.

MLB.com. 2017. "The Commissionership: A Historical Perspective." http://mlb.mlb.com/mlb/history/mlb_history_people.jsp?story=com.

Nadeau, Ben. 2015. "CoachUp Infographic: Are You a Bad or a Good Sports Parent?" *Coach Up Nation* (October 22). www.coachup.com/nation/articles/coachup-survey-are-you-a-bad-or-good-sports-parent.

NCAA Research. 2013. "Estimated Probability of Competing in Athletics beyond the High School Interscholastic Level." www.ncaa.org/sites/default/files/Probability-of-going-pro-methodology_Update2013.pdf.

Omli, Jens, Nicole M. LaVoi, and Diane M. Wiese-Bjornstal. 2008. "Towards an Understanding of Parent Spectator Behavior at Youth Sports Events." *The Journal of Youth Sports Behavior* 3: 30–32. www.cehd.umn.edu/MNYSRC/PDF/Parent-spectator-behavoir.pdf.

O'Sullivan, John. 2013. "Our Biggest Mistake: Talent Selection Instead of Talent Identification." *Changing the Game Project* (December 9). http://changingthegameproject.com/our-biggest-mistake-talent-selection-instead-of-talent-identification/.

O'Sullivan, John. 2015. "Why Kids Quit Sports." *Changing the Game Project* (May 5). http://changingthegameproject.com/why-kids-quit-sports/.

Packer, George. 2013. *The Unwinding: An Inner History of the New America*. New York: Farrar, Straus, and Giroux.

Pathways to the Podium Research Project. 2012. "Faster, Higher, Stronger … and Younger? Birth Order, Sibling Sport Participation, and Sport Expertise Development" (June 19). https://expertadvantage.wordpress.com/2012/06/19/siblings/.

Petitpas, Albert J., Allen E. Cornelius, Judy L. Van Raalte, and Tiffany Jones. 2005. "A Framework for Planning Youth Sport Programs That Foster Psychosocial Development." *The Sport Psychologist* 19: 63–80.

Popper, Nathaniel. 2014. "Committing to Play for a College, Then Starting 9th Grade." *New York Times* (January 26). www.nytimes.com/2014/01/27/sports/committing-to-play-for-a-college-then-starting-9th-grade.html?_r=0.

Riddle, Greg. 2014. "NCAA Coaches Troubled by Recruits Committing at an Early Age." *Dallas News* (February 10). www.dallasnews.com/sports/high-schools/softball-news/headlines/20140208-college-softball-coaches-troubled-by-commitments-coming-at-younger-ages.ece.

Rodriguez, Ken. 2014. "Bruce Bowen: The Long Climb to the Rafters." *NBA.com*. www.nba.com/spurs/features/120222_rodriguez_bruce_bowen.

Scanlan, Tara K., David G. Russell., N.C. Wilson, and Larry A. Scanlan. 2003. "Project on Elite Athlete Commitment (PEAK): I. Introduction and Methodology." *Journal of Sport and Exercise Psychology* 25: 360–376.

Smith, Ronald. 2011. *Pay for Play: A History of Big-Time College Athletic Reform*. Urbana, IL: University of Illinois Press.

Sokolove, Michael. 2010. "How a Soccer Star Is Made." *The New York Times Magazine* (June 2). www.nytimes.com/2010/06/06/magazine/06Soccer-t.html.

Staples, Andy. 2017. "Think Big: 6'9", 396-pound Daniel Faalele Has Coaches Drooling—and He's Never Played a Down." *Sports Illustrated* (March 6). www.si.com/college-football/2017/03/07/daniel-faalele-img-academy-recruiting.

Stevenson, Christopher L. 1990. "The Athletic Career: Some Contingencies of Sport Specialization." *Journal of Sport Behavior* 13: 103–109.

Studeman, Dave. 2005. "Ten Times We Changed the Way We Watch Baseball." *The Hardball Times* (July 14). www.hardballtimes.com/ten-times-we-changed-the-way-we-watch-baseball/.

Taylor, Alan C., John T. Schweichler, Bryce L. Jorgensen, Ember H. McKown, and Melissa Teresak. 2014. "Parental Support Behaviors for Children Participating in Community Soccer Programs." *Contemporary Sports Issues, Sports Studies, and Sports Psychology* (January 21). http://thesportjournal.org/article/parental-support-behaviors-for-children-participating-in-community-soccer-programs/.

The Aspen Institute: Project Play. 2015. "Facts: Sports Activity and Children." https://aspenprojectplay.org/the-facts.

Toppmeyer, Blake. 2014. "Softball Players Making College Choices before Their First High School Games." *Columbia Daily Tribune* (June 30). www.columbiatribune.com/sports/mu/softball-players-making-college-choices-before-their-first-high-school/article_4283eaaa-fa86-5cda-b1b3-fc716c3e1f4a.html.

Trninic, Marko, Slavko Trninic, and Vladan Papic. 2009. "Development Management Model of Elite Athletes in Team Sports Games." *Collegium Antropologicum* 33 (June): 363–372.

University of Florida. 2015. "The Economy of Youth Sports." https://ufonline.ufl.edu/infographics/youth-sports/.

USHistory.org. 2016. "The New England Colonies: Puritan Life." www.ushistory.org/us/3d.asp.

Vecsey, George. 2006. *Baseball: A History of America's Favorite Game.* New York: The Modern Library.

Wallace, Kelly. 2016. "How to Make Your Kids Hate Sports without Really Trying." *CNN* (January 21). www.cnn.com/2016/01/21/health/kids-youth-sports-parents/.

Watterson, John Sayle. 2000. *College Football: History, Spectacle, Controversy.* Baltimore, MD: Johns Hopkins University Press.

Williams, David K. 2014. "How to Become an Elite 'Athlete' in Work and Life." *Forbes* (January 31). www.forbes.com/sites/davidkwilliams/2014/01/31/how-to-become-an-elite-athlete-in-work-and-in-life/#3b42c0cf1a41.

Woitalla, Mike. 2009. "Barcelona's Approach to Youth Development." *YouthSoccerInsider* (May 28). www.youthsoccerfun.com/2009/05/barcelonas_approach_to_youth_d.html.

1

IN THE BEGINNING:
IS IT ENOUGH JUST TO HAVE FUN?

Playing soccer has been a role that has dominated Tyler Ward's life, with his father Kevin, an affluent financier, his fervent supporter. Signed up at age 2 for a toddler soccer class, Tyler joined an actual league at 3, and two years later was designated one of the 15 best players on the 6-and-under team and joined the so-called "pre-travel" program. At 7 Tyler qualified for the club's U8 travel team, competing mainly against 8-year-olds. At that time Kevin declared, "That's when it started to get serious." After Tyler's U9 season, his father moved him to a club considered one of the top teams on the East Coast. Following the move Tyler continued to progress, becoming a leading player on a U11-A team, one of only four such units in the country.

Throughout the fall and spring seasons, Tyler practices three times a week and then plays a game on Sunday. Most recently the 11-year-old made his league's select travel team, which required him to commute an hour-and-a-half each way for Monday evening practice. As a rule Tyler trains or plays six days a week, but unlike adults who have sick days the boy must make up a missed practice, and missing too many in such a competitive setting could readily lead to demotion.

Meanwhile Kevin does everything possible to fuel his son's interest and involvement in soccer, introducing the boy to futsal, a version of indoor soccer, which he plays during the winter when the A-team settles down to a mere two practices a week. Then during the summer Kevin takes Tyler to Europe, where he's enrolled for two-week spans in three different soccer camps. As Tyler's primary agent of socialization, his father denies the prospect of time off. Throughout this chapter agents of socialization and socialization itself are important concepts.

Like Tyler many of the approximately 40 million children enrolled in youth sports are deeply committed to a sport (Matz 2014). As we'll see, some observers consider that such an early specialization poses various physical and psychological problems.

Focus shifts to that topic later in the chapter, but now attention centers on the history of children's organized sports.

The Growth of Young Children's Sports Programs

In the 19th century, the muscular Christians, who emphasized a balance of bodily, mind, and spiritual development, became advocates for young children's, at least young boys' involvement in sports activity, which was organized on playgrounds, in church groups, and in schools. In fact, as education became compulsory, starting in Massachusetts in 1852, the children's day divided between school time and free time, with educators, social workers, and parents often becoming concerned about productive use of free time. Many felt that the most sensible step involved organized leagues for young boys, especially for poor immigrant youths who lived in crowded tenements, spent a lot of time on the streets, and supposedly were untrustworthy unless immersed in supervised activity (Delaney and Madigan 2009, 111–12; Friedman 2013).

At the end of the 19th century, however, public schools did not yet participate in organized sports. School districts refused to support their cost, and so voluntary organizations were largely responsible for any programs that developed (Eitzen and Sage 2009, 63).

Then early in the 20th century, public schools started to emphasize sports, providing physical-education classes as well as a variety of team sports. Outside of school, at least for the opening several decades, the childhood sports experience was largely informal, such as playing with one's neighborhood peers on a nearby field, pavement, or pond, but with the advent of Pop Warner Football in 1929 and then Little League

Baseball in 1939, the most prominent of all organized youth sports programs were established.

The first Little League game took place in founder Carl Stotz's hometown of Williamsport, Pennsylvania, on June 6, 1939, with Lundy Lumber defeating Lycoming Dairy. Local business sponsorship helped keep players' costs low and also encouraged teams to be loyal to their own communities. To date teams must draw from their own locales, prohibited from looking elsewhere for better prospects. While still obtaining about 2.4 million players a year, Little League has fallen off from the 1990s when nearly three million were participating in its baseball and softball divisions (Beauge 2014; Mendell 2014). The program, however, remains active and in the news. In 2016 *ESPN*, *ESPN2*, and *ABC* combined to cover all 32 games in the boys' Little League World Series (Skarka 2016).

Compared to the current era, in the 1950s there was little organized youth sport. Then in 1956 President Eisenhower formed the President's Council on Youth Fitness, establishing an explicit connection between

Little League continues to provide young boys and girls the chance both to learn to play ball and to enjoy it at low cost in their own communities during the summer. (Source: Ryan McVay / thinkstock.com)

the presidential administration and youth sports. This initiative was a high-level response to studies showing Americans' poor health and the importance of improved physical well-being in the Cold War era when, according to the Eisenhower administration, the country needed to convince the rest of the world that its citizenry was more fit and vigorous than its Soviet adversaries (U.S. Department of Health and Human Services 2017).

John Kennedy enthusiastically agreed. As he prepared to enter the White House, Kennedy authored a *Sports Illustrated* article, revealing results from New York's Columbia-Presbyterian Hospital study comparing 4,264 American children's physical fitness with that of 2,870 children from Austria, Italy, and Switzerland. Kennedy wrote, "The findings showed that despite our unparalleled standard of living, despite our good food and our many playgrounds, despite our emphasis on school athletics, American youth lagged far behind Europeans in physical fitness. Six tests for muscular strength and flexibility were given; 57.9% of the American children failed one or more of these tests, while only 8.7% of the European youngsters failed." Kennedy's surprise and concern about these findings wasn't an issue he took lightly. He appointed Bud Wilkinson, the famed University of Oklahoma football coach, as the first physical fitness consultant to the president, emphasizing the growing importance of children's organized sports (Kennedy 1960).

In the intervening years, every presidential administration has taken specific steps to promote youth sports. Because of their prominent launching point, many of these actions have proved influential. The Obama administration was particularly willing to use the President's Council to address national issues involving young people, broadening its agenda and changing its name to the President's Council on Fitness, Sports and Nutrition. For instance, in September 2014 the President's Council called a meeting of school superintendents from around the country to discuss the importance of school-sponsored programs involving various physical activities. Then in January 2015 the President's Council partnered with The Aspen Institute, a distinguished organization cited several times in these chapters, to produce *Sports for All, Play for Life: A Playbook to Get Every Kid in the Game*; this report provided eight strategies to make sporting activities enjoyable, available, and safe for all American children

(U.S. Department of Health & Human Services 2017). As the adjacent Box 1.1 indicates, research has continued to play a role in the development of children's sports programs.

> **BOX 1.1**
>
> **The Controversial "10,000 Hour Rule"**
>
> In the early 1990s, a major investigation focused on whether or not young children making a commitment to some activity by engaging in massive hours of practice could lead to a person becoming an expert. Research involving what journalist Malcolm Gladwell called the "10,000 hour rule" (Gladwell 2008, 38–41) began with musicians and later included mathematicians and chess players (Ferguson and Stern 2014). The 10,000 hour rule is the claim that 10,000 hours of so-called "deliberate practice" in the preteen years are required to become world-class in any endeavor.
>
> Relying on diaries the researchers requested the respondents to keep, K. Anders Ericsson and his associates found that starting at the age of about 8 and continuing to 18, ten violinists with the potential to be international soloists had practiced considerably more than ten of their less accomplished colleagues and that two groups of 12 pianists, one so-called "experts" and the other "amateurs," had followed a similar pattern, with the experts at age 6 starting to accumulate considerably more practice time (Ericsson, Krampe, and Tesch-Römer 1993, 374, 379, 382–83). The researchers concluded, "We view elite performance as the product of a decade or more of maximal effort to improve performance in a domain through optimal distribution of deliberate practice" (Ericsson, Krampe, and Tesch-Römer 1993, 400). The conclusion was that whether it was the violin, the piano, or some other activity such as a sport, deliberate practice starting at an early age and involving lengthy practice over time would produce a superior outcome. To succeed at the highest level in a variety of activities, the researchers claimed, children had to make this commitment.
>
> The most thorough research on this topic involved an examination of 88 studies focusing on whether early deliberate practice had the potential to create world-class output in a variety of fields. In sports as well as the law, medicine, music, and education, the investigators found its impact was modest (Macnamara, Hambrick, and Oswald 2014). In particular, an evaluation of the body of research on young athletes' sports specialization did not support the idea that early deliberate practice can produce elite performers. Neeru Javanthi and his team wrote, "Research in athletes has not consistently demonstrated that early intense training is essential for

attaining an elite level in all sports." The researchers noted that while two studies of rhythmic gymnastics indicated top performers began intense training as young children, athletes in most sports waited until their adolescent years to make such a commitment (Jayanthi, Pinkham, Dugas, Patrick, and LaBella 2013).

Whether or not the President's Council has influenced parents, large numbers of young children join organized sports. The Sports and Fitness Industry Association has estimated that between the ages 6 and 13, 13.52 million children play organized sports a year (Kelley and Carchia 2013). Summary 1.1 lists the major historical issues previously discussed.

SUMMARY 1.1

Historical Factors Influencing the Development of Children's Organized Sports

- Muscular Christians becoming 19th-century advocates of boys' sports on playgrounds as well as in church groups and schools.
- With the development of compulsory schooling, organized leagues formed, especially for poor immigrant boys.
- At the end of the 19th century, school districts considered that the cost and responsibility of sports programs for preadolescents was too great. At that time the only existing programs run by voluntary organizations.
- Early in the 20th century, the public schools began providing children physical-education classes and a number of team sports. In addition, the appearance of Pop Warner Football in 1929 and Little League Baseball in 1939.
- President's Council on Youth Fitness initiated by President Eisenhower and then supported by President Kennedy promoted childrens' improved physical conditioning. The Obama administration was responsible for a number of potentially constructive initiatives.
- Research on the 10,000 hour rule encouraging support for children's deliberate practice in a number of fields including sports, even though no investigations finding that the process produces elite results for athletes.
- Each year about 13.5 million children aged 6 to 13 engaged in organized sports.

The upcoming section examines the three principal categories of participants in youthful organized sports, namely the players themselves, parents, and coaches, and also focuses on several contentious issues that arise in these programs—playing time, injury, and early specialization. Throughout the discussion the impact of parents and coaches as frequent agents of socialization is apparent.

The Terrain for Children's Organized Sports

Are there factors that should determine the age when children should begin sports activity?

Enrollment in Youth Programs

Some sports seem to lend themselves better than others to youthful participation. For instance, swimming, gymnastics, and skating can develop rudimentary skills and enjoyment without requiring competition, which can diminish the experience for young children, who are unlikely to be very competitive or capable of such actions as passing a baseball, shooting a basketball, or playing competent defense in any sport (Grove 2013).

Regardless of young children's capabilities, sports programs for them are widely attended. A nationally representative sample of parents indicated that four in ten of their children aged 5 or younger engaged in organized sports in the year previous to the survey (*PewResearchCenter* 2015).

Data from a Women's Sports Foundation questionnaire revealed that family income has been the most potent factor influencing whether children enroll in programs early. Some specific findings:

- Families earning $100,0000 or more started their children at a mean age of 6.3 compared to 8.1 for families obtaining $35,000 or less.
- Caucasians, whose income overall is higher than other racial groups, had a mean starting age of 6.6 compared to African Americans' 7.7 and Hispanics' 8.2.
- Boys' mean starting age was 6.8 compared to girls' 7.4 (Kelley and Carchia 2013).

As young children enter organized sports, they are likely to have distinct preferences about how their programs should develop.

The Youthful View

It is notable that less than 1 percent of sports-sociology papers written about children's organized sports have examined the topic through the youthful participants' eyes (The Aspen Institute 2017), implying that the young clients' view is not significantly taken into account. That seems to suggest a regrettable oversight since an assessment of children's priorities would appear to be an informative means of grasping their motivation to join and provide commitment to such programs. An academic team specializing in the administration of sports programs described four benefits young children can gain from organized sports during the retention stage:

- Young people enjoy belonging to programs where they can perform quite well. Those who are somewhat to very talented might be motivated by the idea that as they progress in the sport, they might be able to display increasingly better skills.
- Another factor promoting participation in sports programs is the time and enjoyment the players feel being with peers, with team sports appearing to produce a more positive sense of involvement than individual sports.
- In addition, youngsters engage in sports because they want to be physically more active or want to develop their level of fitness (Schwab, Wells, and Arthur-Banning 2010). In order to maximize this benefit, children must receive substantial playing time. Research revealed that 90 percent of children would rather play on a losing team than sit on the bench for a winning unit (O'Sullivan 2015b).
- Finally, organized sport appeals to children because it can be fun (Schwab, Wells, and Arthur-Banning 2010). As the Introduction indicated, 70 percent of children drop out of their programs by the age of 13 because they aren't having fun anymore (Dilworth 2015). Youthful players who enjoy a game are much more likely to be committed to it. As one former pro soccer player and coach wrote, "Chances are, the more they enjoy themselves, the better they play, the more they play, and the harder they will work" (O'Sullivan 2015b).

Two agents of socialization—parents and coaches—form "sports triangles" with youthful athletes, proving particularly influential in their development. While children in organized-sports programs are the focus of sports triangles, each component in the triangle is potentially in communication with the other two.

Sports Triangles in Early Childhood Programs' Retention Stage

It is apparent that parents' behavior is influential in the area of sports programming. A study done with 367 second, third, and fifth graders revealed the extent of parents' influence on their offspring—that mothers' and fathers' beliefs about the children's sports abilities and their degree of emphasis on participation in organized programs were better indicators of the children's sense of self-worth as athletes and their participation rates than the influence of parents' actual involvement in the programs (Fredricks, Simpkins, and Eccles 2005, 57).

In enrolling their children in sports programs, parents tend to make their choices carefully. They generally believe that they are exposing the youngsters to activities that will encourage them to become healthy, hard-working, independent, and goal-oriented citizens. This perception is particularly prevalent in the United States where a widespread belief exists that sports participation makes athletes more confident and resolute (Schwab, Wells, and Arthur-Banning 2010).

As children learn their roles in organized sports, the norms both parents and coaches support have a significant impact on the children. A *norm* is a standard of required or expected behavior. Norms are the rules that people are expected to follow in their relations with each other. Once learned, they can provide individuals a sense of clarity and stability about what to anticipate from others (Doob 2000, 75). In many instances, however, the prevailing norms to which various groups subscribe can clash, and that can apply to parents and their children in sports programs.

Just as researchers writing about children's sports programs often ignore the young athletes' point of view, parents can do the same thing, ruining or at least undermining the young athletes' experience. Two longtime coaches committed to alleviating harmful parental behavior conducted "an informal survey" over three decades with hundreds of college athletes, some of whom became pros, and it included a question about their worst memory playing youthful organized sports. The athletes' most frequent reply: "The ride home from games with my parents."

The writer of the article, a retired NBA player and current coach, said that most parents whom the two coaches involved in the survey had encountered "are well-intentioned folks who can't help but initiate conversation about the contest before the sweat has dried on their child's uniform." In such instances fathers and mothers were failing to acknowledge a previously mentioned issue linked to a norm the children valued—the importance of parents providing their offspring sufficient autonomy so that they could have fun, in this instance backing off with questions and advice right after competition. When asked by the coaches, the young athletes indicated that they would prefer if instead of continuing to respond as spectators, the parents simply returned to being mom or dad.

Toward the end of the survey, the coaches asked the college athletes what statement parents might offer that would make them feel very good—in short, would be a constructive input. The most common response: Something to the effect of "I love to watch you play." Back off and give us space, the young athletes were suggesting. The writer concluded, "There it is, from the mouths of babes who grew up to become college and professional athletes" (Henson 2012).

A well-known researcher on organized-sports programs listed important issues that parents sometimes overlook but need to include in their own set of norms and expectations, making them effective agents of socialization for their children's enjoyable, productive participation in youth programs:

- Often one's children are not as talented as their fathers and mothers believe. As a result it generally makes sense to rely on coaches' assessment of both their ability and decisions about where and how much they should play.
- Parents should recognize their children's resilience, understanding that it can be important and constructive to gain valuable experience from making mistakes.
- It is essential that mothers and fathers recognize that their own athletic careers are over and that they need to see their children's activities as entirely separate from their own.

- Youth coaches, while often unpaid volunteers, tend to act positively in their dealings with children. Parents do well to keep that likelihood in mind, perhaps making occasional complimentary references to the coaching they're doing with the children (Heinzmann 2017).

Besides parents sometimes overreacting to issues related to their children's organized sports, the programs themselves sometimes can pose problems—in particular, proving to be overly rigorous, highly structured, and focused on winning for children who are sometimes unprepared for and uncomfortable with a competitive setting. John O'Sullivan, a coach previously cited, listed several expectations that he felt could be destructive if young athletes had to experience them:

- That teams often schedule an excessive number of games and have too few practices where youngsters can optimally develop skills and understanding of their sport.
- That cuts and all-star selections are made at increasingly early ages, meaning sports for young children becomes a tense, unduly serious venture.
- That programs for even elementary-school aged children are becoming full-year activities, opposing most experts' preference.
- That coaches often emphasize short-term results, particularly winning, at the expense of long-term player development (O'Sullivan 2015a).

In contrast, a pair of researchers mentioned the preferred approach coaches should implement for children ranging from 6 to 12. To begin, it is productive if their plan emphasizes inclusiveness, promoting all participants' enjoyment along with an emphasis on healthy exercise and minimal attention to some players' superior play. To promote inclusiveness with young children, coaches should focus on having fun with simple games that all participants can learn to play effectively and appreciate (Côté and Gilbert 2009, 313–17).

Playing time is one potentially controversial issue that coaches need to regulate.

— About Playing Time

A survey involving children's sports taken by over 700 adult respondents, most of whom were involved with sports programs for four years or more, indicated that among 16 aspects of the programs respondents evaluated, the top factor, which received a mostly positive rating from 40 percent of the research subjects, was equal playing time (Bigelow 2015). There is widespread support for some approximation of this outcome. Clearly playing time is an important issue that children are likely to value and the extent to which they obtain playing time is very likely to affect their motivation for a program.

Brooke de Lench, a well-known writer and lecturer on youth sports, indicated that playing less not only would deprive some children of a chance of catching up, "but, worse, it made being on the team less fun and tended to build resentment … towards the full time players which was clearly destructive of team chemistry and cohesion" (de Lench 2017b).

Bob Bigelow, a former NBA player, veteran coach, and prominent teacher of youth coaching, is hard-hitting on the topic. He noted, "[T]he number one mission for every youth coach … is to make sure kids get meaningful playing time in every game. At my talks and clinics, I am constantly reminding coaches that if playing their less-developed players ends up costing them the game, and if that hurts them too much, they should get out of coaching youth athletes and do something else" (Bigelow 2017).

UPMC Sports Medicine, a large regional center for treating a variety of athletes, has maintained a somewhat different outlook, suggesting that coaches' approach to the topic can vary and that equal time need not be a priority. Without referring to players' age, an organizational statement declared, "In their quest to win, coaches may play the best athletes most of the time, and may even cut or discourage youngsters who do not possess the talent or physical maturity of their peers. A good coach will make sure that every child on the team gets a chance to enjoy the sport" (*UPMC.com* 2016).

While playing time for athletes is largely a coach's decision, the upcoming three issues—burnout, injuries, and early specialization—involve multiple parties.

Young Athletes' Sports-related Struggles

A *dysfunction* is a disruptive or destabilizing consequence produced by an individual, group, or situation and affecting a particular group or society (Doob 2000, 16). The first two issues are unquestionably dysfunctional for young athletes, and early specialization is controversial, with many experts disapproving of it.

Children's Burnout in Organized Sports

The settings producing children's burnout from organized sports involve distinct issues. They include:

- A set of demands, some of which appear excessive: For instance, parents, coaches, league administrators, and trainers pressuring athletes to start specializing during the elementary-school years; or youthful athletes aged 10 to 14 sometimes spending more hours a week at their sport than professionals.
- A volume of injuries produced by high-intensity practice and competition that children seldom received in the past and that are discussed in the next section (Reed 2014; Straus 2017).

When burnout occurs, the young athletes in question are likely to suffer diminished self-confidence and lowered performance goals, to develop increased concern about parental pressures, to endure a persistent sense of anxiety leading to greater vulnerability to injury and loss of sleep, and ultimately to drop the sport (Straus 2017).

Effective coaching can be an antidote to encroaching burnout. Positive Coaching Alliance (PCA) is an organization that has trained over 4,000 coaches and partnered with about 3,500 youth sports programs, schools, education districts, athletic conferences, and park-and-rec departments. A team of researchers found that PCA training encouraged many coaches to change their previous ways, providing their athletes not only a more supportive experience but also raising their level of performance and increasing their retention rate (Agans, Ettekal, and Stack 2016). PCA leaders have been thoughtful and well organized, assuring coaches that achieving a winning record is certainly acceptable as long as their approach provides young players a pleasant, productive experience—that, in fact, a "relentlessly positive" coach most likely will build a successful won-lost record. PCA's approach has received endorsement from high-profile coaches located in one crucible of competition—the NBA. In addition, PCA has painstakingly developed its teaching system, taking research results and distilling them as straightforward lessons that any competent coach can apply.

A journalist concluded that the program worked nicely. "As a father of an 8-year-old who has happily regained his love of soccer thanks to a very positive coach, I can attest to the value of its teachings. Research has found that youth attrition rates are 80 percent lower for children whose coaches practice positive coaching" (Bornstein 2011). PCA appears to be an organization which has provided coaches the ways and means to minimize the relentless pressure of competition—in short, the unwinding that has become so prevalent in children's sports programs.

Burnout and injury are often linked, with injury sometimes a primary reason young athletes suffer burnout in a sport.

Young Athletes' Injuries

In 2012 a Harris Interactive Youth Omnibus online survey interviewed 516 children, who played a variety of sports and included over half who were aged 8 to 12 along with 750 parents and 752 coaches. Three out of four parents stated that they worried about their children getting hurt, and yet many of them failed to examine the issue, with only two in five looking into whether or not the coaches had enough training to provide effective protection. Furthermore about two out of five coaches indicated that some parents had encouraged them to return their injured children to the field of play. Three in four children said that they depended on coaches to protect them from injury, and yet many were quite casual about its occurrence. For instance, three in ten athletes contended that the better players should stay in a game when hurt unless a coach forced them to leave (*Safe Kids Worldwide* 2012).

It is notable that a full two-thirds of youth sports injuries occur during practice. One contributing factor is that parents tend to be more casual about their children's safety during practice, sometimes allowing them to avoid such game-time precautions as the use of protective gear—for

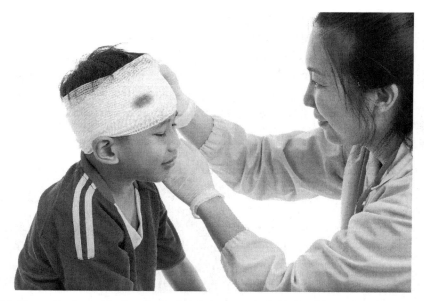

While the greatest number of youth sports injuries occur in football, athletes like this young soccer player also end up in the emergency room after getting hurt playing various other games. (Source: kdshutterman / Shutterstock.com)

instance, mouth guards or helmets (Merkel 2013, 154). Overall research makes it clear that distinct opportunities exist to improve children's protection in organized sports programs.

The injury statistics associated with youth sports are impressive. For the 5 to 14 age group, the number of emergency-room injuries include:

- 215,000 a year for football.
- 170,000 a year for basketball.
- 110,000 a year for baseball and softball.
- 20,000 a year for hockey (Stanford School of Medicine 2016).

The types of youth-sports injuries include the acute, overuse, and reinjury varieties. While younger children's acute injuries tend to be bruises and sprains, they can receive scratched corneas, detached retinas, broken bones, concussions and skull fractures, injured spinal cords, and tears to the anterior cruciate ligament (ACL), with ACL tears disproportionately affecting young female athletes, who are as much as eight times more likely to suffer it than male counterparts. Acute injuries often occur because of the failure to use protective equipment or the use of an inappropriate type. For instance, goggles have become standard fare in basketball and soccer, often preventing eye injuries that can occur when they are absent. A case of improper equipment producing injury could involve softball or baseball players breaking an ankle or leg after sliding into an immobile base. With young children these equipment issues once again raise questions about coaches' role, especially volunteer coaches who need to receive effective training before they are knowledgeable enough to work with players.

Overuse injuries are a second type, occurring because bones and muscles are overly stressed. Children who specialize in one sport are particularly vulnerable to overuse injuries; the relationship of specialization in one sport to injury is discussed at the end of this chapter. Common types of overuse problems are anterior knee pain, which involves tendon or cartilage inflammation, and Little League elbow, which is the result of repetitive throwing and produces pain as well as a possible loss of velocity. The latter injury is most common with pitchers and in the more serious cases requires surgery.

A final type of injury involves reinjury, which is most likely to occur when athletes resume playing a sport before being fully recovered from a previous hurt. After returning they are well advised to resume play carefully, warming up and cooling down thoroughly in order to protect the bodily part previously affected (*KidsHealth* 2016; *Safe Kids Worldwide* 2013). Young athletes often prone to reinjury include those specializing in one sport, producing repeated microtrauma to tendons, muscles, or bones with such repetitive actions as pitchers' throwing motion or gymnastic routines (Malina 2010, 269).

Young children playing sports are generally vulnerable to injury, but that prospect is the most destructive in one sport.

— *The Insidious Case of Young Boys' Tackle Football*

In recent years researchers have been studying the impact of concussions in childhood football. One revealing study involved 42 former NFL players ranging in age from 42 to 69 and displaying contrasting early exposure to the game—those who started tackle football before the age of 12 and those who began at 12 or later. The two groups received a battery of neuropsychological tests, and the results were controlled for the number of years in football and the age when examined. With these factors taken into account, the study produced a chilling conclusion about concussions—that while it took years to reveal the effects, the individuals who started football before the age of 12 were significantly more likely to display impairment in reasoning and planning, memory loss, and verbal IQ (Stamm, Bourlas, Baugh, Fritts, Daneshvar, Martin, McClean, Tripodis, and Stern 2015).

Dr. Robert Cantu, a neurosurgeon who was a colleague of the researchers, indicated that young brains are more vulnerable because they lack myelin, a protective coating on the nerve fibers. With his colleagues' findings in hand, Dr. Cantu began advising families to have their boys stick to flag football until the age of 14 (Farrey 2015). This study and the growing body of research on the topic oppose coaches' and parents' traditional practice of telling young players after a head blow simply to get back in the game. Parents, in fact, are becoming increasingly careful.

A survey conducted by *ESPN* Research and the Global Strategy Group found that once parents heard details about the impact of concussions in football two-thirds of them said it was a serious issue for young players and nearly three in five were less inclined to let their children play in youth leagues (Lavigne 2012).

It's notable that in the late 1970s and early 1980s quarterback Tom Brady's father didn't let his son play tackle football until he reached the age Dr. Cantu advocated—14. Former NFL offensive lineman Randy Cross, who kept his own son from participating until the seventh grade, gave Brady Sr. the idea about delaying his son's entrance into the sport (Rosenthal 2012).

One of the disquieting realities about youth football and concussions is that the coaches are often unqualified to evaluate players' head hits. Pop Warner and many other organizations only require coaches to complete an online course every three years. As Hall of Fame wide receiver Cris Carter concluded, "Our best coaches are coaching our best players, and that's in professional football. Our worst coaches are coaching the most critical position, and that is the 9-, 10-, 11-year-old people" (Barra 2013).

Like the concussion issue, the following topic also links to children's injury.

An Assessment of Childhood Sport Specialization

A team of experts on coaching has contended that young children entering sports at ages 6 to 12 are in the so-called "sampling years" when, they contend, the primary concern should be having fun, allowing the young athletes to be involved in diverse sports because it is simply interesting and satisfying. During these years when coaches provide drills that involve sport-related skills, the emphasis should be on simple, enjoyable, largely noncompetitive tasks. During this phase children should have a chance to develop their roles in the different sports—to experiment with the different tasks or positions and also to develop friendships with their fellow participants (Côté, Young, North, and Duffy 2007, 9–10). They ought to experiment and enjoy themselves, but, according to this team of experts, should decidedly not specialize. It's a focus on "deliberate play" as opposed to a more serious "structured [deliberate] practice" normally associated with more advanced sports activity (Côté, Lidor, and Hackfort 2009, 9)—a gradual, unhurried process in which the athletes become motivated and eventually commit to pursuing their evolving sports roles. Such an outcome is much more likely if parents and coaches cooperate.

Support for the sampling process accompanied by opposition to early specialization is now widespread. A journalist indicated that "[G]rowing numbers of sports physiologists, pediatricians, and psychologists—even coaches and professional athletes ... argue that young people who specialize in one sport before high school are more likely to get injured, stressed out or burned out than those who play multiple sports" (Pichaske 2017).

Further evidence supporting early sampling involves a review of research findings concluding that athletes who don't specialize early tend to have a longer involvement in sports and to develop a greater range of physical and cognitive abilities they can apply productively to their favored sport (Côté, Lidor, and Hackfort 2009, 11, 13).

In addition, a pair of European studies provides evidence supporting early sampling and opposing early specialization. Research involving 735 Belgian boys in three age groups (6 to 8, 8 to 10, and 10 to 12) found that the boys who played multiple sports were more physically fit and had better coordination than their peers who specialized early. It was the senior group—the boys 10 to 12—who benefited the most from multiple sports, showing superior results on several physical tests (de Lench 2017c). Furthermore, an investigation involving 148 elite and 95 near-elite Danish athletes in ten sports found that compared to their near-elite peers, the elite competitors trained less as children and specialized later (Moesch, Elbe, Hauge, and Wikman 2011).

Finally the issue of injury relates to specialization. Research done on over 1,200 child and adolescent athletes who came to one of two Chicago hospitals and their associated clinics indicated that if individuals specialized intensely in a sport at an early age they were more likely to have had a sports-related injury, particularly one involving overuse (American Academy of Pediatrics 2013; Jayanthi, LaBella, Dugas, Feller, and Patrick 2013).

The criticisms against early specialization in sports pile up, and opposition is apparent in well-known individuals' words and actions featured in the nearby Box 1.2.

BOX 1.2

Prominent Sports Figures' Opinions about Children's Sampling or Early Sports Specialization

While the overall evidence firmly opposes early specialization, parents and children often commit to it. For knowledgeable observers that reality can prove frustrating. Joe Maddon, the manager of the 2016 World Series-winning Chicago Cubs, angrily commented on young children's travel teams. What deeply bothered Maddon was "the specialization of kids when they're on these travel squads that are only 12-13-14 years olds that are only dedicated to one thing, traveling all the time, paying exorbitant amounts of money to play baseball with hopes of becoming a professional baseball player. I think that's crazy" (Engh 2015).

Compared to such high-pressure pursuits, many successful athletes experienced a more casual approach from their earliest agents of sports socialization. Mia Hamm, formerly a renowned soccer player, respectfully and fondly recalled the earliest coaching she received as a young child. "The first coaches I had were just dads. And [laughs] probably wearing too small team uniform shirts and a really bad hat or visor on the sideline. And occasionally saying things they got from their days of playing football and trying to apply it to soccer, like 'Get to the end zone.'" But more significant than the shirts or the expressions were the positive goals the dad coaches had in mind. Hamm, attuned to the importance of coaches' positive socialization of youthful players, emphasized that "At a young age it's about development and making sure that the kids really enjoy the environment they're in so they want to come back and continue to learn and listen" (Woitalla 2012).

Steph Curry, a renowned NBA member and twice most valuable player (MVP), had a similarly relaxed introduction to sports. His father Dell, a former NBA veteran, indicated that the young boy started basketball in a rec league at the age of 6 or 7. Becoming a professional was hardly the parents' concern; they just wanted to make sure that Steph learned the fundamentals and had a chance to develop his game. Curry thrived as a child athlete, readily immersing himself in the sampling process. His father explained, "He was energetic, always paid attention to what was going on, eager to learn. He tried several different sports, not just basketball. He played football, baseball, a little soccer. He was always very intuitive of what was going on around him. He just soaked it all up" (*USA Basketball* 2015).

Eventually, without feeling pressure from anyone including himself, Curry narrowed his preferences down to two sports—basketball and baseball. He was 14, an age when many athletes were already specializing. At that point he made his choice. "I liked it [baseball], but I was more interested in basketball," he said. "I was kind of better at it. And I wanted to practice more on it and try to make it to the pros if I have the chance" (Cohen 2016).

The verdict is in from people like the Currys, Mia Hamm, Joe Maddon, and a host of experts in sports-related fields strongly opposed to childhood specialization. It's apparent that they recognize that having fun and playing without pressure, far from restricting young children's capacities as athletes, is clearly advantageous in their development. In contrast, for many parents and children, the elusive rewards of focusing on one sport at a preteen age are too appealing to bypass.

In spite of the strong support for early sampling, some staunch advocacy of early specialization exists. The University of Florida Sport Policy & Research Collaborative indicated that for child athletes and their parents the message received from today's youth culture emphasizes "the idea that high doses of one sport at an early age is the only pathway to athletic stardom." Proponents include many coaches, business people who profit from a variety of youthful sports programs, "and even best-selling authors such as [the previously cited] Malcolm Gladwell who introduced the '10,000 hour rule' of 'deliberate practice' to a mass audience" (University of Florida Sport Policy & Research Collaborative 2013). In concluding that early specialization promotes advancement to more elite levels of play, proponents of this position are likely to either overlook or dismiss both the possible disadvantages to early specialization and the fact that research fails to support the application of the 10,000 hour rule to sports.

The figures on early specialization are noteworthy. The Sports & Fitness Industry Association indicated that while the total for children aged 6 to 17 playing a sport increased three million between 2013 and 2015, the number of sports individual athletes play declined—from an average of 2.09 in 2013 to 1.89 in 2015, representing a 9.6 percent drop and suggesting increased specialization. Many of the specializing athletes were in the preteen group, with the peak age for sports participation being 12 years old (Cook 2016; Langhorst 2016).

Among elite athletes early specialization is common. NCAA survey data involving the sports covered in this book indicated that for Division I participants, 62 percent of women in soccer, 55 percent in basketball, 48 percent in softball, 25 percent in volleyball, and 17 percent in lacrosse started specializing at 12 or younger. For Division I men, the figures were 68 percent of men in soccer, 55 percent in hockey, 49 percent in basketball, 33 percent in football, 32 percent in baseball, and 12 percent in lacrosse (NCAA Convention 2016). It seems instructive to keep in mind that although many youthful elite athletes survive early specialization, preliminary research warns about increased prospects of burnout and injury (Feigley 1984; Jayanthi, Pinkham, Dugas, Patrick, and LaBella 2013; Malina 2010).

It is also clear that the specialization trend does not just involve elite athletes. Seventy-seven percent of high-school athletic directors surveyed indicated that an increase in youngsters' focus on a single sport has been occurring. Furthermore, the number of 6-, 7-, and 8-year-olds' all-star and travel teams has been growing (Berardini 2015).

In enlisting good or perhaps elite athletes in early specialized athletic training, parents are likely to believe they are taking a productive step to obtain a valued college scholarship or even a lucrative professional position or, at the very least, to stay competitive with other prospects (de Lench 2017a). The rewards are more than financial. There is often a special recognition that attaches to elite athletic status, and as parents do all they can to advance their children's sports career the progressions are "a prestigious feather-in-the-cap for both the proud parents and the youth" (Twist and Hutton 2007).

A second parental incentive favoring early specialization is that many of them believe that more is better—that in the tradition of the 10,000 hour rule players improve more quickly by cramming as much deliberate practice as possible into their preteen years and that travel teams for children as young as 6 or 7 are useful skill-developing experiences (de Lench 2017a).

Young athletes' parents, in fact, often believe that early specialization is the road to "competitive survival"—that just as children can lose out by getting behind academically and remain forever disadvantaged, a similar downfall can occur playing sports (de Lench 2017a).

Coaches too can get caught up in the competitive furor early specialization nurtures. A northern California basketball travel team for 10-year-olds, which had won six of seven tournaments, inspired the coach to declare, "I am looking to go to North Carolina and Houston. And there may be a New York tournament" (Keown 2011). When their travel teams are consistently successful, coaches and their youthful players can become channeled into engaging in more and more competitions and in the process almost invariably escalating early specialization. Summary 1.2 provides the principal issues examined affecting children's organized team sports.

SUMMARY 1.2

Significant Issues Affecting Young Athletes' Role in Organized Sports

- Assessment of the age children should start organized sports.
- The chief benefits that preteen athletes are likely to expect from their organized programs.
- Parents' evaluation of their children's athletic performance. When attending games, the guidelines mothers and fathers are advised to have in mind.
- The norms coaches should apply to produce smooth-running programs.
- Coaches' determination of youthful participants' playing time.
- Major factors producing burnout with young players.
- Injury in organized youth sports and its common occurrence during practice.
- The advantages and disadvantages of early specialization and reasons for supporting one of these positions.

While a substantial number of children are deeply involved in sports programs, research has revealed some important and troubling findings about physical fitness over time. The upcoming material carries the discussion beyond children in organized sports, but arguably it's a distinct element in the broad sociocultural context in which current youth sports programs develop and can readily affect them.

Conclusion

Once I had a teaching colleague—Irv, a biologist, who was a child in the 1930s. He never participated in organized sports, Irv told me, but he spent a lot of active time on the Bronx streets, constantly running from place to place. One day on a whim he went to his high school's track to have himself timed for the mile. He ran 4:36, a highly respectable result and quite good enough to have landed him on most modern high-school track teams.

Was Irv's performance a fluke? There has been some relevant investigation, comparing young people's physical conditioning over time and suggesting that in the past there might have been more Irvs than there are now. Researchers at the University of South Australia examined 50 studies involving 25 million children aged 9 to 17 (in short, most of the age range covered in this and the following chapter) from 28 countries and found that their cardiovascular fitness, which measures heart and circulatory system health and endurance, has diminished 5 percent since 1975 and that their time for a mile has averaged a second-and-a-half slower (Armstrong 2012; Shute 2013). A trio of researchers indicated concern, noting that young people's cardiovascular capacity "is important for health and well-being and successful sport participation and this has markedly declined over the last 35 years" (Armstrong, Tomkinson, and Ekelund 2011).

In countries like the United States, Canada, Australia, and the United Kingdom, children are much less inclined to walk or bike to school than in the 1970s and earlier. In addition, the number of people with access to such devices as TVs, VCRs, computers, and video games encouraging a sedentary lifestyle has accelerated (Shute 2013). Admittedly all modern, technologically advanced countries produce distinct numbers of good to elite athletes, but many young people, including the substantial numbers who drop out of organized programs by the age of 13, are at risk for being caught in the ongoing physical decline—seemingly representing evidence of lifestyle unraveling related to young people's health.

The situation brings to mind the era when President Eisenhower initiated the President's Council on Fitness, but the current challenge is perhaps more pervasive. A promising reform might feature fully reorganized sports programs for all children starting at a youthful age, but it seems clear that such an initiative will only have a widespread positive impact if the programs are meticulously organized, effectively established in all locales, and feature well-trained coaches making the activities appealing and worthwhile to both the youthful clients and their parents.

Summary

In the 19th century, muscular Christians became advocates of children's organized sports, particularly as public schooling became compulsory. The organizers wanted young boys to spend their time productively, a concern most emphatically directed toward poor immigrant boys. By the end of that century, however, most school districts still refused to support the cost of athletic programs for preadolescents.

As a result of limited public support for organized sports, some private programs formed early in the 20th century, with two of them—Pop Warner and Little League—continuing to the present.

On occasion politics and sports have combined, with President Eisenhower initiating the President's Council on Fitness, with subsequent administrations also becoming involved. Another important historical influence on children's organized sports has been research, with investigation of the 10,000 hour rule involving youthful performers' deliberate practice offering limited evidence that such activity produces elite athletes.

One important issue involving young children's organized sports concerns the age at which they should enter such programs. In spite of little supportive evidence, some parents feel the younger the better. In fact, a nationally representative sample of parents indicated that four in ten introduced their offspring to organized sports at the age of 5 or younger, with higher income a potent factor promoting early involvement.

Very few sports programs perceive the activities through participants' eyes. There appear to be four benefits such programs offer. On the other hand, dropouts are numerous, with 70 percent leaving organized sports by the age of 13.

In their sports activities, children are part of a so-called "sports triangle," which also involves parents and coaches. Research has shown that parents' views of their children's athletic involvement and ability strongly affects the youngsters' self-worth as athletes. Sometimes, however, parents undermine the sports experience. A researcher on organized sports summarized major program-related issues that parents sometimes overlook.

Coaching too can be problematic. A veteran coach described four distinct drawbacks that often occur in youth programs, producing activities that are highly structured, pressure-laden, and fixated on winning. On the other hand, a pair of researchers described the conditions which coaches of children age 6 to 12 should emphasize.

Some situations in youth sports are difficult to resolve. One involves playing time. Should there be an equitable division, or should the better players receive more time? Coaches, parents, and the players themselves often disagree on this point.

For some athletes organized sport is a struggle, producing various dysfunctions. Excessive time demand and injury can lead to burnout. Effective coaching can alleviate burnout, and the organization Positive Coaching Alliance has been successful in this regard.

Injury is another dysfunction child athletes encounter. A Harris survey cited a number of troubling issues about injuries—for instance, that three in ten young players indicated that good players would stay in a game when hurt unless a coach forced them to leave. In recent years concern about concussions, particularly in football, has soared, and a study of retired NFL players indicated that those who started tackle football before the age of 12 had a greater number of serious aftereffects.

Another issue facing young athletes can be the decision about whether or not to specialize in one sport before the age of 12. A team of researchers on coaching has referred to the "sampling years," assuming the position that it's advantageous for young athletes to develop slowly, engaging in several sports and not specializing until somewhat older. A variety of specialists tend to support this position.

The final topic involves some commentary about international youth fitness over time.

Class Discussion Issues

1. Indicate how the 10,000 hour rule has affected children's sports.
2. What issues should parents keep in mind regarding the age at which their children should start organized sports?
3. Describe the principal benefits young children can obtain from sports programs.

    Choosing both a sport and the player's gender, discuss a hypothetical case in which parents and children might have different expectations about sports programs. What about coaches vs. players?
4. Recall the principal findings two longtime coaches reached with their informal survey conducted over a 30-year period. What does this information suggest about parents' role as agents of socialization in their children's sports programs?
5. Describe a few essential qualities coaches must possess to prove effective agents of socialization working with young children.
6. Do you agree or disagree with Bob Bigelow, who was quoted in the chapter saying that a coach's most pressing responsibility in youth sports is that all players receive meaningful playing time? Explain.
7. Focus on one dysfunctional factor in organized youth sport, also citing one effective means of alleviating the problems that the issue creates.
8. Are you surprised about how many young children are hurt playing sports? What are the most practical steps to cut the number of casualties? Take into account the high percentage hurt in practice.
9. Discuss the pros and cons of early specialization in sports. What's your position on the issue?

References

Agans, Jennifer, Andrea Vest Ettekal, and Caroline Stack. 2016. "PCA Impact Comparison Study." Positive Coaching Alliance. www.positivecoach.org/the-power-of-positive/impact-evaluation/.

American Academy of Pediatrics. 2013. "Sports Specialization, Hours Spent in Organized Sport May Predict Young Athlete Injury." (October 28). www.aap.org/

en-us/about-the-aap/aap-press-room/pages/Sports-Specialization,-Hours-Spent-in-Organized-Sports-May-Predict-Young-Athlete-Injury.aspx.

Armstrong, Neil. 2012. "Young People Are Fit and Active—Fact or Fiction?" *Journal of Sport and Health Science* 1 (December): 131–140. www.sciencedirect.com.

Armstrong, Neil, Grant R. Tomkinson, and Ulf Ekelund. 2011. "Aerobic Fitness and Its Relationship to Sport, Exercise Training and Habitual Physical Activity during Youth." *British Journal of Sports Medicine* 45: 849–858. http://citeseerx.ist.psu.edu/viewdoc/download?doi=10.1.1.966.3135&rep=rep1&type=pdf.

Barra, Allen. 2013. "America's Most Dangerous Football Is in the Pee-Wee Leagues, Not the NFL." *The Atlantic* (August 31). www.theatlantic.com/entertainment/archive/2013/08/americas-most-dangerous-football-is-in-the-pee-wee-leagues-not-the-nfl/279229/.

Beauge, John. 2014. "Little League Baseball, Softball Participation Continues … with One Exception." *Penn Live* (September 26). www.pennlive.com/little-league-world-series/2014/09/participation_in_little_league.html.

Berardini, Kelly. 2015. "Early Specialization? Did We Forget That Sports Are Supposed to Be Fun?" BOC (May 14). www.bocatc.org/blog/at-life/early-specialization-did-we-forget-sports-are-supposed-to-be-fun/.

Bigelow, Bob. 2015. "Bob Bigelow's Youth Sports Survey." *bobbigelow.com*. www.bobbigelow.com/documents/Survey_results.pdf.

Bigelow, Bob. 2017. "Youth Coaches: Meaningful Playing Time for Every Player Is Job One." *momsTEAM*. www.momsteam.com/youth-basketball/youth-coaches-meaningful-playing-time-every-player-job-one.

Bornstein, David. 2011. "The Power of Positive Coaching." *The New York Times* (October 20). http://opinionator.blogs.nytimes.com/2011/10/20/the-power-of-positive-coaching/?_r=0.

Cohen, Ben. 2016. "The Stephen Curry Approach to Youth Sports." *The Wall Street Journal* (May 17). www.wsj.com/articles/the-stephen-curry-approach-to-youth-sports-1463526612.

Cook, Bob. 2016. "Survey Shows Youth Sports Specialization Accelerating." *Forbes* (December 22). www.forbes.com/sites/bobcook/2016/12/22/survey-shows-youth-sports-specialization-accelerating/#28cc25a22fa0.

Côté, Jean, Bradley Young, Julian North, and Patrick Duffy. 2007. "Towards a Definition of Excellence in Sport Coaching." *International Journal of Coaching Science* 1 (January): 3–17.

Côté, Jean, and Wade Gilbert. 2009. "An Integrative Definition of Coaching Effectiveness and Expertise." *International Journal of Sports Science & Coaching* 4: 307–323.

Côté, Jean, Ronnie Lidor, and Dieter Hackfort. 2009. "ISSP Position Stand: To Sample or to Specialize? Seven Postulates about Youth Sport Activities that Lead to Continued Participation and Elite Performance." *International Journal of Sport and Exercise Psychology* 9: 7–17.

Delaney, Tim, and Tim Madigan. 2009. *The Sociology of Sports: An Introduction*. Jefferson, NC: McFarland & Company.

de Lench, Brooke. 2017a. "Early Specialization: Nine Reasons Why It Is a Bad Idea." *momsTEAM*. www.momsteam.com/successful-parenting/early-specialization-in-youth-sports-supported-by-myths-and-competitive-culture-not-facts.

de Lench, Brooke. 2017b. "Equal Playing Time: Should It Be the Rule, Not the Exception?" *momsTEAM*. www.momsteam.com/team-experts/brooke-de-lench/editorials/equal-playing-time-should-it-be-rule-not-exception.

de Lench, Brooke. 2017c. "Kids Who Delay Sports Specialization More Coordinated and Physically Fit, Study Finds." *momsTEAM*. www.momsteam.com/5-7/kids-who-play-multiple-sports-early-more-coordinated-physically-fit-study-finds.

Dilworth, Kate. 2015. "Would You Let Your Kid Quit a Sport Mid-Season?" National Alliance for Youth Sports (February 11). www.nays.org/blog/would-you-let-your-child-quit-a-sport-mid-season/.

Doob, Christopher B. 2000. *Sociology: An Introduction*, 6th ed. Fort Worth, TX: The Harcourt Press.

Eitzen, D. Stanley, and George H. Sage. 2009. *Sociology of North American Sport*, 8th ed. Boulder, CO: Paradigm Publishers.

Engh, Fred. 2015. "Travel Teams: Youth Sports' New Headache." *The Huffington Press* (May 18). www.huffingtonpost.com/fred-engh/travel-teams-youth-sports_b_6887720.html.

Ericsson, K. Anders, Ralph Th. Krampe, and Clemens Tesch-Römer. 1993. "The Role of Deliberate Practice in the Acquisition of Expert Performance." *Psychological Review* 100: 363–406.

Farrey, Tom. 2015. "Study Cites Youth Football for Issues." *ESPN* (January 29). http://espn.go.com/espn/otl/story/_/id/12243012/ex-nfl-players-played-tackle-football-youth-more-likely-thinking-memory-problems.

Feigley, David A. 1984. "Psychological Burnout in High-level Athletes." *The Physician and Sportsmedicine* 12 (May): 108–119.

Ferguson, Brad, and Paula J. Stern. 2014. "A Case of Early Sports Socialization in an Adolescent Athlete." *The Journal of the Canadian Chiropractic Association* 58 (December): 377–383.

Fredricks, Jennifer A., Sandra Simpkins, and Jacquelynne S. Eccles. 2005. "Family Socialization, Gender, and Participation in Sports and Instrumental Music," pp. 41–62 in Catherine R. Cooper, Cynthia C. Garcia Coll, W. Todd Bartko, Helen Davis, and Celina Chatman (eds.), *Developmental Pathways through Middle Childhood*. Mahwah, NJ: Lawrence Erlbaum Associates.

Friedman, Hilary Levey. 2013. "When Did Competitive Sports Take Over American Childhood?" *The Atlantic* (September 20). www.theatlantic.com/education/archive/2013/09/when-did-competitive-sports-take-over-american-childhood/279868/.

Gladwell, Maxwell. 2008. *Outliers: The Story of Success*. Boston, MA: Little, Brown and Company.

Grove, Jim. 2013. "When Is My Child Old Enough for Organized Sports?" *Active for Life* (April 25). http://activeforlife.com/child-old-enough-for-sports/.

Heinzmann, Gregg S. 2017. "Enhancing Parent-Coach Relations in Youth Sports." Rutgers Youth Sports Research Council. http://youthsports.rutgers.edu/programareas/24-articles/61-enhancing-parent-coach-relations.

Henson, Steve. 2012. "What Makes a Nightmare Parent—and What Makes a Great One." *ThePostGame* (February 15). www.thepostgame.com/blog/more-family-fun/201202/what-makes-nightmare-sports-parent.

Jayanthi, Neeru, Cynthia LaBella, Lara Dugas, Erin R. Feller, and Brittany Patrick. 2013. "Risks of Specialized Training and Growth for Injury in Young Athletes: A Prospective Cohort Study." *American Academy of Pediatrics* (October 28). https://aap.confex.com/aap/2013/webprogrampress/Paper21503.html.

Jayanthi, Neeru, Courtney Pinkham, Lara Dugas, Brittany Patrick, and Cynthia LaBella. 2013. "Sports Specialization in Young Athletes: Evidence Based Recommendations." *Sports Health* 5 (May). www.ncbi.nlm.nih.gov/pmc/articles/PMC3658407/?_escaped_fragment_=po=0.909091.

Kelley, Bruce, and Carl Carchia. 2013. "'Hey, Data Data -- Swing!' The Hidden Demographics of Youth Sports." *ESPN* (July 11). http://espn.go.com/espn/story/_/id/9469252/hidden-demographics-youth-sports-espn-magazine.

Kennedy, John F. 1960. "The Soft American." *SI Vault* (December 26). http://armymedicine.mil/Documents/Panel%20C%20-%201960-Kennedy-Soft-American.pdf.

Keown, Tim. 2011. "Where the 'Elite' Kids Shouldn't Meet." *ESPN* (August 24). www.espn.com/espn/commentary/story/_/page/keown-110823/elite-travel-baseball-basketball-teams-make-youth-sports-industrial-complex.

KidsHealth. 2016. "Preventing Children's Sports Injuries." http://kidshealth.org/en/parents/sports-safety.html#.

Langhorst, Paul. 2016. "Youth Sports Participation Statistics and Trends." *EngageSports* (March 8). www.engagesports.com/blog/post/1488/youth-sports-participation-statistics-and-trends.

Lavigne, Paula. 2012. "Concussion News Worries Parents." *ESPN* (August 26). www.espn.com/espn/otl/story/_/id/8297366/espn-survey-finds-news-coverage-concussions-leads-majority-parents-less-likely-allow-sons-play-youth-football-leagues.

Macnamara, Brooke N., David Z. Hambrick, and Frederick L. Oswald. 2014. "Deliberate Practice in Music, Games, Sports, Education, and Professions: A Meta-Analysis." *Psychological Science* (2014): 1–11.

Malina, Robert M. 2010. "Early Sport Specialization: Roots, Effectiveness, Risks." *Current Sports Medicine Reports* 9 (November-December): 364–371.

Matz, Eddie. 2014. "The Kids Are All Right." *ESPN* (February 21). www.espn.com/espn/story/_/id/10496416/are-youth-sports-ruining-kids-childhoods-espn-magazine.

Mendell, David. 2014. "Stealing Home: How Travel Teams Are Eroding Community Baseball." *The Washington Post* (May 23). www.washingtonpost.com/opinions/stealing-home-how-travel-teams-are-eroding-community-baseball/2014/05/23/5af95d34-df6e-11e3-9743-bb9b59cde7b9_story.html?utm_term=.f57a7dc65edb.

Merkel, Donna. 2013. "Youth Sport: Positive and Negative Impact on Young Athletes." *Journal of Sports Medicine* 4: 151–160.

Moesch, K., A. M. Elbe, M.-L. T. Hauge, and J. M. Wikman. 2011. "Late Specialization: The Key to Success in Centimeters, Grams, or Seconds (cgs) Sports." *Scandinavian Journal of Medicine & Science in Sports* 21 (December): 1–9.

NCAA Convention. 2016. "Results from the 2015 GOALS Study of the Student-Athlete Experience" (January). www.ncaa.org/sites/default/files/GOALS_convention_slidebank_jan2016_public.pdf.

O'Sullivan, John. 2015a. "The Enemy of Excellence in Youth Sports." *Changing the Game Project* (January 8). http://changingthegameproject.com/the-enemy-of-excellence-in-youth-sports/.

O'Sullivan, John. 2015b. "Why Kids Quit Sports." *Changing the Game Project* (May 5). http://changingthegameproject.com/why-kids-quit-sports/.

PewResearchCenter. 2015. "Children's Extracurricular Activity." (December 17). http://www.pewsocialtrends.org/2015/12/17/5-childrens-extracurricular-activities/.

Pichaske, Pete. 2017. "In an Era of Specialty Sports, a Growing Consensus Encourages Well-rounded Young Athletes." *The Baltimore Sun* (March 11). www.baltimoresun.com/news/maryland/howard/howard-magazine/ph-mg-ho-multiple-sports-young-athletes-20170104-story.html.

Reed, Ken. 2014. "Burnout and Injury a Major Concern in Youth Sports." *The Huffington Post* (March 31). www.huffingtonpost.com/ken-reed/youth-sports-injuries-and_b_5966664.html.

Rosenthal, Gregg. 2012. "Tom Brady's Father Not Sure He'd Let Son Play Football." *NFL.com*. (May 22). www.nfl.com/news/story/09000d5d82943aba/article/tom-bradys-father-not-sure-hed-let-son-play-football.

Safe Kids Worldwide. 2012. "Coaching Our Kids to Fewer Injuries: A Report on Youth Sports Safety." (April). www.safekids.org/sites/default/files/documents/ResearchReports/Coaching%20Our%20Kids%20to%20Fewer%20Injuries%20A%20Report%20on%20Youth%20Sports%20Safety%20-%20April%202012.pdf.

Safe Kids Worldwide. 2013. "1.35 Million Children Seen in Emergency Rooms for Sports-related Injuries." (August 5). www.safekids.org/press-release/135-million-children-seen-emergency-rooms-sports-related-injuries.

Schwab, Keri A., Mary Sara Wells, and Skye Arthur-Banning. 2010. "Experiences in Youth Sports: A Comparison Between Players' and Parents' Perspectives." *Journal of Sport Administration & Supervision* 2 (April). https://quod.lib.umich.edu/j/jsas/6776111.0002.106/--experiences-in-youth-sports-a-comparison-between-players?rgn=main;view=fulltext.

Shute, Nancy. 2013. "Kids Are Less Fit Today than You Were Back Then." *npr* (November 20). www.npr.org/sections/health-shots/2013/11/20/246316731/kids-are-less-fit-today-than-you-were-back-then.

Skarka, Michael. 2016. "*ESPN* Provides Extensive Coverage of the 32-Game Little League World Series from Williamsport." *ESPN* (August 15). http://espnmediazone.com/us/press-releases/2016/08/espn-provides-extensive-coverage-32-game-little-league-world-series-schedule-williamsport/.

Stamm, Julie M., Alexandra P. Bourlas, Christine M. Baugh, Nathan G. Fritts, Daniel Daneshvar, Brett M. Martin, Michael D. McClean, Yorghos Tripodis, and Robert A. Stern. 2015. "Age of First Exposure to Football and Later-Life Cognitive Impairment in Former NFL Players." *Neurology* 84 (March 17): 114–120. www.ncbi.nlm.nih.gov/pmc/articles/PMC4371403/.

Stanford School of Medicine. 2016. "Sports Injury Statistics." www.stanfordchildrens.org/en/topic/default?id=sports-injury-statistics-90-P02787.

Straus, Lindsey Barton. 2017. "Burnout in Youth Athletes: Risk Factors, Symptoms, Diagnosis, and Treatment." *momsTEAM*. www.momsteam.com/burnout-in-youth-athletes-risk-factors-symptoms-diagnosis-treatment.

The Aspen Institute. 2017. "Ask Kids What They Want." http://youthreport.projectplay.us/the-8-plays/ask-kids-what-they-want/.

Twist, Peter, and Janice Hutton. 2007. "Identifying and Training Youth Athletes. *Idea*

Fitness Journal (September 1). www.ideafit.com/fitness-library/identifying-understanding-and-training-youth-athletes.

University of Florida Sport Policy & Research Collaborative. 2013. "What Does Science Say about Athletic Development in Children?" (September). https://assets.aspeninstitute.org/content/uploads/2016/06/Project-play-september-2013-roundtable-research-brief.pdf.

UPMC.com. 2016. "Pros and Cons of Youth Sports Participation." http://share.upmc.com/2016/02/youth-sports-participation/.

USA Basketball. 2015. "Before They Made It: Stephen Curry." (May 4). www.usab.com/news-events/news/2015/05/before-they-made-it-stephen-curry.aspx.

U.S. Department of Health & Human Services. 2017. "President's Council on Fitness, Sports Nutrition." www.fitness.gov/about-pcfsn/our-history/.

Woitalla, Mike. 2012. "Mia Hamm's Advice for Girls, Parents, and Coaches." *SoccerAmerica* (April 11). www.socceramerica.com/article/46323/mia-hamms-advice-for-girls-parents-and-coaches.html.

2
TEENS IN TRIUMPH AND TURMOIL: ADOLESCENTS' ORGANIZED SPORTS

In the fall of 2008, Elena Delle Donne was a 6-feet-5-inch middle hitter for the University of Delaware women's volleyball team. Just months earlier Delle Donne was the leading female high-school basketball prospect, signing with the vaunted UConn Huskies. But after two days of summer-school classes, the talented player acknowledged what stars of her stature seldom do—that she was burned out playing her game—and she left UConn.

Right after leaving Delle Donne was unclear about what she would do. She kept an open mind about returning to UConn, where the coach said he would hold her scholarship through the summer. In August, however, she gave up her scholarship and went back to her home area to enroll at Delaware as a walk-on for the volleyball team, a sport she only played for the first time the previous year. "She seems a lot happier; she laughs a lot," said Meghan Bonk, a high-school and college teammate (Longman 2008).

Bonny Kenny, the volleyball coach at Delaware, suggested that Delle Donne was a cautionary case about pressure-laden young athletes' programs—much like the deeply committed youthful sports specialists discussed in the previous chapter who were strongly encouraged to focus on a single sport year round and pressured to enter the commercial world of travel teams and tournaments. Aware of her player's history, Kenny said, "From 12 to 18, I bet Elena can count on her hands the amount of weekends she didn't have anything to do related to sport. She's missed the opportunity to be a kid" (Longman 2008).

Admittedly that outcome seems to have largely been Delle Donne's choice. She described herself as a self-starter, committed to developing into the best basketball player in the country and becoming so focused on that plan that she got up at six to exercise and play basketball. By age 7 Delle Donne was on a team with 11-year-old boys. In high school she was all-state at Ursuline Academy, as adept scoring outside the three-point arc as in the paint.

In spite of the high-quality performance, at 13 the young star started finding the game less enjoyable. This surprised and disappointed her because she was the top performer, and Delle Donne interestingly reasoned that the girl who performed best on the court should have the most fun. Performance, in fact, had become a fixation. "I was overdriving myself because I was so into becoming the best," Delle Donne said. "I always thought someone else was working harder than me, which really made me go nuts with it. It wasn't fun. It was like a job, and it was a job I wasn't getting paid for" (Longman 2008). In 2007 she took the summer off and only played basketball her senior year out of a sense of obligation to her teammates.

Clearly Delle Donne was no longer committed to the game and felt comfortable switching to volleyball at Delaware. It was a healthy decision. At Delaware she gradually regained her enthusiasm for basketball, spending four years on the team, leading it to a 104–32 record. Then Delle Donne joined the WNBA and quickly became a top performer (*USA Basketball* 2017). Elena Delle Donne illustrates that elite athletic performance involves more than just mastering physical skills—that even potentially great players can lose their effectiveness as they find it difficult to enjoy and feel satisfied in the pursuit of their sport.

In this chapter considerable emphasis falls on adolescents' sports roles—roles filled by children becoming adults who like Della Donne are experiencing their own sometimes formidable confusions and ambivalences as well as the pressures and supports of such agents of socialization as community, families, peers, coaches, and elite programs.

Before moving on to the contemporary era, however, the focus is on the historical development of high-school sports—activities that originated in a setting far less capable of sustaining extensive sports programming than the current one. In high-school sports as in other areas concerning formal organizations, the nation has displayed a steady growth of programs involving an increasing number of invested and often contesting parties. Advancing through the upcoming section, readers might be able to speculate about why and how adolescents' high-school programs appear to have become not only more prominent but also more competitive and pressure-laden over time.

After a brief look at the history of high-school sports, where student athletes often had considerable involvement in early programs' development, the focus shifts to present-day adolescents' sports and the factors influencing them.

Teen Sports: Historical Growth of High-school Play

In the beginning teens' organized sports were a modest venture primarily involving baseball with activities occurring outside of school. In 1858 New York City, for instance, had at least 60 junior amateur teams organized as clubs with constitutions and bylaws. Following the model that these baseball clubs provided, the first high-school teams developed in such well-known boarding schools as Phillips Exeter, Williston Seminary, and Phillips Andover. In 1859 Worcester High in Massachusetts became the first public high school to produce a team that competed with an opponent outside the school. That opponent was a baseball club named the Eagles, and in the opening game the rules were so rudimentary that Worcester High was permitted to have two players who were not enrolled at the school (Pruter 2004; 2013, 9–11).

In the next quarter century, the development of high-school baseball progressed slowly. In 1885 students often played baseball in the Chicago schools, but few fielded teams. An Oak Park High graduate said, "We had no baseball uniforms. We made one effort at it by the girls starting to make us caps, but after four were finished the attempt died" (Pruter 2013, 14).

By 1890, however, the schools in Cook County, where Chicago is located, did form a high-school baseball league, with student delegates gathering at a local hotel to start a conference—an extension of the student athlete's role that was possible in an era during which most school administrators were often uninterested in initiating and running sports programs. In this case, however, while students did represent their schools, the most influential person in starting the new league was Henry L. Boltwood, the principal and baseball coach at Evanston High, who strongly endorsed the character-building contribution of well supervised high-school sports.

The development of football in secondary schools roughly coincided with baseball. In the late 1850s, Boston private and public schools began play, but the early contests were nothing but crude scrimmages. By the 1870s various New England boarding schools, particularly Phillips Andover and the Adams Academy, were regularly competing.

In the early 1880s, high-school football started developing into an interscholastic sport where games included such key elements as uniforms, on-field officials, and well-prepared playing fields (Pruter 2013, 15–16). Then in 1885, acting with teachers' support, students at five Chicago-area schools took the initiative in creating the legal underpinnings for league play—a constitution, a list of the game's rules, and a schedule. The new league attracted attention, with the local *High School Journal* filled with articles about the games. A North Division High reporter wrote, "We are glad to see so many of the young ladies in attendance at the football games. We don't doubt that they look on us 'footballists' with envy and would like to help us win more games." Support for play was mixed, however, with some contests ending because of darkness or simply never taking place because one or both teams failed to show up.

There were other more serious problems. In its second year, the Chicago league games produced several fairly serious injuries, and soon the importation of ringers (players from outside the school) destroyed the league. Interest in football, however, was becoming intense, and as a result a new structure, the Cook County High School Football League, formed, with, once again, student representatives taking a prominent role by creating a constitution, bylaws, elected officials, and schedules for games. At that time about 200 high schools nationwide had football teams (Pruter 2013, 18–19).

Meanwhile in the 1880s private schools were experimenting with a variety of high-school sports besides football and baseball. In 1882 Phillips Exeter, Phillips Andover, and the Lawrenceville School were the first schools to introduce boys' lacrosse (Majors 2009), and in the 1890s and early 1900s, eastern private schools started to play ice hockey (Pruter 2013, 121).

Private schools also offered girls' unprecedented athletic play. Rosabelle Sinclair, a teacher, introduced lacrosse at the Bryn Mawr School in Baltimore. She became acquainted with the game when she was a student at St. Leonard's School in Scotland, where the headmistress had introduced the sport, describing it as "beautiful and graceful" after seeing it played in Montreal. At the Bryn Mawr School, lacrosse was an immediate success, promoting the development of high-school teams at other schools in the area (Claydon 2013). Unlike early programs in the public-school system, athletics at private schools was under administrative and faculty control.

During this era high-school basketball received its start—in the 1890s in one of the nation's hotbeds of early high-school sports, namely Cook County, Illinois. In 1895 student delegates from Cook County high schools convened to form a league for winter sports. Two fast-growing sports were in contention, basketball and the then popular indoor baseball, and curiously indoor baseball won, by a vote of seven to two. North Division, one of the two dissenting votes, joined the local YMCA basketball league, and at the same time girls' basketball became popular in the county's high schools, with articles covering the games appearing in local newspapers. For several years some chauvinistic supporters of boys' basketball feared that it was considered essentially "a girls' game."

Boys' basketball, however, became increasingly popular, and a permanent league formed in 1901 with eight teams, gradually increasing to 17 in 1910–11. At that time the Chicago schools decided to divide the program into two parts—a lightweight section featuring players under 130 lbs. or possessing a team average of 125 lbs. or less and a heavyweight section. Meanwhile basketball was growing throughout Illinois, which in 1908 became the second state after Wisconsin to start a state tournament (Pruter 2013, 103–06).

The girls' game was also expanding. In 1900 a girls' basketball league was formed, leading to a championship among the contesting teams. Marking that occasion, Frances A. Kellor, a graduate student in sociology at the University of Chicago and a future social reformer, wrote a long article in which she criticized the undue roughness the game produced for adolescent girls but praised the sport as a means of developing bodily control and grace of movement. Meanwhile the exposure of players to spectators produced some prominent opposition. The Hyde Park principal cancelled a scheduled game, saying that "[I]t was too public a place for the young women, who are of the best families in the communities" (Pruter 2013, 151).

Still, the girls' game kept growing. Like that of the boys of that era, the girls' role in high-school sports involved extensive responsibilities, such as locating coaches (usually teachers), establishing rules, creating schedules, and buying uniforms—hardly the kinds of activities generally associated with late-19th-century high-school girls. In various locations throughout the country such as New York, New Jersey, the greater Boston area, and both northern and southern California, the girls' high-school game became popular, often drawing substantial crowds (Pruter 2013, 151–56).

In the turn-of-the-century era, however, girls' high-school basketball only flourished briefly. Many influential educators worried that female players were vulnerable because of smaller hearts and lungs, quite possibly weakening their future "vital force" to have babies. A major problem, critics often believed, was the fact that many female players spurned the fairly gentle girls' norms that had been established, preferring a game that was both physically more demanding (not restricting players to limited sections of the court) and rougher than the official standards permitted. By about 1917 school administrators throughout the country generally concluded that even when leagues maintained rules that addressed girls' allegedly more pronounced vulnerabilities, the game was too physically stressful and too emotionally demanding for female players. It was prudent, they felt, to eliminate girls' interscholastic basketball (Pruter 2013, 164–69).

Boys' sports, however, generally remained popular, but in state after state administrators were troubled. They were concerned that the students who had been running the programs spent too much time involved in sports, jeopardizing their overall development; some officials were concerned about the quality of coaches heading the programs; in many instances educators felt teams had misguided values, overemphasizing winning; finally, there was widespread opposition to the frequent presence of ringers. Additionally, an observer might also consider the possibility that as high-school sports programming expanded, administrators became wary of the power high-school students were wielding. As noted previously, formal organizations such as leagues containing sports teams can involve extensive competition, with participants often grappling among themselves for control.

At any rate, a turning point had arrived, with administrators increasingly believing that it was clearly time to take over the programs and run them more effectively. In 1897 Wisconsin formed the first state high-school athletic association, and in the next two decades state organizations developed in 33 states (Bowen and Hitt 2016; Malina 2016; Pruter 2013, 75–82).

Ever since that time, those associations have played an important role in the regulation of high-school sports. During the Depression and until the end of World War II, declining funding followed by gas rationing and other wartime restrictions limited or simply eliminated organized sports in schools.

The latter half of the 20th century brought shifts in many programs. Following World War II, big cities, which were often enduring financial decline, either severely cut back or eliminated high-school sports, but in the suburbs and small towns public high-school teams often thrived, particularly in basketball and football (Pruter 2013, 315–18). Discussion later in the chapter indicates that these patterns have persisted.

Nowadays high-school athletes no longer have administrative responsibilities; their roles involve performance in programs and decisions about whether they focus on their high-school unit, or additionally or alternatively play for an out-of-school team. Since the late 1990s, the number of so-called "travel" or "select" teams has greatly expanded, with every sport discussed in these chapters producing such organizations.

These clubs operate under the loose control of the Amateur Athletic Union (AAU), an amateur sports organization that, while it represents amateur sports and physical fitness, sponsors many teams which are largely unregulated and sometimes engage in illegal money-making practices. Athletes, who are at least above-average, compete to make these teams, which practice extensively and play tournaments outside their area at locations where college coaches might attend. The tournament system, which requires extensive expenditure by families, has become big business that brings in revenues of about $7 billion a year (Adcox 2017; Christian 2016; Korman 2015).

Participation in travel teams is expensive but often helpful for developing good to elite athletes. African American parents, who tend to be less affluent than white counterparts, often can not afford travel teams for their children, whose development can be affected. In baseball preteen black boys can benefit from fairly inexpensive participation in Little League but are likely to be unable to afford the travel-team phase of high-school baseball. This financially linked disadvantage is one of several reasons why since the middle 1980s the percentage of black players in major-league baseball has declined (Kepner 2014).

In contrast, African Americans have been prominent participants in basketball travel teams and tournaments. When travel basketball teams started, most of the participants were top players, elite performers competing to represent their area in tournaments around the country. The number of prospects was small, making it possible for coaches to view the leading candidates at a selected number of tournaments. Nowadays thousands of youth basketball teams compete almost the entire year in tournaments around the country.

As the travel-team phenomenon has developed, major shoe and apparel companies—Adidas, Nike, Reebok, Under Armour, and others—have become involved, providing many elite teams free shoes and clothing as well as travel and hotel expenses in exchange for wearing their products—items which the company personnel expect top prospects will keep wearing when on scholarship in Division I (if the program they enter has an apparel deal with the company). In addition, for the very best, the future holds an eventual lucrative contract binding them to keep using the company's products when they reach the NBA (Brown 2016; Korman 2015).

This process has provided travel teams a host of benefits, but in the largely unregulated AAU world, there can be costs that players and coaches must confront. A high-school coach with a top prospect said that representatives from several shoe companies attempted to "… basically strong-arm … [him] and say he has to play for this AAU team or we're not sponsoring you. It just felt dirty. In no way, shape or form were we going to do that." Another company, the coach emphasized, had made no such demands, proving a pleasure with which to work (Kleps 2014).

While extensive money and attention have focused on boys' travel teams, girls have also participated, joining units playing basketball, volleyball, soccer, fastpitch softball, and lacrosse.

Boys' football and basketball players are most heavily recruited, and four services—*Rivals.com*, *ESPN*, *247Sports*, and *Scout.com*—provide college coaches assistance by ranking athletes in those two sports. While the various services use somewhat different criteria, all of them rely heavily on game film (Taity 2015). Clearly coaches take these ratings seriously, and the recruiting services recognize that. In fact, since some college recruiters are now observing very young prospects, *Rivals.com* has begun developing player profiles, if not actual rankings, on some sixth-grade football players, with the intention of continuing to monitor them (Elliott 2015).

Whether or not students are elite performers, high-school sports continue to be popular. The National Federation of State High School Associations compiled lists of the ten most popular high-school sports for both females and males. In 2017 nine of the 11 sports discussed in this book were included. The numbers:

- Girls' high-school sports: volleyball, 444,779, basketball 430,368, soccer 388,339, fastpitch softball 367,405, lacrosse 93,473
- Boys' high-school sports: football (11-player team) 1.06 million, basketball 550,305, baseball 491,790, soccer 450,234 (National Federation of State High School Associations 2017).

It is notable that at the top of this list of the most popular female high-school sports, volleyball edged out basketball, traditionally considered the most popular girls' sport. Many players find that volleyball epitomizes a game being fun, the absence of which is a primary reason cited in the previous chapter why many young players drop out of organized sports. One prospect heavily recruited for basketball indicated why she preferred volleyball. "The relationships you build, how together you are, set it apart from basketball," she said. "You come together after every point." Another player, who was involved in basketball as a child, switched to volleyball in high school. "I love basketball – to watch," she said. "I love *to play* volleyball. In basketball, I could post up and score. In volleyball, you have to be good at everything. You have to work together more. In basketball, you can own the court. It can be your show. For volleyball, you need everybody" (Friedman 2017).

SUMMARY 2.1

Historical Issues Involving Teen Sports

- The earliest youth baseball teams located in New York City and during the same era in prominent boarding schools. By 1890 high schools in Cook County, Illinois, established a baseball league, with students running the program.
- Football on a similar trajectory, beginning in Boston's private and public schools and reaching well-known boarding schools in the 1870s. In 1885 students at five Chicago schools promoted a stable football program, producing a constitution, a list of rules, and a schedule of games. In that decade some private schools introduced both boys' lacrosse and ice hockey and also girls' programs, with lacrosse an early entry.
- In the 1890s girls' and boys' basketball became increasingly popular, with students in charge of locating coaches, establishing rules, producing schedules, and purchasing uniforms. The girls' game flourished until about 1917 when it succumbed to claims of females' alleged physical vulnerabilities.
- While boys' programs continued to thrive, the educational officials took control of the programs, forming high-school athletic associations in many states.
- In the 20th century, high-school programs have tended to do better in small towns and suburbs than in cities, which often faced financial decline following World War II.
- Top players in various sports get to choose among an array of travel teams, which can provide them a chance to display their skills, perhaps winning Division I scholarships or eventually even pro contracts.

Summary 2.1 lists the major historical issues covered in this section. Every high-school athlete might tell a story about her or his athletic experience. One account follows.

Adolescents' Efforts to Advance in Organized Sports

Many times in the course of youthful games, it is possible to spot the elite athletic prospects. However, it can be a quirky business, with adolescents' performance of their sports roles turning out to be surprising and provocative. Mark Buehrle was almost emaciated and just five feet tall when he tried out for his high-school baseball team as a pitcher. The first two years he was cut from the team. At that point "I pretty much decided I was done," Buehrle said. "I felt … [discouraged] not being able to make my freshman and sophomore teams. There was going to be no way I'd make the varsity team. I basically decided that baseball wasn't going to be my thing, and I should move on."

Then Buehrle changed his mind, thinking that the coach might have made a mistake and approaching his role as a player much more positively and systematically. "Don't ever give up on your dream," Buehrle emphasized. "Keep trying. I wasn't the biggest kid, but I learned what I needed to do, learned how to work out and stayed focused on getting where I wanted to be" (Tomashoff 2015). Buehrle ended up having a 16-year major-league career, winning 214 games and making the All-Star team five times (*Baseball-Reference.com* 2017).

For Mark Buehrle eventual major-league success seems to have occurred because of his commitment, an essential factor during sports programs' retention stage. For talented adolescent athletes, such agents of socialization as the local community, parents, siblings and teammates, and coaches can affect their success at that stage.

Teen Play in the Community

In many residential areas, organized sports prove beneficial for local youths. Surveys done with teenage respondents indicated that students participating in sports were more likely to have positive self-images; to attend college and complete their degrees; and to display less likelihood of emotional stress, suicidal tendencies, and substance abuse (Harrison and Narayan 2003; The Aspen Institute 2015).

When high-school sports emerge as a positive influence, it is likely that a supportive local community contributes. The following illustration involving a celebrated athlete is a case in point.

In 2005 talk-show host Jay Leno asked 17-year-old hockey phenom Sidney Crosby where he was from, and it would have been understandable, even to his fellow townspeople, if Crosby had said "Halifax"—the well-known city in the vicinity. Instead, the young man answered, "Cole Harbour, Nova Scotia." For many of the 30,000 local residents the reply was deeply meaningful, illustrating the youthful star's sense of community created by playing hockey, attending high school, and involving himself in myriad other local activities (Rosen 2016). The home town has provided a positive setting in which Crosby as an adolescent had been able to become both a world-class hockey player and a well-rounded person.

Eleven years later Crosby made his yearly return to Cole Harbour, where he has helped run a summer hockey camp for the 160 children who were the around-the-world winners among thousands participating in a lottery. At several locations in the town, Crosby displayed the Stanley Cup and the Conn Smythe Trophy for being the most valuable player in the playoffs. When asked why he kept coming back to Cole Harbour,

It is the rare homegrown athlete who receives such public recognition. In this case the appreciation between star and community is distinctly mutual. (Source: Paul McKinnon / Shutterstock.com)

Crosby said, "It just feels right ... Regardless of how busy you are, when you're here, I think for whatever reason, you just feel comfortable and you just feel relaxed. That's why I come back every summer" (Bloom 2016).

Crosby's ongoing relationship with his youthful community appears unusually powerful, contributing to an upbringing which seems to have escaped the ravages of the modern unwinding process. However, his situation has hardly been unique. As ample evidence in these chapters suggests, the setting in which people develop significantly shapes them. That's certainly a standard pattern in sports.

Researchers have found that the locales in which pro athletes grow up often possess positive traits that promote their development as players. In one study investigators used data from official league websites, examining the birth cities of over 2,000 male athletes belonging to three major pro leagues. They found that while about 52 percent of Americans live in cities of over 500,000 people, only 13 percent of their sample from the NHL, 29 percent from the NBA, and 15 from MLB came from cities of that size (Côté, Macdonald, Baker, and Abernathy 2005). In a later study focused on the NFL, the research team found even more distinctive results—that while scarcely one in four Americans were born in municipalities of 50,000 residents or fewer, nearly half of the league's players came from such suburban or rural locales (Macdonald, Cheung, Côté, and Abernathy 2009).

The investigators suggested that smaller municipalities have certain advantages for elite athletes' development; the suburbs or towns provide more space for organized games, offering public facilities that are safer and more comfortable and sponsoring athletic programs that are more relaxed and less tightly structured than those in large cities (Côté, Macdonald, Baker, and Abernathy 2005, 1071).

In the NBA the impact of community of origin has been particularly dramatic over time. In the 1970s and 1980s, a full 90 percent of NBA players came from inner-city neighborhoods, but then as the game expanded and corporate sponsorship increased, colleges and the NBA began a painstaking search for talented players—a move which encouraged many high schools, both American and foreign, to revamp their basketball programs. It was a costly business, requiring effective transportation, cutting-edge facilities and equipment, and improved, often expensive coaching. Inner-city schools were too poor to compete, and as a result their students' basketball development often lagged behind their suburban peers' progress, disadvantaging their access to the NBA (Keating 2011). In short, young players' social class had become a factor affecting their prospect for success in the NBA.

A *social class* is a large category of people who possess similar levels of income, education, and occupational prestige ranking (Doob 2000, 236–37). The impact of families' social-class membership in sports-program participation is apparent in the following discussion.

Families and Support for Their Adolescent Athletes

A pair of studies focusing on families provide further information about the change over time in social class for modern NBA players. One investigation involved 155 NBA players active between 1994 and 2004, with data about their social class and families coming from 245 sources. The researchers learned that an African American child from a low-income background had 37 percent less chance of reaching the NBA than those from middle- or high-income families, and poor white children had a 75 percent lower probability of joining the league than more affluent white prospects (Dubrow and Adams 2012).

A later investigation using data from every county in the nation produced a consistent finding, concluding that for both black and white men the level of affluence for the neighborhood in which they grew up strongly influenced their likelihood of reaching the NBA. Besides the fact that poor boys were likely to face the disadvantage of inferior coaching and facilities, the author concluded that they resided in households and attended schools where encouragement of such job-related general skills as a strong work ethic, commitment, and trust were often deficient (Stephens-Davidowitz 2013). In short, at the retention stage of high-school basketball programs, middle-class players in the suburbs and towns benefited from several advantages over their poor counterparts in the inner-city—advantages that would be likely to make them more accomplished at the retention stage.

While parental influence and affluence can often assist young athletes, the adjacent Box 2.1 indicates that a few NBA prospects benefit from an especially powerful advantage over other candidates.

BOX 2.1

Social Reproduction in the NBA

Social reproduction is the process by which people in certain categories, such as social classes, have differing access to the valuable resources that influence the transmission of inequality from one generation to the next (Doob 2013, 10–11). Some of the valuable resources parents can transmit to their children include financial assistance, networking opportunities, and strategic advice. Just as parents with prominent jobs in such organizations as law firms, corporate enterprises, or political offices can be especially well positioned to help their children establish themselves in their own or related occupations, it is similar in professional sports, for instance the NBA.

Social reproduction, in fact, has been increasing in the NBA. In 2015 there were 24 second-generation NBA players (*HoopsHype* 2015). Specific advantages these players received from their fathers included genetic endowment, particularly their height, and also exposure to years of quality instruction. Steve Kerr, the head coach of the Golden State Warriors, said that it was as if these young men were located in a "basketball think tank" from childhood, benefiting both from their fathers' instruction and time spent in the NBA locker room and on the practice court, with endless tidbits of information offered. "When you grow up in that world, you're exposed to the best teaching and the best coaching," Kerr added (Cacciola 2014). These privileged sons, in short, profited from interaction with a set of first-rate agents of socialization.

Whether it's the NBA or some other pro sport, ex-pro fathers mentoring their children are likely to have a sense of "been there, done that"—a point of view that generally encourages them to be somewhat laid back, acting instructive and supportive to be sure but not zealously committed to even talented youngsters' recruitment to the league since they appreciate that the road ahead is often long and unpredictable. In Chapter 1, Dell Curry's comments on son Steph's productive development as an athlete displays such a cautious, low-key approach.

Sometimes, however, the potential advantages of social reproduction can backfire, creating excessive pressure for a young player. When Marcus Jordan, Michael Jordan's son, went to the University of Central Florida the expectations were enormous. A journalist asked, "How could anyone come close to arguably the greatest player in the history of basketball? Not possible." Marcus played well but hardly at his father's level, and he left the team his senior year (Medcalf 2017). While the younger Jordan faced a particularly formidable comparison, it seems probable that overall having a father who played in the NBA can be distinctly advantageous.

Parents in various social classes tend to view their teen children's sports programs enthusiastically. A nationally representative sample of over 2,500 parents with children in middle school, junior high, and high school, over half of whom were in high school, indicated that 72 percent of these children played sports in the previous year, and 89 percent of those parents believed their children benefited either a great deal or quite a bit from the participation (*npr*, Robert Wood Johnson Foundation, and Harvard T.H. Chan School of Public Health 2015, 14–16).

The same survey revealed that among parents whose high-school aged children played a sport the previous year fully a quarter—26 percent of those parents—hoped their offspring would be recruited to the pros. Parents' education was relevant here. Forty-four percent of parents with a high-school education or less hoped their children would go pro while a mere 9 percent of their counterparts who were college graduates shared that view. In addition, a distinct relationship appeared between family income and that perception, with 39 percent of parents with income under $50,000 a year hoping their children had pro sports in their future while barely half as many—just 20 percent of those with income over $50,000—wanted that outcome.

While less affluent parents were more inclined to hope their children would become professional athletes, they also saw distinctly greater impediments to reaching that goal. Thirty-two percent of those with family income under $50,000 a year said that the cost of travel teams and other expenses was too much, and, in contrast, just half as many—16 percent—of parents with income of $50,000 or more reached that conclusion (*npr*, Robert Wood Johnson Foundation, and Harvard T.H. Chan School of Public Health 2015, 17–18).

Parents often find that their high-school children's athletic expenses are likely to accelerate over time. Hockey is a case in point, costing slightly over $3,000 a year for average teenage hockey players. But then if youngsters continue to improve their play, their families face rising costs with more extensive travel (Mirtle 2014; Turner 2013). At this point parents are an essential financial source, but as the following examples suggest, their frequently unrelenting dedication suggests they are simultaneously an important psychological support.

While some teen athletes' parents are fairly affluent, that is often not the case. Marnie Wiltshire, a Canadian, is a single mom whose 13-year-old son Kyle joined Triple-A Bantam minor hockey as well as two teams that played in the spring. The previous year Wiltshire paid $15,000 (about $11,400 in US dollars) for Kyle's expenses. "Basically, we just save everything we can and everything goes toward hockey," said Wiltshire, whose three younger children also plan to play. "Our whole life is hockey. It's at the point where if you want to stay in the more elite level teams, you have to do the extra stuff."

Jamie Kagan, a partner in a Winnipeg law firm, is more affluent, and while the financial cost of his son's hockey programs is less taxing, he is well aware of the part finances play. "Every parent's nightmare is for their kid to walk out of the dressing room in tears because he got cut," Kagan said. "If it costs another $500 for that not to happen, you'll pay for that. As a parent, you feel you should have done something more. If I give my kid the best stick and that helps him get what he wants and he feels good about himself ...?" (Turner 2013).

Besides parents others can be influential agents of socialization in teen athletes' experience.

Peers' Impact: The Sibling and Teammate Effect

Siblings and teammates are the only agents of socialization who can be fellow players, often providing as a result a uniquely immediate impact. In sports younger siblings appear to be particularly susceptible to older brothers' and sisters' influence, especially if the elders are elite athletes themselves. A questionnaire administered to three levels of athletes—elite, pre-elite, and non-elite—involved 229 individuals engaged in 34 sports and focused on the respondents' siblings. The data revealed that elite athletes' younger siblings were four times more likely to participate regularly in competitive sports than counterparts whose older siblings were non-elite athletes. Furthermore, the study found that elite athletes were more likely to be later-born, raising the possibility that these younger brothers and sisters are particularly well positioned to benefit athletically from their junior location (Pathways to the Podium Research Project 2012).

An illustration of the last trend involves elite women soccer players. In 2015, 17 of 23 members (73.9 percent) of the US national soccer team were younger siblings, and on the youth national team, whose members ranged in age from 13 to 23, a nearly identical 74 percent had at least one older sibling (Longman 2015).

While recognition of sibling influence appears widespread, it is not entirely clear how the process works. What seems apparent is that often at particularly youthful ages younger children find themselves in athletic roles where older brothers and sisters are a frequent presence, teaching them how to play and serving as agents of socialization who provide both inspiration and competition.

The younger athletes are likely to be highly competitive, motivated to mobilize their determination and skills to do well against their older, larger siblings. In particular, they seem willing to take risks to outplay older sisters or brothers and in the process gain precious attention from parents and other onlookers (Longman 2015). As a clear case in point, a study of 700 brothers who played major-league baseball found that when it came to the risky act of stealing bases, younger brothers attempted it an impressive 10.6 times more frequently and were successful 3.2 times as often (Sulloway and Zweigenhaft 2010, 406–08).

In contrast, in a small study of sibling athletes in four families sports researcher Jean Côté reached a different conclusion. The investigator found that among the teenage siblings he interviewed the eldest in three of the four families acted as role models, helping their brothers and sisters decide on the sports they should play (Côté 1999, 404) and working cooperatively to develop both their work ethic and skills (Côté 1999, 407–08). Although Côté's findings downplayed the competitive factor among siblings playing sports, it was consistent with other sources on the topic in emphasizing another point—that younger siblings were often advantaged in athletic opportunity.

Tom Brady, the New England Patriots quarterback, also felt the influence of his siblings in sports. He had three older sisters, all of whom were excellent athletes. In Brady's view, however, there was a distinct problem. In an essay written at 17 Brady explained, "The one and only thing that bothered me about my sisters' accomplishments was that people only recognized me when my sisters were around" (Phillips 2016). While not addressed in the essay, it seems likely that Brady's adolescent subordination to his sisters served as an incentive to become successful in sports.

Certainly teammates can also have a significant influence, with a number of studies offering specifics about their impact. For instance, an investigation that included 27 talented teen athletes found that teammates encouraged the respondents' continuing involvement in sports (Patrick, Ryan, Alfeld-Liro, Fredricks, Hruda, and Eccles 1999). In a survey involving primarily adolescent athletes in 25 sports, teammates' impact on the subjects' outlook and behavior was also considered more positive than negative, supporting team rules and goals and avoiding uncooperative, disruptive behavior (Martin, Ewing, and Gould 2014).

While teammates' influence can often be positive, it sometimes can prove dysfunctional for healthy, smooth-running programs. A study about high-school sports revealed that in a contact sport like football, serious fighting is a more common practice among teammates and friends than in noncontact sports like baseball, basketball, and tennis. It appears that the combined influence of hard-hitting physical contact and teammates' support for fighting help make the game a particularly violent one (Kreager 2007). In addition, teammates' behavioral standards in high-school football can promote other antisocial actions, including cheating during a game, risking injury to an opponent, and even intentionally hurting a player (Steinfeldt, Rutkowski, Vaughan, and Steinfeldt 2011).

On occasion teammates' behavior can be dysfunctional in another way. Alan Goldberg, a sports psychologist, wrote about Jackie, a superlative basketball player who since early childhood had been dedicated to the game and as a freshman was working harder than any of her peers, leading the team in all major statistical categories. It turned out that as early as her freshman year, Jackie, who remained level-headed about her success, ran into problems. Goldberg indicated that this outcome was all too common—that "[S]ometimes these athletes will be teammates whose role on the team is directly, and in their mind negatively affected by you, your work ethic and abilities." He added, "Why would the senior captains on Jackie's team accuse her of being selfish in a game where she had 9 points, 15 assists and 14 rebounds? Are those the stats of a selfish player?" (Goldberg 2017).

In such a situation, a coach is the most obvious individual to address the problem.

The Coaching Influence

Jean Côté and his team of sports psychologists focused on coaching indicated that the development of young athletes involves three roughly age-related phases. In the "sampling years" discussed in Chapter 1 and involving children aged 6 to 12, recreational athletes and their potentially elite peers often have roughly similar priorities, emphasizing having fun and experimenting with different activities and roles the game offers. Coaches must be aware of how the needs of athletes frequently change across the developmental spectrum, from childhood to young adulthood, with coaches' flexible monitoring an essential influence; in particular, in this pleasant, relaxed youthful setting, where children can gain a positive start in organized sports, they need to discourage parents from pushing for early specialization (Côté, Young, North, and Duffy 2007, 9–10).

From age 13 to 15, however, a new phase develops for those hoping to become elite athletes—the "specializing years." The athletes enroll in programs where their fellow participants are also focused on a single sport, and the guidelines distinctly change. While researchers still emphasize the importance of having fun, they now take competition and effective performance seriously, encouraging both motivation and commitment in programs' retention stage. Deliberate practice has become a priority, with coaches introducing training that helps develop sport-specific skills. As the young athletes advance, their instructors will provide them a chance to oppose other teams, offering the prospect of awards and social recognition. In addition, coaches have the responsibility of evaluating players, choosing or nominating participants for elite units such as top travel teams. This is an important if sometimes stressful task because coaches' decisions made at this juncture can significantly shape a young person's sports career.

At age 16 and older, elite athletes enter the "investment years." Now they focus more intensively than previously on one sport and often on playing one position. These athletes require large amounts of sport-specific training, and in order to provide this, a coach must have a detailed knowledge of the athlete's skill set. To make certain that the individual keeps improving, deliberate practice needs to be both physically and mentally demanding. Since the basic intention is to prepare prospects for increasingly more advanced competition, the coach needs to provide ample opportunities for high-level contests.

As the investment years progress, coaches are often inclined to alter their relationships with players, no longer simply telling the individuals what to do but promoting discussion and collaborative outcomes (Côté, Baker, and Abernathy 2007, 186–87; Côté, Young, North, and Duffy 2007, 11–14).

While such a gradual development of elite athletes has widespread support, discussion in the previous chapter's examination of early specialization and in the remaining portion of this chapter indicate that considerable differences of opinion exist about how best to promote the growth of youthful athletic talent. Coaches to be sure remain central to that process.

Representing the National Federation of State High School Associations, Kyle Elmendorf, a two-sport high-school coach, suggested that to help sustain their players' motivation, successful coaches working with adolescents needed to embrace a distinct set of norms:

- One useful standard is "to praise loudly and criticize softly." Elmendorf indicated that when players make mistakes the best approach to use is "the sandwich method"—first mention something positive the athlete has done, then follow with a criticism the coach believes the player needs to address, and then finish with another positive comment.
- An additional norm involves making sure that all program participants feel important. This can be a fairly challenging task, requiring that coaches get to know all of the players and not only learning about them but also recognizing the possibility that communication improves when coaches convey information about their own lives (Elmendorf 2016).

A study that featured 154 varsity high-school coaches in seven sports, six of which are included in this book—girls' basketball, girls' volleyball, football, boys' basketball, girls' soccer, and boys' soccer—seemed to display the kind of sensitive norms cited in the previous two points. Overall the coaches indicated that they were most concerned about their charges' social and psychological development, including their work ethic and goal setting, feeling that while winning is desirable it is a lower-order priority (Gould, Chung, Smith, and White 2006).

- Another standard effective coaches meet is the ability to run a high-level practice. To accomplish that, they generally need to keep things moving—that a common misconception involves stopping and talking to the athletes, believing that it is the best method to overcome any mistakes—but players are likely to become impatient. Better to keep the action going, making terse comments along the way or in-between exercises and appreciating that repetition will reap benefit (Elmendorf 2016).

  According to a pair of studies, it appears that the most effective way that coaches, including high-school coaches, can acquire detailed knowledge about such issues as running effective practices is by observing, listening to, and conversing with experienced, successful colleagues (Cushion, Armour, and Jones 2003, 217–18; Gilbert, Lichtenwaldt, Gilbert, Zelezny, and Côté 2009, 426).

- Finally a useful norm for coaches working with adolescents is the idea of being open to new ideas and approaches. While certain standards might prove dependable over time, it can be productive to consider the possibility of making a change—that just because a certain way of doing things has prevailed, it shouldn't inevitably continue into the indefinite future. In fact, top coaches keep developing, appreciating the importance of addressing ideas and approaches that are currently popular (Elmendorf 2016). The following confrontation between coach and player relates to the last point.

  Indi Cowie was the top player on her high-school soccer team, and in one contest she scored two goals, but after the second the coach benched her. "I got the ball and beat three girls to score a goal, and my coach pulled me off the field," Cowie told a reporter. "He said, 'You should have passed.' I said, 'But I scored a goal, Coach.' He sat me out for the rest of the half. At halftime he asked me, 'Are you ready to play properly?' I said, 'Sure.' I did the same thing, and he took me off the field for the rest of the game." Cowie quit the high-school team and played for a local boys' club.

Did the riff with the coach hurt her recruitment prospects? Hardly. She received a scholarship to the vaunted University of North Carolina. Unlike the high-school coach, the club coach was much more flexible, saying, "All the great Tar Heels are incredibly self-motivated, and they thirst to score goals." He added, "That's Indi, and I believe she has a chance to break boundaries in soccer" (Smith 2011).

To many observers this type of relationship between athlete and coach is troubling, with a highly talented soccer player punished for what most evaluators would consider an exemplary performance of her role. In fact, a study of 106 12- to 15-year-old female soccer players produced an interesting, pertinent finding—that when the girls received a certain amount of autonomy in a context where caring coaches allowed them such rights as free expression of opinions and preferences including the chance to choose their position, they appeared to be more highly motivated to participate in the program (Reynolds and McDonough 2015).

One issue about coaching the previous tiff might bring to mind involves an assessment of whether or not women will be more effective coaching high-school girls than men. Some veteran observers of girls' soccer believe that their young charges not only tend to be more comfortable with female coaches in expressing their concerns and needs but that they are more likely to feel empowered by them, concluding that if a woman who is working with them has attained success in the game, then they can achieve it too.

For girls in soccer and other sports, however, there are more men than women coaches (Mazeika 2016; Scavuzzo 2014; Triton Youth Soccer Association 2016). Sarah Dwyer-Shick, a veteran coach and a member of the Female Coaching Network, which promotes the international expansion of women in coaching, indicated that even though girls' and women's opportunities to play soccer have sharply expanded, the chances to coach are another story. She wrote, "As girls' participation across the country has increased, so has the money involved. Girls' soccer has become a big business. And it is men who run the business. Surprisingly few girls make the transition from girl/player to woman/coach and those that do often do not stay long" (Dwyer-Shick 2015).

While we know nothing about this coach personally, it is clear that she has one important attribute necessary for success—the ability to spark her players' interest and enthusiasm. (Source: Monkey Business Images / thinkstock.com)

It seems important that officials hiring soccer coaches for girls' programs keep a vigilant eye assuring female candidates get a completely fair shake. A similar approach would seem to apply to other high-school girls' sports.

With support from coaches and parents, many athletes move from the sampling years to the specializing and investment years.

Advanced Teen Play

As high-school athletes advance, some demonstrate distinctive qualities which help shape the performance of their role in the recruitment and retention stages of their programs and establish them as elite:

- Drive and commitment

    While most good high-school competitors incorporate training into their lives, a few put their regimen ahead of being a normal teenager, prioritizing their goals and the means to achieve them—training, diet, competition, and sleep—and fueling their work ethic with the realization that there is always something in the game they can manage to make better (Beekman 2016; Mallett and Hanrahan 2004). As a high-school athlete and later as a professional lacrosse player, Mitch Belisle found that "[T]o be truly successful at sports, you need to have a genuine desire to be the best, as well as the drive it takes to fulfill that desire." He added, "So logic would follow that if I wanted to be the best in any of the sports I played, coupling that desire with year-round training would turn me into an unstoppable force, right?" (Belisle 2016).

- Competitiveness

    Competitive as they are, top athletes abhor defeat (Beekman 2016). At Mountain Brook High School, head coach Bucky McMillan explained that lacrosse defender Sean Elmore has been "the ultimate competitor," separated from others by his refusal to lose—whether in a drill, a game, or another sport. McMillan mentioned three players who had gone on to play in college. "All three of those guys, they couldn't stand to lose," he added (Parmley 2017).

- The acceptance of occasional restorative breaks

    As Elena Delle Donne's experience demonstrated, the retention stage of elite high-school programs can be both demanding and exhausting and a potential source of burnout. Elite athletes in such programs need to appreciate that it is important, even essential both psychologically and physically to take occasional time off (Beekman 2016). Since they tend to work so hard at their sports, they would appear to be particularly at risk physically and psychologically if they fail to comply with this suggestion.

Whether or not they are elite, a pair of dysfunctions confront players in advanced high-school programs. First, there is the distinct danger of burnout. When sports administrator Larry Chavez became athletic director at Cleveland High in Rio Rancho, New Mexico, he was stunned to see that year-round training destroyed teams—in particular, volleyball and soccer teams that lost almost all their players by senior year. "I just feel that with kids, they … only have three or four years of high school experience," Chavez said. "And by them being forced, by either high school coaches, parents or club coaches, to specialize so early, I think it's hindering their development, and I think that's why there's such a high rate of burnout for our kids" (Voigt 2016).

An additional dysfunction is injuries. Ray C. Fair, an economist, headed a study of athletes' injuries in high-school and college sports using detailed information on four types—concussions, bone damage, torn tissue, and muscle and cartilage impairment —and found that if investigators substituted the injury rates in four high-school contact sports—wrestling, football, soccer, and basketball—with those obtained in two noncontact sports, namely flag football and baseball, there would be 601,900 fewer injuries a year. Injuries are obviously dysfunctional for players and teams engaged in contact sports, but they can also be a financial detriment for high schools, each year costing as much as $19.2 billion a year, with football accounting for at least a staggering 70 percent of the cost. When the researchers made a similar comparison with male college students, whose numbers in contact sports are considerably fewer than the high-school total, the figures were much smaller but still impressive—49,600 fewer injuries compared to noncontact sports' injury numbers and a savings of between $446 million and $1.5 billion (Fair and Champa 2017, 1–2, 25–29; Kolata 2017).

Across high-school sports certain competitors are more susceptible to injury. Two studies, one involving 29 high schools and the other two, indicated that athletes who specialized in a single sport were more likely to get hurt, particularly receiving lower-extremity injuries involving knees, ankles, hips, and ligament sprains as well as muscle/tendon strains (Bell, Post, Trigsted, Hetzel, McGuine, and Brooks 2016; Howard 2016).

In some sports the impact of intense specialization can be insidious. A study of over 400 female high-school volley players found that even in this noncontact sport lower-extremity injuries are fairly common, largely because players have heard that they will get better simply by playing more. Increased time on the court means subjecting young athletes' ankles, knees, and spine to the potentially damaging impact of repeated jumps on the hardwood floor. "Oftentimes, if you injure your lower extremities, there's what we call a waterfall effect," the researcher explained. "If a volleyball player hurts a knee, she's more likely to hurt an ankle later" (UW Health 2009).

Another female sport appears to be in the throes of change about an injury-related issue. In girls' lacrosse a long-time debate has featured whether or not players should wear helmets. The argument against them has emphasized that the current somewhat limited contact game would become much fiercer—more like the male version, where players have worn helmets for decades. However, with growing fear about head injuries, hundreds of school districts, including programs throughout Florida and New York City, have made headgear compulsory. At a school in Atlanta, two mothers, whose daughters had received concussions, led the initiative and received unanimous support from families. "The girls became better, more confident players," one of the mothers said. "We certainly don't want the girls' game to turn into the boys' game; we want the officials to call the rules as they are. And with the extra protection this past year, we saw a drop in head injuries" (Pennington 2017). For most athletes wearing a helmet is probably a readily acceptable role adjustment—not likely to undermine their commitment to excel in the sport the way an adjustment like cutting back on the amount of practice time might do for zealous competitors.

As far as commitment is concerned, it is commonplace among players in the following context.

— *Travel Teams and Tournaments*

As many families promote their adolescent children's sports advancement, they spend considerable time and money in the process. The costs involve travel team dues, hotels, restaurants, transportation, coaching lessons, and equipment purchase, and can vary widely—anywhere from $1,000 a year up to $15,000 or even more (Mendell 2014; Riddle 2014; Sullivan 2015). Travis Dorsch, a professor in the Department of Family, Consumer, and Human Development at Utah State University, contended that such large expenditures can create tension between parents and their children. For instance, if the family spends $10,000 a year or more on their child's training and travel teams, "What are they expecting in return? Is it a college scholarship?" Dorsch's response was blunt. "The chances are slim to none of a kid getting a scholarship" (Sullivan 2015). So an issue here is not only the sacrifice of spending the money, but the impact that doing so can produce on family relations.

As travel-team members, a select few athletes are distinctly advantaged, such as those invited to attend Nike's Elite Youth Basketball League, the Under Armour Association, or one of the other summer events sponsored by shoe and apparel companies. Unlike their peers who must have families that can afford to pay their various expenses, these elite participants are funded by shoe companies and private donors, and a substantial number will win college scholarships.

While in such programs, these young people generally stay busy and focused. Toward the end of the summer, Noah Morgan was trying to recall how many tournaments he had attended. Was it 11 or perhaps 12? On another issue, however, he was definite. "No time I would have to get a job," he said chuckling. "Basketball is my job. That's my job. That's what's going to pay for me to go to school" (Thomson 2016).

Markelle Fultz, who spent a summer competing at basketball tournaments funded by the Under Armour Association, agreed with Morgan that getting to college was the goal, and his experience was positive. "It was great and I had fun," said Fultz. "There was great competition every game I played. The crowds were good; college coaches were at every game they could come to. Scouts were everywhere" (Jackson 2016).

A study of the travel-team experience produced equally positive respondents. In the summer of 2013, *ESPN* commissioned the University of Florida to conduct a groundbreaking investigation of 1,250 elite athletes aged 10 to 18 participating in summer tournament play in 11 states involving nine different sports, including six covered in these chapters—baseball, basketball, volleyball, lacrosse, soccer, and softball. Regardless of their age, sport, or gender, the respondents, who filled out questionnaires, were enthusiastic. When asked what she liked most about travel sports, a 14-year-old softball player from Texas indicated, "You get to go away from your parents and have fun" (Matz 2014). When the research team asked the respondents what they liked least about travel sports, many recorded one word— "Nothing." A journalist added, "And no, that doesn't mean they left the answer blank. It means they're so content with their sport that they actually took the time to write 'Nothing.'" Interestingly, while the young athletes generally enjoyed the experience, as they grew older they tended to become more realistic about their pro prospects—with 69 percent of the study's respondents aged 10 to 13 believing they were talented enough to become a professional versus a much lower 41 percent picking that optimistic option in the 14 to 18 category (Matz 2013).

It seems a quick review is in order. Research and commentary about youthful athletes in general promotes widespread concern, including various experts' testimony about premature specialization, burnout, and injury. In contrast, the University of Florida questionnaires are virtually unanimous: The respondents contend that these top-level, high-pressure travel teams are a good thing. So who's right?

It appears that there is no single answer—that it depends on the player involved and that some thrive in a high-pressure atmosphere. Chase Bly played baseball and soccer during elementary school, but then in the eighth grade he discovered lacrosse, attending a lacrosse camp that summer. Bly loved the game, and while at the camp he learned that many of the participants belonged to a travel team located near Baltimore. Without telling his parents, Bly arranged for a tryout and made the team. Over the next three summers, twice a week, Bly and his mother made the four-and-a-half-hour trek to practices from their home near Pittsburgh—an investment of time and money that most parents would be either unwilling or unable to make. Seldom did they get home before 2 a.m. For Chase Bly the passion for the game has been fundamental. He said, "If you truly love the sport, then you won't get burned out" (Matz 2014).

But is it that simple? Many involved professionals urge parental caution in overseeing children's sports roles. "Just because the kids are loving it doesn't mean it's what's best for them," said Kristen Dieffenbach, a specialist in exercise science and sports psychology. "If you put them in the kitchen and tell them they can have whatever they want, they'd eat nothing but pizza, chicken wings, burgers and hot dogs." Dieffenbach added, "As the adults in charge ... we have a responsibility to ask ourselves this: In the interest of our kids' long-term development, are we doing all we can do?" (Matz 2014).

Informed observers like Dr. Dieffenbach emphasize such real dangers as burnout and injury that can accompany early specialization, and the following information suggests that many others share similar concerns. Summary 2.2 lists factors affecting adolescents' success in organized sports.

> **SUMMARY 2.2**
>
> **Factors Affecting Teens' Success in Organized Sports**
>
> - Size of community of origin, with professional athletes more likely than the general populace to grow up in rural and suburban areas rather than large cities.
> - Some athletes belong to families that are particularly advantageous for athletic success; the concepts of social class and social reproduction prove relevant here.
> - About nine in ten parents interviewed indicated that their children play organized sports and over a quarter believe they can eventually play pro; the financial cost of teen play can be considerable, making it less probable that lower income families will participate.
> - Siblings, especially athletically active older siblings, tend to encourage their younger brothers' and sisters' involvement in organized sports; younger siblings tend to have more successful sports careers than older brothers and sisters. Teammates can also be a significant influence.
> - Coaches of teen athletes need to understand the complex task of preparing young athletes as they advance into the specialization and investment phases. While coaches vary in their approach, it proves productive for players if coaches commit to a set of norms fairly similar to the one presented in the chapter. It is notable that in recent decades the number of women coaching high-school girls' teams has declined.
> - In looking at elite high-school sports, it is clear that the players have certain distinctive qualities. The participants in travel teams and tournaments are better than average athletes, who, except for the very top candidates, are dependent on families' funding. The most skilled athletes attend leagues funded by large shoe and apparel companies, and many have the distinct possibility of Division I scholarship and some prospect of making it to pro teams. The University of Florida study of travel team players indicated that practically all of them greatly enjoyed the experience. Some professional observers, however, have distinct reservations.

Conclusion

Earlier in the chapter, the focus was on three stages of youth involvement in organized sports, with a team of prominent researchers advocating that the specialization years start around 13 and the investment years at 16 or older. Clearly the researchers writing on the topic were wary of rushing into specialization, and as the following information indicates, it appears that many Americans are reluctant for even more mature athletes to focus on just one sport.

In 2015 a high-school sports site received over a half-million shares in its first three days after touching a nerve with a chart about recruits to Ohio State's national championship football team. While five team members had only participated in high-school football, 42 had played multiple sports. A journalist wrote, "To be an elite level player at a college or professional sport, you need a degree of exceptional athleticism. And the best medically, scientifically, and psychologically recommended way to develop such all around athleticism is ample free play and multiple sport participation as a child" (O'Sullivan 2015).

The last two chapters have cited many experts' concern about early specialization and, in contrast, some parents', coaches', and players' fervent support for it. While Jean Côté and his team of sports psychologists have designated three informative, age-related stages outlining elite athletes' growing commitment to a single sport, there is room for individual choice about when to advance. Above all, it seems productive for players' effective development if they participate in pleasant, upbeat, and informative sports programs where the key agents of socialization provide useful detail about and support for the athletes' progress while allowing the young people themselves to decide when is the best moment to commit to a single sport.

Summary

Early organized youth sports involved junior baseball teams in New York City and in several boarding schools. By 1890 high schools in Cook County, Chicago established a permanent baseball league. The growth of high-school football occurred during the same era. Five Chicago-area schools formed a league, with interest in the contests intense, and representatives from the participating schools drew up a constitution, bylaws, and a schedule for games.

High-school basketball started in Cook County, and by the early 20th century it was played throughout the Chicago area. Interest in the girls' game was also expanding, with a league formed and popularity developing in a number of states. By 1917, however, girls' alleged vulnerabilities to the game led to its elimination.

For boys organized high-school sports continued, but at the turn of the century, administrators took over control of the programs. In the second half of the 20th century, the poverty of cities and the relative affluence of suburbs and small towns meant high-school sports tended to thrive in nonurban areas.

Nowadays high-school students no longer run their leagues and teams, but as players they still have decisions to make—whether to restrict themselves to high-school sports or perhaps, outside of school, to join travel teams if they qualify. Shoe and apparel companies have invested heavily in the travel-team industry, contributing to its expansion. Travel teams and the tournaments associated with them exist for all the sports included in these chapters.

As young female and male teens engage in organized sports, a number of factors come into play, affecting the content of their experience. For instance, research shows that major-league athletes are less likely to come from cities of over 500,000 than the population at large.

Research indicates that the social-class composition of the NBA has changed significantly over time, with players from middle- or high-income families currently more heavily represented than in the past. In particular, sons of former NBA players have become more prevalent.

While survey research indicates that the distinct majority of parents encourage their children to play sports, fully a quarter with high-school age children hope they will play in pro leagues.

Siblings and teammates are other categories of people influencing high-school athletes' development. In fact, elite athletes are more likely to be younger siblings, finding that their older sisters and brothers serve as both inspirations and competitors. Teammates can also be influential in various ways.

A team of specialists on coaching have divided children's organized sports into three phases—the sampling years, the specializing years, and the investment years. For effective programs sports officials need to recognize and address the various requirements at each phase.

While elite athletes have such distinctive qualities as unusual drive and commitment along with competitiveness, they and their parents and coaches need to be aware of the necessity of occasional restorative breaks.

Travel teams and tournaments are staples in elite high-school athletes' lives, and they can prove expensive for families—anywhere from $1,000 to $15,000 a year or more. However, the top athletes, most notably in basketball, pay nothing, with funding provided by shoe companies and private donors. A University of Florida study of travel teams and tournaments indicated that virtually all the players enjoyed the experience.

The final topic involves a few additional observations about young people's specialization in sports.

Class Discussion Issues

1. Indicate what, if anything, you find interesting or remarkable about Elena Delle Donne's role performance as a high-school basketball player.
2. Would it be possible and/or desirable for modern high-school students like their 19th-century predecessors to play some role in running their schools' athletic programs? Discuss.
3. Do you know of any athletes remotely like Mark Buehrle who were minor contributors to their high-school team and ended up having a successful pro career?
4. If you were an elite athlete growing up in the United States, what qualities would you want your community to possess in order to optimize your sports career?
5. Rank and discuss the following four agents of socialization—coaches, parents, siblings, and teammates—for their relative impact on teen players' athletic development.
6. How helpful are siblings likely to be in advancing an athlete's career? From your observations does whether they are older or younger affect their influence?
7. What are several key qualities possessed by a coach for whom you would want to play? On the other hand, what are qualities you hope a coach would not possess?
8. What are the distinctive differences between a good and an elite high-school athlete? Can a good player become outstanding from hard work?

9. Indicate the principal issues that come to mind when considering the pros and cons of teen specialization in sports.
10. Comment on the travel-team system. If you could make one major change in this system, what would it be? Or would you simply leave it the way it is?

References

Adcox, Susan. 2017. "FAQs about Youth Sports and Travel Teams." *The Spruce* (June 3). www.thespruce.com/faqs-about-youth-sports-and-travel-teams-1696030.

Baseball-Reference.com. 2017. "Mark Buehrle." www.baseball-reference.com/players/b/buehrma01.shtml.

Beekman, Jennifer. 2016. "High School Athletes: What Separates the Great from the Good? *Bethesda Beat* (November 23). www.bethesdamagazine.com/Bethesda-Beat/Web-2016/High-School-Athletes-What-Separates-the-Great-from-the-Good/.

Belisle, Mitch. 2016. "Competition, not Specialization, Builds Elite Athletes." *US Lacrosse* (November). www.uslacrosse.org/blog/competition-not-specialization-builds-elite-athletes.

Bell, David R., Eric G. Post, Stephanie G. Trigsted, Scott Hetzel, Timothy A. McGuine, and Alison Brooks. 2016. "Prevalence of Sport Specialization in High School Athletics: A 1-Year Observational Study." *American Journal of Sports Medicine* 44 (June): 1469–1474.

Bloom, Elizabeth. 2016. "Still a Guy from Cole Harbour." *Pittsburgh Post-Gazette* (July 17). www.postgazette.com/sports/penguins/2016/07/17/Pittsburgh-Penguins-captain-Sidney-Crosby-celebrates-Stanley-Cup-win-in-hometown-Cole-Harbour-Nova-Scotia/stories/201607170155.

Bowen, Daniel H., and Collin Hitt. 2016. "History and Evidence Show School Sports Help Students Win." *Phi Delta Kappan* (May). http://kappanonline.org/history-and-evidence-show-school-sports-help-students-win/.

Brown, Derek. 2016. "Choosing the Right AAU Basketball Travel Team." *Inspirational BASKETBALL* (July 11). http://inspirationalbasketball.com/find-right-aau-basketball-team/.

Cacciola, Scott. 2014. "A Generational Wealth of N.B.A. Talent." *The New York Times* (February 15). www.nytimes.com/2014/02/16/sports/basketball/a-generational-wealth-of-nba-talent.html?_r=0.

Christian, Sena. 2016. "Raised for Glory." *COMSTOCK'S* (August 30). www.comstocksmag.com/article/raised-glory.

Claydon, Jane. 2013. "Origin and History of Lacrosse." *Federation of International Lacrosse*. http://filacrosse.com/origin.

Côté, Jean. 1999. "The Influence of the Family in the Development of Talent in Sport." *The Sport Psychologist* 13: 395–417.

Côté, Jean, Joseph Baker, and Bruce Abernathy. 2007. "Practice and Play in the Development in Sport Expertise," pp. 184–202 in Gershon Tenenbaum and Robert C. Eklund (eds.), *Handbook of Sport Psychology*, 3rd ed. Hoboken, NJ: Wiley.

Côté, Jean, Dany J. Macdonald, Joseph Baker, and Bruce Abernathy. 2005. "When 'Where' Is More Important than 'When': Birthplace and Birthdate Effects on the Achievement of Sporting Expertise." *Journal of Sports Sciences* (October 20): 1065–1073.

Côté, Jean, Bradley Young, Julian North, and Patrick Duffy. 2007. "Towards a Definition of Excellence in Sport Coaching." *International Journal of Coaching Science* 1 (January): 3–17.

Cushion, Christopher J., Kathy M. Armour, and Robyn L. Jones. 2003. "Coach Education and Continuing Professional Development: Experience and Learning to Coach." *Quest* 55: 215–230.

Doob, Christopher Bates. 2000. *Sociology: An Introduction*, 6th ed. Fort Worth, TX: The Harcourt Press.

Doob, Christopher B. 2013. *Social Inequality and Social Stratification in US Society*. Boston, MA: Pearson.

Dubrow, Joshua Kjerulf, and Jimi Adams. 2012. "Hoop Inequalities: Race, Class and Family Structure Background and the Odds of Playing in the National Basketball Association." *International Review for the Sociology of Sport* 47 (March): 43–59.

Dwyer-Shick, Sarah. 2015. "When Girls Grow Up; Why So Few Young Female Soccer Players Make It to the Coaching Ranks." Female Coaching Network (December 21). http://femalecoachingnetwork.com/2015/12/21/when-girls-grow-up/.

Elliott, Bud. 2015. "Why Rivals.com Has Recruiting Portraits for Sixth Graders Now." *SBNation* (February 17). www.sbnation.com/college-football-recruiting/2015/2/17/8047771/rivals-middle-school-football-recruiting.

Elmendorf, Kyle. 2016. "Five Habits to Build Successful Programs." National Federation of State High School Associations (July 8). www.nfhs.org/articles/five-habits-to-build-successful-programs/.

Fair, Ray C., and Christopher Champa. 2017. "Estimated Costs of Contact in College and High School Male Sports." Department of Economics, Yale University (September). https://fairmodel.econ.yale.edu/rayfair/pdf/2017A.PDF.

Friedman, Vicki. 2017. "Why Volleyball—not Basketball—Is Winning the Popular Vote." *ESPNW* (February 15). www.espn.com/espnw/sports/article/18659764/why-young-athletes-flocking-volleyball-not-basketball-record-numbers.

Gilbert, Wade, Luke Lichtenwaldt, Jenelle Gilbert, Lynnette Zelezny and Jean Côté. 2009. "Developmental Profiles of Successful High School Coaches." *International Journal of Sports Science & Coaching* 4: 415–431. www.nfhs.org/articles/five-habits-to-build-successful-programs/.

Goldberg, Alan. 2017. "Jealousy and the Uglier Side of Sports." *Competitive Advantage*. www.competitivedge.com/jealousy-uglier-side-sports.

Gould, Daniel, Youngchul Chung, Paige Smith, and Jackie White. 2006. "Future Directions in Coaching Life Skills: Understanding High School Coaches' Views and Needs." *Athletic Insight: The Journal of Sports Psychology* 8 (September). www.athleticinsight.com/Vol8Iss3/CoachingLifeSkills.htm.

Harrison, Patricia A., and Gopalakrishnan Narayan. 2003. "Differences in Behavior, Psychological Factors, and Environmental Factors Associated with Participation in School Sports and Other Activities in Adolescence." *Journal of School Health* 73 (March): 113–120.

HoopsHype. 2015. "24 Current Players Have Fathers Who Played in the League: We Ranked Them." (September 12). http://hoopshype.com/2015/09/12/twenty-current-nba-players-have-fathers-who-played-in-the-league-we-rank-them/.

Howard, Bruce. 2016. "Injury Rates Higher for Athletes Who Specialize in One Sport." National Federation of State High School Associations (December 20). www.nfhs.org/articles/injury-rates-higher-for-athletes-who-specialize-in-one-sport/.

Jackson, Martinis. 2016. "Under Armour Association Circuit: Humble & Hungry." *Slamonline.com* (March 14). www.slamonline.com/college-hs/high-school/under-armour-association-circuihumblehungry/#tMSkZx8y.

Keating, Peter. 2011. "Nothing Is More Important in Sports than a Level Playing Field. Too Bad It Doesn't Exist." *ESPN* (July 11). http://espn.go.com/espn/story/_/id/6777581/importance-athlete-background-making-nba.

Kepner, Tyler. 2014. "M.L.B. Report Highlights Sobering Number of Black Players." *The New York Times* (April 9). www.nytimes.com/2014/04/10/sports/baseball/mlb-report-highlights-sobering-number-of-black-players.html.

Kleps, Kevin. 2014. "It Can Be a Dirty Game When Shoe Companies Get Involved in High School Sports." *Crain's Cleveland Business* (November 30). www.crainscleveland.com/article/20141130/SU.B1/311309977/it-can-be-a-dirty-game-when-shoe-companies-get-involved-in-high.

Kolata, Gina. 2017. "Cost of Contact in Sports Is Estimated at Over 600,000 Injuries a Year." *The New York Times* (September 29). www.nytimes.com/2017/09/29/health/sports-injuries-football-yale.html?rref=collection%2Fbyline%2Fgina-kolata&action=click&contentCollection=undefined&region=stream&module=stream_unit&version=latest&contentPlacement=1&pgtype=collection.

Korman, Chris. 2015. "AAU Basketball Has a Lot of Problems, but It's Still the Best Way to Develop Young Players." *USA Today* (April 15). http://ftw.usatoday.com/2015/04/aau-basketball-scandals.

Kreager, Derek A. 2007. "Unnecessary Roughness? School Sports, Peer Networks, and Male Adolescent Violence." *American Sociological Review* 72 (October): 705–724.

Longman, Jeré. 2008. "At Pinnacle, Stepping Away from Basketball." *The New York Times* (October 18). www.nytimes.com/2008/10/19/sports/ncaabasketball/19athlete.html.

Longman, Jeré. 2015. "Women's World Cup: First Opponents to Face the Fury of U.S. Players? Older Siblings." *The New York Times* (June 14). www.nytimes.com/2015/06/15/sports/soccer/womens-world-cup-looking-up-to-little-sisters.html?_r=0.

Macdonald, Dany J., Max Cheung, Jean Côté, and Bruce Abernathy. 2009. "Place but Not Place of Birth Influences the Development and Emergence of Athletic Talent in American Football." *Journal of Applied Sport Psychology* 21 (January): 80–90.

Majors, Millsaps. 2009. "History of Lacrosse: Where Did It All Begin?" *Gomajors.com* (July 13). http://gomajors.com/sports/mlax/2009-10/releases/MLAX_0713090620.html.

Malina, Robert M. 2016. "School Sports: Overview." *Education Encyclopedia*. http://education.stateuniversity.com/pages/2443/Sports-School.html.

Mallett, Clifford J., and Stephanie J. Hanrahan. 2004. "Elite Athletes: Why Does the 'Fire' Burn So Brightly?" *Psychology of Sport and Exercise* 5: 183–200.

Martin, Eric M., Martha E. Ewing, and Daniel Gould. 2014. "Social Agents' Influence on Self-Perceived Good and Bad Behavior of American Youth Involved in Sport: Developmental Level, Gender, and Competitive Level Effects." *The Sport Psychologist* 28: 111–123.

Matz, Eddie. 2013. "Travel Team Confidential." *ESPN* (June 26). www.espn.com/espn/story/_/id/9422297/elite-youth-athletes-reveal-how-playing-sport-impacts-their-lives-espn-magazine.

Matz, Eddie. 2014. "The Kids Are Alright." *ESPN* (February 21). www.espn.com/espn/story/_/id/10496416/are-youth-sports-ruining-kids-childhoods-espn-magazine.

Mazeika, Vytas. 2016. "Gender Divide: Girls' Soccer Teams Not Likely to Be Coached by a Woman." *The Mercury News* (April 6). www.mercurynews.com/2016/04/06/gender-divide-girls-soccer-teams-not-likely-to-be-coached-by-a-woman/.

Medcalf, Myron. 2017. "A Brief History of the Famous Fathers and Their Hoops-playing Sons." *ESPN* (April 19). www.espn.com/mens-college-basketball/story/_/id/19193669/shareef-oneal-becomes-latest-son-follow-famous-father-basketball-road.

Mendell, David. 2014. "Stealing Home: How Travel Teams Are Eroding Community Baseball." *The Washington Post* (May 23). www.washingtonpost.com/opinions/stealing-home-how-travel-teams-are-eroding-community-baseball/2014/05/23/5af95d34-df6e-11e3-9743-bb9b59cde7b9_story.html?utm_term=.1069f50e631a.

Mirtle, James. 2014. "The Great Offside: How Canadian Hockey Is Becoming a Game Strictly for the Rich." *The Globe and Mail* (January 13). www.theglobeandmail.com/news/national/time-to-lead/the-great-offside-how-canadian-hockey-is-becoming-a-game-strictly-for-the-rich/article15349723/.

National Federation of State High School Associations. 2017. "High School Sports Participation Increases for 28th Straight Year, Nears 8 Million Mark." (September 6). www.nfhs.org/articles/high-school-sports-participation-increases-for-28th-straight-year-nears-8-million-mark/.

npr, Robert Wood Johnson Foundation, and Harvard T.H. Chan School of Public Health. 2015. "Sports and Health in America." (June): 1–47. http://media.npr.org/documents/2015/june/sportsandhealthpoll.pdf.

O'Sullivan, John. 2015. "Can You Guess the One Thing That Elite Athletes Have in Common?" *Active for Life* (February 18). http://activeforlife.com/what-elite-athletes-have-in-common/.

Parmley, Kyle. 2017. "Refusing to Lose." *Village Living* (January 25). www.villagelivin-gonline.com/sports/refusing-to-lose125/.

Pathways to the Podium Research Project. 2012. "Faster, Higher, Stronger ... and Younger? Birth Order, Sibling Sport Participation, and Sport Expertise Development." (June 19). https://expertadvantage.wordpress.com/2012/06/19/siblings/.

Patrick, Helen, Allison M. Ryan, Corinne Alfeld-Liro, Jennifer A. Fredricks, Ludmila Z. Hruda, and Jacquelynne S. Eccles. 1999. "Adolescents' Commitment to Developing Talent: The Role of Peers in Continuing Motivation for Sports and the Arts." *Journal of Youth and Adolescence* 28 (December): 741–763.

Pennington, Bill. 2017. "As Concussion Worries Rise, Girls' Lacrosse Turns to Headgear." *The New York Times* (November 23). www.nytimes.com/2017/11/23/sports/girls-lacrosse-concussions-headgear.html?_r=0.

Phillips, Ian. 2016. "Tom Brady Wrote a Letter When He Was 17 about How His Badass Sisters Overshadowed Him." *Business Insider* (June 23). www.businessinsider.com/tom-brady-wrote-a-letter-when-he-was-17-2016-6.

Pruter, Robert. 2004. "Sports, High School." *Encyclopedia of Chicago*. www.encyclopedia.chicagohistory.org/pages/1185.html.

Pruter, Robert. 2013. *The Rise of American High School Sports and the Search for Control: 1880–1930*. Syracuse, NY: Syracuse University Press.

Reynolds, Amanda J., and Meghan H. McDonough. 2015. "Moderated and Mediated Effects of Coach Autonomy Support, Coach Involvement, and Psychological Need Satisfaction on Motivation in Youth Soccer." *The Sport Psychologist* 29: 51–61.

Riddle, Greg. 2014. "Club Sports Offer Exposure but at a Steep Price." *The Dallas Morning News*. http://res.dallasnews.com/interactives/club-sports/part3/.

Rosen, Dan. 2016. "Sidney Crosby Has Everlasting Impact on Hometown." *nhl.com* (July 16). www.nhl.com/news/sidney-crosby-still-a-star-in-his-hometown/c-281177960.

Scavuzzo, Diane. 2014. "Nicole Farley on Why Female Coaches Are Important in Youth Soccer." *Goalnation.com* (October 6). http://goalnation.com/nicole-farley-female-coaches-important-youth-soccer/.

Smith, Cameron. 2011. "Why One of U.S.'s Best Girl Soccer Stars Won't Play for Her Team." *Yahoo Sports* (March 31). http://sports.yahoo.com/highschool/blog/prep_rally/post/why-one-of-americas-best-girls-.

Steinfeldt, Jesse A., Leslie A. Rutkowski, Ellen L. Vaughan, and Matthew C. Steinfeldt. 2011. "Masculinity, Moral Atmosphere, and Moral Functioning of High School Football Players." *Journal of Sport & Exercise Psychology* 33: 215–234.

Stephens-Davidowitz, Seth. 2013. "In the N.B.A., Zip Code Matters." *The New York Times* (November 2). www.nytimes.com/2013/11/03/opinion/sunday/in-the-nba-zip-code-matters.html.

Sullivan, Paul. 2015. "The Rising Costs of Youth Sports, in Money and Emotion." *The New York Times* (January 16). www.nytimes.com/2015/01/17/your-money/rising-costs-of-youth-sports.html.

Sulloway, Frank J., and Richard L. Zweigenhaft. 2010. "Birth Order and Risk Taking in Athletics: A Meta-Analysis and Study of Major League Baseball." *Personality and Social Psychology Review* 14: 402–416.

Taity, John. 2015. "How Are Recruiting Rankings Determined? ESPN, Rivals, Scout, and 247 Break Out the Process." *al.com* (February 3). www.al.com/sports/index.ssf/2015/02/how_are_recruiting_rankings_de.html.

The Aspen Institute. 2015. "Facts: Sports Activity and Children." www.aspenprojectplay.org/the-facts.

Thomson, Josh. 2016. "The Top High School Athletes Are in a Different Class." *Lohud* (September 21). www.lohud.com/story/sports/2016/09/21/top-high-school-athletes-different-class/90311312/.

Tomashoff, Craig. 2015. "High School Struggles Can Translate to Big League Success." *MLB.com* (September 22). http://m.mlb.com/news/article/151017270/struggling-young-players-succeeded-in-majors/.

Triton Youth Soccer Association. 2016. "Coaching Girls' Soccer." http://tritonyouthsoccer.org/Page.asp?n=40305&org=tysa.

Turner, Randy. 2013. "Parents Who Can Afford It Scramble to Get Kids into Elite Hockey Programs." *Winnipeg Free Press* (February 2). www.winnipegfreepress.com/opinion/fyi/spring-fever-189487451.html.

USA Basketball. 2017. "Elena Delle Donne." www.usab.com/basketball/players/womens/d/delle-donne-elena.aspx.

UW Health. 2009. "Increase in Girls' Volleyball Players Ups Risk of Injury." (April 30).

www.uwhealth.org/news/increase-in-girls-volleyball-players-ups-risk-for-injury/20333.

Voigt, Kurt. 2016. "Where Have the Multi-sport High-school Athletes Gone?" *Associated Press* (April 29). http://bigstory.ap.org/article/140a60118e034abeb06f07abefe080d4/where-have-multi-sport-high-school-athletes-gone.

3

ONE LEVEL DOWN: COLLEGE AND MINOR-LEAGUE SPORTS PROGRAMS

In the wake of Title IX, women's basketball programs have increased in stature, with one team bringing considerable attention to the college game. The University of Connecticut women's basketball program, which started in 1974, had anything but an auspicious beginning, boasting one winning season in its first 11. But then the athletic director hired Geno Auriemma, an assistant at the University of Virginia. The team improved and eventually went undefeated in 1994–95, but other teams had previously done that, making the accomplishment scarcely remarkable. The Huskies, however, were different.

Carla Berube, a sophomore on that undefeated team, said, "There were some really great personalities on our team … [including] our coach … [and] so I think there was a really great story there. It was not just 'a good basketball team.'"

Rebecca Lobo, the star of that team, agreed that Auriemma's contribution was critical for making the team special. "No one other than coach Auriemma could have done it," Lobo said. "It's him, just him. It's his vision. He's the special ingredient that made Connecticut women's basketball what it is" (Prunty 2015).

In the summer of 1994, the coach took the team to Europe on a 12-day, five-game trip, beginning to create team cohesiveness and to ingrain his philosophy which was "It ain't what they do, it's what we do." Auriemma exuded optimism, emphasizing that the impact of his philosophical approach along with the return of all the stars from the previous year when the record was 30–3 made a successful upcoming season highly probable (Shea 1995, 152).

He was right. At that point the squad was well on its way, with Auriemma having overcome what he considered the most important challenge, getting a first-rate recruit to join the team. That occurred in 1991 when Lobo, a *Parade All-American* with almost 100 schools pursuing her, came to UConn. The coach recognized that this young woman at 6-feet-4-inches could play inside or outside, with an effective three-point shot and for someone so tall unusual speed up and down the court. These were the gifts that could help transform the women's college game. "He didn't pitch me," Lobo recalled. "It was just him getting to know me" (Prunty 2015). Lobo indicated that Auriemma was a principal reason she went to UConn. "Obviously he was a good coach. I could tell that by his record and the way practice went. As a person he is very funny and has a great personality. And that is what I was looking for in a coach off the court. Someone who I could go in and see in their office and sit down and talk" (Shea 1995, 174).

Title IX altered the historical reality, providing increased revenues and opportunities promoting women's basketball, but in the UConn case a successful development of the program also required biographical elements—the right coach to direct it and the right player to launch a successful beginning.

Sports programs contain teams, which are formal organizations maintaining clearly stated norms, well defined members' roles, and distinct objectives. Those teams possess *institutional logics*, namely beliefs about what actions are appropriate and acceptable for an organization's members, with an inevitable focus on actions deemed rewarding for themselves and for the organization. In big-time college sports, an emphasis on winning has been paramount in teams' institutional logics. In the 21st century, prominent Division I football and men's basketball teams with their winning traditions have been bringing in increasingly large revenues. – While money is meaningful to the programs' leaders, some upcoming evidence suggests that winning, which bolsters the school's competitive image, is distinctly more important.

Clearly institutional logics shapes college players' development of their roles as team members: The greater their contribution to winning, the more valuable they are, and the better their chances of advancement to the pro level. On some campuses a number of professors and administrators have criticized big-time programs that emphasize winning and financial rewards, but such opposition is unlikely to become dominant at those schools (Southall and Nagel 2010, 68–71).

The upcoming section considers both history and organizational development, providing information about the explosive growth of big-time college programs with their institutional logics directed toward winning and reaping the expanding financial rewards of their success, and also details about the minor-league systems in baseball and hockey, where the focus for institutional logics is on the development of players for the two major leagues in question.

Over time no amateur programs have put more emphasis on winning games than big-time college teams.

The Organizational Growth of College Sports and the Minor Leagues

College sports programs, with football leading the way, have been expanding from the late 19th century to the present.

The Growth of Big-time College Sports

In England the institutional logics governing college sports is very different from big-time American programs, with little, in fact, that is big-time about them. College games between the renowned Oxford and Cambridge universities in soccer attract no more than a sparse audience. The reality is that these college players are not pro prospects; they play for fun while attending the top universities in the country. The nation's truly skilled players, those with a pro future, have been scouted as children and sent to soccer academies, where they train and if progressing well sign contracts at about the age of 16, ending the likelihood of further schooling (Langford 2014).

In contrast, players at many American universities and colleges have contributed to the growth of big-time sports. Officials at these schools have long recognized that football and basketball can make substantial amounts of money and bring attention and glory to the schools. Starting in the 1890s when college administrators saw that the newly aroused public passion for college football could provide the revenues for building their schools, the game "has been torn between the competing demands of marketing and education" (Orland 2009, 1–2)—involved in a struggle between the members of the educational community favoring the recruitment of athletes who would contribute to winning teams and packed stadiums bringing in big bucks versus the opposition committed to bringing in players supporting high academic standards. Certainly the first emphasis involving recruitment continues to exist in many modern programs where top players and teams draw massive crowds and TV audiences and produce millions of dollars for their schools.

As noted in the Introduction, the University of Georgia and the University of Oklahoma, both of which had highly successful football programs, took the NCAA to court, and in the case of *NCAA v. Board of Regents of the University of Oklahoma* the Supreme Court voted seven to two in favor of the universities' making their own deals with TV networks (Rand 1985; Suggs 2010, 131). As a result the historical context in which big-time college sports unfolded changed. Over time the most prominent college football programs sharply increased their revenues, with coaches prominent among those benefiting financially.

From the 1920s when Bill Reid received a bountiful $7,000 a year at Harvard and Tad Jones an even more impressive $15,000 at Yale, college football coaches' salaries have grown. In 1924 after an undefeated season at Notre Dame the renowned Knute Rockne signed a three-year $8,000-a-year contract with Iowa but then reneged, won over by a ten-year $10,000-a-year deal to stay at Notre Dame (Smith 2011, 64–66).

Early in the 21st century, top football coaches' salaries rapidly accelerated. In 2016 Michigan's second-year coach Jim Harbaugh earned $9 million a year, more than any NFL coach. In the course of that year, Harbaugh earned as much as 54 University of Michigan full professors or 79 associate professors (Campos 2014; *theguardian* 2016). Why so much more? Because the unprecedentedly high salaries attract coaches who can produce winning football teams on campuses where the sport's success is highly valued. According to journalist Gilbert Gaul, at the universities where football coaches are highly paid "[I]t is football that dominates the school's profile and is far and away the largest source of revenue in its financial model for athletics" (Gaul 2015).

Indeed, top football programs and their institutional logics provide the coveted standard for college athletic programs, with top winning football teams the distinctly most prominent revenue source followed by men's basketball and women's basketball. A significant contributor to college football programs' revenue expansion has been the formation of the Football Bowl Subdivision (FBS) comprised of 128 elite teams and featuring a four-team playoff for the Division I national championship (Gaines 2014).

In 2016, 24 college athletic programs made $100 million or more, up from 20 the previous year and a mere 13 the year before that. Among the top 25 money-making programs, revenues ranged from UCLA's $96.9 million to Texas A & M's $192.6 million (Gaines 2016). With such substantial revenues, one might simply assume that leading college sports programs would be well-off financially. However, that is seldom the case. In the fierce competition to excel in the recruitment of top players, many sports programs have been building increasingly lavish facilities, which

Like the Penn State football team, other FBS programs provide their players expensive, cutting-edge training facilities. (Source: Fred Vuich / Getty Images)

include state-of-the-art locker rooms and players' lounges containing high-definition TVs and cutting-edge video-game systems. An additional expenditure has involved salaries for leading coaches. In the 2014–15 academic year, less than half of the leading college sports programs—23 of 48 in the so-called "Power Five," the handful of most affluent football conferences—had revenues exceed expenditures (Hobson and Rich 2015a, 2015b).

When Auburn University's chief operating officer David Benedict was asked how his athletic department lost more money in 2014 than in 2004, even though its income had nearly doubled during the decade, he was unapologetic. He indicated that the first clue was the school's uncompromising motto "All in." Benedict added, "When we do something, we're going to do it at the highest level possible." Rutgers athletic director Julie Hermann concurred. She said, "This is a competitive race among some of the biggest universities in this country to compete and achieve at the highest level." Both university officials, in short, were clearly suggesting that their schools' institutional logics were first-and-foremost geared toward winning and that money making was distinctly secondary. A pair of journalists noted, however, that to a host of critics of big-time college athletics "[T]he persistent inability of programs to profit despite continually rising income is evidence of systemic, wasteful spending" (Hobson and Rich 2015a). There seems little evidence to suggest that top athletic programs' financial strategy will change.

In spite of wasteful spending, however, college football along with basketball have been the only two Division I programs with revenues exceeding expenses (McIntyre 2016). Most other sports have lagged behind, far behind.

Whether big-time college sports make money or not, they tend to be popular, with only a select few high-school athletes capable of joining Division I teams. For the 11 sports covered in these chapters, the enrollment percentages are:

Men:
Hockey 4.6%
Lacrosse 2.9%
Football 2.6%

Baseball 2.1%
Soccer 1.3%
Basketball 1%

Women:
Lacrosse 3.8%
Soccer 2.4%
Softball 1.6%
Basketball 1.2%
Volleyball 1.2% (NCAA 2017)

In many cases eventual pro athletes attend college, but in baseball and hockey the minor leagues are a viable option.

The Minor Leagues over Time

For minor-league baseball and hockey teams, institutional logics tends to focus on the development of players—the prevailing sense that if brought along competently, some of these promising candidates can reach a level of performance that permits them to join the parent club and contribute to its success.

Since the 1870s MLB has possessed a minor-league system containing players who can replace major leaguers if they are injured or becoming less productive. Starting in 1920 Branch Rickey, renowned for his leadership role in Jackie Robinson's integration into major-league baseball, initiated a system where a major-league franchise would develop players rising from their lowest level farm clubs up to the highest and finally for the very best reaching the parent club itself. Rickey promoted the farm-club system for two reasons—first, that without it minor-league owners would charge exorbitant prices for their players, generally driving up the cost of talent and making it impossible for low-budget MLB teams like Rickey's St. Louis Cardinals to compete effectively; and second, that once a major-league franchise owned an entire farm system, its owners could make substantial money selling good prospects to other clubs (Morris 2006, 8, 18–19). Saving and making money, in short, were priorities in Rickey's own minor-league institutional logics, and that emphasis reverberated through the franchise.

Rickey traveled widely, especially into areas hard-hit by the 1930s depression. For him frugality was the order of the day. Wanzer Rickey, Branch's brother and equally stingy associate, signed the well-known Enos Slaughter for a bonus of a shotgun and two hunting dogs. Many years earlier the prominent pitcher Dizzy Dean had signed for the identical bonus, and the dogs soon ran away. "Me and Diz always wondered if they were the same two dogs," Slaughter said (Vecsey 2006, 81).

Both MLB and the NHL possess multi-level minor-league systems. In baseball four broad classes exist—Triple-A, Double-A, and A, with the latter possessing three levels, and also the Rookie League. The entire system contains 248 teams (Cronin 2013; *MiLB.com* 2017b).

An official statement from Minor League Baseball reads, "The affiliated Minor Leagues are divided into a structure that allows players to face increasingly difficult competition as they progress in their development" (*MiLB.com* 2018). While minor-league coaches and players would rather win games than lose them—it can prove useful for players or coaches seeking to advance—winning ball games tends not to be a priority.

Typically a journalist wrote, "In years past, winning in the minor leagues was prioritized far below individual development. Winning was very much secondary to developing skills and advancing individuals" (Drayer 2016). However, currently some minor-league officials recognize that besides the improvement of physical skills, players' growth requires insight into how the game works, including recognition of the importance of winning. A long-time baseball executive wrote, "It takes the development of a winning mentality. Players must not only hone their swing or their pitching mechanics, but also they must learn what it takes to win at the game's highest levels" (Dittrich 2013). It's apparent, in short, that minor leagues' contribution to parent clubs' institutional logics can become a topic of discussion and perhaps even debate.

Most likely Bill James, a prominent baseball statistician, would agree with the preceding commentary, but in addition he proposed a substantial change in the minor-league system. He said, "From the standpoint of the game as a whole, there would be huge advantages to restructuring the minor leagues so that the players were not sorted as belonging to teams until they reached a much higher level." James suggested that the best approach to developing baseball talent would be to have all but the top prospects who move quickly to the majors join the minor leagues in an unaffiliated capacity where for varying lengths of time the focus would be strictly on their development, without such interference as higher-level teams abruptly calling up prospects. Then when they were close to major-league caliber, based solely on their performance and not projected major-league team needs, they would enter the draft, prepared if they were truly major-league caliber, to move on up to the show (Brannon 2013). It seems to be a useful proposal, but team owners are unlikely to agree, anticipating a significant loss of control over what previously had been their own minor-league prospects.

Like MLB, the NHL has developed an extensive minor-league system. It started in 1926 when the three-team Pacific Coast Hockey Association folded, and the youthful NHL, soon to enter its second decade, could not absorb the sudden supply of available prospects. At that time there was the formation of four new minor hockey leagues, two of which eventually combined to become the forerunner of the American Hockey League (AHL), the top development league for the NHL containing 30 teams and players who are generally at least 20 years old (Hockey League History 2016).

Prominent developmental leagues include the major juniors comprised of 60 teams belonging to three leagues forming the Canadian Hockey League (CHL), which has teams located in nine Canadian provinces and five American states representing players aged 16 to 20. In addition, 60 Division I NCAA college teams contribute significantly to the NHL (Bitel 2016; Estel 2016; Metter 2013; *The Morning Call* 2014; USHI 2014). It's a complex organizational world, with the NHL 31-team league at the top and in Canada and the United States a grand total of nearly 500 professional and amateur teams displaying highly varied potential (Peter 2011). When players enter the draft, representatives of the top leagues show up round after round.

In hockey's minor leagues, team owners, players, and officials have often found themselves facing public opposition—in particular, in advocating body checking, which involves slamming into an opponent—still a prominent element in the professional game and a major cause of head injuries, including concussions (Hume 2013). Traditionally professional hockey's institutional logics, particularly in the minor leagues, has condoned, even encouraged violence. While the NHL has averaged about one fight every two games, the Canadian minor leagues have produced about one a game, with the unchallenged statistical leader, the Ligue Nord-Américaine de Hockey, averaging 3.2 per game (Klein 2011). Change, however, seems likely, with preliminary research at the minor-league level suggesting a higher concussion rate than generally reported (Echlin, Tator, Cusimano, Cantu, Taunton, Upshur, Hall, Johnson, Forwell, and Skopelja 2010).

Compared to hockey and baseball, pro basketball has a more limited if expanding developmental system—the NBA Development League, renamed the NBA Gatorade (G) League. During the G-League's 17th season in 2017–18, 26 NBA teams had affiliates, each of which played 50 regular-season games. The G-League has been expanding its impact on the senior league, with an all-time highest total of 135 former G-League players on NBA rosters in 2016–17 (NBA Development League 2017).

Although the minor leagues and Division I football, the upcoming topic, pose somewhat different challenges for team officials, a common objective exists: To find top players. Institutional logics emphasizing winning against the best teams in the country necessitates programs' enrollment of such prospects. Summary 3.1 lists broad historical trends involving big-time college and minor-league sports and their institutional logics.

SUMMARY 3.1

Institutional Logics and the Historical Development of American College Sports

Conceptual foundation:

- Teams are a basic unit for analyzing the application of the concept of institutional logics to sports: Teams which, sociologically speaking, are formal organizations possessing clearly stated rules, well defined roles, and distinct goals.
- Institutional logics—belief systems, which determine acceptable actions for organizations' members, who in big-time college sports tend to focus on winning and increasing revenues.

Historical trends:

- Top American college programs, beginning with college football in the 1890s, emphasizing a combination of winning and producing large revenues.

- The arms race to produce facilities and programs to attract top football recruits preventing all but a few university programs from making a profit.
- The formation of minor-league baseball and hockey systems and differences of opinion about which are the more productive options for developing future major leaguers.

The Kingpins: Big-time Football and Basketball

A sample of over 2,000 adults indicated that college football was the nation's third most popular sport after professional football and baseball, distinctly ahead in popularity of all other college sports (Harris Poll 2015).

FBS Teams: Elite College Football

The 128 teams which compete in the FBS receive more television coverage and rake in more revenues than they would have ever anticipated just a few years ago. Are the top coaching staffs so talented and committed that after a few months of hard work with any set of decent athletes they can produce a leading team? Most unlikely. The quality of recruited players has a major effect on a team's record. An examination of FBS programs covering the years 2004 to 2009 indicated that in three of the six participating conferences there was a distinct connection between the recruitment of players and winning—that the data suggested "... between 63% and 80% of the variance in conference winning percentage ... [resulted from] recruiting success." The investigator added, "For programs in these conferences, and really for all programs across conferences, it stresses the importance of making a significant investment in recruiting budgets to drive success on the field" (Caro 2012, 151).

A study of Division 1A teams [what later became members of the FBS] found that not only did the quality of recruited players affect team performance but that performance in turn aided the recruitment process. Coaches appreciate the interaction of these two factors, and as a result each year they excitedly await the new recruits' arrival (Langelett 2003). In recent years no team has been more successful at recruitment than the University of Alabama.

In a decade under Nick Saban's leadership, the Alabama football program has developed 18 first-round players, including a first-round selection in eight straight years, and a total of over 60 draft picks (SEC Football 2016; Weathersby 2013). The head coach has been highly organized, perhaps in demeanor more like an aloof business executive than a hands-on coach. The Alabama team engages in painstaking recruitment and player development, implementing an institutional logics that resolutely pursues winning in a highly competitive college-football setting, producing five national championships for the university during the Saban years.

Recognizing the potential impact of top high-school players on their program, Saban and his staff have worked diligently during the recruitment stage to get the best candidates possible. Over time they have made extensive efforts to build relationships with prospects, their families, and their high-school coaches. The Alabama coaches end up choosing players who are unusually tall and heavy for college prospects. A prominent high-school coach said, "Coach Saban basically has an NFL team playing college football ... [He] recruits the ... guys that have NFL-type bodies, or frames that NFL clubs typically want." Saban has also valued the mental side of the game, seeking prospects who have the strength of character to work with a highly demanding coaching staff as well as the intelligence to understand and implement the team's complicated game plans (Kirpalani 2013).

A distinct indicator of Saban's organizational skill is the team's meticulously assembled program, which features a pro-style offense, defense, and special teams and provides players detailed schooling involving the challenges the best of them must face as NFL candidates (Kirpalani 2013). The Alabama coaching staff has concluded that in order to implement the team's institutional logics most effectively, it is essential to maximize players' outcomes.

In such a carefully planned organizational context, it is hardly surprising that benefits readily appear for individual athletes. Michael Williams, a tight end, was a member of three national-championship teams in his five years at Alabama. As he practiced for the Senior Bowl, Williams, unlike some of his teammates from other schools, was relaxed and poised in facing dozens of reporters, clearly understanding and appreciating the preparation the Alabama staff had provided. Williams said, "Nothing is coming as a surprise. I feel like I can handle every situation they throw at me outside of the field. Coach Saban did well" (Scarborough 2013).

As coaches implement their teams' institutional logics, they are going to make choices about the most effective means to produce winning programs, sometimes making improvements that turn out to be important contributions but are not obvious to many observers. For instance, one such issue involves weight training: It's not only a question of how much to do but also what type of training to pursue.

Stanford University has developed a successful program. In 2006 following a 1–11 record the previous fall, Shannon Turley took over the football team's strength program and began by drawing in upperclassmen who were "borderline obsessed" with improvement. Turley emphasized that rushing yards obtained and rushing yards allowed were the measurements that clearly represent a team's "bully factor," the ability to dominate an opposing defense or offense. The numbers are instructive. On rushing yards obtained, Stanford improved from 115th nationally in 2006 to 39th in 2012, and on rushing yards allowed, the team advanced from 118th nationally in 2006 to 4th in 2012.

Turley has used a no-frills approach that has relentlessly focused on the performances necessitated by a player's position, summarily rejecting the production of strong men with gaudy weight-room numbers. "I don't care how much guys can bench squat or power clean," Turley said. "It has nothing to do with playing football. Football is blocking and tackling. It's creating contact, avoiding contact and gaining separation if you are a skill guy on the perimeter. That's football" (Rausch 2013).

Coby Fleener, later a member of the Indianapolis Colts, was a graduate of the Stanford football program, who arrived on campus in 2007 with a herniated disc and benefited from the strength-building regimen, which the coach developed over a five-year period (Rausch 2013). Like Turley, Fleener recognized that many players and coaches emphasized putting up weight-room numbers. Fleener reacted strongly. "If a coach starts bragging to you about the weight room numbers his guys put up, maybe you should ask him how many of those guys made it through the season without missing games or [getting] a season-ending injury." The Stanford strength-and-conditioning program, he noted, could prevent injury. Fleener added, "There is a reason an NFL locker room was built in the new

Arrillaga Family Sports Center football addition [at Stanford University]. NFL players come back to train with Shannon Turley" (Fleener 2014).

Stanford has been the 17th most successful college football program of the modern era. Using data going back to 2000, Niche, a company which compiles statistical information on schools, neighborhoods, colleges, including top football programs, concluded that the five programs that were most successful in their combination of championships, game attendance, and NFL alumni were:

- Number 5: Louisiana State University, with three national championships, an average attendance of 91,418, and 313 alumni in the NFL
- Number 4: Alabama, with 11 national championships, an average attendance of 101,505, and 298 alumni in the NFL
- Number 3: University of Florida, with three national championships, an average attendance of 87,440, and 278 alumni in the NFL
- Number 2: University of Southern California, with seven national championships, an average attendance of 73,126, and 416 alumni in the NFL
- Number 1: Ohio State University, with six national championships, an average attendance of 104,933, and 409 alumni in the NFL (Martin 2016).

Compared to football prospects, college basketball players face very different qualifications regarding recruitment. The NFL norms are exacting, requiring that a prospect has either graduated from college, used up his college eligibility through participation in football, gone five years since first practicing or playing football at the college level, or passed four NFL seasons since high school without ever playing college football or without attending college (National Football League 2017). In contrast, the NBA only requires that candidates be 19 years old and that one year has passed since high-school graduation (*Draft Site* 2017).

One-and-done Basketball
Kobe Bryant, Kevin Garnett, and LeBron James went directly from high school to the NBA and did brilliantly, but many other young players

struggled and often failed, ending up at best with marginal careers in Europe or the G-League. Valuable talent was being lost, and so in 2005 NBA owners, league officials, and the players' union decided that before high-school graduates could play in the NBA, it would be sensible to require that they be 19, encouraging prospects to spend a maturing year playing in college (LaFauci 2015).

The approach became known as "one-and-done," and its impact on college teams' institutional logics and success has varied. In 2015 after Wisconsin lost the Division I national championship to Duke, coach Bo Ryan criticized Duke and other one-and-done programs when he asserted that he didn't "do a rent-a-player." He added, "I like trying to build from within. It's just the way I am. And to see these guys grow over the years and to be here last year and lose a tough game, boom, they came back" (*WKYT.com* 2015). Ryan was endorsing the traditional college system where top basketball programs almost invariably kept their leading players for four years.

Interestingly, at Kentucky John Calipari, who had coached 13 one-and-done players by 2014, also questioned the system, believing it would be better if NBA prospects had two years to prepare for the league. "Every player that I've recruited, and they will tell you, I say the same thing: 'Don't plan on coming to school for one year. You make a huge mistake,'" Calipari said. "But if after one year, you have options, that will be up to you and your family" (*ESPN* 2014).

At Duke Coach Mike Krzyzewski who, beginning in the early 1990s created a dynasty with star players who remained for four years, won the 2015 national title with two freshmen as mainstays, who right afterwards entered the pro draft (LaFauci 2015). In this era when the salary cap has reached $40 million per team, Krzyzewski suggested that it is reasonable that young players would want to get in on the riches as quickly as possible (Katz 2015).

Using the one-and-done system might be a feasible option for top players, but many observers question its overall effectiveness. In 2017 about a month before a draft that would bring about 20 players into the league after completing one year of college, NBA commissioner Adam Silver declared that often college coaches and athletic directors have been displeased with the current arrangement. He added, "And I know our

[NBA] teams aren't happy either, in part because they don't necessarily think the players who are coming into the league are getting the kind of training that they would expect to see." While Silver's preference appears to involve raising the minimum age for entering the NBA to 20, generally keeping young players in college a year longer, others, like representatives of the players' union, often support an opposing position, allowing 18-year-olds back into the league (Reynolds 2017).

Meanwhile NBA personnel recognize that the one-and-done system, even with its flaws, has had immense value to them—that the arrangement means that league scouts and coaches can observe these promising prospects playing on and against high-profile, successful teams for at least a year-long college stay and that this system is more efficient and revealing than if one-and-done didn't exist and NBA coaches and scouts could only watch draft-headed talent in less revealing high-school contests (Tudor 2015).

The one-and-done program has developed in an era that has been financially beneficial for college sports. In 2011 the NCAA signed an 11-year, $10.8 billion contract with CBS to broadcast men's basketball games. Some of that money goes to fund scholarships in a variety of sports and to help finance various women's and men's sports programs (Beer 2016). In addition, many prominent programs receive large, sometimes multimillion-dollar payments from such companies as Nike, Under Armour, and Adidas for showcasing their shoes and uniforms, and, in addition, coaches can also receive substantial payments (Fantauzzi 2016; Lipsyte 1997).

Shoe companies and leading college basketball programs have benefited during the one-and-done era, but as Commissioner Silver indicated many players have not. In the spring of 2015, 68 recruits had gone from one-and-done in college to the NBA. Only 20 of them, notably many of those included among the top-five draft picks, produced at an above-average rate based on NBA points, assists, and rebounds; top-five draftees were about twice as productive as those in the bottom half of the top 10 (Greenberg 2015).

The following year, recognizing that for many young men the transition from college to the pros had often become a frenetic, nonconstructive experience, the NCAA's Division I Council in collaboration with the

NBA extended the time period an extra five weeks for players deciding whether or not to make themselves eligible for the NBA draft. This is one of a number of issues that can help prospects prepare more effectively for their effort to succeed in the NBA. Policy changes like this one invariably affect the various categories of participants in the game differently. Jim Haney, the executive director of the National Association of Basketball Coaches, said that the earlier, more restrictive policy "was meant to help [college] coaches know for certain what their rosters would look like for the next year, but the reality is, it wasn't helping kids make informed decisions" (Tracy 2016).

That conclusion seems indisputable, but the situation is complicated. As is usually the case with organized sports over time, there are a number of emerging powerful or influential participants—the college coaches with their institutional logics focused on winning but divided on how to go about it, and regardless of their position on the issue often finding that the instability produced by the one-and-done reality complicates the development of a well coordinated approach to successful team play; then the NBA, also with its emphasis on producing a winning, money-making product and sometimes benefiting from the one-and-done system while also losing prospects in the fast-moving process; and then the players, who, though somewhat divided, appear to favor the current approach or might even want to eliminate the one-year-of-college requirement. While this topic is discussed and debated openly, that tends not to be the case for participants involved in the following issues.

— *The Underbelly of Big-time Sports*

It has been noted that as organized sports develop, major participants are going to exert power to gain advantage. In this instance spurred on by their emphasis on winning, coaches and other officials in major college programs sometimes break the rules. Once again, the concept of dysfunction proves useful. When a group, for instance a coaching staff for a prominent college team, violates important norms, it can be dysfunctional if they are caught, adversely affecting the program and both its players and staff. Sometimes in big-time sports programs, coaches, assistant coaches, and players are punished for violations, even dismissed from the organization and the program itself penalized.

A Temple University study of 554 major infractions that occurred at Division I college sports programs between 1954 and 2014 produced interesting findings. In some cases two or more sports were implicated. Men's basketball committed the most violations, closely followed by football, and together they represented 83 percent of the total. Coaches were responsible for 84 percent of the infractions. The most frequent violations involved illicit inducements for prospects and also prohibited, sometimes illegal benefits for players in the program (NCAA 2016b; *The Associated Press* 2016), providing program advantages at the recruitment and retention stages. It seems likely that with huge revenues and media-linked reputations at stake, the pressure on coaches to win is considerably greater in big-time basketball and football than in other programs, unduly encouraging violations that will promote success.

In many instances head coaches publicly appear quite innocent—removed from the process of implementing the dysfunctional outcomes. They tend to pass on the actual performance of violations to subordinates. For instance, when Syracuse head coach Jim Boeheim learned that many of his players had subpar academic performance, he hired a new director of basketball operations and simply ordered him to "fix" team members' academic problems. The director developed an effective if morally and legally challengeable plan: His staff members would obtain access to players' email accounts and then contact faculty members, completing assignments while pretending to be the students. For instance, in one case a member of the team had his eligibility reinstated when a paper written by the director and a basketball facility receptionist led to raising a course grade from the previous year. Meanwhile Coach Boeheim remained aloof from these dealings—an apparent lack of involvement that hardly impressed NCAA officials, who removed 100 wins from the program's total and suspended the coach from nine conference games the following year (New 2015).

The athletes in such prominent, violation-prone college sports programs tend to be valued primarily for the athletic roles they can fill, and while they are also technically students, it is likely that nobody, including the individuals themselves, view them as anything but players, with the priority of plugging them into the team's ongoing institutional logics.

In the course of the retention stage, established college players need to pick a major. Many are likely to follow the path of least resistance, choosing a major reputed to be lenient and easy. A study involving 349 football players in one (eventual FBS) Division I football program, showed a clustering of top athletes into certain academic majors, particularly into one called Apparel, Housing, and Resource Management, which provided the powerful attraction of requiring only a 2.0 average (Fountain and Finley 2011). A journalist commented on the possible negative effect of clustering for students. "If an athlete majors in interdepartmental studies or general studies, either because that's all they could handle or the coach tells them to, has the school done that student a service? Is that athlete really going to have a 'degree to fall back on' if sports don't work out, as the NCAA often touts?" (Trahan 2014).

African Americans are massively overrepresented in Division I football and basketball programs. While between 2007 and 2010 they represented about 2.8 percent of full-time undergraduate students in 76 universities with prominent programs in both sports, they constituted 57.1 percent of football players and 64.3 percent of men's basketball players (Harper, Williams, and Blackman 2013).

Most of these individuals, about 98 percent, do not reach the major leagues, and as a result a team of researchers from the Center for the Study of Race and Equity in Education at the University of Pennsylvania has strongly advised prospects and their families during recruitment to ask coaches the following types of questions that can assess the outcome of playing Division I football or basketball for the vast majority destined not to play pro. The potentially informative questions include "What is the graduation rate for Black men on your team? Besides the few who got drafted, what are recent Black male graduates doing? ... How many players on your team studied abroad or did internships in their fields this past school year? What will happen to me if I don't get drafted? How prepared will I be for a career in my field? Give me specific examples of ways you encourage academic success and the holistic development of your players" (Harper, Williams, and Blackman 2018).

In the fall of 2017 after a federal investigation involving recruiting violations by several major college basketball programs, NCAA president Mark Emmert spoke out, referring generally to both of the underbelly-of-sports issues just covered and saying that they needed to be brought into the open. Referring to major infractions, Emmert declared, "There's always been rumors and innuendo that swirled around about this kind of behavior. I think one of the most disturbing elements of this whole circumstance is it seems to have uncovered, at least in these cases, a code of silence — that people who were aware of these things weren't coming forward" (Tracy 2017). Emmert announced the formation of a committee headed by former secretary of state Condoleezza Rice and charged with a thorough examination of major basketball programs, including cases involving the questionable, even illicit participation of shoe and apparel companies and sports agents (Moriarty 2017). Summary 3.2 sums up how institutional logics affects big-time college sports programs.

SUMMARY 3.2

Institutional Logics in Big-time College Programs

Strategic emphases for top college football teams as exemplified by the Alabama program:

- Conscientious recruitment of high-quality candidates.
- Careful guidance of players' development in the three major phases of the game.
- Preparation for the next level, such as dealing with reporters.

Winning big-time college basketball in the one-and-done era:

- Differing opinions among top coaches as to whether or not to pursue the one-and-done strategy.
- Variation among players as to whether one-and-done is a productive course of action.
- Large revenues received by top college programs from TV coverage and major shoe companies.
- Uncertainty about the continuance of the one-and-done system, with the distinct possibility it could be succeeded by two-and-done.

A dysfunctional outcome linked to leading programs in the two most popular college sports: Temple University study on major infractions in Division I college sports programs showing that men's basketball and football headed the list, suggesting that such dysfunctional behavior resulted because officials within these prominent, financially successful programs felt pressure to cut corners to sustain their winning traditions.

> The focus of big-time sports programs on a win-at-all-cost institutional logics, often failing to emphasize their athletes' academic programs and as a result endangering their largely minority athletes from having a good chance of getting a degree that will help them find well-paying jobs when most of them prove unable to advance to the pro leagues.

While only football and men's basketball produce substantial revenues, other college sports also develop their own institutional logics, often strongly emphasizing winning.

Other Elite Programs in College Sports

In the Temple University study previously cited, women's college basketball tied for third in number of infractions, suggesting that like football and men's basketball, its programs possess some coaches and officials who have not only been highly competitive but willing in a number of cases to cut corners to build and maintain winning teams. The number of infractions in women's basketball teams, however, pales in comparison to the count for men's football and basketball teams (NCAA 2016b; *The Associated Press* 2016).

Like its male counterpart, the women's college basketball game is popular. In the 2015–16 season, Division I women's basketball attendance reached 8.3 million fans, the highest total in the 35 years of NCAA women's basketball (NCAA 2016a).

A highly popular sport, however, does not mean that teams have been making money. In fact, the NCAA has indicated that overall women's college basketball loses $14 million a year (McIntyre 2016). Like most other popular teams, UConn women's basketball has demonstrated that at the pinnacle of college sports persistent winning does not necessarily produce profits: In the 2014–15 season during a run of four-straight Division I championships, the UConn program earned $4 million in revenues and incurred $6.7 million in expenses—hardly an anomaly since a 2013 study of college basketball found no women's programs making a profit (Beer 2016).

The nearby Box 3.1 addresses a modern reality in women's college basketball programs.

BOX 3.1

Where Have All the Women Coaches Gone?

As in girls' high-school soccer discussed in the previous chapter, a limited number of female coaches have headed women's college basketball programs. In 1972 with the advent of Title IX, women represented over 90 percent of the head coaches in more than two dozen women's college sports. Currently the figure has plummeted to about 40 percent (Longman 2017).

Over time more money has come into college sports, drawing increased numbers of male candidates into women's basketball and other women's sports. In addition, such factors as the inordinate demands that the job makes on working mothers and concern about discrimination against lesbian candidates have discouraged some applicants (Longman 2017). In 2015 female head coaches' participation in Division I basketball was 58.6 percent, down over 7 percent from six years earlier (Barrett 2016).

It is notable that a study of 59 Division I female basketball players from two midwestern conferences indicated that respondents showed a decisive preference for male coaches, with players' experience serving as an important contributor: Individuals whose previous coaches were primarily male were much more inclined to favor a male coach than peers with a greater female coaching presence in their past. It does appear than in many cases a vicious cycle appears to have taken hold: Because of the numerical domination of male coaches at lower levels of female basketball, many top college players are unlikely to appreciate women coaches' potential contribution to their teams' institutional logics. Acknowledging the significance of these findings, the researchers advocated a decided push to increase the number of female coaches for youth basketball and other girls' sports, suggesting the utility of such an initiative is apparent in research results indicating that players without previous contact with female coaches will often discard negative attitudes when exposed to them in college (Kalin and Waldron 2015, 310–14).

While most college sports programs are less celebrated than those involving the three just discussed, the participants appear equally committed to and competent at producing high-level individual and team success.

Agents of Socialization and Their Influence on College Athletes' Play

Institutional logics in prominent college sports is concerned with winning, and such agents of socialization as coaches and teammates contribute significantly to the outcomes. Above all, they can provide information and guidance that help players make adjustments that they didn't previously address. The reality is that coaches vary significantly in this capacity—that some lack the knowledge or the interpersonal skills to serve as effective agents of socialization while others do well, providing precise information and assisting players to develop a deeper understanding of themselves and their sport. Consider some settings where coaches' input is likely to be critical for player development.

In fastpitch softball, for instance, it can be tempting to visualize oneself as a dominating pitcher who can take over a game, but such performers are uncommon. An effective pitching coach is likely to convey that information to prospects, counseling that the program can thrive with candidates who possess a variety of effective pitches that frequently allow them to best opposing batters (Silverman 2014).

Detailed, even meticulous instruction based on pitching coaches' research and experience can make a huge difference, creating trust and a positive working relationship between coach and player. Consider two very different strategies for giving advice. Some coaches are likely to tell their pitchers to "just throw strikes," with the result that they lean forward and reach toward the batter. At first this tendency might increase control, but eventually the player is likely to lose speed and even produce a back injury. Instead, competent coaches emphasize, pitchers need to concentrate on a couple of critical details, thinking or saying something like, "As my pitching arm comes down toward the release, I will bring my shoulders back ... and hips forward" (Warner 2016). Without a coach serving as an informative agent of socialization providing detailed guidance and encouragement, a young college pitcher is unlikely to develop such a productive, injury-avoiding release.

Batting in softball can also pose a challenge, with college players often benefiting from coaches' detailed guidance and instruction. Again, it can be tempting to view oneself as a superstar, belting frequent game-winning home runs. However, like the dominating pitcher, few such hitters materialize. Instead coaches need to impress on players the importance of being smart, opportunistic batters—competitors who will scan the defense and try to hit into the open spaces or go with a pitch, sending it to the opposite field.

A prime example of an opportunistic approach is the execution of the slap hit, where batters will unleash a combination of a drag bunt and a grounder, usually executed by left-handed batters, who have a shorter run to first base. Kayla Braud, who was one of the University of Alabama's two slappers, said that the hit needed to be carefully carried out. She explained, "The goal is to [have the bat swing] on a plane and hit the top of the ball and get a nice hop. You don't want to hit it hard, just nice and smooth. It's an art, really." Slap hitting is a complicated skill, requiring painstaking coaching guidance on how to make contact with the ball in the manner that is most advantageous for a particular offensive arrangement along with supervised time spent working on bunts and hitting away as occasional options (Deas 2012).

Whether the focus is pitching or hitting, fastpitch softball is exacting, requiring well-grounded relationships between coaches and players to achieve success. When a prominent softball player became a coach, she consulted her own college coach, describing that woman in terms that suggested someone who is an optimally effective agent of socialization in this ever-challenging sport: "She knows how to get the most out of her players," the younger woman said. "She pushed her kids to be the best they can be. She was real, authentic, honest—a coach you never wanted to disappoint" (Sorg 2015).

Lacrosse has become another popular college sport, where agents of socialization can prove critical. At Cornell Max Siebold was a celebrated midfielder. Toward the end of his senior year, Siebold had a point-scoring streak of 48 games, the second longest in the nation, and a knack for scoring at key times, either tying games, breaking ties, or forcing overtime. But besides producing the offensive numbers, Siebold served as an agent of socialization, displaying a standard of commitment for others to embrace. Chris Finn, a teammate, knew Siebold well. "On the field, in practice and especially in games, he has this intense focus," Finn said. "You look at him and you just know he's ready to go as hard as he can – offense, defense, faceoff. For the guys on the field, it's a calming influence. You just know you can count on him in big moments" (Kekis 2009).

Like lacrosse teammates, coaches can also provide emotional support, helping players adjust to the stressful conditions that accompany their play. Goaltending is a distinct case in point. Trevor Tierney, who was an All-American goalie and competed six years professionally, indicated that any young person playing the position who is afraid of the ball is smart. He wrote, "It's a hard rubber ball traveling at an incredibly fast speed, and it is often hitting your body." Tierney indicated that concussions forced him to retire—"the last of which was suffered on a shot to the dome" (Tierney 2012).

For their physical welfare, goalies protect themselves, wearing a top-of-the-line helmet, a throat guard, a cup, and protection for all exposed body parts, but once on the field they need to recognize that they simply can't do their job if they are scared. It's best if one's mind remains blank, removed from fear. A coach taught Tierney to visualize a plate of glass about the size of the goal three feet in front of him and to keep his eyes fixed in a relaxed manner on that spot, not focusing on the opponent, zoning out any fears about him, and saying "yes" when the ball reached the imaginary glass. The drill trains the goalie to focus on the one zone where he must focus to prevent a score, simultaneously teaching him to reject fear of the shooter bearing down on him. Effective coaches working with goalies also provide suggestions about goalies' positioning their knees, back, and head; maintaining eye contact with the ball as it enters the zone and moving toward it; and holding the stick's shaft with the fingers to insure maximum flexibility (*Lacrosse Monkey* 2011; Nissi 2015; Tierney 2012). Tierney and other goalies have found that as agents of socialization, coaches and older goalies were essential, both in alleviating the sense of vulnerability that Tierney felt exposed to in front of the goal and providing pointers making it possible for goalies to complete their difficult role.

Not surprisingly Trevor Tierney, who had the chance to learn from some of the great goalies of his era and eventually won two national lacrosse championships at Princeton, was heavily recruited out of high school (LXTC 2015). However, unlike some promising baseball and hockey prospects discussed in the upcoming section, he did not have to deliberate about two quite different types of programs.

College or the Minor Leagues?

As talented teens in baseball and hockey head toward the advancement stage in high-school sports, they must make a choice that can shape their

A goalie in a Division I championship lacrosse game like the one played here must not only be skillful but also courageous. (Source: Mike Broglio / Shutterstock.com)

career. The institutional logics they face varies, with the Division I teams committed to winning but the minor-league clubs generally emphasizing the development of a limited number of prospects who can move toward the majors.

The Baseball Options

In 1923 as a sophomore at Columbia, Lou Gehrig, who played just seven college games, was in full glory, setting three school records by batting .444, slugging .937, and smashing seven home runs. A full half-century afterwards, George Moisten, a Columbia teammate, spoke about one of the most memorable moments. "That right field at Cornell had a high fence, then there was a road back of it, then a forest. Lou lifted his home run into the forest. I looked over at Coach Coakley, sitting near me on the bench, and he was slapping his head in wonder" (Ray 2009). Soon afterwards the Yankees became interested, and a scout approached Gehrig, setting up a meeting with the team's GM. The Yankees were happy to sign him, offering Gehrig a $1,500 bonus and $400 a month—huge sums for a young man who wanted to help his impoverished family (Ray 2009).

Nearly a century later, the majority of pro baseball prospects continue to drop out of college, with about 4 percent of MLB players graduating. They become eligible for the draft after their junior year if they are 21 years old, and then, if signed, head for the minors, willing to face the roughly 10 percent odds of making it to the show for at least one game (*Campus Explorer* 2016; *Chasing the Dream* 2017; Morosi 2012).

An issue college baseball players must face is their limited financial support. The NCAA permits Division I baseball programs 11.7 scholarships for a 27-member squad, without establishing distinct amounts for individual players but setting a minimum for scholarship recipients of 25 percent of basic expenses. Dan Hartleb, the University of Illinois baseball coach, was blunt. "It's an expensive sport. We give partial scholarships where football and basketball are full rides" (Castle 2015).

Still, in spite of the limited financing for playing baseball in college and the modest percentage of college graduates in MLB, a number of college programs consistently send players to the majors. For instance, in 2016 Long Beach State had 12 former players in MLB, Arizona ten, Vanderbilt nine, and North Carolina, Miami, Texas, and Virginia eight each (Selbe 2016).

Some major leaguers have committed both to playing pro ball and to getting college educated, obtaining a degree which can be a necessity for many future jobs. Curtis Granderson, who has had a solid 13-year MLB career and whose parents are teachers, graduated from the University of Illinois at Chicago with a degree in business management and marketing. Drafted after his junior year by the Detroit Tigers, Granderson asked team officials if he could keep attending college while playing on their

Class A team. "It [was] very difficult to do," Granderson told a reporter. "A lot of stuff had to line up for me to get the opportunity to go back to school." He ended graduating only a semester after his original class. Occasionally players ask Granderson about attending college, and he tells them that to be successful, they must make the demanding commitment to both the team and to college. He explains that once they sign a pro contract, however, baseball comes first (Morosi 2012).

Minor-league baseball is a distinctly different experience from college. While the prospect doesn't need to concern himself with academic demands, he faces a more formidable competition than in either the high-school or college game. Prospects who pass successfully through the recruitment stage into MLB must produce results that are much better than most minor leaguers'. In a study of 343 professional baseball players, major leaguers tended to be superior to their minor-league counterparts in tests of speed, vertical jump, and grip strength—abilities that make a substantial contribution to predicted baseball performance (Hoffman, Vazquez, Pichardo, and Tenenbaum 2009). The pattern was similar with visual function—a critical issue in a sport where batters' precise sighting of world-class pitches is a premium. In three visual tests involving 387 professional baseball players, major leaguers obtained better results than minor leaguers (Laby, Davidson, Rosenbaum, Strasser, Mellman, Rosenbaum, and Kirschen 1996).

The journey to the majors can be a difficult one, with the number of minor-league competitors often staggering. Players might arrive at spring training filled with optimism, but when assessing the depth of talent ahead of them, they can become uneasy about their ability to progress (Gmelch 2001, 75). In 2015 Tyler Glasnow was one of 52 pitchers at the Pittsburgh Pirates spring training. Clint Hurdle, the Pittsburgh manager, praised his performance, highlighted by his fastball, curveball, and changeup, but he was concerned about the young pitcher's command of his pitches. Glasnow appreciated the praise but was looking ahead. He said, "My ultimate goal is to get off all those prospect lists and make the major leagues" (Dill 2015). Competition on the cusp of the majors can be tough. It turned out that Glasnow remained in Triple-A for the entire season. When rosters expanded in September, his performance was good enough so that the parent club might have brought him to the majors, but he remained in Triple-A and validated that decision, starting against Columbus in his first game following the September call-up and striking out one batter but giving up five walks and a double before being pulled from the contest. With command of the fastball missing, a journalist said it was painful to watch him struggle (Wilmoth 2015).

One of the challenges novice minor leaguers starting spring training face is dealing with a number of new and often unexpected norms. George Gmelch, who spent three years in the minors, wrote, "I still remember arriving in Lakeland, Florida, for my first spring training ... and receiving a sheet of regulations telling me when I had to be in bed, when the lights went out, what time I had to get up, and how I was to dress, all in sharp contrast to the freedoms I enjoyed in college and even at home" (Gmelch 2001, 47).

Historically the minor leagues have been more rule-prone than the majors. Joe Maddon, the popular coach of the Chicago Cubs, said, "Back in the day, minor league managers would have all these rules up on the wall, man." Dress codes were a favorite focus, and the season the Cubs won the World Series Maddon scoffed at such norms, declaring, "If you think you look hot, wear it ... That's our dress code." Maddon said he never grasped why managers had traditionally stressed that on the road players should wear collared shirts and avoid wearing shorts. He added that the entire team faced more important issues if they were going to be successful. "I'm here to manage the team, not make rules," Maddon declared (Berg 2016).

While minor-league players generally feel motivated to excel, low draft picks or undrafted candidates often must endure low pay and difficult working conditions. Garrett Broshuis was a University of Missouri pitcher selected by the San Francisco Giants in the fourth round of the 2004 draft. The Giants sent Broshuis to the Salem-Keizer Volcanoes of the Class A Northwest League, where his job involved playing ball six or seven days a week from about three in the afternoon until midnight, and then often spending many hours on run-down, cramped buses traveling to the next site. His salary was $1,100 a month. "Professional baseball," Broshuis said, "was disappointing from the first week I was there" (Gordon 2014).

Since 1976 the minimum salary in the major leagues has risen 2,500 percent while in the minors it has risen about 70 percent, providing between $1,100 and $2,150 a month for a five-month season, a significant loss when inflation is considered. The income decline has been particularly apparent among the lowest paid players. In 1974 at the bottom of the pay scale in low-level Class A ball, a minor leaguer made $500 a month in his first year in the pros—the inflation-adjusted equivalent of $2,300 in 2014, more than twice the updated maximum for modern minor-league equivalents (Rymer 2014).

Dirk Hayhurst, who reached the major leagues after a lengthy minor-league stay, indicated that while players often face a painful economic and competitive struggle during the retention stage of minor-league programs, the prospect of failure can be more disturbing. "I say this as one of the lucky ones. I was able to hang on long enough to get my shot at the bigs .... When my minor league season was over, I worked two, sometimes three, jobs while sleeping on someone's floor. I lived next to a school that let me work out in their gym for free because I couldn't afford a gym membership. I had parents who could mortgage their house to help me ... It was hard, damn hard, but I did it" (Hayhurst 2014).

Besides low pay, minor leaguers face other conditions that can prove pivotal in their quest to make the majors. Immersed in the retention stage of a minor-league program, young players need competent assistant coaches—effective agents of socialization who not only can help sharpen playing skills but also acquaint them with the challenges and stresses they will face in this new, formidable world.

In addition, it can be very helpful for players if the administrators in Double-A and Triple-A run their operations, everything from their pre-game preparation to their nutrition instruction, much like the parent club, making it more familiar and comfortable for players to adjust if called up (Coulter 2016).

Minor-league players, of course, are aware of the formidable odds against reaching the majors. Wynter Phoenix, an outfielder for the Yakima Bears, a Class A short-season team, was thoughtful about his dreams of reaching the show, realizing that the game is humbling and that his progress could slow down or stalemate. Phoenix said, "In your heart, if you love the game and believe in yourself, you never lose confidence. But in your mind, you ask, am I going to make it, what are my chances really?" (Gmelch 2001, 74).

In the lower level minor leagues, coaches and managers see players' doubts. Interviews with six Rookie League managers suggested that most figured that no more than a quarter of their players believed "deep down" that they would eventually reach the majors. Doug Davis, the manager of the Class A short season Pittsfield Mets, addressed many prospects' inability to remain confident. "I find that even at this level, with kids who have been successful all the way up [as amateurs], they still have a difficult time believing in their abilities, difficulty believing that they can go out there and be consistent every day" (Gmelch 2001, 74). Some, however, become more confident when they receive expert minor-league training for several years, a distinct advantage, for instance, over prospects in one-and-done college basketball.

At the Triple-A level in particular, competitors can feel somewhat more optimistic about their prospects. Players often feel they are just one accident away from making it to the majors. John Lindsey, a first baseman, who spent 18 years in the minor leagues, said it was not as if prospects hoped major leaguers would get hurt, but the fact was that sometimes they did. Lindsey added, "The phone is going to ring. The manager is going to call someone into his office. You just hope that when it happens it will be you. When you're in Triple-A, you're 'this close,' but you can also be a million miles away" (Feinstein 2014, 47). Certainly Lindsey with nearly two decades in the minors qualified as an authority on the prospect of closeness to the show.

Like their counterparts in minor-league baseball, hockey players trying to reach the NHL face an important choice.

The Hockey Options

A substantial number of professional hockey players go to college, often after having played first in the major juniors for 16- to 20-year-olds. Sixty Division I schools provide scholarships for 18 male team members averaging $15,704 per year. For Division II a sharp drop-off occurs, with scholarships paying $5,238 per player. About 10.8 percent of male high-school hockey participants play the game in college, with about 3.2 percent of that high-school total entering Division I (*Scholarshipstats.com* 2017). Freshmen hockey players average 20 years old, with college coaches often observing what they consider the best of them from high school and also for two years through the juniors and gaining considerable information before deciding whether or not to make scholarship offers (College Sports Scholarships 2016).

About 30 percent of NHL members arrive from US colleges. When hearing that figure, New Jersey Devils forward Mike Cammalleri, who spent three years at the University of Michigan, said it was about what he would have expected. Camalleri said college hockey not only develops playing skills "... but there's a social and outside-the-classroom aspect to developing a personality and a comfort within your own skin and enabling players to enter the NHL and be successful" (Morreale 2015).

One apparent reason for the comfort is that the players are less pressured to perform in college. Candidates in the minor-league system generally must be signed to the parent club or be rejected within two years. Sometimes teams feel they need more time to develop young prospects, but the system doesn't allow it. The college retention stage extends up to four years. A coach explained how it was particularly useful to give defensemen the extra time college provided. "For defensemen, it may take you a little bit longer to get up to speed for the NHL level, and being in a situation where their game-to-practice ratio is more in favor of practice, that's when they can spend more time developing their body, mature as a player. I feel that helps defensemen" (Morreale 2015).

Never has college hockey been more popular. Top American prospects face an increasingly competitive situation. While the number of Division I programs has stabilized at 60, the recruitment stage draws a growing number and diversity of applicants. Nowadays coaches can track promising candidates with their computers. One successful coach explained, "Good players have a tendency to get found now." Europeans' growing presence in Division I hockey seems to support that conclusion, with 82 European players in 2017 compared to just 32 five years earlier (Santaniello 2017).

For the first time, in 2015, three of the top eight draftees were college students, and 26 of the league's 30 teams chose a total of 56 picks from 28 colleges (Weinreb 2015). Jack Eichel, a Boston College defenseman, commented on his college years. "I'm super happy with my decision to go to college; I never regretted it and got a lot of experience off the ice," Eichel said. "I learned a lot and matured as a person by going through a lot of the experiences you go through in college like living on your own" (Morreale 2015). It is notable that among Division I hockey players, 92 percent who enrolled in college in 2007 graduated, a full eight percentage points over the NCAA average for college athletes (College Hockey Inc. 2014).

Other prospects have pursued a prominent alternative. Historically the most frequent route to the NHL has been the major juniors. Since 2006–07 the major juniors with 60 CHL teams have contributed over half of the players joining the NHL. The CHL helps smooth the transition from the largely amateur lower levels of junior hockey, providing a schedule and playoff structure that is similar to those in the senior league. Supporters of the major-junior program emphasize that their prospects play about twice as many games as their college counterparts, arguably preparing them more effectively for a NHL future (Bitel 2016; Peters 2012).

Major juniors' supporters contend that besides the advantage of more games, their players experience a faster, more aggressive style of play than the colleges, additionally preparing their fledglings better for the NHL. A journalist summarized the CHL's supposed assets when he said,

> [This league's advantages include] the speed and style of play, … the length of schedule, [and] the playoff best-of-seven series format. The CHL is more like a pro atmosphere with the 'in your face' attitude that many feel is [the] best development road to the NHL. Players wear half-shields or visors, plus fighting is accepted. Just another aspect to the CHL that makes the major juniors quite attractive for a r[is]ing young star looking to someday get his payday in the NHL.
>
> (Bitel 2016)

A number of factors, in short, arguably prepare CHL players better than their college counterparts for the NHL's institutional logics. Notably the above quote included a reference to fighting, which remains largely absent from the college game but continues in the minor leagues.

During the 1990s and early 2000s, Rob McCaig was a tough defenseman for the Louisiana Ice Gators of the East Coast Hockey League. When an opponent took a cheap shot or perhaps just to liven play, "I would get a tap on the shoulder, go on out and rattle someone's cage," he explained (O'Brien 2017).

Research on the American Hockey League, the most prominent developmental league for the NHL, indicated that minor-league hockey crowds love violence. During the 2010–11 season (1,200 games), the study found that if at any point in the course of a season, a home team averaged a one-fight increase per game, home attendance expanded by nearly 1,000 spectators and that the more common increase of a fight every four home games produced a consistent finding, raising home attendance about 250 people per game (Paul, Weinbach, and Robbins 2013, 23, 31).

While to some extent fighting is still acceptable, opposition, as noted earlier, has been building. As a result the minor-league game has been changing, becoming less violent but also faster and more polished, and, not surprisingly, less well attended. In fact, nowadays most minor-league teams are not profitable, and a substantial number have folded, including 16 in the American-based East Coast Hockey League (O'Brien 2017).

Elite hockey prospects face a world of shrinking possibilities. Not only have more candidates for a nonexpanding Division I materialized, but, in addition, the minor leagues are declining, offering fewer positions. Summary 3.3 lists issues influencing baseball and hockey prospects in choosing between college and the minor leagues.

SUMMARY 3.3

Issues Confronting Baseball and Hockey Players in Choosing between College and the Minor Leagues

A question worth pondering: The college route is less attuned to major leagues' institutional logics than minor leagues', but does that mean that one path is better than the other?

Baseball options:

College: Limited Division I financial aid compared to football and basketball; pursuit of a college degree which can be a valuable requirement for many future jobs.

Minor leagues: A formidable competition, which increases in intensity as candidates advance toward the majors; a regulated life often involving low pay and a difficult

> lifestyle; importance of minor-league clubs providing assistant coaches serving as agents of socialization not only for skill development but also for guidance about the pressures to be faced in the pro baseball world; an asset in preparing prospects for the majors if higher-level teams in the minors run their operations as much as possible in a manner similar to the parent clubs.
>
> *Hockey options:*
>
> College: For 60 Division I programs a less pressured atmosphere than the minor leagues, with prospects having more time, four years if necessary, to develop.
>
> Minor-league hockey: Major juniors, with over half of candidates making the NHL arriving from the major juniors as a member of one of 60 teams; widespread belief in pro hockey that the major juniors along with the AHL play a faster, more aggressive game than the colleges, better preparing young men for the NHL.

Prospects in both baseball and hockey have options as they seek to join the major leagues, but the residents of one small country have just a single choice and pursue it exceptionally well.

A Special Case

While players join Major League Baseball from such locations as Venezuela, Cuba, Puerto Rico, Japan, Korea, Canada, and Mexico (Thornburg 2016), one international source is particularly notable: the Dominican Republic, a country with a population of barely 10 million people, with about one thirty-third as many inhabitants as the United States and barely more than the total living in New York City. Yet since Ozzie Virgil became the first major leaguer in 1956, at least 708 Dominicans have played in MLB. In the past two decades, the number of Dominicans in the majors has nearly tripled. Most likely those numbers will continue to grow. More than a quarter of the upper minor-league rosters and nearly half of the lower rungs are Dominicans (*Baseball-Reference.com* 2017; Ghosh 2014; Thornburg 2016; Rojas 2015; Thorn 2013). The Dominican Summer League, which is part of minor-league baseball, contains 40 teams (*MiLB.com* 2017a).

It might cross one's mind that somehow a disproportionate number of Dominicans possess a baseball-proficiency gene. While that seems unlikely, it does appear that several conditions make this small nation particularly adept at developing talented players who can contribute to major-league teams' success. First, since Cuban refugees introduced the sport to the island in the 1860s, Dominicans have been passionate about playing and watching baseball. The game's first advocates were the sons of affluent families, who early in the 20th century studied in the US when that nation was celebrated as a rising economic and political power, and they brought both knowledge of and enthusiasm for one of its attractive products back to the island. Nowadays ball parks and playing fields exist in all cities and towns throughout the country, including poor areas, and beginning with the very young, children of all social classes participate in the game, giving themselves a chance to join local, regional, and eventually national teams. Investment in the institutional logics of playing expert winning baseball, in short, has become entrenched in the country's culture.

Second, skilled young players have a chance to join baseball academies. At the age of 12 or 13, Dominican prospects, whose families must sign consent forms, are recruited by scouts to play in one of the many baseball academies for young adolescents scattered around the country. Scouting has been a highly competitive enterprise, with the men involved in it attempting to identify a candidate's ability, starting to develop his skills, and getting him signed without another scout intervening.

These academies are basically baseball farms, run by men called "buscones" (street agents), who combine the functions of trainers and agents. Existence focuses on two activities—playing baseball and sleeping. The buscones' academies have no books, no computers, but perhaps, if the recruits are lucky, an old TV. For the youthful candidates, all formal education has ceased. While some buscones do their job well, others are more hustlers than mentors—stealing from the boys, encouraging them to lie about their age to be contract eligible, or providing performance-enhancing drugs (PEDs) claimed to be B-12 shots in order to add power to a bat or speed up a fast ball. In fact, players in the Dominican summer league have had the highest rate of positive PED use in pro baseball (Bautista 2015; Kurlansky 2010, 96; Ruck 2011).

In addition, all 30 MLB teams have academies on the island that talented players can join at the age of 16. Fifteen of those major-league academies have been built since 2005 at an average cost of about

$4 million. Raúl Mondesí, a long-time major leaguer, described the excitement of recruitment to one of the academies. "The first time I got to Campo Las Palmas I thought I was in baseball heaven. I had never seen anything like that in my life. Everything in order and clean and completely level fields," recounted Mondesí, who was the National League Rookie of the Year in 1994 (Rojas 2015). In 1987 the Los Angeles Dodgers developed Campo Las Palmas, offering a distinctly state-of-the-art facility for other MLB teams to emulate. It contains two full baseball fields, two half fields for infield practice, a gym, a dining hall with high-quality food, a study chamber, and a dormitory for as many as 100 prospects. At modern MLB academies, coaches and teachers serve as competent agents of socialization, developing not only baseball skills but also providing "English lessons, leadership workshops, stress-management sessions, and information about American life" (Rojas 2015).

Third, an incentive for developing prospects has been the list of major-league ballplayers who were born on the island and escaped the poverty of their youth, becoming both wealthy and renowned—Felipe and Matty Alou, Juan Marichal, Pedro Martinez, David Ortiz, and Albert Pujols among the most prominent. These top performers have become heroic role models for young countrymen trying to follow in their wake (Jozsa 2009, 32). A Dominican baseball official explained, "It's more than a game … It's a national fever. It's almost our way of life" (Thorn 2013). But it's hardly an easy road to success.

The organizers at Campo Las Palmas have decided that it is necessary to be tough with their young charges, preparing them by conveying a distinct sense of how difficult their lives will be if they reach the minors. Typically they explain that in the American minor leagues:

> … you travel in buses with no air conditioning, sleep in lousy hotels, eat strange food with people you can't talk with. You have a manager, and you don't know if he don't like you as a Black or as a Latino. You don't know who you're going to be facing. The four or five years you spend in the minors, you're going to be suffering. And that's even if you get there. Most of you won't.
>
> (Klein 1999, 100)

In 2006, in fact, less than 3 percent of Dominican prospects who joined major-league academies made it to the big leagues while 11.5 percent of Americans signed in the United States reached MLB that year (Rojas 2015).

Compared to American candidates, Dominicans are distinctly second-class citizens, paid considerably less and denied such standard minor-league resources as health insurance and professional staff support. While Americans must complete high school, Dominicans have no such requirement and can be signed at 16 when their bodies and playing ability are less developed. The renowned David Ortiz, an eight-time All Star and native Dominican, said, "A 16-year-old doesn't know how to play baseball ... I don't care what they say. When I signed at 16, I didn't know what the fuck I was doing" (Gordon 2013). What happens is that Ortiz and other talented Dominicans have found themselves in a high-powered, academy-centered, player-producing system.

José Bautista, a Dominican major leaguer, suggested that most Americans are likely to consider the above picture a painful one. However, the candidates from the buscones' academies realize that the best of them have a chance at 16 to sign a MLB contract and then move to a MLB training academy with not only the developmental benefits previously cited but also what these boys consider relatively luxurious conditions—perhaps four or five instead of 10 in a room and a computer lab with internet and video games. In addition, critical for future success, they receive three nutritious meals a day and competent weight training (Bautista 2015).

Dominicans' achievements playing baseball are clearly established, with no minor leagues outside that nation able to rival their proficiency. It appears that the combination of a culture fixated on baseball and young, talented, often poor boys with almost no other options for interesting, well-paid jobs encourages the development of a small number of first-rate players who can eventually find themselves contributing to major-league teams' winning ways.

Like Dominican baseball, the world of American college sports features various contexts in which the athletes' rights are distinctly limited.. The two upcoming issues are cases in point, and in both instances adjustments would seem productive.

Conclusion: A Pair of Issues about College Athletes' Just Treatment

Before Title IX legislation, only a handful of colleges played women's soccer. In the two decades that followed its enactment, in fact, many girls joined in boys' games, but when reaching age 7 or 8, parents sought leagues exclusively for girls, sometimes needing to create them on their own. By 2007 there were 18 million youth soccer players, half of whom were girls. Meanwhile many colleges found that with its cheapness and relative safety, soccer was a good sport to help address Title IX requirements. By 2012 more female college students were engaged in soccer than any other sport (Grainey 2012, 4–7). One indication of an encouraging response to its growth has been the expansion in soccer scholarships, generally partial ones—with Division I women's programs offering 14.1 per school compared to the men's 9.9 involving 314 teams for women and a mere 204 for men (*Athnet* 2016).

One powerful idea associated with Title IX has been women athletes' growing conviction that they should receive equitable treatment and, according to Bonnie Hagerman, a lecturer on gender and sports, "[W]here equity and equality are lacking, we see increased numbers of women pressing their schools to comply fully with Title IX, often through legal recourse" (Bromley 2016). In short, the forces promoting equal opportunity in college sports seem to have grown stronger.

Will women's soccer and other major women's college programs continue to grow? A half-century in the future, will the leadership in women's college sports still be able to point to discriminatory conditions, or will such gender-related second-class citizenry have become a distant reminder from the past?

A second issue involves money-making NCAA programs and the often financially strapped athletes who fill the players' roles. Taylor Branch, a well-known writer, suggested that while players' illegal recruitment or payment are troublesome, the core problem is that two of the noble principles the NCAA uses to justify its existence—"'amateurism' and the 'student-athlete'—are cynical hoaxes, legalistic confections propagated by the universities so they can exploit the skills and fame of young athletes" (Branch 2011).

As he researched big-time college sports, Branch found that many of the college athletes, who were obviously essential for the programs' success, were financially deprived. Speaking from experience Heisman Trophy winner Desmond Howard said, "And you walk around and you can't put gas in your car? You can't even fly home to see your parents?" A few big-time coaches are distinctly sympathetic. After Alabama coach Nick Saban furiously referred to players' agents as pimps, Dale Brown, a retired LSU basketball coach, spoke bluntly about his peers. "Look at the money we make off predominantly poor black kids ... We're the whoremasters." Furthermore, as noted earlier, Division I athletes routinely receive substandard education that fails to prepare them for the job world (Branch 2011).

Branch admitted that he "reflexively recoiled" at the prospect of paying players but that in an increasingly commercialized college-sports world, where many of the top athletes were impoverished, reform was essential. Branch concluded, "The time has come for a major overhaul. And whether the powers that be like it or not, big changes are coming" (Branch 2011).

Summary

The content of institutional logics differs in the various organizational settings examined in this chapter, with Division I teams focused on winning and the baseball and hockey minor leagues often concentrated on player development for their parent clubs' success. Recent history has shown that leading college football teams have sharply increased their winning percentages, head coaches' salaries, and revenues, but fairly few top college sports programs have made a profit. Whether it's the heavy-revenue sports or other Division I teams, the numbers show that it's only an elite few who are recruited from high school to these top college teams.

The minor-league baseball system contains four broad classes and 248 teams. Minor-league hockey started in 1926 and is larger than its baseball counterpart, with three leading developmental leagues and a total of nearly 500 professional and amateur teams.

Data on three FBS conferences indicated that the quality of the players recruited accounted for 63 percent to 80 percent of the variance in conference winning percentage. Under Nick Saban the highly successful

Alabama team has prepared its athletes for the distinct possibility of NFL play with meticulously planned offensive, defensive, and special-team units.

While Division I college basketball remains popular, the one-and-done system has produced mixed results, with some prospects succeeding and many floundering.

The current college football and basketball scene features pressure and competition—a setting where big-time programs sometimes break the rules in recruiting and providing illegal benefits. A troublesome issue is that recruited players for major college sports programs seldom receive much guidance in organizing their academic programs, often leaving them adrift when the vast majority of them fail to make the pros.

Other elite college sports include women's basketball, which has become increasingly popular for players and spectators. One noteworthy issue has been that over time the number of male coaches in women's college basketball has increased, with higher pay and several other issues contributing to the trend.

The concept of agents of socialization seems useful in analyzing how coaches and teammates can contribute to institutional logics. Illustrations of the concept's relevance are apparent in examining both softball and lacrosse.

Higher education is a limited option for elite baseball players, with fewer than 5 percent having graduated from college, where financial support is much less extensive than for Division I football or basketball. Minor-league prospects face fierce competition, with those eventually making the majors possessing superior physical attributes. In addition, they often must deal with poor pay and difficult working conditions. Players find it helpful if their coaches not only assist them in sharpening their skills but can also guide them in coping with this new, taxing world.

A substantial number of hockey players attend college after first playing in the major juniors. About 30 percent of NHL prospects arrive from American colleges, where they have more time to mature as players than in the minor leagues. Alternatively over half of NHL members have joined the league directly from the major juniors, with prospects saying that they experienced several advantages over the college game.

Dominican baseball is a special case, with a poor country of barely 10 million people over time turning out over 700 major leaguers. Several conditions make the island a particularly successful location for developing fine ball players. While Americans might find the Dominican baseball system depressing and destructive, it has turned out well for a number of highly talented prospects.

Finally, the chapter ends with examination of two thought-provoking issues—the future development of women's college sports and the plight of some big-time Division I athletes in major college programs. The two situations are both in flux, with pressure for change mobilized by past injustices.

Class Discussion Issues

1. Define institutional logics and provide a detailed example.
2. Discuss the difference between English college sports programs and those in Division I.
3. Comment on the fact that while a number of football programs rake in substantial revenues, few athletic programs make a profit. Are there productive steps to alter this situation?
4. If you had the authority to develop the institutional logics for either a minor-league baseball or hockey team, what issues would you emphasize? Make sure to address the topic of winning.
5. Summarize research findings about the impact that recruitment has on winning in big-time football. What are the principal factors influencing Division I football programs' institutional logics?
6. Is the one-and-done approach to college basketball a good idea? Discuss its impact on college programs, coaches, players, and the NBA.
7. Summarize the study on major infractions in college sports programs and also the principal findings about the deficient education many athletes in Division I receive. What specific administrative reforms could prove productive here?
8. Why has the percentage of female head college coaches declined? Discuss the different factors coming into play here.

9. Examine the relationship of the concept of agents of socialization to institutional logics. Give an illustration of how agents of socialization affect intercollegiate play, perhaps a situation you experienced yourself or someone told you.
10. In order to succeed and advance through the different classes of the minor-league baseball system what are the principal attributes a player requires?
11. Why has college hockey become so popular? Do you think college hockey represents a productive option for competing to join the NHL or is it better to play minor-league hockey?
12. What, if anything, does the Dominican story of baseball success suggest about the development of quality players and the contribution to major-league teams' institutional logics?

References

Athnet. 2016. "College Soccer Scholarships and Recruiting." www.athleticscholarships.net/soccerscholarships.htm.

Barrett, J.C. 2016. "There Are Fewer Women Coaches in College Basketball Now than There Were a Decade Ago." *ESPN* (January 19). https://fivethirtyeight.com/features/there-are-fewer-women-coaches-in-college-basketball-now-than-there-were-a-decade-ago/.

Baseball-Reference.com. 2017. "Players by Place of Birth." www.baseball-reference.com/bio/.

Bautista, José. 2015. "The Cycle." *The Players' Tribune* (April 2). www.theplayerstribune.com/jose-bautista-dominican-baseball-prospects-mlb.

Beer, Jonathan. 2016. "The Financial Impact of Championship Basketball." *CBSNews* (April 6). www.cbsnews.com/news/the-financial-impact-of-championship-basketball/.

Berg, Ted. 2016. "Joe Maddon Defines Cubs' 2016 'Dress Code: 'If You Think You Look Hot, Wear It.''" *USA Today* (March 20). http://ftw.usatoday.com/2016/03/joe-maddon-chicago-cubs-dress-code-look-hot-mlb.

Bitel, Russ. 2016. "Major Juniors vs. College Hockey: What's the Better Choice?" *Hockey Family Advisor*. http://hockeyfamilyadvisor.com/major-juniors-vs-college-hockey-whats-the-better-choice-2/.

Branch, Taylor. 2011. "The Shame of College Sports." *The Atlantic* (October). www.theatlantic.com/magazine/archive/2011/10/the-shame-of-college-sports/308643/.

Brannon, Jason. 2013. "Bill James on How to Fix Minor League Baseball." *SB Nation* (June 3). www.sbnation.com/hot-corner/2013/6/3/4392678/bill-james-on-how-to-fix-minor-league-baseball.

Bromley, Anne E. 2016. "Equity in Sports: UVA's Bonnie Hagerman Explains the Impact of Title IX." *UVAToday* (September 9). https://news.virginia.edu/content/equity-sports-uvas-bonnie-hagerman-explains-impact-title-ix.

Campos, Paul. 2014. "A Brief History of Coaching Football Salaries in the Context of the New Guilded Age." *Lawyers, Guns & Money* (December 30). www.lawyers gunsmoneyblog.com/2014/12/brief-history-college-football-coaching-salaries-context-new-gilded-age.

Campus Explorer. 2016. "Major League Baseball Players Finish Their Degrees." www.campusexplorer.com/college-advice-tips/899B0F09/Major-League-Baseball-Players-Finish-Their-Degrees/.

Caro, Cary A. 2012. "College Football Success: The Relationship between Recruiting and Winning." *International Journal of Sports Science & Coaching* 7 (March): 139–152. http://journals.sagepub.com/doi/abs/10.1260/1747-9541.7.1.139.

Castle, George. 2015. "Why 11.7 Is a Terrible Number for College Baseball Scholarships." *youthletic.* www.youthletic.com/articles/why-117-is-a-terrible-number-for-college-baseball-scholarships/?page=2.

Chasing the Dream. 2017. "About Chasing MLB Dreams." https://chasingmlbdreams.com/about-chasing-the-dream/.

College Hockey Inc. 2014. "Hockey Leads in NCAA Grad Rate." (October 28). http://collegehockeyinc.com/articles/hockey-leads-ncaa-grad-rate.

College Sports Scholarships. 2016. "NCAA Ice Hockey Scholarships." www.collegesportsscholarships.com/ice-hockey.htm.

Coulter, Darrell. 2016. "Elite Baseball Pitching Instruction." *Pitching Habits.* http://pitchinghabits.com/whats-wrong-with-the-minor-league-baseball-system/.

Cronin, John. 2013. "Truth in the Minor League Class Structure: The Case for Restructuring the Minors." *SABR* (Spring). http://sabr.org/research/truth-minor-league-class-structure-case-reclassification-minors.

Deas, Tommy. 2012. "Slap Batting a Strategic Weapon for UA Softball." *TideSports.com* (May 22). https://alabama.rivals.com/content.asp?CID=1368531.

Dill, Jason. 2015. "Top Pittsburgh Pirates Prospect Tyler Glasnow Soaking Up First MLB Spring Camp." *Bradenton Herald* (February 24). www.bradenton.com/sports/mlb/pittsburgh-pirates/article34799853.html.

Dittrich, John. 2013. "What Makes Minor League Baseball So Important? Why Do Some Organizations Never Win?" *ballparkbiz*.com (November 14). https://ballparkbiz.wordpress.com/2013/11/14/what-makes-minor-league-baseball-so-important-why-do-some-organizations-never-win/

Draft Site. 2017. "NBA Draft Rules." www.draftsite.com/nba/rules/.

Drayer, Shannon. 2016. "Mariners' Emphasis on Winning in the Minors Quickly Produced Results." *710 a ESPN* (October 20). http://sports.mynorthwest.com/202224/mariners-emphasis-on-winning-in-the-minors-quickly-produced-results/.

Echlin, Paul Sean, Charles H. Tator, Michael D. Cusimano, Robert C. Cantu, Jack E. Taunton, Ross E. G. Upshur, Craig R. Hall, Andrew M. Johnson, Lorie A. Forwell, and Elaine N. Skopelja. 2010. "A Prospective Study of Physician-observed Concussions during Junior Ice Hockey: Implications for Incidence Rates." *Journal of Neurosurgery* 29 (November): E4+.

ESPN. 2014. "NCAA against-One-and-Done Rule." (April 7). http://espn.go.com/mens-college-basketball/story/_/id/10740125/ncaa-officials-john-calipari-kentucky-wildcats-oppose-one-done-rule.

Estel, Dick. 2016. "The Professional Hockey Leagues of North America." National Hockey League (September 22). www.dickestel.com/hockeyleagues.htm.

Fantauzzi, Damian. 2016. "Who Owns College Sports?" *Saratoga Today* (January 21). http://saratogatodaynewspaper.com/index.php/today-in-saratoga/sports/item/5041-who-owns-college-sports.

Feinstein, John. 2014. *Where Nobody Knows Your Name: Life in the Minor Leagues of Baseball.* New York: Doubleday.

Fleener, Coby. 2014. "The Best Decision I've Ever Made." *Cobyfleener.com* (January 27). https://cobyfleener.com/blog/2014/01/27/stanford-university-the-best-decision-ive-ever-made/.

Fountain, Jeffrey J., and Peter S. Finley. 2011. "Academic Clustering: A Longitudinal Analysis of a Division I Football Program." *Journal of Issues in Intercollegiate Athletics* 4: 24–41.

Gaines, Cork. 2014. "College Football Reaches $3.4 Billion in Revenue." *Business Insider* (December 7). www.businessinsider.com/college-football-revenue-2014-12.

Gaines, Cork. 2016. "The 25 Schools That Make the Most Money in College Sports." *Business Insider* (October 13). www.businessinsider.com/schools-most-revenue-college-sports-2016-10/#23-washington--1035-million-3.

Gaul, Gilbert M. 2015. "How College Football Coaches Became Multi-million-dollar Money Pits." *Time* (August). http://time.com/4006558/college-football-coach-salaries/.

Ghosh, Palash. 2014. "Huge Salaries and a Poverty-Stricken Country: The Economics of Baseball in the Dominican Republic." *International Business Times* (January 24). www.ibtimes.com/huge-salaries-poverty-stricken-country-economics-baseball-dominican-republic-1546993.

Gmelch, George. 2001. *Inside Pitch: Life in Professional Baseball.* Washington, DC: Smithsonian Institution Press.

Gordon, Ian. 2013. "Inside Major League Baseball's Dominican Sweatshop System." *Mother Jones* (March/April). www.motherjones.com/politics/2013/03/baseball-dominican-system-yewri-guillen.

Gordon, Ian. 2014. "Minor-League Baseball Players Make Poverty-Level Wages." *Mother Jones* (July/August). www.motherjones.com/politics/2014/06/baseball-broshuis-minor-league-wage-income.

Grainey, Timothy F. 2012. *Beyond Bend It like Beckham: The Global Phenomenon of Women's Soccer.* Lincoln, NE: University of Nebraska Press.

Greenberg, Neil. 2015. "A Look at How One and Done Players Perform in the NBA." *The Washington Post* (April 8). www.washingtonpost.com/news/fancy-stats/wp/2015/04/0.

Harper, Shaun, Collin D. Williams Jr., and Horatio W. Blackman. 2018. "Black Male Student-Athletes and Racial Inequities in NCAA Division I College Sports." *Center for the Study of Race and Equity in Education.* https://equity.gse.upenn.edu/sports.

Harris Poll. 2015. "Pro Football is Still America's Favorite Sport." (January 26). www.theharrispoll.com/sports/Americas_Fav_Sport_2016.html.

Hayhurst, Dirk. 2014. "An Inside Look into the Harsh Conditions of Minor League Baseball." *Bleacher Report* (May 14). http://bleacherreport.com/articles/2062307-an-inside-look-into-the-harsh-conditions-of-minor-league-baseball.

Hobson, William, and Steven Rich. 2015a. "Playing in the Red." *The Washington Post* (November 23). www.washingtonpost.com/sf/sports/wp/2015/11/23/running-up-the-bills/?utm_term=.e869cf1b2a66.

Hobson, William, and Steven Rich. 2015b. "Colleges Spend Fortunes on Lavish Athletic Facilities." *Chicago Tribune* (December 23). www.chicagotribune.com/sports/college/ct-athletic-facilities-expenses-20151222-story.html.

Hockey League History. 2016. "Minor Professional Hockey Leagues: Exploring the Past Hockey Leagues of North America." www.hockeyleaguehistory.com/minor_professional_hockey_leagues.htm.

Hoffman, Jay R., José Vazquez, Napoleon Pichardo, and Gersho Tenenbaum. 2009. "Anthropometric and Performance Comparisons in Professional Baseball Players." *Journal of Strength and Conditioning Research* 23 (November): 2173–2178.

Hume, Stephen. 2013. "The Trouble with Canadian Hockey Starts with the Minor Leagues." *The Vancouver Sun* (January 4). www.vancouversun.com/sports/stephen+hume+trouble+with+canadian+hockey+starts+with+minor+leagues/7776668/story.html.

Jozsa, Jr. Frank P. 2009. *Global Sports: Cultures, Markets, and Organizations.* Hackensack, NJ: World Scientific Publishing Company.

Kalin, Jacqui L., and Jennifer J. Waldron. 2015. "Preferences toward Gender of Coach and Perceptions of Roles of Basketball Coaches." *International Journal of Exercise Science* 8: 303–317.

Katz, Andy. 2015. "One and Done Culture Feeds Urgency to 'Leave as Early as Possible.'" ESPN. http://espn.go.com/mens-college-basketball/story/_/id/13923267/duke-blue-devils-coach-mike-krzyzewski-says-one-done-culture-not-going-away.

Kekis, John. 2009. "Cornell's Max Seibald, a Four-Year Leader." *Bleacher Report* (May 15). http://bleacherreport.com/articles/176227-cornells-max-seibald-_-a-four-year-leader.

Kirpalani, Sanjay. 2013. "Nick Saban's Secret Recruiting Recipe." *Bleacher Report* (June 3). http://bleacherreport.com/articles/1649924-nick-sabans-secret-recruiting-recipe.

Klein, Alan A. 1999. "Coming of Age in North America: Socialization of Dominican Baseball Players," pp. 96–103 in Jay Coakley and Peter Donnelly (eds.), *Inside Sports.* New York: Routledge.

Klein, Jeff Z. 2011. "No Fights. No Checking. Can This Be Hockey?" *The New York Times* (March 5). www.nytimes.com/2011/03/06/weekinreview/06hockey.html?_r=0.

Kurlansky, Mark. 2010. *The Eastern Stars: How Baseball Changed the Dominican Town of San Pedro de Macorís.* New York: Riverhead Books.

Laby, Daniel M., John L. Davidson, Louis J. Rosenbaum, Charles Strasser, Michael F. Mellman, Arthur L. Rosenbaum, and David G. Kirschen. 1996. "The Visual Function of Professional Baseball Players." *American Journal of Ophthalmology* 122 (October): 476–485.

Lacrosse Monkey. 2011. "How to Play Goalie in Men's Lacrosse." July 8. www.google.com/webhp?sourceid=chrome-instant&ion=1&espv=2&ie=UTF-8#q=how+to+be+a+better+goalie+in+lacrosse&start=10.

LaFauci, Trevor. 2015. "Broken System: How the One-and-Done Philosophy Is Ruining Men's College Basketball." *Politicus Sports* (May 21). http://sports.politicususa.com/2015/05/21/broken-system-how-the-one-and-done-philosophy-is-ruining-mens-college-basketball.html.

Langelett, George. 2003. "The Relationship between Recruiting and Team Performance in Division 1A College Football." *Journal of Sports Economics* 4 (August).

Langford, Jon. 2014. "America's Big Business of College Football? It's a Foreign Concept for Brits." *BBC* (March). www.bbcamerica.com/anglophenia/2014/03/americas-big-business-college-football-alien-concept-brits/.

Lipsyte, Robert. 1997. "If It's Gotta Be the Shoes, He's Gotta Be the Guy." *The New York Times* (July 6). www.nytimes.com/1997/07/06/sports/if-it-s-gotta-be-the-shoes-he-s-gotta-be-the-guy.html?pagewanted=all.

Longman, Jeré. 2017. "Number of Women Coaching in College Has Plummeted in Title IX Era." *The New York Times* (March 30). www.nytimes.com/2017/03/30/sports/ncaabasketball/coaches-women-title-ix.html.

LXTC. 2015. "LXTC Goalie Evolution Academy." www.lxtclacrosse.com/goalie-evolution-academy/.

Martin, Emmie. 2016. "The 20 Most Dominant Football Programs in the Modern Era." *Business Insider* (September 17). www.businessinsider.com/best-college-football-programs-in-america-2016-9.

McIntyre, Jason. 2016. "Women's College Basketball Loses $14 Million a Year, Says Mark Emmert." *USA Today* (April 20). http://thebiglead.com/2016/04/20/womens-college-basketball-loses-14-million-a-year-says-mark-emmert/.

Metter, Anatoliy. 2013. "Top Ten Best Developmental Ice Hockey Leagues (North America)." *The Hockey Writers* (July 10). http://thehockeywriters.com/top-10-best-developmental-ice-hockey-leagues-north-america/.

MiLB.com. 2017a. "Dominican Summer League." www.milb.com/index.jsp?sid=l130.

MiLB.com. 2017b. "Teams by Classification." www.milb.com/milb/info/classifications.jsp.

MiLB.com. 2018. "MiLB.com Frequently Asked Questions." www.milb.com/milb/info/faq.jsp?mc=business.

Moriarty, Morgan. 2017. "NCAA Forms Commission to Make 'Substantive Changes' to College Basketball." (October 11). www.sbnation.com/college-basketball/2017/10/11/16460212/ncaa-commission-on-college-basketball-fbi.

Morosi, Jon Paul. 2012. "College Grads in Baseball a Rare Breed." *FoxSports* (May 17). www.foxsports.com/mlb/story/curtis-granderson-college-grads-in-baseball-a-rare-breed-051712.

Morreale, Mike G. 2015. "College Hockey's Impact on NHL Continues to Grow." *NHL.com* (June 25). www.nhl.com/news/college-hockeys-impact-on-nhl-continues-to-grow/c-772290.

Morris, Peter. 2006. *A Game of Inches: The Stories behind the Innovations That Shaped Baseball*. Chicago, IL: Ivan R. Dee.

National Football League. 2017. "Eligibility Rules." www.nflregionalcombines.com/Docs/Eligibility%20Rules.pdf.

NBA Development League. 2017. "Frequently Asked Questions: NBA Development League." http://dleague.nba.com/faq/.

NCAA. 2016a. "Women's Basketball Sets Attendance Record across All Three Divisions." (June 8). www.ncaa.com/news/basketball-women/article/2016-06-07/womens-basketball-sets-attendance-record-across-all-three.

NCAA. 2016b. "Temple Study Examines Penalty Consistency of NCAA Infractions." (August 9). www.ncaa.org/about/resources/media-center/news/temple-study-examines-penalty-consistency-ncaa-infractions.

NCAA. 2017. "Estimated Probability of Competing in College Athletics." (March 10). www.ncaa.org/about/resources/research/estimated-probability-competing-college-athletics.

New, Jake. 2015. "Academic Fraud at Syracuse," *Inside Higher Ed.* (March 9). www.insidehighered.com/news/2015/03/09/ncaa-suspends-syracuse-u-basketball-coach-vacates-108-wins.

Nissi, Taylor. 2015. "How to Play Goalie in Lacrosse." *Howcast.* www.howcast.com/videos/498200-how-to-shoot-from-a-stationary-position-lacrosse/.

O'Brien, Rebecca Davis. 2017. "Minor-League Hockey: Less Violent Hockey – Also Less Popular." *Wall Street Journal* (April). www.wsj.com/articles/minor-league-hockey-is-getting-less-violentand-less-popular-1491411116.

Orland, Michael. 2009. *Bowled Over: Big Time College Football from the Sixties to the BCS Era.* Chapel Hill, NC: The University of North Carolina Press.

Paul, Rodney J., Andrew P. Weinbach, and Daniel Robbins. 2013. "American Hockey League Attendance: A Study of Fan Preferences for Fighting, Team Performance, and Promotions." *International Journal of Sport Finance* 8 (February): 21–38.

Peter, Bruce. 2011. "The North American Hockey System." *Puck Worlds* (June 10). www.puckworlds.com/2011/6/10/2212875/the-north-american-hockey-system.

Peters, Chris. 2012. "A Beginner's Guide to the CHL vs. NCAA Recruiting Battle." *The United States of Hockey* (July 18). https://unitedstatesofhockey.com/2012/07/18/a-beginners-guide-to-the-chl-vs-ncaa-recruiting-battle/.

Prunty, Brendan. 2015. "The 1995 Connecticut Huskies, the Team That Made Women's Basketball." *USA Today* (March 12). http://thebiglead.com/2015/03/12/the-1995-connecticut-huskies-the-team-that-made-womens-basketball/.

Rand, Suzanne E. 1985. "The Commercialization of College Football: The Universities of Oklahoma and Georgia Learn an Antitrust Lesson in NCAA v. Board of Regents." *Pepperdine Law Review* 12 (January 15): 515–534. http://digitalcommons.pepperdine.edu/cgi/viewcontent.cgi?article=1895&context=plr

Rausch, Max. 2013. "How to Build a Bully: Inside the Stanford Football Strength Program." *Bleacher Report* (August 16). http://bleacherreport.com/articles/1739903-how-to-build-a-bully-inside-the-stanford-football-strength-program.

Ray, James Lincoln. 2009. "Lou Gehrig." SABR. http://sabr.org/bioproj/person/ccdffd4c.

Reynolds, Tim. 2017. "Commissioner Adam Silver Wants the NBA Drafts One-and-Done Rule Changed." *Business Insider* (June 2). www.businessinsider.com/ap-changes-coming-nba-commissioner-wants-draft-rules-amended-2017-6.

Rojas, Enrique. 2015. "Baseball Academies Thrive in the Dominican Republic." *ESPN* (July 1). http://espn.go.com/blog/onenacion/post/_/id/710/baseball-academies-thrive-in-the-dominican-republic.

Ruck, Rob. 2011. "Baseball's Recruitment Abuses." *Americas Quarterly* (Summer). http://americasquarterly.org/node/2745.

Rymer, Zachary D. 2014. "MLB Must Finally Answer for Exploitation in the Minor Leagues." *Bleacher Report* (February 12). http://bleacherreport.com/articles/1957838-mlb-must-finally-answer-for-exploitation-in-the-minor-leagues.

Santaniello, Gary. 2017. "College Hockey Has a Glut of Top Talent but Nowhere to Grow." *The New York Times* (March 24). www.nytimes.com/2017/03/23/sports/hockey/ncaa-college-teams.html.

Scarborough, Alex. 2013. "Players Appreciate Saban's Ability to Develop Off-Field Needs for NFL." *ESPN* (January 25). www.espn.go.com/colleges/alabama/football/story/_/id/8879417/alabama-crimson-tide-players-nfl-ready-field-thanks-nick-saban.

Scholarship.com. 2017. "College Hockey & Scholarship Opportunities." www.scholarshipstats.com/hockey.html.

SEC Football. 2016. "51 SEC Players Selected in the 2016 NFL Draft." www.secsports.com/article/15385639/51-sec-players-selected-2016-nfl-draft.

Selbe, Nick. 2016. "College Baseball: Schools That Produce the Most MLB Players." NCAA. www.ncaa.com/news/baseball/article/2016-06-09/college-baseball-schools-produce-most-mlb-players.

Shea, Jim. 1995. *Husky Mania: The Inside Story of the Rise of UConn Men's and Women's Basketball Teams.* New York: Villard Books.

Silverman, Steve. 2014. "What Do College Softball Coaches Look For?" *Livestrong.com* (March 15). www.livestrong.com/article/378019-what-do-college-softball-coaches-look-for/.

Smith, Ronald. 2011. *Pay for Play: A History of Big-Time College Athletic Reform.* Urbana, IL: University of Illinois Press.

Sorg, Lisa. 2015. "Softball Coach Makes Her Best Pitch." *Duke Magazine* (Winter). http://dukemagazine.duke.edu/article/sports-softball-coach-makes-her-best-pitch.

Southall, Richard M., and Mark S. Nagel. 2010. "Institutional Logics Theory: Examining Big-Time College Sport," pp. 68–80 in Earl Smith (ed.), *Sociology of Sport and Social Theory.* Champaign, IL: Human Kinetics.

Suggs, Welch. 2010. "Football, Television, and the Supreme Court: How a Decision 20 Years Ago Brought Commercialization to the World of College Sports," pp. 130–134 in Robert E. Washington and David Karen (eds.), *Sport, Power, and Society: Institutions and Practices.* Boulder, CO: Westview Press.

The Associated Press. 2016. "Key Findings in Temple University Study on NCAA Infractions." (August 9). http://bigstory.ap.org/article/26ed7d4de37d44ab981b1ee39742edf8/key-findings-temple-university-study-ncaa-infractions.

the guardian. 2016. "Jim Harbaugh Is Football's Highest Paid Coach at $9m a Year." (October 26). www.theguardian.com/sport/2016/oct/26/michigan-jim-harbaugh-highrs-salary-coach-college-football.

The Morning Call. 2014. "AHL Is One Step Away from NHL." (September 29). www.mcall.com/sports/hockey/phantoms/mc-phantoms-minor-league-explanation-10172014-20140927-story.html.

Thorn, John. 2013. "Pride and Passion: Baseball in the Dominican Republic." *MLB.com* (January 25). http://mlb.mlb.com/dr/pride_passion_dr.jsp.

Thornburg, Chad. 2016. "Opening Day Rosters Feature 238 International Players." *MLB.com.* www.mlb.com/news/mlb-rosters-feature-238-international-players/c-170477992.

Tierney, Trevor. 2012. "How to Become a Fearless Lacrosse Goalie." *Lacrosse AllStars* (April 19). http://laxallstars.com/how-to-become-a-fearless-lacrosse-goalie/.

Tracy, Marc. 2016. "College or the N.B.A.? New Rule Gives Players More Time and Feedback." *The New York Times* (May 28). www.nytimes.com/2016/05/28/sports/ncaabasketball/nba-draft-college-basketball-players.html?_r=0.

Tracy, Marc. 2017. "Amid Scandal, N.C.A.A. Forms Commission to Reform Men's Basketball." *The New York Times* (October 11). www.nytimes.com/2017/10/11/sports/ncaa-college-basketball-reform.html.

Trahan, Kevin. 2014. "Athletes Are Getting Degrees, but Does That Actually Mean Anything?" (July 9). www.sbnation.com/college-football/2014/7/9/5885433/ncaa-trial-student-athletes-education.

Tudor, Caulton. 2015. "Don't Expect NBA Owners, Union to End One-and-Done Era." *Wralsportsfan* (April 8). www.wralsportsfan.com/don-t-expect-nba-owners-union-to-end-one-and-one-era/14568176/.

USHI. 2014. "The Junior Hockey Landscape: What You Need to Know." (November 12). www.ushi.com/news_article/show/446473-the-junior-hockey-landscape-what-you-need-to-know.

Vecsey, George. 2006. *Baseball: A History of America's Favorite Game*. New York: The Modern Library.

Warner, Gerald. 2016. "How to Correct the 'Leaning Forward' Problem." *PitchSoftball.com*. www.pitchsoftball.com/HowtoStoptheLeaningForwardProblem.html.

Weathersby, Edwin. 2013. "15 College Football Coaches Who Are the Best Recruiters." *Bleacher Report* (April 25). http://bleacherreport.com/articles/1617801-15-college-football-coaches-who-are-the-best-recruiters.

Weinreb, Josh. 2015. "Notebook: 27 College Teams Represented over 56 Picks in 2015 NHL Entry Draft." *USCHO.com* (June 27). www.uscho.com/2015/06/27/notebook-27-college-teams-represented-over-56-picks-in-2015-nhl-entry-draft/.

Wilmoth, Charlie. 2015. "Cannonballs Coming: Tyler Glasnow Dreadful in First Start since September Call-ups." *SB Nation* (September 1). www.bucsdugout.com/2015/9/1/9243075/cannonballs-coming-tyler-glasnow-dreadful-in-first-start-since.

WKYT.com. 2015. "Wisconsin's Bo Ryan: 'We Don't Do a Rent-a-Player.'" (April 7). www.wkyt.com/home/headlines/Wisconsins-Bo-Ryan-refers-to-one-and-dones-as-rent-a-players-298884811.html.

4

SCALING THE HEIGHTS: PLAYERS IN THE FOUR MAJOR LEAGUES

It was a magical moment when in 2002 *ESPN* did the then unprecedented, nationally televising a high-school basketball game featuring a still largely unknown 17-year-old—LeBron James. Afterwards Jay Bilas, a sports journalist, was prophetic in writing about the young man. He declared, "His current talent level, ability and future potential is clearly worthy of being covered by national media outlets, scouted by professional teams, coveted by marketers of products, and pursued by game promoters and shoe companies that hope to make him the next Jordan or Iverson as a shoe pitchman" (Bilas 2002).

The contest was highly publicized ahead of time, covered by a team composed of well-known sports personalities, followed by a 30-minute program focused on James, and also provided coverage on *ESPN The Magazine* and on ESPN's *SportsCenter* following the game. During the telecast attention fixed on James and his play, with no mention of either team's offensive or defensive schemes and often no reference to other players' scoring or their entrance into or departure from the game. Besides *ESPN*, *USA Today* and *Sports Illustrated* gave James major coverage.

Bilas was not particularly concerned about the attention overwhelming James, feeling that he was as prepared to make the leap successfully to the NBA as any teen. Instead the writer's concern was other players—celebrated by the media and, while falling short of the exquisite talent and drive that James displayed, deciding to make the same huge jump from high-school competition to the NBA (Bilas 2002).

A distinct case in point would be Sebastian Telfair, a high-school senior who attended Lincoln High School in New York City, graduated a year after James, and led his team to three straight state championships, becoming the all-time points leader in state history. His breathtaking play, featuring pinpoint, no-look passes and flashy dribbling that could leave opponents immobilized, fascinated onlookers, attracting celebrities like Jay Z, Ahmad Rashad, and Spike Lee to his games. An *ESPN* film crew followed Telfair, detailing his achievements to that point. *Sports Illustrated* did a cover story showing the 18-year-old grasping a basketball and leaping over the Coney Island pier and the surrounding skyline with the headline "Watch me now."

Drafted in the first round, Telfair immediately became eligible for a five-year, $10 million deal with Adidas. The future seemed bright until he started playing in a league where the opponents were infinitely better than those against whom he had previously competed. The most positive factor was that midway through his first year when he became a starter he managed a few games with decent scoring and assist totals. However, his jump shot was erratic, especially facing expert defenders. Yes, he could dribble well, but his passes, so effective in high school, simply failed with large, fast-moving pro defenders. And speaking of defense, Telfair, who had always focused almost exclusively on offense, was worthless. Overall he simply didn't seem ready for the NBA. Furthermore, at 6 feet, 170 lbs. he was small by NBA standards, hardly comparable to celebrated players like Kevin Garnett, Dwight Howard, or James whose massive stature helped them successfully jump from high school to the pros.

Telfair played nine years with seven teams, never catching on with any of them and spending ample time on the bench. Clearly, many critics suggested, the young man, who did have talent, would have been smart to have pursued the option of going from high school to Louisville and improving for at least a year with a program featuring a competent set of coaches/teachers (Gonzalez 2013; Mangiaracina 2014).

Before making the leap, both of the high schoolers seemed like sure bets for the NBA, but the realities of that league indicated that it was true for one but not the other. To be successful, young prospects must not only possess high-level playing skills but also be able to engage in *adaptation*, which entails individuals understanding the setting in which they are located and learning to perform their role effectively within it (Battochio, Schinke, Battochio, Halliwell, and Tenenbaum 2010, 283). It's a response players need to keep in mind as they enter the recruitment or retention stages in the major leagues. Adaptation is necessary for athletes at all programmatic levels, but a consistent reality applying to the major leagues is that the quality of play is distinctly higher than at lower levels, meaning that players are almost invariably more severely challenged to make performance improvements than ever before. Major-league play, it seems, involves a survival of the fittest, with the fittest almost certainly adept at adaptation.

Momentarily the focus shifts to players' experiences in the four major pro sports as they adapt to the challenges of entering and staying in their league. First, though, some historical material providing a background for that discussion and indicating some of the significant changes in those leagues that have taken place over time.

The Historical Growth of the Top Professional Leagues

In the four big leagues' opening years, players made little money—a sharp contrast with the current situation. In the 1870s in the newly formed National League, salaries comprised over 60 percent of a club's budget. At that time teams would compete with each other for top prospects. It was a costly situation for these cash-challenged businessmen, and in 1879 owners secretly agreed that each team would have five players (about half the roster) who were reserved, that is, off-limits for other clubs. The so-called "reserved" players who tried to leave their teams were blacklisted, and a team which signed someone from a competitor's reserved list was ousted from the league. Owners started to make a profit for the first time, and by 1883 what became known as "the reserve clause" covered a team's entire roster. Publicly team officials sought to present their action in a positive light, asserting that the new policy promoted fairer competition by preventing the richer clubs from buying up all the best players (Reiss 1995, 157; Scully 1989, 2–3).

The reserve system persisted largely unchallenged until 1969, and players simply accepted it—made an adaptation to low pay, believing that resistance would only arouse owners' wrath and their eventual banishment from the game. When St. Louis center fielder Curt Flood finally resisted the system and went to court, the individuals called to testify in the case almost unanimously opposed him (Barra 2011).

Active players feared reprisal from the owners and provided Flood no public support—a situation he later recalled. He said, "I spent six weeks in New York during the trial ... and not one player who was playing at the time came to see just what was going on because it involved them so dramatically ... . No one came to just sit and say, 'Hey, this is pretty important'" (Chass 1977, 77). Flood realized he probably wouldn't win his case, but he pursued it knowing it would ultimately benefit players. In 1972 he lost in a close Supreme Court vote. He never played again, but his case mobilized players and the Players' Association to oppose the reserve system (Barra 2011).

Successful adaptation requires that initially individuals need to understand the setting in which they are located, and until the 1970s that was hardly the case for MLB players on the issue of salaries. Traditionally baseball administrators had convinced players that when they signed their first contract, they had given up control over their career; in truth, if the two sides couldn't reach a follow-up agreement, the club could renew the old contract for just one year, but then the individual was allowed to sign elsewhere. Soon that system was tested. Pitcher Andy Messersmith completed the option year on his contract when he could not reach an accord with his team, and at that moment he was free to sell his services to any club, exercising a right that previously owners had not revealed to players. Seeking resolution, the owners declared a lockout in the spring of 1976 during which deliberations between team officials and the players' representatives led to an agreement recognizing free agency after five years of service. Players' financial prospects immediately improved.

Salaries soared for the newly declared free agents. Messersmith, who had made $90,000 the previous year, signed a three-year contract for $1.75 million. The major-league payroll would expand from $32 million in 1976 on the eve of free agency to a massive $284 million a decade later (Vecsey 2006, 144–46). In 2017 the Los Angeles Dodgers' payroll was only $42 million less than the league total in 1986. At the latter date, 23 teams had payrolls of $100 million or more, with the league ranging from the Dodgers' $242.1 million down to the Milwaukee Braves' $63.1 million (Perry 2017).

Besides players' salary advancement over time, the early pro leagues changed in other significant ways. Consider the NHL, which in 1942 consisted of a half-dozen franchises, only two of which, the Montreal Canadiens and Toronto Maple Leafs, existed at the league's foundation in 1917. Still, that set of six teams was whimsically designated the "Original Six" when expansion to 12 teams occurred in 1967 (Sapienza 2011). During the Original Six's era, games were popular, with attendance at 95 percent capacity.

The Original Six played in an era when the haves, especially the two founding Canadian teams, were decisively positioned to stay dominant over their four American rivals. Between 1927 and 1967, the Montreal Canadiens captured 12 Stanley Cups, during an era when the so-called "50-mile rule" gave each team automatic access to all players within a 50-mile radius—for the two Canadian teams abundant, high-quality candidates playing the world's best youth hockey while for American teams such as the New York Rangers, a distinctly underprivileged member of the Original Six, unrestricted access to nearby prospects from such hockey wastelands as the Bronx or Westchester County.

To compensate for lack of access to top players, underprivileged franchises had the right to sign youngsters outside their locale, binding them to the club indefinitely. Such transactions required a skilled, mobile scouting force, a major expense, but sometimes it proved worthwhile. In 1962 Boston Bruins officials, hundreds of miles from home in Ontario, struck gold, convincing future superstar Bobby Orr's parents to sign with them when their son had reached the age of 13 (Caggiano 2011; Eskenazi 1976, 171; Montville 1994).

When the NHL expanded to 12 teams, league officials were seeking to build American TV coverage, locating all of the new entries in the United States. At the time bids from such Canadian cities as Edmonton, Winnipeg, and Calgary were not seriously considered, probably because their inclusion would not have bolstered the American viewing audience. While those three cities are now represented in the league, the bias against Canadian franchises persists, with the lure of American TV revenues outweighing the advantages of forming franchises in such midsized Canadian cities as Quebec City, London, or Saskatoon, where interest in local minor-league clubs has often been strong and viewing audiences most likely would prove substantial. Currently seven of the NHL's 31 teams are Canadian, representing 22.6 percent of the total—a decline from the Original Six era when the two Canadian teams constituted 33.3 percent (Gaines 2013; Miller 2012; Plagenhoef 1999; Wilkins 1985, 149–56).

Like the NHL the NBA has expanded significantly over time, and it has also altered in other respects. By the 1970s the NBA was much less popular than pro baseball, pro football, and college football. When David Stern became commissioner in 1984, he took specific steps to make the NBA more appealing, promoting his top players more effectively than executives in other sports and also encouraging the signing of top international prospects (Hughes 2004; Wiedeman 2012).

At the beginning of Stern's tenure, the NBA provided little TV coverage, with the league finals usually appearing late at night on tape-delay (*ESPN* 2012). According to economist David Surdam, NBA owners had been wary of TV "not realiz[ing] ... that exciting, fast-paced basketball was tailor-made for television" (Surdam 2012, 168). During Stern's first six years in office, he negotiated deals with NBC and *Turner Broadcasting System* for $875 million, helping to make the league a source of wealth for many owners and players (Simmons 2009, 151). The massive media payment has continued into the post-Stern era. Starting in 2016–17 and extending to 2024–25, *ESPN* and *Turner* will pay the NBA $2.66 billion annually, an increase of 21 percent from the previous contract (Draper 2014). The league has also expanded internationally. In 2017 fans in 215 countries saw the NBA finals in 49 languages on televisions, computers, tablets, and mobile phones (*NBA.com* 2017).

The growth of the major leagues is apparent in teams' steadily rising values, with the leading American professional teams the Dallas Cowboys worth $4 billion and the New York Yankees $3.4 billion (Badenhausen 2016a). All four US major sports illustrate institutional logics at its most developed—leagues in which painstaking strategies for improving teams and winning have produced massive revenues and public acclaim.

Another significant historical issue about professional sports has involved the racial integration of baseball, football, and basketball. MLB's integration occurred in a league where racial segregation was informal, not supported by law but nonetheless unchallenged. The impact of the league's integration has been momentous. Each spring the MLB community and sports media review the events that occurred when Branch Rickey, the president of the Brooklyn Dodgers, sent Jackie Robinson to the Dodgers after a year spent with the Montreal Royals' Triple-A club (Hanssen 1998, 605; Simon 2002, 54–55). The significance of this racial experiment was apparent when Martin Luther King, Jr., told an aide that without Robinson "I never would have been able to do what I did" (Falkner 1995, 237).

Seven decades later, however, MLB contained a relatively small number of African Americans. In 2017 major-league baseball rosters possessed 7.7 percent blacks, 31.9 percent Latinos, 1.9 percent Asians, and 57.5 percent whites (Lapchick 2017a). The black percentage was less than half what it was in 1986 —18.3 percent of major leaguers. One contributing factor has involved the reality that since black families tend to be less affluent than their white counterparts, they are often unable to finance travel-team participation, which can be an influential experience in players' development, especially between the ages of 12 and 15 (Kepner 2014). In addition, as noted in the previous chapter, another contributor to the decline of blacks in MLB has been that college baseball can't provide significant financial aid. Unlike college football and basketball, which can use some of their substantial revenues for full scholarships, college baseball can afford only modest financial support, meaning that college-bound athletes who play baseball and one of those other two sports are often more likely to opt for the free ride football or basketball can provide (J. Powell 2016).

Compared to MLB, racial integration of the NFL and NBA was much less publicized. During the Great Depression, NFL team owners planned new divisional alignments which they expected would create a financial bonanza, including sufficient payoff for high-salaried players. In this new league, they reasoned, it would be unseemly to integrate, allowing what the owners perceived as the humiliating prospect of some blacks making more money than some whites (Ross 1999, 49–50). Gradually, however, integration proceeded.

In 1946 the NFL color line was first crossed but under conditions distinctly different from those involving Robinson's entrance into MLB.

Owners of the Los Angeles Rams, the team taking the step, were hardly proponents of integration. However, the commissioners of the Los Angeles Coliseum, where the team played, required that any team renting their stadium had to include African Americans. So the Rams signed two black players—signed them but hardly played them (Ross 1999, 82–83). That season Kenny Washington, a celebrated college player, ran a paltry 114 yards on 23 attempts for the Rams. In contrast, the Cleveland Browns, which was in the All-America Conference and joined the NFL four years later, often ran Marion Motley, an African American who was the team's second-leading runner, gaining a substantial 601 yards on 73 carries (Ross 1999, 96).

Two persistent conditions helped maintain discrimination. First, many African American players were "stacked," limited to positions which coaches felt required less intelligence and initiative and were well suited for blacks' alleged superior strength and athletic ability. The 20 African Americans who had played in the two professional football leagues by the end of 1949 were almost entirely confined to halfback, defensive back, and end and prohibited from such leadership roles as quarterback, center, and middle linebacker that were more cerebral and physically central on the field. Second, many teams engaged in deceitful practices, adding African Americans to their rosters as a means of preventing bad publicity and then releasing them when the heat was off.

The black press and civil-rights organizations like the National Association for the Advancement of Colored People and the Congress of Racial Equality were relentless in criticizing African Americans' discriminatory treatment. Calling for boycotts and picketing, they eventually focused on the Washington Redskins, the league's most determined opponent of integration, and with the aid of a Kennedy administration official forced that last all-white holdout to sign three black players (Basen 2012; Lomax 1999, 165).

In modern times the number of black players in the NFL has been substantial. In 1992 they represented about 60 percent of players (Lapchick 1992), and by 2016 African Americans were 69.7 percent, with whites 27.4 percent and others 2.9 percent (Lapchick 2016).

As in the NFL and MLB, racial integration met resistance in the NBA. In 1949 shortly before the formation of the NBA, the famed

In the early 1950s, the popularity of the Harlem Globetrotters promoted the racial integration of the NBA. The Globetrotters continue to tour, not only in the US but in many other countries as illustrated by this exhibition match in Budapest, Hungary. (Source: Ferenc Szelepcsenyi / Shutterstock.com)

Harlem Globetrotters, with their crowd-pleasing showmanship, visited Minneapolis Auditorium to play George Mikan and pro basketball's top team—the Minneapolis Lakers. Over 10,000 fans showed up, until then the largest crowd in Laker history, a benchmark that remained until the team moved to Los Angeles in 1960. It was a telltale sign.

Like the leadership in the other two leagues, NBA executives eventually concluded that pronounced enthusiasm for black players made it abundantly clear that it was financially masochistic to exclude them. The Boston Celtics led the way, with Walter Brown, the Celtics owner, picking Chuck Cooper in the second round of the 1950 draft. "Walter," some intellectually challenged individual wailed, "don't you know he's a colored boy?" Brown snarled, "I don't give a damn if he's striped, plaid or polka-dot! Boston takes Chuck Cooper of Duquesne!" (Kamp 2006). In the ninth round, the Washington Capitols chose a second black player —Earl Lloyd from West Virginia State. That summer Nat "Sweetwater" Clifton, a member of the Harlem Globetrotters, also joined the NBA. Clifton had learned that the members of the white team competing against the Globetrotters in their multi-city tour received more money. He told his teammates, and soon the owner learned about Clifton's message, angrily informing the New York Knicks that the player was available, and the Knick happily bought his contract (Kamp 2006).

During that era black players were few in number and were often maltreated. In 1956 when Bill Russell was recruited by the Boston Celtics, he was the team's only black player. It was difficult. A biographer recorded, "In most cities, Bill was taunted with racial epithets—baboon, coon, and nigger —but he remembered what [Bob] Cousy told him and did not respond to the ignorant comments, except through his play" (Nelson 2005, 46–47). The play displayed aggressive defense and shot blocking that were spectacularly effective (Halberstam 1981, 115–16).

Blacks continued to be recruited, with the best of them becoming leading NBA performers. In 1961–62 with most teams having only two or three African Americans, seven of the league's top ten rebounders were black. Three years later with about three or four African Americans on a roster, nine of the leading ten rebounders and six of the top seven assist men were black.

In spite of not receiving high-quality weight training and food, top African Americans seemed better suited for the game than their white colleagues. Discreetly, black players would mock the whites' frailer physiques, accusing those who were weak jumpers as having "white legs" and those who were slower as having "white man's disease" (Halberstam 1981, 30–31). The highly competitive Larry Bird, the top white player of the 1980s and 1990s, readily admitted that blacks were superior athletes and "really got irritated" when a white man guarded him "because it's disrespect to my game" (Smith 2011, 23).

Over time racial diversity has developed within the NBA, and in recent decades the numbers have stabilized. By the 2003–04 season 76 percent of players were black, and by 2017 the league was 80.9 percent people of color, with 74.4 percent black, along with 19.1 percent white, many of whom were foreign (Lapchick 2005, 2017b).

In modern pro sports, racial diversity on teams generally prevails. There is, however, one additional issue worth mentioning. Curtis Granderson, an 11-year MLB veteran who has been active in various poverty- and race-related charities, has consistently emphasized the importance of understanding and improving race relations both within pro sports and elsewhere. Granderson indicated that if observers look at the dispersion of players warming up before a MLB game, they are likely to see separation into "a perfect pie chart: [Self-segregated sections of] all Latinos, all blacks, all whites" (M. Powell 2016).

Granderson's observation might prompt one to consider that if to a large extent racial groups in MLB tend to remain apart, the relative isolation probably limits the extent to which teammates serve as agents of socialization for those outside their own racial/ethnic group. An observer might wonder whether chances to improve individual skills and/or team morale are appreciably limited in MLB and other top pro leagues as a result. Some adaptation might prove constructive.

Racial relations represents one of many issues that can impact on new players coming into one of the top leagues. This new life can be difficult, producing stress, injuries, and, all too often, brief careers. It can also be exciting as a chance for success and the fame and fortune that can go with it beckon.

Distinctive Careers by the Numbers

Athletes who reach the four most prominent sports leagues are a tiny percentage of the prospects. Do they actually have careers? Conventionally a *career* is an occupation pursued for a significant number of years and offering prospects for advancement (*Oxford Dictionaries* 2016). In pro sports prospects for advancement certainly exist, but compared to most careers, the length, even for the most successful players, is distinctly short—5.6 years for MLB, 5.5 for NHL, 4.8 for NBA, and 3.5 for the NFL (RAM Financial Group 2017). On the other hand, salaries are significantly greater than those for most careers—on average per year $6.2 million for the NBA, $4.4 million for MLB, $2.9 million for the NHL, and $2.1 million for the NFL (Badenhausen 2016b).

Players who have pro sports careers must have superior athletic abilities such as high-level motor skills and hand-eye coordination along with knowledge of their sport developed from years of practice and play. In addition, pro athletes must possess such capacities as discipline, fitness, and facility in dealing with stress. The retention stage requires persistent commitment. During the season players generally train every day, and often their work week is over 40 hours, regularly including evenings, weekends, and holidays (Bureau of Labor Statistics 2015; National Career Services 2016). Adaptation is likely to be essential, especially in the beginning as new major leaguers begin to grasp the demands and adjust if possible to a level of play that is distinctly superior to any they previously encountered.

Upcoming information indicates that pro athletes generally find pursuing a pro sports career a highly challenging endeavor. The large numbers of young candidates interested in progressing in organized sports inevitably mean that the majority of them will not advance too far, probably not to the college level, particularly not within Division I, and very seldom to the professional ranks. The upcoming statistics are impressive, signifying the annihilation of many athletes' dreams of fame, glory, and wealth. For each of the four most prominent pro sports, NCAA data provided here supplies the percentages of players managing to move from college to pro teams followed by the percentage going from high school to pro teams:

NFL: 1.5 percent and 0.08 percent
MLB: 9.1 percent and 0.50 percent
NBA: 1.1 percent and 0.03 percent
NHL: 5.6 percent and 0.07 percent (NCAA 2017; NCAA Research 2013).

Several numbers require commentary: The proportions of baseball players making it to the pros either from college or high-school units and hockey players from college to the pros are relatively high because, as Chapter 3 discussed, both of these pro sports support a large professionalized minor-league system, where the majority of youthful pros in those sports both start and end their careers.

But a curious twist is apparent. Although the likelihood is small that a given athlete will make it to the pros, NCAA surveys demonstrate that Division I prospects remain unrealistically confident that they will reach the major league in their sport. Here are the numbers for athletes' perception of their chances of making it versus the reality for the four sports previously cited:

NFL: The perception 52 percent; the reality 1.5 percent
MLB: The perception 60 percent; the reality 9.1 percent
NBA: The perception 76 percent; the reality 1.1 percent
NHL: The perception 63 percent; the reality 5.6 percent (NCAA Research 2013; New 2015).

The disparity between players' personal sense of their chances and the research-based outcomes is impressive. It seems likely that various agents of socialization promote unrealistic projections. Parents, siblings, teammates, and coaches can be encouraging, even convincing in their assertions that a player in question has what it takes to make the pros. Sometimes, in fact, an influential person can even initiate the belief.

About halfway through his football career at the University of California at Los Angeles, a coach told Ramogi Huma, an undersized linebacker, that he "was an NFL guy with real potential." It was a surprise. "I was going to make sure I got my degree, and I really didn't think the NFL was much of a possibility for me," Huma said. "But then it got into my head that maybe it actually was." Huma's hopes were aroused, but then he hurt his hip, ending football for him. Afterwards he was dubious about the prospect of playing in the NFL, even if he had stayed healthy. "If you had to generalize, you could easily say no one goes pro," he said. "That's how slim the chances are" (New 2015). And yet circumstances in a substantial number of Division I college players' lives, including the powerful impact of agents of socialization, often encourage them to believe otherwise.

Huma was undersized, and while a coach still thought he could make the NFL, being undersized in football can be a distinct disadvantage. It's also true in other prominent professional sports. A strength-and-conditioning coach concluded that in MLB "[M]uch like natural selection the biggest, fastest and strongest survive" (Guadagni 2015). A two-year study of 343 professional baseball players cited in Chapter 3 endorses that conclusion, revealing that overall major leaguers proved superior to minor leaguers in speed, jumping ability, and grip strength (Hoffman, Vazquez, Pichardo, and Tenenbaum 2009).

Major leaguers' superior physical assets are only one reason why young athletes entering the major leagues discover an abruptly different sports world from their previous one.

The Big Leagues: Taking on the Challenge

It is possible to consider a pro-sports career as a process, revealing itself in sequential steps each of which requires adaptation—the draft and related matters, the first encounter with the league, adjustment to involvement in the majors, and termination. A small study of NHL players, in fact, supported a roughly similar set of steps, indicating that prospects enter the league facing such challenges as the NHL entry draft and training camp; then new players compete to make the team by accumulating productive statistics and holding their own against opponents; veterans sometimes join the NHL elite by becoming one of the team's top players in point production of goals and assists and even occasionally emerging as a star throughout the league; and finally older players attempt to remain important to the team during training camp and the regular season, with top performers concerned about maintaining high-level play such as stellar point production. In the NHL, in short, players' priorities change as the years unfold (Battochio, Stambulova, and Schinke 2016). Inevitably the other major leagues display a similar sequence. For many prospects the draft represents an early challenge.

The Draft and Related Issues

In MLB's reserve era, owners could control salaries once a man signed with a club, but they still faced the unresolved challenge of signing young recruits, who were free to accept the highest bid. This issue became particularly publicized in 1964 when outfield prospect Rick Reichardt and his attorney encouraged a bidding war for his services, enticing most of the major-league teams to take part. The temptation was understandable. Reichardt seemed very talented, and he was also a large, handsome man who appealed to both the media and fans. Joe Garagiola, a former player and TV personality, declared, "The first time I saw him, I thought he fell off a Wheaties box" (Crowe 2007). Reichardt, who signed with the Los Angeles Angels, received a bonus of $205,000—more money than Willie Mays's, Mickey Mantle's, or any other contemporary star's salary.

When the young man signed his contract in the penthouse of Gene Autry's Hotel Continental in front of reporters and TV cameras, he was perplexed. "I don't think any athlete is really worth all that money," he said. "But if they're going to pay it, then I'll take all I can get. I'd be foolish not to" (Shrake 1964). The modest statement turned out to be prophetic. Reichardt was much less successful than projected, in part because illness forced the removal of a kidney in 1966. Owners, informed by the experience, recognized they'd received a wake-up call, and the next year they started the draft (Halverson 2012; Myers 1994).

The so-called "First-Year Players' Draft" started in 1965, much later in baseball than in pro football (1936) and basketball (1947). A major factor in the lengthy delay was that without the draft the wealthier clubs like the New York Yankees and St. Louis Cardinals were able to capitalize more effectively on such advantages as more extensive scouting teams than their competitors (Manuel 2010).

Nowadays a yearly players' draft occurs in all four major professional leagues and for many players represents a major step in the recruitment process. In MLB the First-Year Players' Draft is large, currently 40 rounds and a total of about 1,200 draftees along with compensatory picks for free agents lost. In contrast, the NHL Entry Draft involves seven rounds and about 215 picks, the NFL also has seven rounds with no more than 256 choices, and the NBA provides two rounds and a mere 60 draftees (*Baseball Almanac* 2015).

In 1936 NFL officials conducted the first pro draft at Philadelphia's Ritz-Carlton Hotel. Nine owners chose players from lists of the nation's leading amateurs. Just 31 of the 81 draftees signed with a team because the salaries offered were too low (Williams 2006, 41–42). Nowadays with the rich contracts available, most drafted NFL prospects readily sign, and the NFL and NBA drafts are highly publicized media events.

In the NFL some traits make it more likely certain prospects will be drafted. One issue involves candidates' colleges, with those from schools having higher Associated Press rankings standing a better chance—Alabama, Ohio State, Michigan, Florida, LSU, Southern California, etc.

Another issue influencing NFL prospects' draft potential has been their coaching. Some coaches have managed to get 20 to 30 percent of their prospects into the NFL (Rask 2015). To determine coaches' relative impact, *Rivals.com* personnel decided that they needed to take into account players' evaluation when entering a college program. It was a revealing decision. Mack Brown, a former Texas coach, had the most recruits in the NFL, but their quality was sufficiently high that Brown's role in helping them reach the pros seems to have been less significant than the contributions some other coaches made working with recruits who arrived at their colleges less accomplished.

While Chris Petersen, coach at Boise State and later Washington, hardly led the coaching parade in the number of players making the NFL, *Rivals.com*, controlling for the quality of Petersen's recruits upon arrival at college, designated him the coach who made the greatest contribution to their success—16.3 percent more likely to get them drafted than the average FBS head coach (Rask 2015).

At Boise State Petersen sent over 20 players to the NFL, with four first-round draft picks. The coach has a formula which he drums into his team members: "Talent + Character = Our Kind of Guy (O.K.G.)." Petersen has focused on both elements in the formula. On talent: "The biggest misconception when people hear about this O.K.G. thing is it's all about being just a really good person and that's not true," Petersen said. "It's having really good talent we think has a big upside in addition to all the intangible things [the character elements] that come with it." Then on character: "We're not into those guys we just like on Saturdays," Petersen said. "We need to like them Sunday-Friday as well, that they're doing all the things right in the classroom and off the field, that they're growing and becoming a better person, preparing themselves for the rest of their lives" (Kelley 2014). For Petersen, in short, acting as coach and mentor (agent of socialization), the development of his players doesn't simply involve football but their totality of outlooks and activities. Apparently he feels that success comes when team members not only emphasize adaptation to the game setting but to life generally.

In 2010 *Rivals.com* assessed the approximately 4,500 Division I candidates who would become eligible for the 2014 NFL draft. The numbers were instructive, showing *Rivals.com*'s consistent predictive capacity, with rough estimates of success rates:

- Of five-star candidates 16 of 27 drafted, a three in five chance
- Of four-star prospects 77 of 395 chosen, a one in five prospect

- Of three-star players 92 of 1,644 picked, a one in 18 likelihood
- Of two-star recruits 71 of 2,434 selected, a one in 34 chance (Elliott 2014).

Players' background can affect their draft prospects, but their performances for pro scouts and coaches can also be influential. Before the NFL draft, about 300 top players attend the National Invitation Camp, which features the NFL Scouting Combine or simply "the combine," and involves four days of activities with such drills as a 40-yard dash, bench press, and a vertical jump. The players also receive a physical, a Cybex test to determine knee flexibility, and a 50-question, multiple-choice IQ test known as "the Wonderlic" with a 12-minute time limit (*NFL.com* 2014; Williams 2006, 149). In addition, during the combine a team's representatives can schedule up to 60 15-minute interviews with prospects. "It's a real chance to figure out the guy's vibe," Miami Dolphins GM Chris Grier said. "How they come across; how they will fit into a program. You wouldn't want a quarterback to come in and have no personality. You want to get a sense of what kind of energy he will bring to your team" (Vrentas 2016).

NBA prospects face similar challenges. They often wonder if it is productive to participate in such activities as the NBA Draft Combine or the Portsmouth Invitational Tournament. For college prospects, especially the marginal ones, it is a chance to display themselves to team officials. After a full physical, the candidates complete several personality tests, physical-fitness assessments, and skill drills such as spot-up shooting from various distances, NBA three-pointers, or off-the-dribble shooting. The camps last several days, and as they proceed the players engage in scrimmages and even full-fledged games featuring referees and recorded stats. The information teams obtain can significantly influence whether or not they decide to draft a prospect (*NBA.com* 2014; *Topend Sports* 2015).

It tends to be a physically and psychologically exhausting process. As the two-day NBA Draft Combine was finishing, a journalist wrote, "One by one, potential NBA draftees filed into the press center last Friday, sweat dripping from their faces, the look of enthusiasm that they arrived at the combine with replaced by the drained look of overwhelming exhaustion." He added, "Glen Rice Jr. answered another round of

Defensive back Gareon Conley of Ohio State caught this pass during the sixth day of the 2017 NFL Scouting Combine. It became one bit of data contributing to the Oakland Raiders' body of information about him, eventually leading to the team's decision to draft him in the first round as the 24th pick. (Source: Joe Robbins / Getty Images)

questions about his problems at Georgia Tech, Ricky Ledo his problems at Providence and Shabazz Muhammad on the appearance that he is a selfish, one-dimensional player" (Mannix 2013).

It is hardly surprising that candidates find the experience difficult. Chris Herren, who was an eventual second-round draft pick, noted that "[S]howcasing yourself for NBA teams at the combine is extremely nerve-racking." He added, "How relaxed do you think you'd be working out in front of Pat Riley with all his NBA title rings and his star power?" (Herren and Reynolds 2011, 141). It is usually a tense, risky business, certainly a situation featuring unprecedented challenges, but marginal players like Herren have little alternative to making a comprehensive adaptation to the challenges of the draft, performing as well as possible.

Most definite first rounders declare for the draft in April and instead of participating in the combine or other such events spend the two months beforehand getting in shape to play in the NBA and visiting interested teams. "I went out and trained in Santa Barbara," former Wisconsin Badger and Naismith award winner Frank Kaminsky said. "I stayed there probably five or six weeks with some workouts in between. I wanted to learn about myself as an athlete." Other top players did running, yoga, or changes in diet—early steps in preparation for the pro game (Jeyarajah 2015).

Scouts assessing NBA prospects have a recruitment challenge that NFL personnel don't face—that with the exception of a few tournaments, they have been banned since 2005 from watching high-school contests, including summer games and AAU events. That means that within the current one-and-done system, these besieged evaluators have only an eight-to-nine month opening to decide about purchasing high-priced Division I talent that can affect their team for a decade a more. No surprise that scouts are known to lust for any additional sources of information about players of interest—whether it comes from newspaper or magazine articles or limited first-hand observations (Parrish 2015; Titus 2014).

What do scouts look for in NBA prospects? Physical qualities include a high skill level in such areas as shooting, passing, and dribbling as well as athleticism—a combination of speed, quickness, and strength that will permit the player to excel at the basic tasks of the game. Another highly valued trait is basketball intelligence, the ability to avoid errors by choosing an effective play, particularly one that fits well with the game's tempo and does not force either turnovers or defensive blunders. In addition, scouts are interested in sportsmanship, the capacity, even if suddenly angered, to keep one's composure, focusing on what must be done to achieve success and avoiding distraction, ill-advised choices, and a decline in momentum (*USSportsCamps* 2015).

During the recruitment stage, scouts and executives observe prospects, they evaluate and discuss them, but usually, even with high picks, some doubt persists. Usually but not always. A case in point would be Lebron James and another Connor McDavid, a hockey player. Within the NHL collective, a consensus exists that about once a decade a superstar will emerge who not only displays special skills but also an acute appreciation of the game which he shares with the public at large. Wayne Gretzky was "The Great One" and Mario Lemieux "The Magnificent One," and then as teenagers Eric Lindros, John Taveras, and Sidney Crosby were designated "The Next One." Most recently Connor McDavid has received that same label and been the object of the hype that goes with it. "Pressure is something I've been dealing with for a long time," McDavid said after the Oilers chose him No. 1 overall in the 2015 NHL draft. "It's something I'm comfortable with" (Maaddi 2015).

Most seasoned observers seem convinced about McDavid's potential. Crosby, his immediate predecessor as The Next One, spoke about McDavid's stellar attributes. "I feel he does everything well; he's a smart player, sees the ice and can beat guys 1-on-1 if he needs to," Crosby said. "He uses his teammates and makes a lot of plays to set them up" (Morreale 2015a).

Chris Peters, a sports writer and broadcaster, indicated that the first time he saw McDavid the player was 15 years old, at least two years younger than most of the competition at the World Under-18 Championship in Russia. Peters indicated that McDavid's special qualities burst forth in a game against Switzerland. "He had the puck on the left wing and was going 1-on-1 with Mirco Mueller, who just a few months later would be selected in the first round by the San Jose Sharks. McDavid turned him inside out so fast with a move along the boards that he was three steps past from Mueller before the Swiss defenseman knew what happened" (Peters 2015). Like others commenting about McDavid, Peters seemed to suggest that this latest once-a-decade superstar's adaptation for the NHL was well advanced even before he arrived. Compared to McDavid, however, most draftees have much less promising pro prospects.

A study of nearly 4,900 former players drafted into MLB, the NFL, the NBA, and the NHL between 1980 and 1989 indicated that for all the leagues except MLB the round in which individuals were drafted correlated quite well with playing in the major leagues. For MLB that pattern did not hold. The researchers suggested that time spent in minor league baseball might mitigate against the effect of draft position. Overall, the study indicated that while in three of the four leagues the draft round did correlate with making it to the majors—the higher the round, the better the chances—that factor accounted for only a modest portion of the total variance, with such issues as injury, late "blooming," and team environment also influential (Koz, Frazer-Thomas, and Baker 2012, e64-e69).

Later statistical data compiled by *Bleacher Report* indicated that MLB shared the other leagues' pattern, with players taken in higher rounds displaying a greater likelihood of making it to the top league (Cornelius 2014; Rosenbaum 2012). The researchers in the original study concluded, "These findings provide a foundation for future analyses to inform our understanding of the drafting process and improve the accuracy of professional franchises in predicting potential" (Koz, Frazer-Thomas, and Baker 2012, e68).

The nearby Box 4.1 suggests one surprising factor that has affected predictions about NHL players' performance.

BOX 4.1

Youthful Players' Date of Birth and Its Effect on the NHL Draft

The previous findings suggest that overall the drafts in major pro sports are somewhat predictive in locating talented players. However, as the following discussion suggests, the possibility exists that unexpected, even subtle factors can intervene, limiting the effectiveness of the draft. Consider Canadian hockey and the choice of young boys picked for youth teams. To begin, it's necessary to look back in time.

In 1954 the Soviet Union surprisingly won the World Hockey Championship, defeating Canada, which had won the prestigious tournament nine of the previous eleven times. Then two years later in the Olympics semifinal, the Soviet Union defeated Canada, which had won six of the previous seven gold medals (Addona and Yates 2010, 1, 13). It was a moment of crisis, and Canadian hockey officials and coaches rapidly mobilized, starting to favor, in programs involving boys born in a given year, those whose birthday came in the early months over their peers born later in the year. At the tender age of 5 or 6, the coaches found, the more senior enrollees could often skate faster and more expertly and pass and shoot more accurately, and in the furor of the 1950s Canadians' youth hockey programs such superiority seemed critical to defeat the upstart Soviets.

The *relative age effect* is coaches' preference to recruit and to provide more playing time for slightly older children in a sport, with this early advantage sometimes carried into more advanced programs including the professional ranks. In youth hockey five- and six-year-olds born in the first quarter of the year have quite often benefited from the relative age effect, and studies document the process from that point of entry to the NHL (Addona and Yates 2010, 1).

For instance, among the NHL players drafted between 1980 and 2012, 36 percent of draftees were born in the first quarter of the year and a much more modest 14.5 percent in the fourth quarter. Focusing on individuals drafted in 2007 or earlier, the researchers assessed productivity over time by calculating the number of games played—a clear indication of coaches' value placed on players' contribution. The number used was 400 games, which is the total required to qualify for the NHL Player Pension and widely considered to be the minimum in games for having completed a career in the league. Did the players born in the first quarter have a greater percentage of their numbers reaching 400 games? No, it was 13 percent, with, perhaps not surprising, the other three quarters higher—18, 21, and 25 percent. The researchers were impressed. They wrote, "This bias is remarkable because it is exhibited by professional decision makers evaluating adults in a context where ... [relative age equalities] have been widely publicized." The process by which this age-related bias develops is not entirely clear. The researchers suspect that if prospects reaching their early teens have been the victims of the age-related effect, then its impact is likely to persist, adversely affecting access to elite junior teams and eventually draft selection (Deaner, Lowen, and Cobley 2013). One might wonder whether the other major sports have similar hidden or somewhat hidden factors, age-related or linked to some other trait, affecting the results of their draft.

Unless an athlete appears to be a bona fide superstar, the draft process can be precarious. Tommy Lasorda, the Los Angeles Dodgers' manager and a childhood friend of Mike Piazza's father, wanted the young man drafted. Lasorda explained, "I sent five of my friends from five different organizations out to see Michael play, and nobody wanted to sign him. I *ordered* the Dodgers to draft him. I said, 'I don't give a shit where you draft him but *draft* him'" (Piazza and Wheeler 2013, 50). Dodgers officials obeyed, taking Piazza in the 62nd round of the 1988 draft (*Baseball-Reference* 2017). This was the inauspicious beginning of a Hall of Fame career during which Piazza became a capable catcher and top hitter for the Los Angeles Dodgers and New York Mets.

Piazza's career was much more successful than his draft status predicted. In fact, such an outcome is fairly common because young prospects' careers are often hard to anticipate. A pair of researchers examined the records of 1,200 pitchers over 20 years to evaluate whether performance in the minors predicted the outcome for the majors (Longley and Wong 2011, 197–201). They indicated that in spite of the fact that pitchers operate in situations where their output is "easily measurable and highly quantifiable, and where the nature of the work at the developmental level is identical to that at the advanced level," their performance capacities only become apparent once they enter the majors (Longley and Wong 2011, 201).

In one sport a composite measure predicted the extent of pro success more effectively than a draft. A study of over 300 NBA prospects who attended the NBA Draft Combine between 2001 and 2006 found that age (younger players were more productive), college performance, the quality of the college program, and several measures of both physical traits and physical performance predicted NBA success in the first three years better than draft status (Kaufman 2014; Moxley and Towne 2014). That's a noteworthy finding, but have NBA scouts and coaches acted upon it? A team of researchers concluded that while NBA evaluators have more predictive data available, "… decision-makers often consider factors … that are … [less] relevant to future performance" (Kaufman 2014). Those factors are the traditional ones for assessing prospects—the combine results and information from scouts' and coaches' observations and interviews with the candidates.

The reality is that considerable difference of opinion exists regarding what combination of factors most effectively predicts NBA success as well as success in the other top pro leagues. Perhaps as in the cases of the Standard Aptitude Tests (SAT) and American College Testing (ACT) for students facing the college-admissions process, the outcomes of the various tests for pro prospects are no more than crude indicators of their potential for future performance. However, like students dealing with admissions officials, the players, regardless of their personal feelings about combines and other evaluations, realize that pro officials take the results very seriously, considering them a major factor in a team's decision about whether or not to draft an individual, and so players see no alternative to adaptation to the situation, studiously preparing to do as well on them as they possibly can.

With the limited effectiveness of traditional assessments of draftees in mind, T.J. Allan, a critic of organized sports programs, suggested using a simpler approach. Instead of favoring traditional issues that supposedly reveal prospects' potential for success, scouts and coaches should heavily weigh one distinct element—namely, the determination and effort players currently show. Michael Jordan would be a definite case in point. As a sophomore 5-foot-9-inch Jordan was not particularly skilled, and he failed to make the varsity (Gordon 2017). Even then, however, he believed in making a relentless effort—that if he or anyone else did so, positive results would occur. Those qualities remained front and center throughout his career as the following quote emphasizes. Jordan declared, "I've missed more than 9,000 shots in my career. I've lost almost 300 games. Twenty-six times, I've been trusted to take the game winning shot and missed. I've failed over and over and over again in my life. And that is why I succeed" (Allan 2015). The author of the article suggested that first and foremost NBA team officials seeking players to add to their rosters should look for a semblance of the relentless spirit Jordan displayed. It's a provocative suggestion.

Another, distinctly unusual approach that has been used for choosing pro prospects has been sabermetrics—the pursuit of objective information about baseball players or teams based on their statistical records (Birnbaum 2016). Bill James, a pioneer in the endeavor, first publicized the term in 1980. While analysis of the wealth of baseball data has been around since the sport's early days, the sabermetrics experts have started to challenge established use—for instance, questioning the extensive attention traditionally paid to such measurements as batting average and pitching wins, which teammates' input significantly affects (Birnbaum 2016).

Billy Beane, the Oakland Athletics' GM, has been a strong proponent of the practice. The book *Moneyball* recounts how Beane and his assistants spent their opening years in Oakland struggling with a set of traditional scouts who often recruited players with magnificent physiques, latter-day

Rick Reichardts. "This guy may be the best body in the draft," a scout might say, suggesting it qualified him as a high draft pick. Soon Beane began retorting, "We're not selling jeans here" (Lewis 2004, 31). For me the scouts' approach was familiar. In the late 1970s and early 1980s, I occasionally attended a local Double-A team's games and saw the results of what appeared to be a similar strategy. Many of the prospects were fine physical specimens—Schwarzenegger-like body types who looked impressive speaking to reporters or charming female fans, but the distinct majority of them soon disappeared, victims of the game's relentless trimming-down process.

In contrast to the scouts' traditional approach, Beane and his associates employed sabermetrics, using experts' conclusion that hitters' two most important contributions for scoring runs are getting on base and advancing runners (Mandelbaum 2004, 88). Later Paul DePodesta, a statistician who worked for Beane, settled on one issue, namely on-base average (OBA), which calculates the percentage of hitters' times at bat that they make it safely on base by any means except an error. It is a measurement highlighting batters' contribution, providing valuable information about their role in scoring runs (Lewis 2004, 127–28). It's perhaps needless to add that sabermetricians are unconcerned about whether hitters are skinny, pudgy, or hypermuscular. Impressed by the insights provided in MLB, statisticians working for NBA, NHL, and NFL teams have also begun using sabermetrics (Cyrgalis 2011; Laws 2016; Ryan 2016).

Whether drafted or not, new arrivals in the major leagues are likely to find that some distinct adjustments are necessary to succeed at this retention stage.

First Encounters with the Big Time

Doug Glanville had spent an entire season as the centerfielder for the Iowa Cubs, a Triple-A team. One day he realized that something was up because he was moved to left field, probably because the Chicago Cubs, the parent team, was going to call him up and wanted him to practice the position. After the game Glanville received a call to go to the manager's office, and when he and two teammates arrived, he learned that the call up was going to occur. The next few hours seemed surreal. Glanville spent the night packing, calling friends and family, and then caught a crack-of-dawn flight to Chicago. He wrote, "Six hours later, when the Cubs took the field against the Montreal Expos in front of thirty-thousand-plus fans, I sprinted out to left. It was like floating on air with two tons of butterflies in my stomach" (Glanville 2010, 82). But such discomforts were well worth it, with each move up the ladder from Class-A to the majors offering distinct improvements — "the cities got bigger, the hotels got nicer, our seat options on the plane no longer included the dreaded 'middle' seat, and the clubhouse food tasted a little better" (Glanville 2010, 83). In short, it wasn't difficult for Glanville to remain motivated as he entered the retention stage.

The move upward, however, can also include a downside—in Glanville's emphatic phrase, it produces "the chronic sense of being temporary" (Glanville 2010, 18), suggesting that almost all players have persistent doubts about achieving a sustained stay in the majors and that those doubts can play havoc with their sense of well-being (Glanville 2010, 37). At the major-league level, the recruitment stage and early years in the retention stage require psychological as well as physical adaptation, and players can readily flounder in the process.

Besides the well publicized shortness of pro careers, several factors contribute to players' anxiety and sense of temporariness. Rookies reaching the NHL often fail to appreciate how much they need to alter the way they play. Sam Bennett, for instance, scored 91 points in his last full season of junior hockey, but when he joined the NHL's Calgary Flames, where he played center, scoring was only one of his duties. "Kids rate their game on the score sheet," pointed out Flames head coach Bob Hartley. "If their name is on the score sheet, they feel they have a good game, but that's not always the case. Especially at centre [sic] where there are so many responsibilities. We're asking Sammy to make sure he plays the game in the three zones [into which the rink is divided]. We want him to be responsible. That confidence can come overnight. You need to get a feel" (Odland 2015). Bennett agreed on the last point, suggesting that the formidable schedule and frequent travel required adjustment. When commenting on his performance to date in his rookie year, Bennett was critical of his play, emphasizing the necessity of adaptation to the NHL game. "Mediocre," he said. "Definitely I have a lot more to bring. I want to do more and help my team win more" (Morreale 2015b).

But besides facing a more complex game, new arrivals find that the players are more formidable, distinctly so in the NFL's unrelentingly physical context. Ryan Riddle, a sixth-round draftee, who became a journalist after his NFL career, wrote about the contrast between playing football in college and the pros. The difference, he claimed, is huge, with college competition against "boys fresh out of high school" whose bodies are still developing. In stark contrast, the NFL provides "the biggest, strongest, toughest men you will ever see in your entire life," representing "the absolute best 2,000 football players in the entire world." Furthermore, from college to the pros, the performance setting has changed. In college individuals are competing for positions against teammates whose skills and motivational level vary considerably. In the pros, in contrast, competition is against talented men "who are fighting to feed their families and prolong a career of glory, fame and wealth beyond their wildest dreams."

Another important distinction between college and professional players is that the former don't need to be as committed to and prepared for the game (Riddle 2012). Quarterback Brady Quinn illustrated the contrast, pointing out that in college the playbook was about an inch in width while in the NFL it was about six times thicker (Haddock 2014). Both offensive and defensive NFL strategies are so complicated that new participants must engage in extensive study and practice before they are trustworthy in a game (Riddle 2012).

Research involving 11 current or retired NHL members suggests that like Doug Glanville's anxieties about sticking with the Chicago Cubs, Sam Bennett's expanded duties when moving up to the Calgary Flames, and Ryan Riddle's comments about players making the leap from college to the NFL, each of the featured hockey players found that arriving in the NHL was a challenging reality, requiring significant adaptation (Battochio, Schinke, Battochio, Halliwell, and Tenenbaum 2010, 283).

While that response is most applicable to rookies, it is likely to prove necessary throughout players' careers. One psychological element that illustrates adaptation is self-enhancement —developing a distinct sense of how to execute a task and carrying it out. When players engage effectively in self-enhancement, they feel a distinct improvement both mentally and physically. For instance, a NHL goaltender learned that he played much better if he got enthusiastically aroused before a game. He explained, "I start visualizing when I am getting dressed. I make a film in my head with about 7 or 8 big saves and I play it at least three times" (Battochio, Schinke, Battochio, Halliwell, and Tenenbaum 2010, 294).

Besides developing outlooks and skills that enhance performance, players are likely to recognize the importance of various agents of socialization—family, friends, coaches, and teammates who can facilitate their adaptation, providing emotional support and knowledge. The respondents in the hockey study just cited often referred to the importance of teammates, especially in their first year. A rookie said, "I was fortunate to play with [name withheld] and I would watch him on the ice and see how he handled certain situations." Another new arrival said, "When you look at the older guys in the league, they are trusted because they have been doing their jobs for many years" (Battochio, Schinke, Battochio, Halliwell, and Tenenbaum 2010, 295).

Pro athletes usually must elevate their level of performance in order to secure themselves in the retention stage with a major-league team.

Survival in the Majors

Once on a big-league team, players need to develop basic skills and outlooks that promote good performance and improve their survival chances. A study of 62 Baseball Hall of Fame inductees with average MLB career spans of a lengthy 17.6 years and covering the years from 1956 to 2005 produced some informative findings. The study focused on position players, who face broadly similar demands on offense and defense, excluding pitchers whose performance requirements are distinctly different. Inductees from the Negro Leagues were not included because the majority of their playing time was not in MLB (Cotton, Shen, and Livne-Tarandach 2011, 20). The research, which used the inductees' acceptance speeches as its primary source of data, made a distinction between first-ballot and later-ballot inductees. While the performance statistics between the two groups were fairly similar, the first-ballot players were more likely to obtain such coveted awards as batting championships, all-star selections, or most valuable player citations (Cotton, Shen, and Livne-Tarandach 2011, 25).

Perhaps more revealing and surprising, the researchers found that while both categories of Hall of Famers mentioned receiving support during their career, the first-ballot inductees emphasized it more. Comparing the inductees' speeches, the investigators found several measures showing that the first-ballot group indicated more extensive involvement with what the researchers called "developers," who provided various types of support and involved family members, peers and teammates, coaches, and other valued individuals. For instance, the first-ballot inductees received more support on the various emotional and career issues listed—such issues as friendship, role modeling, counseling, coaching, job-related feedback, and career strategizing (Cotton, Shen, and Livne-Tarandach 2011, 31–32). In addition, the first-ballot group cited almost twice as many support personnel as later inductees—22.4 versus 11.7 (Cotton, Shen, and Livne-Tarandach 2011, 35). Finally, it is hardly shocking to learn that in their speeches the first-ballot contingent referred 22 times on average to psychological support (involving such issues as emotional backing or friendship) while the second set of colleagues made just 12 such references (Cotton, Shen, and Livne-Tarandach 2011, 29).

The most potent developers were individuals who provided what the researchers called "hybrid multiplexity," interactions in which a single person supplied various types of assistance. Ex-catcher Carlton Fisk, for instance, cited Walt Hriniak, his hitting coach, who not only helped him improve as a hitter but was a staunch friend and an expert informant about emotional clarity. Fisk said, "Walt Hriniak is the single most important person in my baseball life. He taught me a lot of things, [such as] … regardless of what goes on around you, maintain your focus, and your desire, and your motivation. But most of all be honest to yourself. Man, the time we spent in the bowels of every stadium, the sweat, the blood, the tears, the conversation, the relationship, the friendship, the closeness. I wouldn't be here if it wasn't for you, Walter" (Cotton, Shen, and Livne-Tarandach 2011, 34).

People like Walt Hriniak can be considered exemplary agents of socialization, helping players, whether future Hall of Famers or those less elevated, to deal with the diverse kinds of physical and psychological challenges that they face in adaptation to the major leagues. Such challenges provide the subject matter in the remainder of this section, with some of the situations focused on individual efforts and others involving team endeavors.

Major-league baseball is demanding, with participants required to invest large amounts of time and energy into improving their skills. Technology, which has advanced over time, has sometimes helped players develop those skills and thus to improve their chances of entering and remaining in the leagues.

Asked about the use of video equipment when he joined the Atlanta Braves in 1993, eight-time All-Star Chipper Jones indicated that it didn't exist. He added, "You basically relied on word of mouth from your teammates to get the pitcher's repertoire and what their tendencies might be" (*MLB.com* 2009).

It's very different now. Doug Glanville emphasized that videotape and later digital video have allowed batters to study details of their opponents and, perhaps more important, of themselves. As part of the video package, there can be a record of either a player's every at-bat or pitch during a game. For instance, Glanville noted, "I could sit in front of the computer, click on GLANVILLE, then click on [former pitcher] CURT SHILLING, and voilà. Every at-bat where I faced Curt would come up. Did I want to know what he threw me on 2–2 counts? Do I want to see how I looked against his slider? I could sort the data by count, pitch type, player, pitcher, whatever I needed" (Glanville 2010, 27).

Terence Newman of the Minnesota Vikings has also benefited from recent technology, bolstering his knowledge and enhancing performance. At 38, five years older than any other NFL cornerback, he has played a position most appropriate for young men—where, for instance, the defender facing a speedy receiver must run backwards and then abruptly turn and sprint into coverage.

To give himself an edge, Newman has spent many hours before each game at a computer which connects to a large projection screen, carefully watching, and, if necessary, stopping and repeating film of the opposing team. During these endeavors Newman has either been alone or with fellow cornerbacks who respect both his concentrated effort and demand for silence. Watching film has been a highly informative process. The footage, for example, might reveal subtle tips from body language—that a certain team would run every time a receiver's hands remained on his knees or in another instance that the defense could rule out some routes if a receiver had his outside foot forward. "You see how their bodies move and how their feet are," Newman said. "You understand there's only certain places ... [they] can go" (Shpigel 2016).

At times it is apparent that in performing their roles, successful pro athletes often develop a different mental approach from less elevated players. Brian Hamm, a thoughtful college baseball coach, has offered the following conclusion: "High school players are focused for every meaningful inning, college players are focused for every inning, minor league players are focused for every at-bat, and major league players are focused for every pitch" (Hamm 2016). Hamm seems to have suggested an important issue related to MLB's retention stage—that a significant element in major leaguers' adaptation is unabated commitment.

The following illustration seems to epitomize Hamm's sense of the major-league focus. About 145 games into the season when he accomplished the rare feat of winning the Triple Crown, the Detroit Tigers' Miguel Cabrera came to bat in a game his team was handily winning. While at that moment his team needed nothing more from him, Cabrera was furious when he flied out softly to right field, throwing his bat to the ground in disgust. The announcers who covered the team all year said they had never seen him so aroused. Asked about his reaction, Cabrera said, "That's the first at-bat I gave away all season, and I'm not happy about it" (Hamm 2016). Like other ball players, Cabrera knew that he would make outs the majority of the time; while his adaptation to his role had prepared him to accept that reality, what he couldn't abide was the momentary loss of commitment in performing his role at an optimal level. Inexplicably he, the relentless fighter to get on base, had done the unforgiveable, giving in pathetically to a pitch.

Individual players' skill development is one issue, but in all team sports, emphatically in basketball, a sense of group cohesion can develop, providing a display that is both productive and breathtaking to watch. On the Golden State Warriors, a journalist indicated, the players tend to be spread out and constantly moving, all displaying the basic skills of dribbling, passing, and shooting. Seldom does anyone hold the ball long enough to read the logo. "We play a certain style where everybody's involved," Steph Curry said. "There's a lot of skill involved — skill that's showcased by ball movement and flow. Based on the strength that we have on our roster, we try to highlight that."

"They're the team that everybody wants to be," said Tara VanDerveer, the Stanford women's coach, a Hall of Famer who attends as many Warriors games as possible and records the others. "They know what pretty looks like. It's beautiful basketball" (Branch 2016b).

In fact, VanDerveer's compliment was notable. While it is generally agreed that NBA members are fine athletes individually, top women's coaches have seldom praised them for their team play—at least not until that moment. Sociologically the Warriors demonstrate sociologist George Herbert Mead's provocative concept of *play*—a process in which individuals become attuned to others' roles, learning the rights and obligations involved (Mead 1934, 150). On offense, for instance, Warrior teammates recognize two shared qualities featured in their collective role performance—that they are highly skilled distributors who can readily get the ball to others and that individually they are frequently moving without the ball, seeking open spaces to receive passes.

Effective coaches are critical for winning teams, but a huge boost for a team can also come from an exemplary leader in the game—a player who might be considered a "quasi-coach." The advantage these particular leaders have over actual coaches is that besides instructive commentary, they also lead by example—agents of socialization whose successful actions can sometimes prove more impactful than words. Team leaders tend to be accomplished performers, but beyond such shared qualities as extensive experience, effective decision-making, a sense of discipline, and the capacity to motivate their peers, they differ widely in personality and style (Harmer 2015).

The New York Rangers' Mark Messier was a highly successful team leader, with an unparalleled grasp of the game of hockey. Once when Messier got hurt, a player on the bench turned to another and said half-jokingly, "What do we do now?" The implication of the question seemed to be that with Messier gone, team cohesion was in shreds. "I guess," the other replied tentatively, "we keep playing." Fortunately for the team Messier soon returned. He was a team leader in a highly physical sport that has an 82-game regular season followed by (for the top teams) two months of playoffs. In this exhausting sport, Messier was unrelenting in the demands he made of himself and his teammates (Farber 1996).

At the core of a successful team, Messier asserted, is trust, meaning that as team leader he had to find a way to connect to all the players. Messier said, "It's a people issue, not a sports issue. The way to find that common thread is compassion. The odd threat doesn't hurt." Messier laughed and added, "[B]ut with compassion the appeal to the player is much deeper than the old hard-ass line that you're going to get reprimanded if you don't play well. We try to build a team, to bond, through the course of a year." Messier's teammates were convinced that he created that bond, and in 1994 he led the New York Rangers to their only Stanley Cup victory since 1940 (Farber 1996).

Research done in the NFL also indicates the importance of key players. A study using data involving members of all 32 NFL teams between 1999 and 2009 found that signing elite talent, especially at quarterback, was the most productive step for improving teams' outcome (Zimmer 2016, 64–65). Not surprisingly NFL scouts and coaches are acutely aware that quarterbacks are critical for success. As journalist Andy Benoit wrote, "Virtually the entire league agrees: In order to compete for a Super Bowl, you have to have a star quarterback" (Benoit 2012).

While top players obviously exist in all four of the major professional sports covered in this chapter, the nearby Box 4.2 indicates that in basketball a superstar can sometimes take over the game to a greater extent than counterparts in baseball and football.

BOX 4.2

Supreme Performance in the Three Most Popular Team Pro Sports

What follows concerns athletes and the roles they play in different sports. In 2016 LeBron James and the Cleveland Cavaliers won the NBA championship from the Golden State Warriors, overcoming a three to one deficit. In the seven-game finals, James led all participants in points, rebounds, assists, blocks, and steals (*Fox Sports* 2016). With two minutes to go in the seventh game and the score tied, two Warrior players brought the ball up, and as one of them drove toward the basket for what appeared to be (in spite of an opponent slowing him down) a certain two-points lead, James sprinted toward him from deep in the court and leaped up, making a monumental block that gave the ball back to Cleveland and soon led to the basket that won the Cavaliers the game and the championship (Nadkarni 2016).

> Unquestionably James's 2016 finals was an astounding performance, but something to keep in mind is that he couldn't have been so dominant, so individually successful in either baseball or football. Because of the way players' roles in those two games are structured, nobody, even the most magnificent performer, has the opportunity to dominate play as in basketball, where, though admittedly such performances are unusual, rules permit individuals to remain active for the entire game or close to it.
>
> In contrast, in the other two sports, athletes' roles are substantially different, requiring them to remain on the sidelines for extensive periods of time. In baseball a batter, no matter how well he's hitting, is locked into a position in the team's rotation on offense and remains in the dugout until his turn to bat comes up. Pitchers, to be sure, can dominate the opposing team, but their focus is on defense, with either little or no role on offense.
>
> Baseball analyst Tim Kurkjian has considered this difference between basketball and baseball. He said, "When LeBron James is in a shooting slump, he just puts the ball to the floor and goes to the rack. He dunks a couple of times, and all of a sudden, his slump is over; whereas baseball players ... stand out in right field wondering, 'Am I ever going to get another hit?'" (Levin 2016). Kurkjian's comment suggests that there couldn't be a performance like James's 2016 finals in baseball, or, in fact, in football. A quarterback can be the major force on offense, but then he's on the sidelines when the defensive and special-teams units take over.
>
> In contrast, in the 2016 NBA finals, James's statistical supremacy split quite evenly between offensive and defensive categories—scoring and assists are offensive, blocks and steals are defensive, and rebounding is both. In sports-media settings where athletes from different sports and eras are often compared, it seems feasible to argue that occasionally top NBA players can be more individually dominant throughout a game than their counterparts in MLB and the NFL.

Whether they are stars or marginal performers, pro athletes face retirement, a new experience. Since they were children, leaving a sports program involved an advancement stage leading to a higher-level program. Now the advancement stage entails an often painful withdrawal from active participation in the sport.

Bowing Out: The Close of the Career

Pro-sports careers, as previously noted, are short, ranging for the four major leagues on average from 3.5 to 5.6 years (RAM Financial

Group 2017). However, many of those who get recruited to these leagues barely manage to play.

In the NHL over half the men who make it to the league participate in fewer than 100 games, and 5 percent must leave after a single contest, barely experiencing the NHL before being forced to depart (*QuantHockey.com* 2016a). Some NFL recruits have an equally brief stay. Tony Dye, a Cincinnati Bengals safety for only one game, felt as if "I was never officially solidified as an NFL player." Dye found adaptation to his abrupt departure from the team's highly structured regimen painful and difficult (Shpigel 2017).

Only about 4 percent of NHL players dress for more than 1,000 games. While on average NHL members participate for 5.5 years, Chris Chelios and Gordie Howe lasted 26 seasons. The mean age at retirement covering play between the years 1917–18 and 2015–16 has been 28.2 years (*QuantHockey.com* 2016a, 2016b) —an age when people in most occupations are barely getting started. Summary 4.1 covers the stages players experience in the four most prominent pro leagues.

SUMMARY 4.1

Stages Players Experience in the Top Four Pro Leagues

Factors affecting a prospect's placement in the draft:

- AP rating for one's school, *Rivals.com*'s assessment, and scouts' or coaches' input affecting candidates' draft prospects.
- Effective preparation for and performance at the league's combine or some other predraft events.
- The traditional pro team's approach to the draft: Scouts' input varies by sport, with the NBA contingent highly restricted in the one-and-done era; limited success of draft systems in all four major sports, with the possible utility of alternative sources of information about incoming players such as sabermetrics.

First encounters with the major leagues in the early retention phase:

- Adaptation to a more affluent, high-profile environment in which players are often doubtful about their capacity to remain with the parent clubs.

- Factors contributing to rookies' anxiety: The necessity of making adjustments such as a hockey center's need to broaden his previous duties; the anxiety of facing bigger, stronger, faster players in a more complicated game.

Living the career:

- During the retention stage, the use of technology such as digital video to improve a MLB player's skill in batting.
- Development of a team's fast-moving, multi-skill game such as Golden State's glittering collective offense: Illustration of Mead's concept of play.
- The mental side of pro sports involving players' well developed ability to focus on the detail of the game: Miguel Cabrera's fixation on maintaining consistent, high-level performance.

Bowing out: The close of the career:

- Major-league players' length of time in the retention stage of the four most prominent sports ranging from 3.5 to 5.6 years.
- The significant influence of injury on career length and the necessity for players, coaches, and team executives to engage in resocialization, notably after recognition of and response to concussions.

The inevitable shortness of pro sports careers occurs because of a barrage of factors that include a relentless competition for positions, the unavoidable impact of aging, and the ever-present threat of injury. Many players must make adaptations involving reduced playing time or, sooner more likely than later, face permanent departure from the game. The prospect of retirement from pro sports can be painful. In a study of retired NHL members, one respondent explained, "My identity became the hockey player. You're signing autographs, you're on TV and in the print, and your identity gets wrapped up in that. And I don't think it's necessarily an ego thing. It's more how you're identified with people. My identity was stripped from me when I retired and I had to reinvent myself" (Caron, Bloom, Johnston, and Sabiston 2013).

With their identity wrapped up in the game, some individuals make every possible effort to play as long as possible. After 24 years in MLB during which he became the all-time hits leader, Pete Rose famously said, "I'd walk through hell in a gasoline suit to keep playing baseball" (*Baseball Almanac* 2016).

Injuries, however, often force retirement. A University of Michigan research group conducted a study with a stratified random sample of 1,063 retired NFL players in two age categories—30–49 and 50+. Overall 30 percent of the older and just 11 percent of the younger retirees ruled out injuries as a major factor influencing their decision to leave the game (Weir, Jackson, and Sonnega 2009). With the impact of injuries so prevalent, some NFL players prefer to retire before being forced to do so. After 14 years playing linebacker for the Indianapolis Colts, Robert Mathis, who made 122 sacks, declared, "I want to walk away, not limp away … The rest of my body goes to my kids" (Soong 2016).

Injury also produces retirement in other sports. Basketball players sometimes suffer career-ending Achilles tendon tears. A study of 18 NBA members requiring Achilles tendon surgery found that seven were forced to retire afterwards and eight of the remaining 11 played less than an additional two years (Amin, Old, Tabb, Garg, Toossi, and Cerynik 2013).

Concussions in the NFL, however, are a particularly lethal injury, that in recent years has gained extensive public attention and concern. Not only is the pro football job experience shorter than in other major sports, it is also more violent, threatening serious head injuries. Peter Davies, a neuropathologist who has studied the physically dangerous effects of playing NFL football, indicated that in other major sports "[Y]ou don't go out on the field with the intent to hit somebody on every play … like football players do" (McCarthy 2015).

"It really is hard to put into words just how violent and how intense those hits are," said Boomer Esiason, the TV personality who played quarterback for three NFL teams. "I will say this, that when I would hand the ball off and I would watch a guy go into the pile, what you hear and what you see, you wonder how guys are coming out of that," Esiason added. "They're all in there together, the arms, the legs, the helmets, the shoulder pads, everything is all just in a giant pile … And what that sounds like, it sounds like a car accident" (McCarthy 2015).

As a result of repeated blows to the head, a number of NFL veterans have suffered chronic traumatic encephalopathy (CTE) producing such symptoms as headaches, cognitive dysfunction, memory loss, erratic behavior, dementia, depression, and suicidal impulses (Mayo Clinic 2018). While such symptoms can suggest the likelihood of CTE, only an autopsy can undeniably establish its presence.

The symptoms, however, are potent indicators of the disease. In 2017 scientists at Boston University's renowned CTE Center found that 110 of 111 former NFL players' brains donated to their research program from individuals who doctors believed suffered from CTE contained evidence of the disease (Boston University School of Medicine 2017).

Forty-four of the 111 (40 percent) were linemen—hardly a surprise since they are the players experiencing the most frequent head collisions (Newman 2017). Two days after the CTE Center issued its report, John Urschel, an offensive lineman for the Baltimore Ravens, announced his retirement at the age of 26. Besides playing football, Urschel is a gifted mathematician, who pursues a doctorate in mathematics at MIT. In 2015 he received a concussion, and while he returned to the game three weeks later, his ability to do high-level math was temporarily impaired. Soon after the concussion, Urschel told an interviewer that he wanted to keep playing football and pursuing his Ph.D in math. He said, "I recognize that this is somewhat irrational ... [b]ut I am doing it" (Belson 2017a). That dual involvement, however, is no longer the case.

A few months later, Chris Borland, a former NFL linebacker who retired after only a single fine season because of the serious risk of head injury, did a public-service announcement blasting the NFL for playing down and trying to discredit research on CTE. Borland said that the league's response to the risks "is especially sad when you think about the fact that there are 5-year-old kids out there playing tackle football" (Belson 2017b). In short, for Borland and Urschel, no adaptations that they could devise would lessen the threat that continuing to play posed.

Other former NFL players have also responded decisively to the concussion issue. In April 2015 three-and-a-half years after more than 5,000 retired players had filed suits against the league, the NFL agreed to pay the medical expenses for retired players, whether part of the suit or not, who could establish that their symptoms from CTE and from other diseases related to head injuries such as Alzheimer's or Parkinson's were the result of league play. The settlement will extend for 65 years, potentially involve over 20,000 former players, and will cost the NFL about $1 billion (Belson 2015; Draper 2017; Groves 2017; Mihoces and Axon 2015). The enormity of the problem, both the number of casualties and the cost involved, would have seemed inconceivable just a few years ago.

In the NHL too, injuries can be both serious and destructive for careers. In spite of the fact that modern athletes train harder than ever to be stronger and more durable, the number of career-ending casualties has been increasing. The list has included many unknowns but also such superstars as Bobby Orr, Mario Lemieux, and Eric Lindros (Clipperton 2017).

Like the NFL, the NHL has faced litigation involving concussions. The family of Steve Montador, a former player whose autopsy showed that he suffered CTE, has sued the league, and surviving former players have also initiated additional suits, in all instances alleging that the league failed to protect its employees from long-term lethal injury (Waldron 2015). Support comes from Canadian hockey fans, about two-thirds of whom want to ban fighting during games, which can produce dangerous injuries.

Fighting, however, has been a traditional element in pro hockey and usually players and officials have favored it. Surveys with NHL players regularly indicate that a high percentage of them—around 98 percent— oppose a ban on fighting. Many players believe that fighting contributes little to the occurrence of concussions and that it has been a positive, necessary part of the game where selected tough guys, the enforcers, stick up for teammates and make it clear that no opposing club is going to push their guys around (Kennedy 2015; Whyno 2013).

Leading NHL officials agree, claiming no substantiated connection exists between hockey play and brain damage, including CTE. In fact, autopsies have indicated only a handful of ex-NHL players who had CTE compared to hundreds from the NFL. While neither the league leadership nor the NHL Players' Association has moved to eliminate fighting in the game, the number of fights has appreciably declined— from 645 in 2010–11 to 317 toward the end of the regular season in 2015–16 (Branch 2016a).

In spite of the decline, criticism of the NHL's approach to concussions has been unrelenting, especially when individuals with apparent serious effects return to the ice almost immediately after a head injury. Malcolm Davis, a former right-winger and one of over two dozen ex-players suing the league, commented, "We never saw a doctor for these injuries, and I rarely knew someone to be formally diagnosed with a concussion." Davis added, "I certainly wasn't. During our playing days, the League would lay out the red carpet if a player broke his finger or hurt a muscle in his leg. The treatment for a head injury? Smelling salts and the terse advice to 'keep your head up'" (Waldron 2015).

Both concussion-plagued leagues, however, have been forced to recognize that smelling salts won't do the trick. Not only are NHL and NFL players' concussions shortening careers, they are also prompting extensive resocialization, with players, trainers, coaches, medical personnel, and executives alerted to the recently recognized dangers and costs and the necessity both during players' careers and afterwards to take steps to deal with the long-term fallout.

While injuries are generally less serious in baseball, aging players are increasingly vulnerable to them and are unlikely to keep participating in their 40s or even their late 30s. When at 37 Joe DiMaggio was asked what was the main factor prompting his retirement, he answered quickly—injuries. "The old ones were catching up with me, and I've had some new ones. Mainly, it was my shoulders." He touched his hand first to the right collarbone, then to the left saying: "It pained me right here, when I'd swing and when I'd throw. I've been having trouble with my right shoulder ever since 1939. In the last three years, I'd get off one or two good throws early in the game, and then I'd have nothing left. They knew it, and they were running on me. I threw a lot of them out, but a lot more of them made it." When DiMaggio had finished talking about the shoulder, he mentioned his right knee, which would often stiffen and impede his throws from the outfield (Young 2014). It's possible that a less proud individual might have continued, at least for a while. "I don't want them to remember me struggling," DiMaggio told a *New York Times* photographer when he retired. His brother Tom poignantly added, "He quit because he wasn't Joe DiMaggio any more" (Barnes 1999).

Many other players have found that a combination of injury and age ended their pro careers. Like DiMaggio, Michael Cuddyer was an outfielder and about the same age facing retirement—36. He had twice been an All-Star and had a year remaining on a two-year contract worth $21 million. It was a very difficult decision, but after 15 years he decided to retire. He spoke forthrightly. "I've always run out every hit like it was my last. As an untested high school kid drafted with a dream, I've never taken a single moment in the majors for granted. It goes against every grain in my body to consider a future without the game. But after 15 years, the toll on my body has finally caught up with me." Cuddyer mentioned several injuries including a damaged shoulder, a banged-up knee, and a bulging disc in the neck that had put him on the disabled list six times in recent years. The moment to retire had arrived. He concluded, "Mentally, I was able to overcome it for a long time, but the physical and emotional taxation took its toll. Part of being a professional is to know yourself and to know your limits" (McCarron 2015).

In contrast to the players who want to remain in the major leagues in spite of troubling injury, a few quit because they simply have had enough. In his 13th year, the celebrated Bill Russell emerged during a game from a huddle on the basketball court chuckling. When teammates asked what was so funny, he replied that it was "a bunch of grown men running around in short pants in front of 15,000 people." The others saw little humor in the situation, and Russell realized that he was getting out of touch and had better leave (Nelson 2005, 87). Avoiding the fanfare of a press conference, Russell wrote an article published in *Sports Illustrated* entitled "I'm Not Involved Anymore." His interest in the game was gone. Throughout his career he had thrown himself into the action, but now the shots, the screens, the rebounds seemed distinctly humdrum (Goudsouzian 2010, 238). Russell turned out to be one of the very few who after many years managed to leave the game entirely on his own terms.

The previous focus has been on details about players reaching the end of their careers, but the discussion about the big four major leagues ends with selected observations about the changing pro sports world. Summary 4.2 lists concepts and ideas that appear throughout the chapter.

> **SUMMARY 4.2**
>
> **Ideas and Concepts Used to Examine Pro Careers in the Top Pro Leagues**
>
> *Low probabilities of achieving sports careers:*
>
> - Statistical long shot of reaching the majors from Division I programs and much lower chances from high-school teams.
> - Division I prospects offering overly optimistic claims of making the pros: Likelihood of impact from agents of socialization.
>
> *Socialization experiences coming into play during the four stages of the pro career:*
>
> - Major leaguers engaging in ongoing adaptation as they encounter new information and experiences.
> - The impact of such sources of socialization as coaches and team leaders.
> - The concept of play and its application to team sports such as the Golden State Warriors on offense.
> - Over time adaptation for players, coaches, and other team personnel to deal with updated responses to injuries, partivcularly concussions.

Conclusion: What Happens in Pro Sports Seldom Stays in Pro Sports

The sports journalist's role has drastically changed, a member of the profession claimed. He explained, "Once, all we had to do was trundle down from the press box, stick a digital recorder under an athlete's nose and grunt, 'Your thoughts?' Quotes were recorded, meaningful conclusions drawn, lessons on the life-affirming properties of fair play presented." Now, the journalist lamented, "Sports has become an unrelenting Twitter feed of dysfunction and dismay" (Hoffer 2014, 12).

Survey data suggest that the public's outlook toward pro athletes has changed. When a sample of about 1,000 adults were asked whether they serve as better or worse role models than a decade or two earlier, 62 percent said worse, 22 percent the same, and only 12 percent better (Cohn 2015).

Retired pitcher Steve Blass was hardly surprised by the numbers. "I think it's absolutely true because the world has changed," he said. "The scrutiny is incredible. Back in the day, for better or worse, we didn't know as much as we know now. The technology has stripped every degree of privacy from everyone."

Pro athletes are aware of the changes and sometimes look back nostalgically. Renowned former tackle Joe Greene indicated that in 1975 prior to Super Bowl IX he and two fellow linemates left the plane and stopped at an outdoor café for some liquid refreshment. "We had a wonderful time talking and reminiscing about our season," Greene said. "And nobody bothered us. Nobody took our pictures. Nobody asked for autographs" (Cohn 2015).

For celebrity athletes privacy can be difficult to preserve in a modern world where the appetite for information about them often appears to be insatiable and journalists relentlessly investigate. When Kansas City Royals pitcher Yordano Ventura was killed in an auto accident, rumors abounded that he was still alive after the collision and was robbed of jewelry and left for dead. A day later in order to refute some of the rumored information, a reporter, who had obtained photos from a forensic scientist, tweeted out images of Ventura's body, including pictures of his bloody, badly injured face, suggesting that survival would have been impossible. Angrily a journalist asked, "Did the public need to see Ventura's lifeless body in order to prove that he ... [died in the accident]? Why does the public feel that the mourning process of an athlete should be viewed for the world to see?" (Morello 2017).

Sometimes more than just people's curiosity supports the quest for information. Pro athletes' contracts often contain waivers permitting teams to release to the public details about their injuries. A physician who generally supports doctor-patient confidentiality suggested the unusual pressures in this situation. He wrote, "Professional sports are essentially an entertainment industry that fuels merchandise sales, cable deals, websites, fantasy leagues, and—importantly—point spreads. Are we, as fans and customers of this industry, owed information regarding any issues—health-related or otherwise—that could impair the performance of our favorite player or our fantasy team?" (McCarthy 2013).

Notably the media attention can also produce distinct benefits. For instance, the massive amount of research and publicity about concussions in football and other sports has led to a number of constructive steps; the coverage of events involving discrimination and sexual abuse toward women has contributed to some productive actions against the guilty parties and increased vigilance about those issues. As a result of increased scrutiny, some pro athletes undoubtedy needed to make significant adaptation in their personal behavior.

For young players aspiring for advancement to Division I or even professional ranks, the constant buzz about athletes, especially celebrity athletes, can be an incentive—just one more impetus to make every effort to defeat the massive odds against their rising to elite status.

In fact, there is evidence that some established pros have been making a profitable adaptation to the modern era's inquiring media. Dave Finocchio, a founder of the prominent *Bleacher Report*, indicated that athletes working with the media can benefit financially—that in particular prominent players, sometimes with their spouses, will reveal their private lives, particularly in the NBA "where a lot of the athletes view themselves as entertainers or half-athletes, half-entertainers." Finocchio indicated that "Steph Curry and his wife [Ayesha] ... have built this massive brand where she ... has become a celebrity in the United States. And I'm sure she in her own right will end up making a ton of money [with] her own cookbook, meal-kit delivery service, and ... her own cooking show on the Food Network" (McAlone 2016).

Clearly prominent modern athletes respond to media attention in different ways. While it's not apparent whether or not further major changes in journalists' approach to covering sports will soon occur, one conclusion seems indisputable—that the public appetite for information about celebrity players will remain robust.

Summary

Historically the baseball clubs in the newly formed National League made little money. For the owners the financial situation improved when they established the reserve system, which the players overturned in the 1970s, leading to sharply increased salaries. Other leagues also introduced significant new practices over time such as the NHL's elimination of the 50-mile rule and the NBA's signing of international stars and negotiation of large TV deals.

In 1947 Jackie Robinson became the first African American to play in the major leagues. While the percentage of black players gradually increased over time, it has recently dropped, in part because top athletes can't get full college scholarships in baseball as in football and basketball. The NFL and the NBA also eventually integrated, and nowadays the distinct majority of players in both leagues are African American.

It's reasonable to consider whether given the modest length of time players spend in the major leagues they actually pursue careers. Candidates for the top pro leagues face almost impossible odds to make it to the majors—in most of the sports about one chance in 1,000 as a high-school student of eventually reaching the majors. Survey data demonstrate that Division I prospects have a greatly inflated expectation of making it to the majors. Players reaching the big leagues must engage in adaptation to be successful.

In facing the challenge of joining a major-league team, top players in all four of the major sports face a draft. A couple of studies concluded that a distinct correlation exists between the round in which players entering the major leagues are drafted and their playing time in those leagues.

Other approaches to assessing candidates for the major pro leagues exist. In particular, sabermetrics has proved useful in predicting players' success, and while its application began in baseball, the other three major leagues have also begun using its statistical measures.

As rookies arrive in the major leagues, they find that significant adaptation is often necessary. Compared to the minors, major-league players find that their roles are more complicated, often involving a greater number of responsibilities, and that the participants are more physically gifted and more committed to intense play. A study of NHL members focused on the importance of adaptation — grasping what it entails and performing their revised roles.

Recruits to the big leagues have certain distinctive qualities, beginning with the top players. A study of 62 MLB Hall of Famers found that the first-ballot inductees were more likely to have received prized individual awards than the later-ballot contingent and to have had a greater number of supporters. Committed pros, with the use of digital video or some other modern technology, spend a lot of time improving their basic skills. While skill refinement occurs on the individual level, it can also be a collective process involving a team like the Golden State Warriors, whose spread offense is both a beautiful and efficient display of dribbling, passing, and shooting. In major pro sports, one position stands out for its importance in contributing to a team's supremacy; it appears essential to have a star quarterback in order to compete for the Super Bowl.

Finally, the end of the career is difficult for players in the top leagues, involving loss of a valued identity and the necessity to find a new one. Injury often contributes to retirement. A University of Michigan study indicated that in two age groups composed of ex-NFL players, the majority of respondents felt that injuries played an important role in their leaving the game. Concussions in the NFL and NHL are receiving growing public attention and concern. Following a suit settled in April 2015, ex-NFL players who can establish that the head blows they received playing in the league left them somewhat or seriously incapacitated will obtain substantial payment from the league. While fewer ex-NHL members have suffered from CTE and other debilitating brain conditions, concussion-related reform has also been occurring in hockey. Players' motivation to retire can occur for distinctly different reasons as the contrasting cases of Joe DiMaggio and Bill Russell demonstrate.

The chapter ends with a brief discussion about the changing media world modern pro athletes encounter.

Class Discussion Issues

1. Have you ever observed a "can't miss" prospect in one of the four major professional sports? What were his outstanding traits? Are you aware of anything notable in his socialization as a player? Can you comment on either his adaptation or commitment to the game?
2. Discuss the impact that the development of the reserve system and its eventual elimination had on MLB.
3. Consider the effects that the racial integration of baseball, football, and basketball have had on the respective pro leagues.
4. Compare a sports career in one of the four prominent sports discussed in this chapter with some other well-known career, discussing both the similarities and the differences.
5. What are the major hurdles players face in their adaptation to one of the four top leagues? Name two successful prospects you

particularly admire, indicating some steps they needed to take in order to establish themselves in their league.

6. Does the discrepancy between the statistical likelihood of making it from Division I to a major pro sport versus Division I athletes' disproportionately high expectation of accomplishing that feat surprise you? Comment, tying in the concept of agents of socialization.

7. Examine the pros and cons of the draft system in the four most prominent pro leagues. If you could make a single change in one league's system or perhaps all four leagues' systems, what would it be and why?

8. When players enter the major leagues, what feelings are they likely to experience? In addition, discuss what agents of socialization would be likely to provide career support for newly arrived prospects and what would that support entail.

9. A study of NHL players indicated that they engage in adaptation. Discuss the kinds of actions they took.

10. Pick out one or two players in the top four major leagues and indicate in detail what makes them remarkable. Is it performance skills, social abilities, or a combination of both? What traits encourage the NHL to designate a player "The Great One" or "The Next One," and are there reasons why other leagues don't make a similar distinction?

11. Has the approach to dealing with such serious injuries as concussions changed over time in pro sports, or are we, the members of the public, seeing largely superficial adjustments that will not significantly curtail the dangers players face? In addition, indicate what further developments in dealing with injuries, if any, are likely to occur in upcoming decades.

References

Addona, Vittorrio, and Philip A. Yates. 2010. "A Closer Look at the Relative Age Effect." *Journal of Quantitative Analysis in Sports* 6: 1–17.

Allan, T.J. 2015. "How Michael Jordan's Mindset Made Him a Great Competitor." *USA Basketball* (November 24). www.usab.com/youth/news/2012/08/how-michael-jordans-mindset-made-him-great.aspx.

Amin, Nirav H., Andrew B. Old, Loni P. Tabb, Rohit Garg, Nadir Toossi, and Douglas L.

Cerynik. 2013. "Performance Outcomes after Repair of Complete Achilles Tendon Ruptures in National Basketball Association Players." *The American Journal of Sports Medicine* 41: 1864–1870.

Badenhausen, Kurt. 2016a. "Dallas Cowboys Head the World's 50 Most Valuable Sports Teams of 2016." *Forbes* (July 13). www.forbes.com/sites/kurtbadenhausen/2016/07/13/dallas-cowboys-head-the-worlds-50-most-valuable-sports-teams-of-2016/#7159758ff330.

Badenhausen, Kurt. 2016b. "Average Player Salaries in American Sports Leagues." *Forbes* (December 15). www.forbes.com/sites/kurtbadenhausen/2016/12/15/average-player-salaries-in-major-american-sports-leagues/#4dbd83f41050.

Barnes, Bart. 1999. "American Icon DiMaggio Dies at 82." *The Washington Post* (March 8). www.washingtonpost.com/wp-srv/sports/baseball/daily/march99/08/dimaggioobit.htm.

Barra, Allen. 2011. "How Curt Flood Changed Baseball and Killed His Career in the Process." *The Atlantic* (July 12). www.theatlantic.com/entertainment/archive/2011/07/how-curt-flood-changed-baseball-and-killed-his-career-in-the-process/241783/.

Baseball Almanac. 2015. "Baseball Draft." www.baseball-almanac.com/draft/baseball_draft.shtml.

Baseball Almanac. 2016. "Pete Rose Quotes." www.baseball-almanac.com/quotes/quorose.shtml.

Baseball-Reference.com. 2017. "Mike Piazza." www.baseball-reference.com/players/p/piazzmi01.shtml.

Basen, Ryan. 2012. "Fifty Years Ago, Last Outpost in N.F.L. Fell." *The New York Times* (October 6). www.nytimes.com/2012/10/07/sports/football/50-years-ago-redskins-were-last-nfl-team-to-integrate.html?pagewanted=a.

Basketball-Reference.com. 2016. "Lebron James." www.basketball-reference.com/players/j/jamesle01.html.

Battochio, Randy C., Robert J. Schinke, Danny L. Battochio, Wayne Halliwell, and Gershon Tenenbaum. 2010. "The Adaptation Process of National Hockey League Players." *Journal of Clinical Sport Psychology* 4: 282–301.

Battochio, Randy C., Natalia Stambulova, and Robert J. Schinke. 2016. "Canadian National Hockey League Players." *Journal of Sports Sciences* 34: 278–288.

Belson, Ken. 2015. "Judge Approves Deal in N.F.L. Concussion Suit." *The New York Times* (April 22). www.nytimes.com/2015/04/23/sports/football/nfl-concussion-settlement-is-given-final-approval.html.

Belson, Ken. 2016. "Dementia Care, Tailored to N.F.L. Retirees." *The New York Times* (March 23). www.nytimes.com/2016/03/23/sports/dementia-care-tailored-to-nfl-retirees.html.

Belson, Ken 2017a. "For Ravens' John Urschel, Playing in the N.F.L. No Longer Adds Up." *The New York Times* (July 27). www.nytimes.com/2017/07/27/sports/football/john-urschel-baltimore-ravens-retires-nfl-cte-study.html?_r=0.

Belson, Ken. 2017b. "Chris Borland Blasts N.F.L. for Hiding C.T.E. Risks." *The New York Times* (October 24). www.nytimes.com/2017/10/24/sports/football/chris-borland-nfl-cte.html?_r=0.

Benoit, Andy. 2012. "N.F.L. Evolution: Good Isn't Good Enough for Quarterbacks." *The New York Times* (April 23). https://fifthdown.blogs.nytimes.com/2012/04/23/n-f-l-evolution-good-isnt-good-enough-for-quarterbacks/.

Bilas, Jay. 2002. "Did 'LeBron Mania' Go Too Far?" *ESPN* (December 17). http://espn.go.com/columns/bilas_jay/1477784.html.

Birnbaum, Phil. 2016. "A Guide to Sabermetric Research." *SABR* http://sabr.org/sabermetrics/single-page.

Boston University School of Medicine. 2017. "New Study of 111 Deceased Former NFL Players Found 99 Percent Had CTE." www.bumc.bu.edu/busm/2017/07/25/new-study-of-111-deceased-former-nfl-players-finds-99-percent-had-cte/.

Branch, John. 2016a. "In E-Mails NHL Officials Conceded Risk of Fights." *The New York Times* (March 29). www.nytimes.com/2016/03/29/sports/hockey/nhl-emails-link-concussions-fighting-bettman.html?_r=0.

Branch, John. 2016b. "The Golden State Warriors Play the Beautiful Game." *The New York Times* (October 25). www.nytimes.com/2016/10/26/sports/basketball/golden-state-warriors-nba-stephen-curry-kevin-durant.html.

Bureau of Labor Statistics. 2015. "Athletes and Sports Competitors." (December 17). www.bls.gov/ooh/entertainment-and-sports/athletes-and-sports-competitors.htm.

Caggiano, Greg. 2011. "The Great Expansion: Interview with Alan Bass." *WorldPress.com* (March 31). https://gcaggiano.wordpress.com/tag/the-great-expansion-the-ultimate-risk-that-changed-the-nhl-forever/.

Caron, Jeffrey G., Gordon A. Bloom, Karen M. Johnston, and Catherine M. Sabiston. 2013. "Effects of Multiple Concussions on Retired National Hockey League Players." *Journal of Sport & Exercise Psychology* 35: 168–179.

Chass, Murray. 1977. "Curt Flood—Baseball's Forgotten Man." *Baseball Digest* (January) 77.

Clipperton, Joshua. 2017. "NHL 100: Mario Lemieux among NHL Players Who Left the Game Early." *CBS Sports* (February 7). www.cbc.ca/sports/hockey/nhl/mario-lemieux-injuries-nhl-careers-1.3970394.

Cohn, Bob. 2015. "Survey Shows Perception of Athletes Has Changed in the Age of Increased Exposure." *TRIBLive* (February 14). http://triblive.com/sports/otherlocal/7766668-74/athletes-role-public.

Cornelius, Emily. 2014. "How Hard Is It to Make It to the MLB?" *The Huffington Post* (October 7). www.huffingtonpost.com/emily-cornelius/how-hard-is-it-to-make-it_1_b_5947308.html.

Cotton, Richard D., Yan Shen, and Reut Livne-Tarandach. 2011. "On Becoming Extraordinary: The Content and Structure of the Developmental Networks of Major League Baseball Hall of Famers." *Academy of Management Journal* 54: 15–46.

Crowe, Jerry. 2007. "Tip Money Now, It Was Top Money for Reichardt." *Los Angeles Times* (May 28). http://articles.latimes.com/2007/may/28/sports/sp-crowe28.

Cyrgalis, Brett. 2011. "Hockey Finds Its Own Type of Sabermetrics." *New York Post* (October 12). http://nypost.com/2011/10/12/hockey-finds-its-own-type-of-sabermetrics/.

Deaner, Robert O., Aaron Lowen, and Stephen Cobley. 2013. "Born at the Wrong Time: Selection Bias in the NHL Draft." PLOS (February 27). http://journals.plos.org/plosone/article?id=10.1371/journal.pone.0057753.

Draper, Kevin. 2014. "What the NBA's Insane Deal Means for the NBA and You." *Deadspin* (October 6). http://deadspin.com/what-the-nbas-insane-new-tv-deal-means-for-the-league-a-1642926274.

Draper, Kevin. 2017. "The Billion Dollar Concussion Suit Is a New Kind of Disaster."

Deadspin (March 29). http://deadspin.com/the-billion-dollar-nfl-concussion-settlement-is-a-new-k-1793787616.

Elliott, Bud. 2014. "How Sleeper Recruits Still Make the NFL despite Blue-chip Dominance." *SB Nation* (May 12). www.sbnation.com/college-football-recruiting/2014/5/12/5696710/nfl-draft-recruits-five-stars-two-stars.

Eskenazi, Gerald. 1976. *A Thinking Man's Guide to Pro Hockey*. New York: E.P. Dutton & Co.

ESPN. 2012. "David Stern, the Highs and the Lows." (October 26). http://espn.go.com/nba/story/_/page/5-on-5-121026/

Falkner, David. 1995. *Great Time Coming: The Life of Jackie Robinson, from Baseball to Birmingham*. New York: Simon and Schuster.

Farber, Michael. 1996. "The Look One Glimpse Tells You That Mark Messier Is the Best Leader in Sports." *Sports Illustrated Vault* (February 12). www.si.com/vault/1996/02/12/209898/the-look-one-glimpse-tells-you-that-mark-messier-is-the-best-leader-in-sports.

Fox Sports. 2016. "This Unbelievable Stat Illustrates Just How Great LeBron James Was in the Finals." (June 19). www.foxsports.com/nba/story/lebron-james-cleveland-cavaliers-nba-finals-game-7-061916.

Gaines, Cork. 2013. "How the NHL Has Evolved since the 'Original Six' NHL." *Business Insider* (June 12). www.businessinsider.com/chart-how-the-nhl-has-evolved-since-the-original-six-2013-6.

Glanville, Doug. 2010. *The Game from Where I Stand: A Ballplayer's Inside View*. New York: Times Books.

Gonzalez, Bansky. 2013. "So Long, NBA! Sebastian Telfair's Heading to China." *UPROXX* (October 15). http://uproxx.com/smokingsection/2013/10/sebastian-telfair-basketball-china/.

Gordon, Jeff. 2017. "A Biography of Michael Jordan as a Basketball Player." *Livestrong* (September 11). www.livestrong.com/article/450727-a-biography-of-michael-jordan-as-a-high-school-basketball-player/.

Goudsouzian, Aram. 2010. *King of the Court: Bill Russell and the Basketball Revolution*. Berkeley, CA: University of California Press.

Groves, Roger. 2017. "Study That 110 Out Of 111 NFL Former Players Have Brain Disease May Hurt Future Player Lawsuits." *Forbes* (July 26). www.forbes.com/sites/rogergroves/2017/07/26/study-that-110-out-of-111-nfl-former-players-have-brain-disease-may-hurt-future-player-lawsuits/#6bac01467efd.

Guadagni, Steven. 2015. "What Separates You from Major League Baseball Players." *Top Velocity*. www.topvelocity.net/what-separates-you-from-major-league-baseball-players/.

Haddock, Steven. 2014. "Is It Difficult for Football Players to Transition into the NFL Once They Are Drafted? Why or Why Not?" *Quora* (May 18). www.quora.com/Is-it-difficult-for-college-football-players-to-transition-into-the-NFL-once-they-are-drafted-Why-or-why-not.

Halberstam, David. 1981. *The Breaks of the Game*. New York: Alfred A. Knopf.

Halverson, Joe. 2012. "Rick Reichardt: The Most Important Baseball Player You've Never Heard of." *Los Angeles Angels Stream* (May 24). http://bleacherreport.com/articles/1194670-rick-reichardt-the-most-important-baseball-player-youve-never-heard-of.

Hamm, Brian. 2016. "What Separates High School, College, and Professional Baseball Players." *baseballtoolshed.com* (April 18). http://baseballtoolshed.com/what-separates-high-school-college-and-professional-baseball-players/.

Hanssen, Andrew. 1998. "The Cost of Discrimination: A Study of Major League Baseball." *Southern Economic Journal* 64 (January): 603–627.

Harmer, Alfie Potts. 2015. "Top 20 Greatest Leaders in Sports." *TheSportster* (September 11). www.thesportster.com/entertainment/top-20-greatest-leaders-in-sports-history/.

Herren, Chris, and Bill Reynolds. 2011. *Basketball Junkie: A Memoir*. New York: St. Martin's Press.

Hoffer, Richard. 2014. "Broken News: Bad Sports Are Dominating Headlines and Making Us Throw Up Our Hands." *Sports Illustrated* (September 22) 12–13. www.si.com/vault/2014/09/22/106636996/broken-news.

Hoffman, Jay R., Jose Vazquez, Napoleon Pichardo, and Gershon Tenenbaum. 2009. "Anthropometric and Performance Comparisons in Professional Baseball Players." *The Journal of Strength and Conditioning Research* 23 (October): 2173–2178.

Hughes, Glyn. 2004. "Managing Black Guys: Representation, Corporate Culture, and the NBA." *Sociology of Sport Journal* 21: 163–184.

Jeyarajah, Shehan. 2015. "2015 NBA Draft: Preparing for Draft Day." *SIKIDS.com* (June 25). www.sikids.com/blogs/2015/06/25/2015-nba-draft-preparing-for-draft-day.

Kamp, David. 2006. "Only the Ball Was Brown." *GQ.com* (September 4). www.byliner.com/david-kamp/stories/only-the-ball-was-brown.

Kaufman, Scott Barry. 2014. "What Predicts NBA Success?" *Scientific American* (August 5). http://blogs.scientificamerican.com/beautiful-minds/what-predicts-nba-success/.

Kelley, Mason. 2014. "Talent + Character = O.K.G." *Gohuskies.com* (October 8). www.gohuskies.com/ViewArticle.dbml?ATCLID=209703741.

Kennedy, Ryan. 2015. "Fighting in the NHL: Should It Stay or Go?" *The Hockey News* (January 18). www.thehockeynews.com/blog/fighting-in-the-nhl-should-it-stay-or-go/.

Kepner, Tyler. 2014. "M.L.B. Report Highlights Sobering Number of Black Players." *The New York Times* (April 9). www.nytimes.com/2014/04/10/sports/baseball/mlb-report-highlights-sobering-number-of-black-players.html.

Koz, D., J. Frazer-Thomas, and J. Baker. 2012. "Accuracy of Professional Sports Drafts in Predicting Career Potential." *Scandinavian Journal of Science and Medicine in Sports* 22 (August): e64-e69.

Lapchick, Richard. 1992. "Race and Sport in the 1990s." *The Christian Science Monitor* (April 10). www.csmonitor.com/1992/0410/10181.html.

Lapchick, Richard. 2005. "The 2004 Racial and Gender Report Card: National Basketball Association." *The Institute for Ethics and Diversity in Sports* (May 4). http://nebula.wsimg.com/45f0c0ea011c3c94cdba4b955f7fb533?AccessKeyId=DAC3A56D8FB782449D2A&disposition=0&alloworigin=1.

Lapchick, Richard. 2016. "The 2016 Racial and Gender Report Card: National Football League." *The Institute for Ethics and Diversity in Sports* (September 28). http://nebula.wsimg.com/1abf21ec51fd8dafbecfc2e0319a6091?AccessKeyId=DAC3A56D8FB782449D2A&disposition=0&alloworigin=1.

Lapchick, Richard. 2017a. "The 2016 Racial and Gender Report Card: Major League Baseball." *The Institute for Ethics and Diversity in Sports* (April 18). http://nebula.

wsimg.com/d96daf1e011b077b2fd9ff4cfe4bf1bc?AccessKeyId=DAC3A56D8FB7 82449D2A&disposition=0&alloworigin=.

Lapchick, Richard. 2017b. "The 2017 Racial and Gender Report Card: National Basketball Association." *The Institute for Ethics and Diversity in Sports* (June 20). http://nebula.wsimg.com/74491b38503915f2f148062ff076e698?AccessKeyId=DAC3A56D8FB782449D2A&disposition=0&allow.

Laws, Will. 2016. "Top 30 Most Valuable Players in the NBA." *PointAfter* (May 2). http://basketball-players.pointafter.com/stories/13098/top-30-nba-player-rankings.

Levin, Michael. 2016. "Why Tim Kurkjian Says Baseball's Still the Best Game Bar None." *TheHuffingtonPost.com* (August 23). www.huffingtonpost.com/michaellevin/why-tim-kurkjian-says-bas_b_11654732.html.

Lewis, Michael. 2004. *Moneyball: The Art of Winning an Unfair Game*. New York: W. W. Norton & Company.

Lomax, Michael E. 1999. "The African American Experience in Professional Football." *Journal of Social History* 33 (Autumn): 163–178.

Longley, Neil, and Glenn Wong. 2011. "The Speed of Human Capital Formation in the Baseball Industry: The Information of Minor-League Performance in Predicting Major-League Performance." *Managerial and Decision Economics* 32: 192–204.

Maaddi, Rob. 2015. "Before McDavid Others Wore 'The Next One' Label." *USA Today* (October 7). www.usatoday.com/story/sports/nhl/2015/10/07/before-mcdavid-others-wore-the-next-one.label/73500654/?utm_source=feedblitz&utm_medium=FeedBlitzRss&utm_campaign=usatodaycomnhl-topstories.

Mandelbaum, Michael. 2004. *The Meaning of Sports: Why Americans Watch Baseball, Football, and Basketball and What They See When They Do*. New York: PublicAffairs.

Mangiaracina, Marina. 2014. "The Story of Sebastian Telfair." *SB Nation* (July 15). www.welcometoloudcity.com/2014/7/15/5877621/sebastian-telfair-is-getting-ridiculous.

Mannix, Chris. 2013. "Winners, Losers from the 2013 Draft Combine." *Sports Illustrated* (May 20). http://sportsillustrated.cnn.com/nba/news/20130520/nba-draft-combine-2013-winners-losers-cody-zeller-shabazz-muhamm.

Manuel, John. 2010. "The History and Future of the Amateur Draft." *SABR* (Summer). http://sabr.org/research/history-and-future-amateur-draft.

Mayo Clinic. 2018. "Chronic Traumatic Encephalopathy." www.mayoclinic.org/diseases-conditions/chronic-traumatic-encephalopathy/symptoms-causes/syc-20370921.

McAlone, Nathan. 2016. "The CEO of Bleacher Report Indicates Which Athletes Make the Most Money and Why." *Business Insider* (August 16). www.businessinsider.com/private-lives-of-athletes-equal-celebrity-bucks-2016-8.

McCarron, Anthony. 2015. "Michael Cuddyer Writes 'I Gave You Everything I Had' as Retiring Mets Slugger Explains His Decision." *Daily News* (December 12). www.nydailynews.com/sports/baseball/mets/michael-cuddyer-writes-gave-article-1.2463670.

McCarthy, T.C. 2015. "Life after Football." *Newsday* (January 22). www.data.newsday.com/projects/sports/football/life-football/.

Mead, George Herbert. 1934. *Mind, Self and Society*. Chicago, IL: University of Chicago Press.

Mihoces, Gary, and Rachel Axon. 2015. "Judge Approves Settlement—at Least $900 Million—to NFL Concussion Lawsuits." *USA Today* (April 22). www.usatoday.

com/story/sports/nfl/2015/04/22/concussion-related-lawsuits-judge-settlement-nfl/26199011/.

Miller, Ed. 2012. "NHL Expansion Celebrates 45th Anniversary." *The Hockey Writers.* http://thehockeywriters.com/nhl-expansion-celebrates-45th-anniversary/.

MLB.com. 2009. "How Video Is Changing Baseball." (November 16). http://mlb.mlb.com/news/print.jsp?ymd=20091115&content_id=7670358&vkey=news_mlb&fext=.jsp&c_id=mlb.

Montville, Leigh. 1994. "The Curse of the Cup." *Sports Illustrated* (June 6). www.si.com/vault/1994/06/06/131244/the-curse-of-the-cup-could-this-be-the-year-that-the-rangers-break-the-jinx-and-put-an-end-to-more-than-half-a-century-of-heartache#.

Morello, Breanna. 2017. "Reserving an Athlete's Right to Privacy Even after a Tragedy." *NY Sports Day* (January 26). www.nysportsday.com/2017/01/26/morello-reserving-an-athletes-right-to-privacy-even-after-a-tragedy/.

Morreale, Mike G. 2015a. "McDavid Deserves All the Comparisons to Crosby." *NHL.com* (May 28). www.nhl.com/ice/news.htm?id=769050.

Morreale, Mike G. 2015b. "Eichel, Bennett Continue to Adjust to Pro Game." *NHL.com* (December 29). www.nhl.com/news/eichel-bennett-continue-to-adjust-to-pro-game/c-794737.

Moxley, Jerad H., and Tyler J. Towne. 2014. "Predicting Success in the National Basketball Association: Stability and Potential." *Psychology of Sport and Exercise* (June). www.researchgate.net/publication/264123950_Predicting_success_in_the_National_Basketball_Association_Stability_potential.

Myers, David W. 1994. "Where Are They Now?: Rick Reichardt." *Los Angeles Times* (May 3). http://articles.latimes.com/1994-05-03/sports/sp-53197_1_rick-reichardt.

Nadkarni, Rohan. 2016. "The Block: An In-depth Look at LeBron James's Altering Play." *Sports Illustrated* (June 20). www.si.com/nba/2016/06/20/nba-finals-game-7-lebron-james-block-andre-iguodala-highlights-video.

National Career Services. 2016. "Sports Professional." (October 6). www.ncaa.org/sites/default/files/2015-16RES_Probability_Chart_Web_20170314.pdf.

NBA.com. 2014. "Basketball 101: NBA Draft." www.nba.com/hornets/draft_basketball_101.html.

NBA.com. 2017. "2017 Finals: By the Numbers." (May 30). www.nba.com/article/2017/05/30/2017-nba-finals-numbers.

NCAA. 2017. "Estimated Probability of Competing in Professional Athletics." (March 10). www.ncaa.org/about/resources/research/estimated-probability-competing-professional-athletics.

NCAA Research. 2013. "Estimated Probability of Competing in Athletics beyond the High School Interscholastic Level." www.ncaa.org/sites/default/files/Probability-of-going-pro-methodology_Update2013.pdf.

Nelson, Murry R. 2005. *Bill Russell: A Biography.* Westport, CT: Greenwood Press.

New, Jake. 2015. "A Long Shot." *Inside Higher Ed.* (January 25). www.insidehighered.com/news/2015/01/27/college-athletes-greatly-overestimate-their-chances-playing-professionally.

Newman, Katelyn. 2017. "Study: 110 of 111 Ex-NFL Players' Brains Had C.T.E." *U.S.News* (July 25). www.usnews.com/news/national-news/articles/2017-07-25/110-of-111-deceased-nfl-football-players-brains-had-cte-study-finds.

NFL.com. 2014. "What Goes on at the Combine." www.nfl.com/combine/workouts.

Odland, Kristen. 2015. "Scoreless Bennett Adjusting to the NHL." *Calgary Herald* (October 14). http://calgaryherald.com/sports/hockey/nhl/calgary-flames/scoreless-bennett-adjusting-to-the-nhl.

Oxford Dictionaries. 2016. "Career." https://en.oxforddictionaries.com/definition/career.

Parrish, Gary. 2015. "The Nike-Under Armour Battle for High School Stars Is Heating Up." *CBS Sports* (August 6). www.cbssports.com/collegebasketball/eye-on-college-basketball/25261949/the-nike-under-armour-battle-for-high-school-stars-is-heating-up.

Perry, Dayn. 2017. "Here's Every Team's Opening Payroll for 2017." *CBS Sports* (April 7). www.cbssports.com/mlb/news/heres-every-mlb-teams-opening-day-payroll-for-2017/.

Peters, Chris. 2015. "Best since Mario? How Connor McDavid Will Change the NHL." *CBS Sports* (October 8). www.cbssports.com/nhl/eye-on-hockey/25331541/best-since-mario-how-connor-mcdavid-will-change-the-nhl.

Piazza, Mike, and Lonnie Wheeler. 2013. *Long Shot*. New York: Simon & Schuster.

Plagenhoef, Scott. 1999. "The Times to Remember." *Hockey Digest* 27 (April): 34–40.

Powell, Jackie. 2016. "The Declining Number of Black Players Is a Huge Problem." *SB Nation* (June 2). www.overthemonster.com/2016/6/2/11806176/mlb-black-players-decline-red-sox-chuck-d.

Powell, Michael. 2016. "Curtis Granderson Is a Man on a Generous Mission." *The New York Times* (November 28). www.nytimes.com/2016/11/28/sports/baseball/most-valuable-person-the-title-belongs-to-curtis-granderson.html.

QuantHockey.com. 2016a. "Average Length of an Average NHL Player Career." www.quanthockey.com/Distributions/CareerLengthGP.php.

QuantHockey.com. 2016b. "NHL Player Average Retirement Age." www.quanthockey.com/Distributions/RetireeAgeDistribution.php.

RAM Financial Group. 2017. "Athlete Services." www.ramfg.com/RAM-Financial-Group-Solutions-Professional-Athletes-Athletes-Services.

Rask, Kevin. 2015. "Coach Influence on Player Development." *Winthrop Intelligence*. http://winthropintelligence.com/2014/01/02/coach-influence-player-development/.

Reiss, Steven A. 1995. *Sport in Industrial America, 1850–1920*. Wheeling, IL: Harlan Davidson, Inc.

Riddle, Ryan. 2012. "The Difference between College and the Pros in the NFL." *Bleacher Report* (September 6). http://bleacherreport.com/articles/1324537-the-difference-between-college-and-the-pros-in-the-nfl.

Rosenbaum, Mike. 2012. "Examining the Percentage of MLB Draft Picks Who Reach the Major Leagues." *Bleacher Report* (June 12). http://bleacherreport.com/articles/1219356-examining-the-percentage-of-mlb-draft-picks-that-reach-the-major-leagues.

Ross, Charles K. 1999. *Outside the Lines: African Americans and the Integration of the National Football League*. New York: New York University Press.

Ryan, Brennan. 2016. "Paul DePodesta and the Incoming Football Sabermetrics Revolution." *The State Press* (February 3). www.statepress.com/article/2016/02/paul-depodesta-and-the-incoming-football-sabermetrics-revolution.

Sapienza, P.J. 2011. "NHL Hockey: Does the Original Six Really Mean Anything Anymore?" *Bleacher Report* (May 26). http://bleacherreport.com/articles713721-nhl-hockey-does-the-original-six-really-mean-anyting-anymore.

Scully, Gerald W. 1989. *The Business of Major League Baseball*. Chicago, IL: University of Chicago Press.

Shpigel, Ben. 2016. "Playing in the N.F.L. at 38." *The New York Times* (November 30). www.nytimes.com/2016/11/30/sports/football/terence-newman-minnesota-vikings-cornerback.html?_r=0.

Shpigel, Ben. 2017. "One Game to Remember. Just One." *The New York Times* (November 22). www.nytimes.com/2017/11/22/sports/football/one-nfl-game.html.

Shrake, Edwin. 1964. "The Richest Bonus Baby Ever." *Vault Beta* (July 6). www.si.com/vault/1964/07/06/607968/the-richest-bonus-baby-ever.

Simmons, Bill. 2009. *The Book of Basketball: The NBA According to The Sports Guy*. New York: Ballantine Books.

Simon, Scott. 2002. *Jackie Robinson and the Integration of Baseball*. Hoboken, NY: John Wiley & Sons.

Smith, John Matthew. 2011. "Gifts That God Didn't Give: White Hopes, Basketball, and the Legend of Larry Bird." *Massachusetts Historical Review* 13: 1–30.

Soong, Kelyn. 2016. "Longtime Colts Linebacker Robert Mathis Will Play His Last Game Sunday." *The Washington Post* (December 30). www.washingtonpost.com/news/early-lead/wp/2016/12/30/longtime-colts-linebacker-robert-mathis-will-play-his-last-nfl-game-sunday/?utm_term=.27a838ed109c.

Surdam, David G. 2012. *The Rise of the National Basketball Association*. Champaign, IL: University of Illinois Press.

Titus, Mark. 2014. "My Trip to NBA Scout School." *Grantland.com* (July 30). http://grantland.com/features/nba-scout-school-las-vegas-summer-league-fran-fraschilla-dallas-mavericks-new-york-knicks/.

Topend Sports. 2015. "NBA Pre-draft Combine Camp." www.topendsports.com/sport/basketball/nba-draft.htm.

USSportsCamps. 2015. "What NBA Scouts Look for in Players 20 and Younger." www.ussportscamps.com/tips/basketball/what-nba-scouts-look-for-in-athletes-20-and-younger.

Vecsey, George. 2006. *Baseball: A History of America's Favorite Game*. New York: The Modern Library.

Vrentas, Jenny. 2016. "Behind Closed Doors at the NFL Combine." *MMQB* (March 1). http://mmqb.si.com/mmqb/2016/03/01/nfl-combine-miami-dolphins-formal-interview-quarterback.

Waldron, Travis. 2015. "Concussions Are at the Heart of a New Lawsuit against the NHL." *ThinkProgress* (May 15). http://thinkprogress.org/sports/2015/05/15/3659487/family-deceased-former-hockey-player-will-sue-nhl-concussions/.

Weir, David R., James S. Jackson, and Amanda Sonnega. 2009. "Study of Retired NFL Players." National Football League Player Care Foundation (September 10). http://ns.umich.edu/Releases/2009/Sep09/FinalReport.pdf.

Whyno, Stephen. 2013. "NHL: Fighting Survey Shows Many Hockey Fans Want Ban, Players Don't." *The Canadian Press* (November 7). www.thestar.com/sports/hockey/2013/11/07/nhl_fighting_survey_shows_canadian_hockey_fans_want_ban_players_dont.html.

Wiedeman, Reeves. 2012. "David Stern's Legacy." *New Yorker* (October 26). www.newyorker.com/online/blogs/sportingscene/2012/10/david-sterns-legacy.html.

Wilkins, Charles. 1985. *Hockey: The Illustrated History*. Toronto, Canada: Doubleday Canada Limited.

Williams, Pete. 2006. *The Draft: A Year Inside the NFL's Search for Talent*. New York: St. Martin's Press.

Young, Dick, 2014. "Joe DiMaggio Ends His Legendary Yankees Career in 1951—Dimag Quits as Player for a TV Post." *Daily News* (November 25). (Originally published on December 12, 1951). www.nydailynews.com/sports/baseball/yankees/dimag-quits-player-tv-post-article-1.2010069.

Zimmer, Timothy E. 2016. "The Impact of NFL Salary Cap Concentration on Team Success." *Sport Management International Journal* 12: 53–66.

5

WITHOUT FAME AND FORTUNE: PRO TEAM SPORTS AT THE MARGINS

At 26 Amber Patton was a fastpitch softball star, who played for the Chicago Bandits, one of the league's top teams. Talking about being in National Pro Fastpitch (NPF), Patton started sobbing—not because she was declining as a player but because the salary was simply too low to sustain her, prompting her to consider quitting. "I just really, really hope that this league takes off and people aren't faced with this decision," Patton explained. "It's tough, but you have to make a living" (Seminara 2013).

Amber Patton's experience is hardly unusual in NPF or, in fact, in any of the five so-called "niche" pro sports covered in this chapter. The participants in a pro niche sport represent a distinct subsegment of organized sports, drawing modest revenues from ticket sales and TV programming (Buning, Coble, and Kerwin 2015, 53) and sometimes featuring financially challenged owners who are hard-pressed or simply unable to meet teams' expenses.

Generally players in niche pro sports suffer *structural vulnerability*—a condition where individuals, groups, or larger units like sports leagues face deficiencies in such critical resources as money, productive networks, or strategic information, inhibiting positive outcomes for the participants and the organizations to which they belong (Doob 2013, 225–26; Rank 2004). In short, the victims of structural vulnerability suffer not only a financial deficit but like Amber Patton the psychological effects of living a severely disadvantaged life. In particular, players in niche sports know that they are considerably less affluent, less known, and less acclaimed than their counterparts in the major leagues.

This chapter clearly illustrates the history-and-biography perspective—that though distinctly talented, athletes in these six pro leagues are pursuing their sports in historical settings that make them structurally vulnerable, perhaps even unable to earn a living. For hard-working athletes and coaches it proves frustrating: The commitment to their teams' institutional logics appears to be as fierce and unrelenting as their counterparts in the major leagues display, and yet the financial rewards and public acclaim are considerably more modest.

Most of the salary issues involve individual leagues and their separate struggles, but in one modern instance, a comparison of female and male salaries in the same sport has been highlighted.

In 2016 five members of the US women's national soccer team, all of whom played in the pro National Women's Soccer League (NWSL), filed a wage-discrimination suit with the Equal Employment Opportunity Commission against the US Soccer Federation, citing figures for 2015 indicating that the women's team with its World Cup victory produced nearly $20 million more in revenue than their male counterparts but received only about a quarter of the men's pay. The World Cup final against Japan drew 26 million US viewers, the most to ever watch a soccer game.

In comparison, since finishing third in 1930, the men's team never advanced beyond the World Cup quarterfinals (Fagan 2016; Robinson and Futterman 2016; U.S. Soccer 2002). Hope Solo, the team's goaltender was forthright. "The numbers speak for themselves," said Ms. Solo. "We are the best in the world, have three World Cup championships, four Olympic championships, and the [men's national team] get[s] paid more to just show up than we get paid to win major championships" (Robinson and Futterman 2016). The US Soccer Federation countered, claiming that the differing rates of pay were based on the fact that from 2008 to 2015 men's national-team revenues were nearly three times as great as women's and that no gender discrimination occurred (Goldberg 2016a).

Top players Carli Lloyd and Megan Rapinoe joined head coach Jill Ellis and Mayor Bill DeBlasio on Broadway in New York City's parade to celebrate the victory of the US women's soccer team in the 2015 World Cup. (Soucre: lev radin / Shutterstock.com)

In April 2017 the women's national soccer team reached an agreement with the US Soccer Federation, providing a sharp increase in compensation and benefits and covering five years, including the 2019 World Cup and the 2020 Olympics. While the compensation remains less than men's, some players might find their income doubling, with earnings between $200,000 and $300,000 a year—a rare, significant victory for players in the less affluent pro sports (Rios 2017).

As the focus shifts to the history of the niche leagues, it becomes apparent that they are not only less well-off than the top four but also less established, facing struggles to get started and to remain in business.

The History of the Niche Leagues

Before the WNBA's debut in June 1997, there was the Women's Professional Basketball League (WBL), which began in 1978 and contained 300 players, most of whom came from 26 colleges possessing fairly well-developed basketball programs (Porter 2006, 38–39). The WBL coaches were generally men, with only a small number of qualified female coaches available at the time. Most of those women were already settled in established college programs and were unwilling to trade stable, well-paying positions for jobs in the new, unpredictable league (Porter 2006, 238).

Because many of the owners lacked sufficient cash to support their teams, the players were often poorly paid. Marshall Geller, the owner of the league's San Francisco Pioneers, addressed the potentially dire prospects of a league exposed to structural vulnerability. He declared, "You are never going to get anywhere if you present an image to the public that you are living hand to mouth ... Players are sleeping in cars. Girls are going to the press and telling them they haven't been paid. Arenas are shutting down unless the league wired them money tomorrow" (Porter 2006, 239). It was a hopeless situation, with the athletes persistent victims of structural vulnerability, and after three years the league ceased. In contrast, the WNBA eventually proved superior.

At its start the WNBA was pitted against the American Basketball League (ABL), which had a debut in the fall of 1996. The ABL officials chose cities where teams could build on the presence of strong women's college programs. Players received a surprisingly good financial package, with salaries averaging $80,000 a year along with medical insurance and stock-purchase options. The opening year nine of 12 Olympians and most top collegians signed with the ABL. It was an encouraging start, and league officials spoke about their independence, bragging that they were free of control from the NBA (Basketball Research 2016).

The ABL's triumph, however, was short-lived. In the spring of 1997, three recent Olympic gold medalists, Sheryl Swoopes, Rebecca Lobo, and Lisa Leslie, snubbed the ABL and joined the WNBA. They realized the WNBA was less independent, but they saw a distinct advantage coming from NBA commissioner David Stern's support. Stern said, "I had no doubt about it. Here was an opportunity to develop new fans, more programming, have arena content outside the NBA season, give more girls an incentive to play basketball. Because if you play, there's more chance you'll be a lifelong basketball fan. So we thought it was an ultimate winner. But we knew it was going to be a long haul" (Voepel 2016).

With NBA backing, the WNBA lined up telecasting deals with *NBC*, *ESPN*, and *Lifetime Television* as well as such sponsors as Sears,

Coca-Cola, and McDonald's. Meanwhile during the ABL's second year, investors began losing faith in the league, recognizing the WNBA had a much more robust marketing future. WNBA attendance averaged over twice the ABL turnout. A third of the way through its third season the ABL folded (Slusser 1998).

The WNBA is clearly the most successful women's professional league in US sports history, possessing a six-year contract with *ESPN*, a steady influx of graduated college stars, and 20 years completed. After the WBL's mere three years, it was notable that the WNBA would last more than six times as long and still be going strong.

On the other hand, several factors indicate that the league is hardly as successful as the men's major pro leagues, displaying, in fact, indications of being structurally vulnerable. Attendance has settled at about 7,500 per game, a bit less than half the NBA turnout. Women's salaries are a tiny fraction of men's. Furthermore, with six teams folding in the first decade of the 21st century, instability has been an ongoing concern. In addition, critics sometimes emphasize the extent of NBA involvement, including the outright ownership of six of the league's 12 teams; most notably, Los Angeles Dodgers owners bought the high-profile Los Angeles Sparks (*ESPN* 2017; Rohlin 2014). Such an arrangement, some observers say, makes the women's league just a vanity project subjected to those wealthy businessmen's control. Debate about NBA involvement in the league currently persists.

Men's pro soccer is the other niche sport that has a fairly lengthy history. The North American Soccer League (NASL) was a semi-pro operation from the late 1960s to the middle 1970s. Then in 1975 Pelé, the Brazilian superstar and three-time World Cup winner, came out of retirement to play for the New York Cosmos, an expansion team owned by the media conglomerate Warner Communications (*Qz.com* 2014). Pelé's impact was immediate. Previously the team had provided Burger King vouchers and bumper stickers to draw even modest turnouts—only 5,277 at the home game before the superstar's initial appearance.

Now with Pelé in the lineup, the stadium possessing a capacity of 22,500 was quickly filled, with as many as 50,000 more turned away. Shortly afterwards the team switched its home games to Giants' Stadium with its 77,000 seating. In addition, during the Pelé years, the club could do the previously impossible—induce several major European players to join the Cosmos. On the road the team sold out all their games, and at home such celebrities as Mick Jagger, Henry Kissinger, Robert Redford, and Steven Spielberg became ardent regulars. Press conferences, which had previously occurred in locker rooms, now moved to the 21 Club or the Grand Ballroom of the Plaza Hotel with growing swarms of journalists following a team seemingly bound for international renown (Newsham 2005; 2006, 66).

Pelé did well financially, earning in his three-year Cosmos stint more than he had in 19 years with Santos, his famed Brazilian club. In October 1977 Pelé retired after his last game at Giants Stadium. The impact was pronounced, emphasizing the importance of one player's presence for the league's sudden success and, once he left, highlighting NASL's structural vulnerability. In the following years, attendance plummeted, an important television deal in the works collapsed, and prominent European stars headed home as hard times promoted salary-cap enforcement. By 1985 the NASL had expired (Newsham 2005).

Soccer has generally been a tough sell in the US. One reason it has trouble securing a foothold has been the nature of the competition—the fact that on the field players tend to remain consistently positioned in relation to teammates, generally doing little that spectators find remarkable or surprising. Because of the size of the playing area, for example, there is little chance for defenders to emulate some NHL counterparts, suddenly driving deeply into the offensive end. In addition, prospective American fans tend to feel soccer lacks the statistical wealth that is available when examining other major sports; it is a low-scoring game, with players at just a few positions obtaining the lion's share of the goals and assists. Furthermore soccer has suffered an additional disadvantage, being a fast-moving, pass-oriented game that with the advent of radio in the 1920s required special verbal agility to broadcast effectively while baseball, inevitably slow-paced, readily allowed easy-going, detailed commentary (Apostolov 2012, 525; Scott 2011, 834–36). Yet in spite of the drawbacks, American professional soccer has recently done quite well.

The upturn began when the US hosted the 1994 World Cup. While many foreigners questioned if the nation could effectively run a big-time soccer tournament, the results were impressive, with a total of 3.6 million spectators and an average turnout per game of 68,991, making it to date the best attended World Cup ever. In addition, the American team entry was respectable. The United States Soccer Federation (USSF) had established a training program that produced a steadily improving unit, which made it past the first round, holding eventual champion Brazil to a scoreless tie until the 70th minute of their round-of-sixteen match. The US defense was stellar, yielding just four goals in four games. Following the tournament, players like Tab Ramos, Cobi Jones, Eric Wynalda, Claudio Reyna, and Alexi Lalas were recognized in public. At this time the leadership in American soccer felt it was opportune to make another attempt to establish a soccer league (Litterer 2010; U.S. Soccer 2017).

Major League Soccer (MLS) features separate franchises, 22 in 2017, with owners who are financially responsible for their clubs. However, unlike other American pro sports, the league office controls all player dealings such as signings and salaries. Unlike the NASL, MLS leaders have promoted parity, which they believe is essential to create and maintain fan interest. The original team owners endorsed these ideas, contributing $75 million to meet the league's expenses for the opening five years. Business support was robust, with MLS obtaining ten corporate sponsors as well as TV contracts with *ABC*, *ESPN*, *ESPN2*, and *Univision*.

Recognizing a niche league's precarious state, the MLS leadership planned carefully. While prominent European players would draw fans, it was essential to display a distinct American majority. The league limited each team to five foreign players, along with 15 Americans. To maintain parity, clubs faced an overall salary cap of $1.25 million per year and a relatively low player maximum of $175,000 a year, with exceptions for four well-known members per team. MLS also included a farm system to promote player development, working out agreements with two active lower-level leagues (Apostolov 2012; Badehausen 2012; Dure 2010, 208; Gonzalez 2017; Wahl 2009, 5).

MLS started in 1996, and it did fairly well, displaying endurance as nine of 11 teams remained stable operations over time. Trying to accelerate league attendance and prestige, MLS in 2007 engaged in a Pelé-like initiative by enticing the renowned David Beckham to join the LA Galaxy for a package composed of salary supplemented by endorsement and merchandising deals that totaled about $32.5 million over five years.

In addition, Beckham signed on for two more years in MLS but only played one more year. During the Beckham era, MLS started or completed four new stadiums and made major renovations of three others, and, in addition, European stars like Thierry Henry and Robby Keane followed him to the US. While TV coverage expanded during Beckham's stay, attendance was mixed—increasing initially, then falling off, and once again increasing during his final year. Finally, Beckham appears to deserve some credit for the fact that when he arrived, teams were worth about $35 million—a figure which rose steadily during his six years, and by 2017 a handful of clubs were valued at over $200 million (DeShriver, Rascher, and Shapiro 2014; Rosenblatt 2017; *USA Today* 2017).

Three other pro leagues involving fastpitch softball, women's soccer, and men's lacrosse have also encountered constant financial struggle. In 1997 the Women's Pro Softball League (WPSL) consisted of four teams located in the eastern United States; former Olympians, collegiate all-Americans, and all-conference players highlighted the squads' 15-member rosters. After four years structural vulnerabilities involving limited funding, high travel costs, and inadequate playing facilities closed down the league (International Softball Federation 2015; McKinney 2016).

From its beginning in 2004 National Pro Fastpitch (NPF), WPSL's successor, has grown slowly. The league leaders have been eager to expand, but survival has been the priority. Commissioner Cheri Kempf indicated that between 2004 and 2007, the leadership was allowing teams to join NPF without making certain that their owners could afford to finance them. For several years Kempf cut back to a four-team league, recognizing that the growth of a niche league needed to be a carefully controlled process. She said, "It was painful, but I knew that we had to shrink before we could grow" (Westly 2016).

The current impediment to growth is the absence of well-heeled owners. Locating talented players is hardly a problem. With about 300 Division I programs graduating players each year, there seem to be enough quality candidates to quadruple the size of the league and still keep the level of performance high (Westly 2016). In 2017 the league had six teams, each of which played 25 regular-season games followed by a four-team playoff. NPF's own digital platform streamed all the games, and *MLB.com* and several channels covered selected contests (National Pro Fastpitch 2017).

Women's pro soccer has displayed a similar struggle. In 1999 Mia Hamm and her teammates on the US women's team hosted the World Cup and won the event, which averaged over 37,000 spectators for 32 matches and surprisingly produced a profit of nearly $2 million. Observers could readily appreciate that this group of bright, energetic women cared about each other, their sport, and the public. It was particularly unusual to see such prominent players give so much attention to their adoring young fans (Grainey 2012, 26–32).

It seemed to be the moment to start a women's pro soccer league—the Women's United Soccer Association (WUSA). Most marketing efforts featured Mia Hamm, and the demands soon overwhelmed her, making her play ineffective and adversely affecting her team, which won only six of 21 games. The other discouraging news the first year was typical of a team with structural vulnerability —that the league's $40 million in investment money was used up before the playoffs (Grainey 2012, 49–50).

Through the league's three years, attendance declined steadily—from an average of 8,116 in 2001 to 6,667 in 2003. WUSA officials never had a clear strategy about how both to promote their enthusiastic effort to get young girls interested in soccer and also to sell their product to a target audience. While it was fine to interest the girls, the league desperately needed to start filling seats with paying adults (Grainey 2012, 58–60).

WUSA folded, and in 2009 the Women's Professional League (WPL) formed and never effectively got off the ground. To attempt to keep the operation going, officials cut the regular schedule and the All-Star game. During the league's three years, its modest attendance (4,518 in 2009) steadily dropped, and its minimal TV coverage received low ratings (Grainey 2012, 57–59). WPL's most emphatic lesson seemed clear: That even though a women's pro league is important to Americans and that even if the players are very good, a niche team will not succeed unless a strong business plan guides it (Galarcep 2014).

As the National Women's Soccer League (NWSL) formed, its leaders stayed focused on that idea. Soccer officials for the current league have fully recognized that their players are challenged financially. At the same time, however, they are painfully aware that two earlier leagues failed after three years, and relatively high salaries contributed. Christie Rampone, who played in all three leagues, said that the two previous ventures "went a little big on salaries and the way we traveled." She added, "We lost a lot of money quick" (Quon 2014).

Another new venture has been a men's pro lacrosse league. The two men who formed Major League Lacrosse (MLL) in 1998 have been pleased with how they did it: 14 years later in a book they wrote about founding the league. Jake Steinfeld, one of the partners, related, "We shook hands, and that was that. No contract, no lawyer, no partnership agreement—just a handshake. To this day that's all Dave and I have ever had—a handshake" (Steinfeld and Morrow 2012, 24). A similar energy and camaraderie is apparent in the current league, even though it remains small and struggling.

In 2017 MLL had nine teams and a total of 63 regular-season games, meaning seven games per team between April and August. In addition, there was the MLL All-Star Week-end, two semi-finals, and the MLL Championship Game. The league contained 230 players, who had attended the most renowned lacrosse-playing colleges. In 2016 attendance at games averaged 3,733 spectators (Major League Lacrosse 2016a). The following year the Lax Sports Network televised the league's regular-season games; in addition, there were partnerships with various regional sports networks along with availability on *ESPN3* (Major League Lacrosse 2016b).

An indoor league also developed. In 2016 each of the nine teams in the National Lacrosse League (NLL) played 18 games in the regular season, averaging 9,152 spectators a game, an increase of 2 percent from the previous year (*Inside Lacrosse* 2016).

The female counterpart, the United Women's Lacrosse League (UWLL), started in 2016 and has been composed of four teams, which are all located in eastern states. Its 80 members have not received salaries, only compensation for travel. Between 2012 and 2015, average attendance declined 21 percent (Shaffer 2016).

While women's lacrosse has a pro league, women's professional volleyball has failed to develop in the United States. In 1987 Major League Volleyball formed and received some TV coverage, but it featured players who were not good enough to join top foreign leagues in Italy and Japan and ran on a tiny budget that forced closure in 1989 (Smith 2017). For women it was the only pro indoor volleyball league that even got off the ground. However, in recent years American women have entered foreign pro leagues in large numbers, with USA Volleyball, the governing body for the sport, processing international transfer certificates for 217 American women allowing them to compete in foreign volleyball leagues in at least 32 countries for the 2017–18 season. Some of those women play on the US Women's National Volleyball Team, which has compiled a 126–24 record since the celebrated Karch Kiraly, the only individual to win Olympic gold medals in both indoor and beach volleyball, became head coach in 2012 (Kauffman 2017a, 2017b).

As upcoming references indicate, elite performers in three women's pro leagues along with volleyball have a chance to play for good salaries abroad, but for lacrosse, which is primarily a North American game, no such option exists.

With discussion shifting from the past to the present, the focus falls on some of the challenges these marginal leagues face.

Growing Pains for the Niche Sports

The six pro leagues vary considerably in their revenue intake and players' salaries. This section presents material that demonstrates how structurally vulnerable players in these leagues have adjusted to their often challenging careers. To date little information is available about the United Women's Lacrosse League, which is barely underway. MLS, the oldest of the niche leagues, had its inaugural season in 1996.

Major League Soccer (MLS)

Among second-tier pro leagues, MLS leads the way financially, obtaining contracts in 2015 with *ESPN*, *Fox Sports*, and *Univision* that run through 2022 and provide about $90 million annually, tripling payments from the preceding contract (Marcin 2016). Meanwhile players' earnings have been increasing. In 2016 the mean salary was $316,777 a year, a boost of 8.5 percent from the previous year. The mean calculation, however, requires commentary, reflecting the impact of the small number of star players who receive multiple millions. In this instance the median figure

MLS has been a particularly successful niche sport. The league has 23 teams, with 20 in the US and three in Canada. This photo shows Michael Bradley, a top American player for Toronto FC, controlling the ball in a game against the New York Red Bulls. (Source: lev radin / Shutterstock.com)

avoids that distortion and not surprisingly is much lower —$117,000 (Carlisle 2016).

Among the sports discussed in this book, soccer is the only one in which a host of other countries are more accomplished than the US. As the adjacent Box 5.1 indicates, how to improve men's soccer is an issue that concerns and often divides MLS and national team officials.

BOX 5.1

US Male Soccer Pros' Role: Is Playing Abroad an Essential Requirement?

Fédération Internationale de Football Association (FIFA), the world governing body for soccer, indicated in 2017 that the US men's national team ranked 35th, considerably below its average of 20th since FIFA started its rating system in 1993 (*FIFA.com* 2017). The most accomplished nations play what is widely known as "the beautiful game," displaying expert, elegantly orchestrated, and visually captivating play with which they can confront the US in international competition and usually dominate the upstart, a relatively recent arrival to the world scene. So far American entries have hardly been an embodiment of the beautiful game. Theirs has been a difficult challenge worth examining and a case where a national team has an ongoing, sometimes controversial influence on the domestic pro league.

As foreign experts observe the American soccer scene, they can readily see major defects. So when Jurgen Klinsmann, the rare combination of a former world-class player and an astute coach and organizer, became US men's national soccer team coach, he was bluntly critical about the length of the MLS season, saying that a seven- or eight-month span per year was too short and that instead they should be active ten or even 11 months. Referring to a hypothetical national team member, Klinsmann said, "If he comes and says that [he needs a break after the MLS season], then I give him a hug and say, 'Have fun the six weeks, but don't come back here'" (Schaerlaeckens 2011).

Lengthening the season might prove useful, but Klinsmann has argued that the most important step to improve top American players is constant competition against quality players—Europeans, who represent top-level competition. At first glance an evaluator might say that Klinsmann is unquestionably correct—that his approach can simply make leading American players better in a soccer world where they have a long way to go to equal many other countries' leading competitors. A difficulty, however, is that sending top Americans abroad will lose some or perhaps many of them to European leagues. MLS personnel are particularly concerned that a number of the best MLS academy graduates, who trained since childhood with high-quality coaches under the costly sponsorship of a league team, will simply find the European level of play more appealing and lucrative, leading to their departure from domestic hire (Carlisle 2014; Schaerlaeckens 2011). In their structurally vulnerable league, MLS leaders contend, they can simply not afford to lose top performers.

So angry or at least irritated exchanges occurred as the two sides emphasized opposing priorities. The MLS commissioner considered it "detrimental" to the league when Klinsmann said that top players Michael Bradley and Clint Dempsey would have trouble maintaining their superior form after leaving Europe and returning to play in MLS. Klinsmann, in turn, basically held his line, asserting that the experience appropriate for different players often varied: "Some kids would benefit from the environment in Europe, while others are best suited to continue their growth in MLS" (Carlisle 2014).

Klinsmann's designation of two player categories seems to have been a discreet suggestion that while the most gifted American athletes needed European exposure to become adjusted to the top international level, the less gifted were better suited to play in the somewhat inferior US league. Such an outlook is hardly unique. When Italy manager Antonio Conte was assembling a team for the European championships, he left off two potential candidates who were in MLS. When asked why, Conte was blunt, saying that he and his associates assessed the two performers and felt they were below standard. He was equally direct about the American league. "It's normal that if you go and play there then you can pay the consequences in footballing terms" (Doyle 2016).

Such low opinions of MLS will not go away until US officials dedicated to bringing American soccer into the forefront of the game have achieved a level of domestic play that is competitive with top European and Latin American performance. In June 2016 the national team composed of players in various leagues produced mixed results. With 12 members in MLS and the other 11 in European leagues (MLS 2016), the national team lost 4 to 0 to top-ranked Argentina in the semifinals of Copa América Centenario, so fully outplayed that they never even managed a single shot on goal. And yet earlier in the tournament the US team did well, winning three times and achieving the coach's pretournament objective of reaching the semifinals. Klinsmann, seemingly accepting that the results were mixed, said, "There will always be a step backwards and then two more forward."

To promote that advancement, he resumed his standard argument, advocating team members' frequent play against top international competition. Speaking hypothetically to the president of the US Soccer Federation, Klinsmann urged, "If ever we can get a friendly with Argentina, please do it. With Brazil, please do it. Even if we get [harsh] lessons here and there, that's part of our process. You've got to take those teams on in order to learn" (Waldstein 2016).

That can be a challenging task because modestly performing national teams have limited opportunities to face top competition. In 2016 the US men's soccer team seeking to qualify for the Olympics and composed of all but three members 23 and under failed to be one of the 16 squads that made it. In this instance the opportunity denied seemed especially significant. Alexi Lalas, a soccer analyst who played in the 1992 and 1996 Olympics, indicated that the lasting value of that participation is not so much the games themselves as it is the experiencing of the tournament atmosphere. "You learn the way to play in a tournament," he said. "The way you play in a tournament is very different than the way you play ... friendlies and certainly in a club situation. It is a unique and specific type of skill. That's part of why Germany is so good — yes, they're good at soccer in general, but they're also very good at tournament play" (Murray 2016). As Lalas emphasized, the development of individuals' roles can sometimes benefit significantly from exposure to certain specific experiences. A few weeks later Lalas's statement about the quality of German soccer was corroborated when its men's Olympic team narrowly lost the gold medal in the finals to Brazil in a hotly contested penalty shootout. Meanwhile it is apparent that the US men's national team continues to fall short of top international standards.

In 2016 following a streak of poor team performances, Klinsmann was fired. His overall record as head coach was 55-27-16, and his 12-straight wins, 16 victories, and 76.1 winning percentage in 2013 are American national-team records (Tansey 2016;

> U.S. Soccer 2016). Following Klinsmann's dismissal Bruce Arena, a former US soccer head coach, replaced him, serving for 11 months but then stepping down soon after the team lost to Trinidad and Tobago and for the first time since 1986 failed to qualify for the World Cup (*CNN* 2017). At that time it seemed that the deficiencies in the national program Klinsmann had emphasized were still painfully apparent.

Like MLS the WNBA has had a two-decade existence.

Women's National Basketball Association (WNBA)

This league has proved quite successful, though through the years it has encountered many struggles. Finances to be sure have been a constant concern. In 1998 and 2009, attendance averaged over 10,000 spectators a game, but in 2015 it was 7,318, the lowest in league history. Certain encouraging signs have been apparent—for instance, in 2015 the league had 25 sellouts, 14 more than the previous season (*Las Vegas Review-Journal* 2015), and in 2016 attendance averaged 7,655 spectators, the highest in five years (*WNBA.com* 2016).

The low turnouts can be disturbing to players, bringing to mind the psychological challenge of structural vulnerability. In 2014 Maya Moore, the league's top draftee in 2011, wrote an article about playing in the WNBA. Elite players like her, she explained, went from exciting AAU travel teams to high-school All-American games, and then college, which in her case included two national championships at UConn. Moore wrote,

> In college, your coaches tell you to stay focused on your team and the game—not the media attention. But you know you're on national television. You know people are following you. You can feel the excitement. And then as a professional, all of that momentum, all of that passion, all of that support—the ball of momentum is deflating before my eyes.
>
> (Payne 2015)

The structural vulnerability of playing in a niche league, Moore was suggesting, can be distressing—especially for someone like her, who came from a highly acclaimed college program with rabid fans. League leaders, however, have worked hard to keep making improvements.

A fairly encouraging development is that in 2013 the WNBA signed a six-year TV deal with *ESPN*, covering the years 2017 through 2022 and paying about $12 million a year or about $1 million per team (Lefton and Ourand 2013). However, the league's total revenues are modest, and as a result women's salaries are low, averaging about $75,000 a year (Berri 2015), with a rookie minimum of $34,500 and a maximum of $95,000 (*Best Basketball Tips* 2017).

As a result many players find themselves strapped for funds. A common response for the better performers is to follow up the WNBA season by playing abroad, depriving themselves of any significant offseason. Tamika Catchings, who played ten years in the WNBA and eight abroad, explained, "I know some of my teammates, we lost on a Tuesday and some of them were overseas on that Friday and they'll get back in April" (Lebron 2014). Then WNBA preseason practice would start in May. In the 2016 offseason, 63 players from all 12 WNBA teams joined leagues in Russia, Turkey, China, Italy, and several other European and Asian countries (Barker 2016).

In February 2015 Diana Taurasi, who was MVP in the league finals and led the Phoenix Mercury to a third WNBA championship the previous year, chose to sit out the upcoming season. In fact, UMMC Ekaterinburg, the Russian team for which she played in the offseason, prompted that decision by paying her more than her WNBA salary to take the summer off and rest (*Fox Sports* 2015). Taurasi was grateful for the Russian team's support and the benefit its officials provided her. She said, "I'm really lucky to even have these options. It speaks volumes on how UMMC values our relationship, and vice versa. For ten years, I have never had any significant time off" (Fagan 2015).

Besides the inordinate time on the court each year, the WNBA members abroad often face difficult travel conditions, taking buses and not airplanes the way they do at home, and must endure fairly primitive training methods, which sometimes can make them more vulnerable to injury than in the WNBA. On that subject Tamika Catchings said, "It takes a toll on my body. You look at my knees and my ankle, and injuries have been bad for me" (Steele 2012). Catchings was hardly alone.

Michelle Snow, who besides the WNBA played in five foreign countries, provided an inventory of her injuries. "I don't think there's anything left to break," she said, pointing out past fractures to her tibia, toe, nose, cheekbone, and finger (Ryan 2011). But the money is quite good, and so many in this niche league keep playing abroad.

Leading WNBA members like Diana Taurasi, who has earned $1.5 million a year playing abroad, receive unusually high salaries because they can contribute to top finishes in one of the European leagues, which can qualify the team for participation in one of two elite competitions—either the Euro League or the Euro Cup. Teams which win either one of these championships gain considerably in prestige and pride and, to some extent, increased revenue (Mumcu 2015).

Besides foreign play WNBA members sometimes develop original plans for bolstering their income. Like other top league competitors, Angel McCoughtry, an eight-year veteran, spent the offseason playing abroad. In 2017, however, she couldn't keep it up, and she took a year off. "My body was speaking to me," McCoughtry said. "I was always tight. I was always mentally drained from playing all year round. I had plantar fasciitis [inflammation of the thick tissue on the bottom of the foot]. It was tough and I knew that it was time to recover if I wanted longevity in my career" (Andrews 2017). McCoughtry, however, didn't just relax but spent the year setting up an ice cream parlor in Atlanta. Her fiancé said that starting the business had made McCoughtry very happy, showing her "that she can be responsible for something else outside of basketball." McCoughtry planned to keep the ice cream parlor going after playing (Andrews 2017).

The WNBA and MLS hardly compare in salaries, facilities, media coverage, and public attention with the top four men's pro leagues, but their various assets are considerably greater than those of the upcoming three niche leagues.

National Pro Fastpitch (NPF)

Women's pro fastpitch softball is a highly skilled game, which has drawn limited spectator support. In 2014 Cat Osterman, a top pitcher, threw a shutout against the Chicago Bandits. Media darling and retired NPF pitcher Jennie Finch was on hand, along with two other former Olympic stars, to sign autographs and bolster attendance. Nonetheless just 1,552 spectators showed up (*Sportspagemagazine.com* 2014).

In 2012 attendance averaged about 1,000 fans a game (Riddle 2012), but then in 2015 it increased 26 percent from the previous year (Daniel 2016). That year the league signed a TV deal with *ESPN2* and *ESPN3* for the following year covering 16 games, including the final two contests from the Championship Series, and for 2017 *CBS* agreed to a 25-game TV arrangement with the league (National Pro Fastpitch 2015b; Westly 2016).

In spite of such encouraging signs, however, it's a league where structural vulnerability is a relentless reality. Most players need to hold full-time jobs outside their league. Natalie Villarreal, a second baseman and two-time Big-12 defensive player of the year, missed all but one day of practice as the Dallas Charge prepared for its season. "It's tough," said Villarreal who was getting certified to be a teacher. "No one wants to miss practice, especially with a new team and the first week" (Riddle 2015).

Average NPF salaries have been just $3,000 to $10,000 a year, with stars making at least several times more, notably one superstar. In the spring of 2016, the Houston-based Scrap Yard Dawgs received national attention when the team leadership decided to pay ace pitcher Monica Abbott $1 million for six years, which is believed to be the highest salary ever for a female athlete in US pro team sports (Lombardo 2015; National Pro Fastpitch 2015a; Westly 2016).

Meanwhile an indication of players' economic vulnerability is that they face a decidedly nomadic existence. Most of the teams do not have a home stadium, playing at minor-league baseball fields or college softball parks. The exception has been the Chicago Bandits, which had its own 2,000-seat softball facility opened in 2011 (Menaker 2012; Placek 2017).

For top performers the nomadic experience has often stretched farther afield, with the chance to play in Japan, where the best Americans can receive $60,000 or more a season as members of corporate-sponsored teams. It can be an eye-opening experience. Pitcher Keilani Ricketts said that while the Japanese display less power, "[T]heir defense is amazing, [and] I don't even have to field a ground ball because they field everything behind me" (*Soonersports.com* 2013).

Kristen Butler, a member of the Akron Racers, has spent several offseasons in Japan playing for the Denso Bright Pegasus. The Japanese teams, which can only recruit two foreigners each, are primarily inclined to sign pitchers and catchers, and Butler is a catcher. At the games, pep bands and cheerleaders are often present. Butler was enthusiastic. "It's phenomenal," she said. "They treat you like a rock star over there" (Williams 2009). She embraced the new tradition, living in the Denso team house while learning the language, the training regimen, and the country's customs. "I just feel very blessed that I've been given the opportunity to be able to pursue the sport that I love in the way that I'm able to do it," Butler said (D'Agruma 2015). This was a case of a player who in a foreign setting was able to escape some of the disheartening effects her NPF peers normally suffer as participants in a niche sport.

Like NPF members, NWSL players can find that in spite of the limited pay, the pro experience is rewarding.

National Women's Soccer League (NWSL)

In 2013 as the NWSL developed, the leadership assessed its structural vulnerability, taking some unprecedented steps to keep the league solvent: Having the three North American federations pay for stars from their respective countries, thereby sparing the league that major expense; and, in addition, convincing US Soccer to assume the burden for the myriad front-office expenses the league has produced. When developing its business plan for running the front office, US Soccer emphasized the necessity of keeping expenses down, ending up with a feasible budget that was less than a third that of WPL, NWSL's short-lived predecessor (Foudy 2013).

While NWSL is well organized, its revenues make it a modest operation. Almost all of its ten teams play in small facilities, drawing modest crowds—in 2016, 16,945 on average for the Portland Thorns with most other clubs attracting many fewer spectators—an average of 5,585 (*Soccer Stadium Digest* 2016). In 2017 *Lifetime* televised 22 regular season games (Anderson 2017).

Predictably players' salaries are low—$7,200 to $39,700 a year, with the majority toward the lower end of the scale. To compensate for their limited income, most of the participants must work second jobs or receive financial support from families and friends. In addition, many stay with host families during the season. What players manage to survive with such salaries? Primarily college students or recent college graduates and generally athletes with little national-team experience (McCann 2014; McCauley 2016; Mendola 2015). Kate Deines, who retired at 25, said that she could not afford to keep turning down business opportunities to play in the low-paying league. "It definitely feels like an extension of college life, and it is way less glamorous than college," Deines concluded (Mendola 2015).

In certain respects, however, NWSL contains an exceptional team. In each of its five years, the Portland Thorns has increased attendance, averaging 17,653 fans in 2017—surprisingly more than 15 NBA teams, 13 NHL teams, and one MLB team. Precisely why is not clear, but some distinct suggestions are apparent (Murray 2017). Since the 1970s the city of Portland has been a strong supporter of professional soccer. In fact, in 1975 as the Portland Timbers, a men's team, won a playoff game in the now defunct North American Soccer League, a franchise executive designated Portland "Soccer City, USA" (Goldberg 2016b).

Unquestionably a major reason the Thorns has been successful has been its affiliation with the modern version of the Timbers. As NWSL formed, the head of US Soccer approached several MLS executives about supporting the new women's teams in their cities, and the Timbers' owner was the only one to respond. In fact, he bought the club, allowing the Thorns to make full use of the Timbers' 130 front-office employees. The Timbers connection, however, is more than administrative. Throughout the city people gain a sense of the two pro soccer teams in partnership; entering Providence Park, where both teams play their home games, people see a marquee with equal-sized logos of the Thorns and the Timbers on its opposite sides.

In addition, Portland possesses what many feel have become very special fans. A player explained. "They're almost a community outside of what's happening on the field," Thorns midfielder Tobin Heath said. "They love us and support us, but they love each other and support each other, which is cool. What we're doing on the field is inspiring this idea of community" (Murray 2017). Unquestionably the Thorns has been a major success, but observers need to consider a distinct reservation—that as participants in a niche league, the team invariably experiences the same limitations as the other teams in limited attendance at away games and modest TV coverage.

One more issue about women's pro soccer: What about the option of playing abroad, which some basketball and softball players are able to do? It exists for top players. In 2017 three of them signed with European clubs. These short-term deals can pay substantial salaries, over $100,000 for several months of play in two cases, and provide the participants superior training and playing facilities compared to those in the United States (Goff 2017; Withiam 2017). The athletes indicated that the experience was productive. Crystal Dunn, who joined Chelsea in London, said, "I've only been there four weeks, but I already feel a change in how I view myself as a player." She added, "It has been eye-opening. I'm not used to working 9 to 5, but I'm going in there early and I'm not leaving the training ground until … [the workout is completed]. They are true professionals and I feel like I'm part of a team that lives and breathes and dies soccer" hBell 2017). The quote suggests that because of its distinct assets, women's pro soccer in England might be escaping its niche status.

The final pro league involves men's pro lacrosse.

Major League Lacrosse (MLL)

In 2016 MLL salaries ranged between $10,000 and $25,000 a year (*Altius Directory* 2017). Players realize they are involved in a niche sport and that pay is going to remain minimal. Brett Schmidt, a defender for the Charlotte Hornets, received $10,000 for the season. He explained, "It's more a summer part-time job. Guys are just grateful to be able to play in a league, but the money isn't something you truly rely on" (Garcia 2015). Without exception players need second jobs, but these tend to be distant from the team's location, often creating, as in some other niche sports, a nomadic existence for MLL members. Most of the athletes only appear on the weekends, flying or driving in, playing the game, and then returning to the site of their other job. Matt Danowski, a four-time All-American at Duke, explained, "I wish this were our full-time job." He added, "I wish we could practice five days a week and play Saturday. We're not there yet, but we're pioneers in this thing" (Garno 2014).

While Danowski and most other players earn starvation wages, a rare star receives much more. Paul Rabil has become known as "lacrosse's first million-dollar man." That achievement has primarily resulted from endorsements—Red Bull, New Balance, Go Pro, Polk Audio, and others. Rabil's marketability has developed because of unceasing high-speed, expert play in the league for a half-dozen years, a 111-mph shot, and, most recently, his potent pairing with Rob Pannell at attack for the New York Lizards. Rabil, no longer forced to attack the goal with little help, has often become a feeder, a member of a nearly unparalleled offensive pair reminiscent of top combinations in other sports (Ciampaglia 2013; Flannery 2013; Soshnick 2013; Vaccaro 2015).

Many of Rabil's peers, however, find they earn too little to keep playing the game they love. Summary 5.1 lists factors promoting job instability for the athletes encountering structural vulnerability discussed in this chapter. It appears that the future for these leagues remains uncertain.

SUMMARY 5.1

Job-threatening Challenges for Athletes in Niche Pro Leagues Resulting from Structural Vulnerability and Related Factors

- Limited salaries, tiny in comparison to their counterparts in the four major sports.
- Frequently ineffective plans for league and team development, meaning the players can readily face the impending threat of leagues' demise.
- Elite athletes sometimes displaying uncertain career plans because leaders in a niche league can disagree about key strategies: Most prominently, the debate on whether American men's professional soccer should make its priority the improvement of top players' quality by extensive involvement in European leagues or alternatively those players should stay put in MLS, bolstering its quality.
- Exhaustion and/or repeated injury resulting from lengthy work demands, including WNBA, NPF, and NWSL elite performers each year playing a second season abroad.

Conclusion

It would be interesting to look ahead several decades and see the state of the niche leagues. How many of them will still exist, and how many of those will be healthy financially? Will the US women's national soccer team, perhaps the most militant sports group, continue to protest receiving lower income than male counterparts? Will MLS be any closer to displaying world-class soccer?

Then there's the WNBA, perhaps because of its players' extensive international involvement, the most likely league to undergo a major change. When Diana Taurasi decided to sit out the WNBA with the financial support of her Russian team, it came to light that Taurasi's was not a unique case—that dozens of top American players had been offered bonuses from their foreign clubs to take the season off from WNBA play. Until Taurasi's move, however, that hadn't happened because the players both wanted to keep competing against the world's strongest teams as members of the WNBA and also remained loyal to an American league which they consider has fairly strong ownership, a stable set of 12 teams for a half-dozen years, and the financial backing of a strong TV deal with *ESPN*. Taurasi, however, made a significant move, and in the years ahead others might follow her lead, perhaps forcing the WNBA to change its remuneration structure by finding ways of increasing elite players' salaries, thereby discouraging them from planning to take leaves of absence (Fagan 2015). While prediction here seems difficult, it appears quite certain that current instabilities will produce many changes.

All in all, the prospect of these leagues eliminating structural vulnerability in the future seems limited. However, some encouraging signs are apparent. A study conducted with 215 students enrolled in physical-activity classes at an urban midwestern university indicated that niche pro sports like those featured in this chapter can take steps to increase their attendance and support.

Fans' accessibility to team officials and players can be a potent means of building support for teams in smaller leagues. A given sport's supporters well might feel greater affinity for such athletes than for major leaguers—the shared sense of not being celebrities, just ordinary people—and over time that shared sense can promote loyalty to a team (Greenhaigh, Simmons, Hambrick, and Greenwell 2011, 48–49).

John Arlotta, the co-owner and GM of the Georgia Swarm, has clearly grasped the importance of such a relationship. When he moved his lacrosse team to Atlanta, he explained at his opening press conference that a priority "is getting into the community and giving back, while building support." He added that the team wants to develop "a long-term relationship with the community which we can build on." Later on Arlotta noted, "We don't make money in this business. We're doing this because we're passionate about lacrosse and growing the sport—that's the rationale for doing it" (Hudson 2017). In 2017 the passionate effort paid off when the Swarm won the NLL championship.

Summary

The leagues covered in this chapter face structural vulnerability, often lacking such valued resources as money and productive networks. Yet in spite of the financially linked problems they face, many competitors keep playing, and sometimes a payoff appears. In 2017 the members of the women's national soccer team received a significant boost in compensation and benefits for a five-year period during which both the World Cup and Olympics occur.

The leagues' history is fairly brief. The WNBA began in 1997, proving more appealing to top stars than the ABL. While the WNBA has survived for two decades and has had a lengthy contract with *ESPN* to broadcast games, attendance has been erratic, salaries are small, and six teams folded in the first decade of the 21st century.

Following the successful American hosting of the World Cup, MLS started in 1996. In 2017 the league possessed 22 teams. While the owners are financially responsible for their clubs, MLS has a unique arrangement in which the league office controls all player allocations, signings, salaries, and trades.

In 2016 NPF had six teams, each of which played 25 regular-season games followed by a four-team playoff. With about 300 Division I softball programs graduating players each year, the league has access to enough quality players to expand considerably, but it currently lacks funding for such a venture.

Women's pro soccer has been encountering a similar struggle. NWSL is the third women's pro soccer league since 2001. Its organizers have recognized that to succeed the league requires a much stronger business plan than its predecessors.

Both men and women have pro lacrosse leagues. Men, in fact, have two leagues—an indoor and an outdoor version. In 2017 MLL, the outdoor entry, had nine teams and a total of 63 regular-season games, meaning just seven games per team. The UWLL, the women's pro league, started in 2016 with four teams; the only payment is compensation for travel expenses.

While no women's professional volleyball league currently exists in the United States, top players can join over 30 leagues in European and Asian countries.

In considering the niche leagues' growing pains, a number of issues stand out. While MLS has the most revenues and highest salaries of these six leagues, it faces the challenge of representing a rare sport where many European and Latin American countries are much more proficient at playing the game. Criticism of MLS players' development is widespread, but MLS officials have not been particularly receptive.

While the WNBA has survived for over two decades, its players have received modest pay. The top participants have had a chance to play in foreign countries during the offseason—Turkey and Russia in particular. It can be a tiring way of life, returning home a mere month before the WNBA preseason training starts.

Players in the NPF league not only receive low salaries, but most of the teams don't possess a home stadium. Like WNBA members, some of the top players join foreign teams during the offseason, earning considerably more from corporate-sponsored teams than in the NPF league.

Like their pro counterparts in women's basketball and fastpitch softball, top performers in the NWSL have found that they can earn more money in selected foreign leagues. In pro lacrosse there are no foreign options. One player suggested that they were paid like workers hired for a part-time summer job.

Class Discussion Questions

1. If you were a pro athlete in one of the leagues discussed in this chapter, how would structural vulnerability affect your life? If you loved the sport, would it prove satisfying to take part in it?
2. Does it take a special kind of person to start and nurture a professional sports league in a niche sport? What about team

ownership? Indicate both the principal qualities required for ownership and those to be avoided.
3. Would you be willing to participate in a pro league where teams play in front of small crowds for modest salaries? Are athletes likely to be highly motivated in such a situation?
4. What is your position on the debate about whether top MLS players should remain in the league or alternatively play at least some of the time abroad? Explain.
5. Do you have any information about professional female athletes who have played abroad in one of the four sports discussed here? What was particularly interesting or notable about their experience?
6. Single out one of these leagues that is most likely to do well in the future and one that is likely to fail. In both cases indicate why, referring to specific sources of structural vulnerability.

References

Altius Directory. 2017. "MLL Salaries." www.altiusdirectory.com/Sports/mll-salaries.php.

Anderson, Jason. 2017. "NWSL Announces 2017 National TV Schedule." *SB Nation* (March 30). www.blackandredunited.com/washington-spirit-womens-soccer/2017/3/30/15118290/nwsl-2017-tv-schedule-lifetime.

Andrews, Malika. 2017. "A Way to Extend Her W.N.B.A. Career? Opening an Ice Cream Parlor." *The New York Times* (July 22). www.nytimes.com/2017/07/21/sports/basketball/angel-mccoughtry-wnba-ice-cream-atlanta.html.

Apostolov, Steven. 2012. "Everywhere and Nowhere: The Forgotten Past and Clouded Future of American Professional Soccer from the Perspective of Massachusetts." *Soccer & Society* 13 (July): 1–47.

Badenhausen, Kurt. 2012. "David Beckham Departs MLS after Earning $255 Million." *Forbes* (November 30). www.forbes.com/sites/kurtbadenhausen/2012/11/30/david-beckham-departs-mls-after-earning-255-million/.

Barker, Barbara. 2016. "For WNBA Players, the Real Money Is Overseas." *Newday* (November 19). www.newsday.com/sports/columnists/barbara-barker/wnba-players-are-underpaid-shouldn-t-have-to-play-overseas-1.12639553.

Basketball Research. 2016. "Women's Professional Basketball League." https://sites.google.com/a/asu.edu/womensbasketball/Home.

Bell, Jack. 2017. "3 U.S. Women Embrace European Adventure." *Empire of Soccer* (March 9). www.empireofsoccer.com/3-u-s-women-embrace-european-adventure-58980/.

Berkman, Seth. 2017. "Kelsey Plum Is a Lot Like James Harden. But Is It a Left-Handed Compliment?" *The New York Times* (April 13). www.nytimes.com/2017/04/13/sports/basketball/kelsey-plum-wnba-draft-james-harden-comparisons.html.

Berri, David. 2015. "Basketball's Gender Wage Gap Is Even Worse than You Think." *Vice*

Sports (August 12). https://sports.vice.com/en_us/article/basketballs-gender-wage-gap-is-even-worse-than-you-think.

Best Basketball Tips. 2017. "WNBA Players' Salaries." www.best-basketball-tips.com/wnba-player-salaries.html.

Buning, Richard J., Cassie Coble, and Shannon Kerwin. 2015. "The Progressive Involvement of Youth in Niche Sport: The Perspective of Youth Participants and Their Parents." *Journal of Amateur Sport* 1: 52–80. http://www.jamsport.org/Buningetal2015%20JAS%20PDF.pdf.

Carlisle, Jeff. 2014. "Jurgen Klinsmann Firm on Young Player Advice as MLS Frustration Grows." *ESPN FC* (November 14). www.espnfc.us/team/united-states/660/blog/post/2145959/jurgen-klinsmann-firm-on-young-player-advice-as-mls-frustration-grows.

Carlisle, Jeff. 2016. "Average MLS Salary Goes Up, with Surprising Value Available Leaguewide." *ESPN FC* (May 19). www.espnfc.us/major-league-soccer/19/blog/post/2876311/average-mls-salary-goes-up-with-surprising-value-available-league-wide.

Ciampaglia, Dante A. 2013. "Lacrosse Superstar Paul Rabil Aims to Extend the Sport's Reach." *Sports Illustrated* (September 10). www.sikids.com/si-kids/2016/01/12/paul-rabil-big-shot.

CNN. 2017. "USMNT Head Coach Bruce Arena Resigns after World Cup Humiliation." (October 13). www.theindychannel.com/news/national/usmnt-head-coach-bruce-arena-resigns-after-world-cup-humiliation.

D'Agruma, Mike. 2015. "Kristen Butler Returns to Akron after Off-season in Japan." *Akron.com* (May 5, 20). www.akron.com/akron-ohio-business-news.asp?aID=2841.

Daniel, P.K. 2016. "NPF Enjoying Expansion, TV Exposure and Uptick at the Gate." *X Band Sports*. https://xbandsports.com/a-conversation-with-npf-commissioner-cheri-kempf-npf-enjoying-expansion-increased-television-exposure-and-uptick-at-the-gate/.

DeShriver, Timothy, Daniel Rascher, and Stephen Shapiro. 2014. "The Beckham Effect: David Beckham's Impact on Major League Soccer, 2007–2012." North American Society for Sport Management Conference. www.nassm.com/files/conf_abstracts/2014-044.pdf.

Doob, Christopher B. 2013. *Social Inequality and Social Stratification in US Society*. Boston, MA: Pearson.

Doyle, John. 2016. "Conte and Italy Send Message with an Emphatic Win." *The New York Times* (June 14). www.nytimes.com/2016/06/15/sports/soccer/italy-euro-2016-roster.html?_r=0.

Dure, Beau. 2010. *Long-range Goals: The Success Story of Major League Soccer*. Washington, DC: Potomac Books.

ESPN. 2017. "WNBA Teams." www.espn.com/wnba/teams.

Fagan, Kate. 2015. "Diana Taurasi's Decision to Sit Out Should Spark WNBA Salary Changes." *ESPN* (February 4). http://espn.go.com/wnba/story/_/id/12272036/diana-taurasi-decision-sit-spark-wnba-salary-changes.

Fagan, Kate. 2016. "U.S. Women's Team Files Wage-Discrimination Action vs. U.S. Soccer." *ESPNW* (April 1). http://espn.go.com/espnw/sports/article/15102506/women-national-team-files-wage-discrimination-action-vs-us-soccer-federation.

FIFA.com. 2017. "Men's Ranking." (July 6). www.fifa.com/fifa-world-ranking/associations/association=usa/men/index.html.

Flannery, Jim. 2013. "Paul Rabil of the Philadelphia Wings Becomes Lacrosse's First Million Dollar Man." *Bleacher Report* (April 2). http://bleacherreport.com/articles/1588296-paul-rabil-becomes-lacrosses-first-million-dollar-man.

Foudy, Julie. 2013. "Will NWSL Be a Success? … Well." *ESPNW* (April 13). http://espn.go.com/espnw/news-commentary/article/9161421/espnw-latest-women-professional-soccer-league-success.

Fox Sports. 2015. "Mercury's Diana Taurasi to Rest, Sit Out 2015 WNBA Season." (February 3). www.foxsports.com/arizona/story/phoenix-mercury-diana-taurasi-to-sit-out-2015-wnba-season-020315.

Galarcep, Ives. 2014. "Women's Professional Soccer Shuts Down." *Fox Soccer* (May 21). www.foxsports.com/foxsoccer/usa/story/womens-professional-soccer-league-shut-down-051812.

Garcia, Ahiza. 2015. "The Pro Athletes with Full-time Day Jobs." *CNN Money* (September 28). http://money.cnn.com/2015/09/28/smallbusiness/major-league-lacrosse-salaries/.

Garno, Greg. 2014. "Exhausting Travel and No Pay: Major League Lacrosse Players Stick with It." *Sporting News* (August 15). www.sportingnews.com/other-sports/news/major-league-lacrosse-charlotte-hounds-matt-danowski-nba-mlb-miguel-cabrera/3olqatf1phgl1j3jt0pkhupxm.

Goff, Steven. 2017. "Here's Why U.S. Women's Soccer Stars Are Taking Their Talents to Europe." *The Washington Post* (February 19). www.washingtonpost.com/news/soccer-insider/wp/2017/02/19/heres-why-u-s-womens-soccer-stars-are-taking-their-talents-to-europe/?utm_term=.8a238b8a96aa.

Goldberg, Haley. 2016a. "U.S. Soccer Is Saying There Isn't a Gender Wage Gap." *Trending* (June 3). www.self.com/trending/2016/06/u-s-soccer-is-saying-there-isnt-a-gender-wage-gap/.

Goldberg, Jamie. 2016b. "Portland Thorns' Fan Support Stands Alone in Women's Soccer." *The Oregonian* (June 26). www.oregonlive.com/portland-thorns/2016/06/portland_thorns_fan_support_st.html.

Gonzalez, Roger. 2017. "MLS Expansion: Here's What to Know about the 12 Cities to Submit Franchise Bids." *CBS Sports Digital* (February 1). www.cbssports.com/soccer/news/mls-expansion-heres-what-to-know-about-the-12-cities-to-submit-franchise-bids/.

Grainey, Timothy F. 2012. *Beyond Bend It like Beckham: The Global Phenomenon of Women's Soccer*. Lincoln, NE: University of Nebraska Press.

Greenhaigh, Greg P., Jason M. Simmons, Marion E. Hambrick, and T. Christopher Greenwell. 2011. "Spectator Support: Examining the Attributes That Differentiate Niche from Mainstream Sport." *Sport Marketing Quarterly* 20: 41–52.

Hudson, Phil W. 2017. "Why the Georgia Swarm's NLL Championship Cup Win Should Matter to Atlanta Sports Fans." *Atlanta Business Chronicle*. (June 11). www.bizjournals.com/atlanta/news/2017/06/11/georgia-swarm-brings-atlanta-nll-championship-by.html.

Inside Lacrosse. 2016. "NLL Attendance Climbs 2 Percent in 2016." (June 23). www.insidelacrosse.com/article/nll-attendance-climbs-2-in-2016/35644.

International Softball Federation. 2015. "History of Softball." www.athleticscholarships.net/history-of-softball.htm.

Kauffman, Bill. 2017a. "Preview: New Blood for U.S. Highlights 2017." *USA Volleyball*

(June 7). www.teamusa.org/USA-Volleyball/Features/2017/June/07/Preview-New-Blood-on-Womens-National-Team-to-Highlight-2017.

Kauffman, Bill. 2017b. "U.S. Women's Update: Overseas Pro Season Starts with Bang." Team USA (October 16). www.teamusa.org/USA-Volleyball/Features/2017/October/16/US-Womens-Update-Overseas-Pro-Season-Starts-with-Bang.

Las Vegas Review-Journal. 2015. "2015 WNBA Season Sees Lowest Attendance in League History." (September 16). www.reviewjournal.com/sports/sideline/2015-wnba-season-sees-lowest-fan-attendance-league-history.

Lebron, Steven. 2014. "How Much Women's Basketball Players Make in the U.S. vs. China." *SportsMic* (June 10). http://mic.com/articles/90845/how-much-women-s-basketball-players-make-in-the-u-s-vs-china#.l7gRgyiOJ.

Lefton, Terry, and John Ourand. 2013. "ESPN Signs Six-Year Extension with WNBA Which Is Worth $12M Per Year." *SportsBusinessDaily* (March 28). www.sportsbusinessdaily.com/Daily/Issues/2013/03/28/Media/WNBA.aspx.

Litterer, David. 2010. "An Overview of American Soccer History." *American Soccer History Archives* (May 30). http://homepages.sover.net/~spectrum/overview.html.

Lombardo, Kayla. 2015. "NPF 'Charges' toward Expansion, Establishes a Team in Dallas." *The Kay-Zone.* http://thekayzoneblog.com/tag/national-pro-fastpitch/.

Major League Lacrosse. 2016a. "About MLL." www.majorleaguelacrosse.com/about.

Major League Lacrosse. 2016b. "Watch MLL." (March 29). www.majorleaguelacrosse.com/article/watch-mll.

Marcin, Tim. 2016. "MLS 20/20 Expansion: Is the League's Rapid Growth Plan Too Much Too Soon?" *International Business Times* (April 16). www.ibtimes.com/mls-2020-expansion-leagues-rapid-growth-plan-too-much-too-soon-2354737.

McCann, Alison. 2014. "Low Pay Limits Players' Experience in National Women's Soccer League." *FiveThirtyEight* (March 24). http://fivethirtyeight.com/datalab/low-pay-limits-player-experience-in-national-womens-soccer-league/.

McCauley, Kevin. 2016. "NWSL Has Survived Longer than Any Other Women's Soccer League. When Do Players Get Paid?" *SB Nation* (April 15). www.sbnation.com/soccer/2016/4/15/11409908/nwsl-2016-season-wages-cap-salary-minimum.

McKinney, Kelsey. 2016. "When Will the Women of Professional Softball Get the Attention They Deserve?" *Slinter* (September 5). https://splinternews.com/when-will-the-women-of-professional-softball-get-the-at-1793861662.

Menaker, Elise. 2012. "Pro Softball: 'Not a Lemonade Stand.'" *Medill Reports* (May 30). http://newsarchive.medill.northwestern.edu/chicago/news.aspx?id=206205.

Mendola, Nicholas. 2015. "NWSL Players Open Season 'Chasing the Dream'—Rapinoe Scores Three versus WNY." *NBC Sports* (April 13). www.prosoccertalk.nbcsports.com/2015/04/13/nwsl-players-open-season-chasing-the-dream-rapinoe-scores-3-vs-wny/.

MLS. 2016. "National Team Roster for Copa America." (May 22). www.mlssoccer.com/copa-america/usa/roster.

Mumcu, Ceyda. 2015. "Overseas Opportunities Could Be a Boon for WNBA, Players." *Sports Business Journal* (August 31). www.sportsbusinessdaily.com/Journal/Issues/2015/08/31/Opinion/Ceyda-Mumcu.aspx.

Murray, Caitlin. 2016. "Does It Matter That the USA Men's Soccer Team Didn't Qualify for the Olympics?" *foxsports.com* (August 4). www.foxsports.com/soccer/story/does-it-matter-that-the-usa-men-didn-t-qualify-for-olympics-soccer-080416.

Murray, Caitlin. 2017. "A Blueprint for Women's Sports Success. But Can It Be Copied?" *The New York Times* (October 13). www.nytimes.com/2017/10/13/sports/soccer/portland-thorns-nwsl.html.
National Pro Fastpitch. 2015a. "FAQ's." www.profastpitch.com/about/faqs/.
National Pro Fastpitch. 2015b. "National Pro Fastpitch Reaches 16-Game Deal with ESPN: Six Games to Air on ESPN2; Additional 10 Games Streamed Live on ESPN3." www.profastpitch.com/news/?article_id=1906.
National Pro Fastpitch. 2017. "Official Website of the National Pro Fastpitch League: Home." www.profastpitch.com/.
Newsham, Gavin. 2005. "When Pelé and Cosmos Were Kings." *The Guardian* (June 9). www.theguardian.com/football/2005/jun/10/sport.comment.
Newsham, Gavin. 2006. *Once in a Lifetime: The Incredible Story of the New York Cosmos*. New York: Grove Press.
Payne, Marissa. 2015. "Former U-Conn Star Maya Moore Laments the Current State of the WNBA." *The Washington Post* (May 6). www.washingtonpost.com/news/early-lead/wp/2015/05/06/former-u-conn-star-maya-moore-laments-the-current-state-of-the-wnba/.
Placek, Christopher. 2017. "Rosemont Assumes Ownership of Chicago Bandits Softball Team." *Dailyherald.com* (February 1). www.dailyherald.com/article/20170201/news/170209957/.
Porter, Karra. 2006. *The Story of the First Women's Professional League, 1978–81*. Lincoln, NE: University of Nebraska Press.
Quon, Kasey. 2014. "Women's Soccer Pros Playing for the Love of the Game — not the Paycheck." *Peninsula Press* (August 4). http://archive.peninsulapress.com/2014/08/04/maddie-thompson-pro-womens-soccer.
Qz.com. 2014. "A Brief History of Soccer in the US, and Why It Might Finally Have Found Its Place in the American Psyche" (May 10). https://qz.com/206259/a-brief-history-of-soccer-in-the-us-and-why-it-might-finally-have-found-its-place-in-the-american-psyche/.
Rank, Mark R. 2004. "The Disturbing Paradox of Poverty in American Families: What We Have Learned over the Past Four Decades," pp. 469–490 in Marilyn Coleman and Lawrence H. Ganong (eds.), *Handbook of Contemporary Families: Considering the Past, Contemplating the Future*. Thousand Oaks, CA: Sage.
Riddle, Greg. 2012. "Four Locals Show Off Their Skills in National Pro Fastpitch League." *The Dallas Morning News* (July 27). www.dallasnews.com/sports/high-schools/headlines/20120725-four-locals-show-off-their-skills-in-national-pro-fastpitch-league.ece.
Riddle, Greg. 2015. "Dallas Charge Pro Fastpitch Softball Players Love the Sport, but Can't Afford to Quit Their Day Jobs." *SportsDay* (June). https://sportsday.dallasnews.com/other-sports/moresportsheadlines/2015/06/02/dallas-charge-pro-fastpitch-softball-players-love-the-sport-but-can-t-afford-to-quit-their-day-jobs-1.
Rios, Edwin. 2017. "The US Women's Soccer Team Scored a Much-needed Pay Bump." *Mother Jones* (April 5). www.motherjones.com/media/2017/04/equal-pay-day-us-womens-soccer-team-earns-pay-bump.
Robinson, Joshua, and Matthew Futterman. 2016. "U.S. Women's Soccer Team Stars Allege Pay Discrimination." *The Wall Street Journal* (March 31). www.wsj.com/articles/u-s-womens-national-team-accuses-u-s-soccer-of-pay-discrimination-1459429306.

Rohlin, Melissa. 2014. "Magic Johnson and Other Dodgers Owners Purchase the Sparks." *Los Angeles Times* (February 4). http://articles.latimes.com/2014/feb/04/sports/la-sp-sn-sparks-sold-magic-dodgers-20140204.

Rosenblatt, Ryan. 2017. "Don Garber Reflects on David Beckham's MLS Ten Years after His Signing." *Fox Sports* (January 11). www.foxsports.com/soccer/story/david-beckham-mls-don-garber-10-years-011117.

Ryan, Shannon. 2011. "Travel No Foreign Concept in WNBA: NBA Stars Planning on Playing Overseas Could Learn a Thing or Two." *Chicago Tribune* (August 6). http://articles.chicagotribune.com/2011-08-06/sports/ct-spt-0807-wnba-over seas--20110806_1_wnba-besik.

Schaerlaeckens, Leander. 2011. "MLSers Flock to Europe for Training." *ESPN* (December 12). http://espn.go.com/sports/soccer/news/_/id/7338036/major-league-soccer-mls-players-training-abroad-season.

Scott, Ian. 2011. "From NASL to MLS: Transnational Culture, Exceptionalism and Britain's Part in American Soccer's Coming of Age." *Journal of Popular Culture* 44 (August): 831–853.

Seminara, David. 2013. "Loving Softball Is Easier than Living It." *The New York Times* (August 31). www.nytimes.com/2013/09/01/sports/loving-softball-is-easier-than-living-it.html?_r=0.

Shaffer, Jonas. 2016. "'Fledgling' United Women's Lacrosse League Trying to Find Footing with Fans, Sponsors." *The Baltimore Sun* (July 29). www.baltimoresun.com/sports/college/lacrosse/bs-sp-professional-womens-lacrosse-0730-20160729-story.html.

Slusser, Susan. 1998. "American Basketball League Folds/WNBA Alone after 'Sad Day' for Women's Sports." *San Francisco Chronicle* (December 23). www.sfgate.com/news/article/American-Basketball-League-Folds-WNBA-alone-2971096.php.

Smith, Ernie. "The Story of Major League Volleyball, a Failed Sports League That Was Quietly Groundbreaking." *Tedium* (May 23). https://tedium.co/2017/05/23/obscure-sports-leagues/.

Soccer Stadium Digest. 2016. "2016 NWSL Attendance." http://soccerstadiumdigest.com/2016-nwsl-attendance/.

Soonersports.com. 2013. "Catching Up with Keilani Ricketts" (November 26). www.soonersports.com/ViewArticle.dbml?ATCLID=209324525.

Soshnick, Scott. 2013. "Paul Rabil, Lacrosse's Million-Dollar Man." *BloombergBusiness* (April 4). www.bloomberg.com/bw/articles/2013-04-04/paul-rabils-lacrosses-million-dollar-man.

Sportspagemagazine.com. 2014. "Osterman, Pride Shut Down Bandits Offense in Game Two for 3–0 Victory" (August 1). www.sportspagemagazine.com/content/os/sb-os/c-sb-os/art-c-sb-os/osterman-pride-shutdown-bandits-offense-in-game-tw.shtml?60214.

Steele, Michele. 2012. "WNBA Players Cash in Overseas." *ESPNW* (February 6). http://espn.go.com/espnw/news-commentary/article/7538075/wnba-players-cash-overseas.

Steinfeld, Jake, and Dave Morrow. 2012. *Take a Shot!: A Remarkable Story of Perseverance, Friendship, and a Really Crazy Adventure*. Carlsbad, CA: Hay House.

Tansey, Joe. 2016. "Where the USMNT Stands after the Firing of Jurgen Klinsmann." *Bleacher Report* (November 21). http://bleacherreport.com/articles/2677465-where-the-usmnt-stand-after-the-firing-of-jurgen-klinsmann.

USA Today. 2017. "David Beckham: He Came, He Sold, He Conquered the USA" (December 2). www.usatoday.com/story/sports/mls/2012/12/02/david-beckham-future-major-league-soccer/1741355/.

U.S. Soccer. 2002. "Where It All Began: The Story of the U.S. World Cup Squad, 'The Shot Putters'" (January 9). www.ussoccer.com/stories/2014/03/17/11/25/where-it-all-began-the-story-of-the-1930-u-s-world-cup-squad-the-shot-putters.

U.S. Soccer. 2016. "Where a Nation Joins a Team" (November 21). www.ussoccer.com/stories/2016/11/21/19/34/161121-mnt-us-soccer-parts-ways-with-jurgen-klinsmann.

U.S. Soccer. 2017. "History." www.ussoccer.com/about/history/us-soccer-as-host/1994-fifa-world-cup.

Vaccaro, Chris R. 2015. "The Lax Bros of Long Island." *Rolling Stone* (August 6). www.rollingstone.com/sports/features/the-lax-bros-of-long-island-20150806.

Voepel, Mechelle. 2016. "WNBA Oral History: Moving the Ball Forward." *abcNEWS* (May 19). http://abcnews.go.com/Sports/wnba-oral-history-moving-ball-forward/story?id=39232337.

Wahl, Grant. 2009. *The Beckham Experiment: How the World's Most Famous Athlete Tried to Conquer America.* New York: Crown Books.

Waldstein, David. 2016. "Copa América: After U.S. Is Thrashed, Coach Asks for More." *The New York Times* (June 22). www.nytimes.com/2016/06/23/sports/soccer/copa-america-us-argentina.html.

Westly, Erica. 2016. "With a Million-Dollar Arm, a League Makes Its Pitch." *The New York Times* (July 30). www.nytimes.com/2016/07/31/sports/with-a-million-dollar-arm-a-softball-league-makes-its-pitch.html?_r=0.

Williams, Joe. 2009. "Butler Embraces Japan." *Orlando Sentinel* (June 16). http://articles.orlandosentinel.com/2009-06-16/sports/hsbutler16_1_butler-japan-softball.

Withiam, Hannah. 2017. "Why Are Women's Soccer Superstars Fleeing the US?" *New York Post* (April 15). http://nypost.com/2017/04/15/why-are-womens-soccer-superstars-fleeing-the-us/.

WNBA.com. 2016. "WNBA's Record-Breaking Season Scores Highest in Five Years" (September 21). www.wnba.com/news/record-breaking-attendance-five-years-digital-social-retail/.

6

STARS WHO WEREN'T SUPPOSED TO MAKE IT

At one extreme we might consider players like Mia Hamm and LeBron James, who from their teen years have had superior skills making it possible to dominate competition. It's crystal clear to any mildly competent observer that they will inevitably excel at any level of their sport. In sharp contrast there are athletes coming out of high school or college who go either unnoticed or nearly so by officials at the next level but who turn out to be successful or even very successful (Zak 2015).

This chapter is less concerned than its predecessors about entire sports programs, instead zeroing in on players' roles—in some instances athletes' own perceptions of and expectations about them and in other cases coaches' judgments, whether effective or ineffective.

A prominent case in the latter category involved Tom Brady, who is renowned as a low NFL draft choice. What is less well known is that the Patriots were not just lucky in getting such a quality quarterback as a low pick but that they chose him in the course of a carefully calculated strategy.

As draft day in 2000 approached, Patriots officials looked back on a season where they had lost six of their last eight games and fired the head coach. Bill Belichick replaced him, and in his first draft with the Patriots, before he ever coached a game for them, he picked Tom Brady in the sixth round—the most important key to winning three Super Bowls in the next five years and five by 2017.

Before the draft, however, Brady's prospects didn't look good. Other teams tended to emphasize his negative points—his slowness, skinniness, and generally unathletic appearance. In contrast, Belichick and his assistants were high on Brady. Quarterbacks coach Dick Rehbein was sent to scout the quarterbacks in the draft, and he reported that Brady was "the best fit for the [Patriots'] system," and other team officials preparing for the draft agreed, emphasizing Brady's meticulous approach to game preparation as well as his leadership abilities, which he had clearly demonstrated as a college quarterback. Jason Licht, a scout for the team, said, "It's not that we said we wanted to draft a tall, lanky quarterback that ran a 5.3 [time in the] 40 [yard dash]. Those weren't the traits we were looking for." He added, "But we were looking for the mental makeup ... Belichick did a lot of homework on him, along with our staff, on his mental makeup. Watching the tape, he was the guy that would go in and lead [the University of Michigan] back to victory" (Gaines 2015).

Brady was a prospect Belichick and company wanted, but at the beginning of the draft other needs took precedence: The Patriots were a decimated team, one with deficiencies at most positions but not in any obvious way at quarterback. They already had three, led by the capable Drew Bledsoe, seemingly just entering his prime, and a fourth qb was a distinct luxury, sacrificing a player slot that could meet a pressing need at another position. In the draft's opening rounds, the Patriots took several high picks, but then in the third round they started keeping a sharp eye out for Brady's status, often examining their draft board and realizing by the sixth round that his was the sole name on its left side where they had listed the still undrafted prospects whom they considered valuable picks.

So Belichick and company made the unheralded but momentous choice, picking Brady as the seventh quarterback in the draft. The first year he only played in one game, but early in the next season, Bledsoe was hurt, and Brady instantly proved a capable replacement, winning 11 of 14 games that year (*Biography.com* 2016c; Gaines 2015).

The quarterbacks coach's contention that Brady was the quarterback in the draft who was the best fit for the Patriots' system illustrates a dominant perspective running through this chapter: That team officials, whether in the pros or college, try to visualize how effectively a given player would fit into their system. What is singular about this issue is that from one team to another, officials vary significantly in their assessment of players, meaning that, as in the Brady case, they reach very different conclusions about a particular prospect's potential contribution to and fit with their team.

The content of this chapter focuses on the recruitment stage in organized sports, analyzing how this critical moment involves small-group interaction between a player and one or more coaches and/or scouts. A useful concept here is cultural fit. Borrowed from the interdisciplinary field of human relations, which concerns itself with the compatibility between prospective employees and work organizations, *cultural fit* refers to a job candidate's ability and willingness to commit to the beliefs, attitudes, and activities that an organization maintains, thereby making it likely that the prospect in question will relate well with others in the workplace and prove productive on the job (Bouton 2015; Koen, Klehe, Van Vianen, Zikic, and Nauta 2010; MSG Presentations 2017).

Unlike the earlier chapters which examine organized programs, this one concerns individual players in the context of the team, notably their struggles to surmount various challenges that allow them to succeed during the recruitment and retention stages. Sometimes, as in the Brady case, it requires coaches' acute perception to visualize their potential cultural fit.

The chapter divides into two parts. The first section considers settings where for various reasons some fine players were initially excluded from college or pro teams. The second segment examines the impact of coaching on young prospects' success, analyzing contexts in which the idea of cultural fit seems applicable in two senses—that the coaches, like the Patriots contingent previously mentioned, are searching for players who can effectively move into their schemes and contribute to team performance and that the players, in turn, are making a maximum effort to provide a positive fit, contributing to those units.

Reasons Why Some Prospects Are Excluded, at Least Temporarily

Athletes can encounter various conditions that can deny them a place on teams: They simply don't appear to make a potential contribution. In some instances, however, team officials belatedly figure out that certain prospects rejected by other teams are well suited for theirs.

Crowded Out by the Competition

Invariably drafting prospects is an inexact science, with coaches and scouts who must make many choices in a fairly short time often facing the stressful combination of limited information and high stakes. Players can get lost in the shuffle, including some who are really capable if not flashy. In the NHL each year a large number of talented prospects emerge out of junior hockey. From 2002 to 2004, Dan Girardi, a defenseman was eligible for the draft, and while 13 teammates were selected in those three years, he remained overlooked. Yet he persevered, playing on several minor-league teams and eventually drawing the attention of the New York Rangers, who signed him to a contract, first sending him to their Hartford affiliate and then finally bringing him to the parent club at the beginning of 2007.

Girardi's persistence paid off. He became a first-rate defender for the New York Rangers, very effectively matching against such top scorers as Sidney Crosby and Alex Ovechkin—according to a journalist, an "under-the-radar workman whose blue-collar approach to the game is a bedrock of the franchise."

Marc Staal, a fellow defender, supported the idea that a player could readily be overlooked coming out of the juniors—that "[I]f you don't catch their attention right out of the gate and have that spotlight on you, it's pretty tough to be noticed." Staal added, "Coming from where ... [Girardi] did to what he is for us, that's pretty impressive" (Brooks 2015).

Graduating from high school, Curt Warner, a quarterback, faced a situation fairly similar to Girardi's, where his decent but unspectacular performances, especially early on, led scouts and coaches to overlook him. He was rejected by top college programs, spending four of five years mainly on the bench for his Division I-AA college. Warner was passed over in the draft but improved steadily over the next five years, which involved a preseason stay with the Green Bay Packers, three years in the Arena Football League, and one year in NFL Europe. Eventually he joined the Los Angeles Rams, where his painstakingly developed skills eventually led to stardom (*Biography.com* 2016a; Ohebsion 2016). Commenting on the player the quarterback had become, a reporter noted that he had developed an "amazing array of passes he can throw with chilling accuracy" (*Biography.com* 2016a). In 2017 Warner's rise from obscurity reached its zenith when he was inducted into the Pro Football Hall of Fame (D'Andrea 2017).

At that time Cris Collingsworth, a NBC analyst and former player, appeared dumbfounded by Warner's accomplishments. "It couldn't happen," Collingsworth said and then repeated the phrase. "It couldn't happen. There's no way this guy that's stocking shelves in an Iowa grocery store is going to go play Arena Football and figure out, 'I've got to get this ball out of my hand pretty quickly here and make it out.' He wasn't going to play in St. Louis. Trent Green gets hurt, and he goes on to throw the game-winning touchdown in the Super Bowl. Come on" (Bender 2017). Like many pro athletes who are long shots as effective cultural fits with their teams, Warner was able to make it happen by relentless practice, steadily improving over time until he achieved high-quality play.

The following set of athletes also face conditions that can cause them to be overlooked.

During preseason training camp, Dallas Cowboys players competing to make the team realize that survival is likely to require unrelenting effort in confronting constant challenges (Source: Arthur Eugene Preston / Shutterstock.com)

Trapped in the Wrong Sport

In some instances potentially productive athletes are involved in a sport where they lack the abilities to contribute effectively to their team. Often they don't realize that it would prove promising to change sports, but sometimes they do. Jimmy Graham spent a four-year college career playing basketball at the University of Miami and averaging an undistinguished 4.3 points and 16 minutes. At the end of that modest career, he played a season for the Hurricanes at tight end, hardly flooring the scouts with his season total of 17 catches and 213 yards.

However, his potential must have shone through because Graham received an invitation to the 2009 NFL Scouting Combine. His speed wasn't great compared to some of the NFL's top stars, but he was faster than most linebackers. At 6-feet-8-inches in height he was fairly short for a NBA forward but towered over most NFL defenders. He also possessed large, soft hands (Clark 2012; Zac 2015).

Following the combine the official assessment of Graham read, "Graham is a very raw tight end that left the basketball team to turn out for football in time for the 2009 season. He is extremely athletic and has a huge upside but still needs a ton of technique work from running routes to blocking" (*NFL.com* 2016). Graham was happy to put in the time and effort. Looking back three years after the combine he said, "It's a very weird circumstance ... The road it took to get here, all the things that had to have fallen in place, it's almost a miracle. Being invited to the combine with 17 career catches is incredible" (Clark 2012).

Near miracle or not, Graham's switch to football provided him a role he developed and executed well, producing statistically good results for the New Orleans Saints and Seattle Seahawks. In six years he caught 434 passes, averaged 12.3 yards a catch, totaled over 5,300 yards, and had two seasons with over 1,200 yards in catches (*NFL.com* 2016).

Graham indicated that throughout his career about ten basketball players had approached him, asking about making the shift from basketball to football. Most of the time he discouraged their making the move, feeling that they were simply in it for the money and were unprepared for the grueling transition required. Graham believed that to make the shift, the player needed to love the game. He said, "My first training camp, in

August, I'm getting dominated, the first time you've ever blocked a 300-pound man isn't fun. It was fun for me though" (Clark 2012).

Graham is part of a short list of athletes who successfully transitioned from basketball to stardom at tight end in the NFL—in particular, San Diego Chargers' Antonio Gates, a Pro Bowler who played only basketball at Kent State; and Atlanta Falcons' Tony Gonzalez, who starred in both sports in high school and at the University of California at Berkeley and was a perennial Pro Bowler (Clark 2012). Later in the chapter, discussion focuses on the role that coaches can take in selected players' shift from basketball to football.

Sometimes what traps an athlete in the wrong sport is not the skills required but the nature of the sport itself. Successful players need to feel comfortable in the role they perform, and if that comfort is lacking, then a mismatch between the player and the game exists. Micaya White clearly had the skills to be a fine basketball player, but she simply couldn't fit into the game. "When I tried to show aggression, I'd end up hurting another player or fouling out of the game." Apprehensive at first about trying a new sport, she quickly became comfortable with volleyball, which seemed as competitive as basketball. "Only there was a net in between," she said. "You can put in all this aggression toward one object and let it out" (Friedman 2017). White was hardly alone in finding volleyball much more appealing than basketball. In 2015 for the first time, more high-school girls played volleyball than basketball. "There's a whole lot of girls out there who like to be powerful, who like to be strong and assertive and aggressive, but they also like having a net between them," said Kathy DeBoer, executive director of the American Volleyball Coaches Association. "They don't enjoy checking each other or boxing each other out or slide tackles" (Friedman 2017).

While some athletes have started out in what turned out to be the wrong sport, others participated in one for which they were potentially well suited but initially found themselves at a position that didn't match up effectively with their abilities.

Locked into the Wrong Position

Football fans watching J.J. Watt terrorize the Houston Oilers' opposing offenses might find it surprising that scouting reports on him before the

NFL Draft were filled with negatives. Appearing in 2016 on *The Dan Patrick Show* after his third selection as Defensive Player of the Year, Watt paraded some of the most damning indictments:

- "Won't consistently get the edge on (offensive) tackles with his get-off or quickness."
- "Lacks some lateral mobility, both rushing the passer and playing in space."
- And the most damning of them all: "He won't ever be a stud pass rusher" (Goodbread 2016).

Considering Watt's overall performance in the NFL, the statements appear almost eerily inaccurate. So what happened? In high school Watt played decently as both a tight end and a defensive back and signed with Central Michigan University, which in spite of *Rivals.com*'s lowly two-star rating offered him a scholarship. His freshman year he played extensively at tight end but caught only eight passes. At the end of the year, he left the school, not accepting the coach's idea that he would be more effective on the offensive line (Berkes 2015; Kertscher 2016; *Rivals.com* 2007).

Watt gave up his scholarship and became a walk-on at the University of Wisconsin, starting a weight program that would reshape his body to perform at an elite level (Corbett 2012). In spite of the fact that at first some of the coaches felt the young man was not big or fast enough to make the team, he persevered, motivated in part by having promised his parents he would earn a scholarship and eventually fitting in well as a defensive end. Watt was unrelenting. "At that time, failure was not an option. I was gambling on myself. There was just no option but to make it work," Watt said. "There was a belief in myself to start with. And I put in the work. When you put in the work, you start to believe in yourself even more" (Kertscher 2016). Like many other young male athletes, Watt was still maturing physically during his early college years, and there seems little doubt that the weight program was an important contribution, helping the Wisconsin coaches appreciate his growing potential.

Watt was dedicated to fulfilling the role expectations for a top defensive end. He said his case was typical of successful walk-ons at

Wisconsin, who had a chip on their shoulder and as a result needed "to go above and beyond what the other scholarship players have to do." The approach succeeded. By his third year as a Badger, Watt not only had a scholarship but was second-team All American and was the 11th overall pick in the 2011 draft (Kertscher 2016). Still, as the previously cited scouting reports indicated, he had improvements to make before he eventually became a major star in the NFL.

Watt is hardly the only two-star football prospect who attained stardom after switching positions. At Kansas State Jordy Nelson was a walk-on as a defensive back, who coach Bill Snyder felt would fit much more productively at wide receiver. It was a splendid move, with Nelson soon becoming a star and gaining over 1,600 receiving yards his senior year. In 2008 he was a second-round choice of the Green Bay Packers and became quarterback Aaron Rodgers' favorite target and one of the top NFL receivers (Kaylor 2015).

These two players represent notable cases of college football players changing position and attaining stardom when shifting from offense to defense or vice versa. Consider the process that unfolds. It seems to involve a distinct gamble where the players and coaches seek a better fit, betting big on the possibility of substantial rewards but also facing the prospect of a full-fledged wipeout. As was indicated, one winner was J.J. Watt, who was an indifferent tight end and yet became a ferocious, nearly unstoppable defensive end. The skills at the two positions are very different, and in this case the shift to defense has been much better attuned to Watt's abilities.

One might compare the position shifts from offense to defense or vice versa in football to changes of position in several other popular sports, notably basketball and baseball. In those cases most or sometimes all players engage in both offense and defense, developing a roughly similar skill set to teammates; for instance, basketball players as a rule must dribble, shoot, pass, and guard opponents and most baseball team members do all of the following—bat, throw, and catch—and so if they change position the carryover skills are more extensive and thus the adjustments required are less than football players shifting between defense and offense.

Sometimes players' failure to fit is not about the position they play but their physical attributes.

Considered Too Small, Too Slow, Too Puny, or Simply Too Ordinary

In various sports, scouts and coaches look for a combination of size, speed, and skillful performance. Young players, especially youthful males, often take considerable time to mature, and in middle school or even the beginning of high school they might barely display a suggestion of what they will become.

At my Division III college, an above-average basketball player told me that as a high-school senior in his team's man-to-man defense he was matched in a game against a sophomore who later became a two-time NCAA Player of the Year as well as a member of both the Basketball Hall of Fame and the 50 Greatest Players in NBA History (selection in 1996). At the time when the celebrated career was barely beginning, my informant explained, "The kid was skinny and slow, two years younger than me, and still hadn't grown into his body—awkward as hell. I owned him, but within a year or so, the result would have been reversed."[1] The situation illustrated that even future great players can be fairly ineffective in their youth. This eventual star was fortunate that much of his physical and skill development occurred in high school while playing for a team where he was good enough to get a chance to improve. Others aren't as lucky.

At 19 Dennis Rodman was homeless, and the following year he was a janitor on the graveyard shift. But during those two years after high school he was growing rapidly—a total of nine inches from 5-feet-11-inches to 6-feet-8-inches. "All of a sudden I could do things on a basketball court I'd never dreamed of doing," Rodman said. "It was like I had a new body that knew how to do all this shit the old one didn't" (Burka 1998).

Following a year at Cooke County Junior College, the coach for Southeastern Oklahoma State University offered him a scholarship and after three years the Detroit Pistons drafted him in the second round, beginning a celebrated career where Rodman was a prominent player on five championship teams and eventually entered the Hall of Fame (*Land of Basketball.com* 2016).

Scotty Pippin, one of Rodman's teammates with the Chicago Bulls and a fellow Hall of Famer, had a similar experience. In high school Pippin was also relatively short, about 6-feet-1-inch, and weighed a mere 150 lbs. —traits that seemed more important to scouts and coaches than his leading the team to the state finals and winning all-conference honors. However, as a favor to Pippin's high-school coach, Don Dyer, the head coach at the University of Central Arkansas offered Pippin a chance to become its team manager; instead he chose to be a walk-on (*Biography. com* 2016b).

Through his college years, the young man was definitely a work in progress, adapting to his enlarging body and improving gradually. In 1983 two players quit, and Dyer put Pippin, who'd grown to 6-feet-3-inches, on the roster and on scholarship. It seemed a worthwhile gamble. "He was real gangly," Dyer recalled. "The coordination just wasn't there yet, but you could see underneath that even then he had the skills" (Demirel 2013). Like perceptive coaches discussed later in the chapter, Dyer could spot important abilities before they fully materialized. During his college years, Pippin reached 6-feet-8-inches and blossomed as a player, averaging 23.6 points and 10 rebounds his senior year. As Pippin's college career ended, scouts and coaches paid attention, impressed by his massive wingspan and relentless defensive skill as well as his ability to score and rebound. The Seattle Supersonics took Pippin with the fifth overall pick in the 1987 draft, and a few weeks later he was traded to the Chicago Bulls, where he and Michael Jordan became the core of one of the all-time best NBA teams (*Biography.com* 2016b; Demirel 2013).

A modest stature can also be a turnoff for coaches in other sports—hockey for instance. At any level of play, it can be useful if defensemen are tall with long arms to reach around opponents and grab the puck and heavy in order to push their men against the boards or away from the crease. In his youthful career, Brian Molloy was decidedly neither—considered too short and light by the high-school coach at 5-feet-4-inches, 130 lbs. Nonetheless after breaking his ankle as a sophomore, Molloy retuned to a team that was deficient in defenders, and he became the third defenseman on a Hamden, Connecticut team that won the New England championship his junior year. Recruited to play at Brown University, Molloy conveniently grew four inches and put on 30 lbs., much of it muscle, in the months after his last year of high-school hockey and before his first year of college play. Though still somewhat small, Molloy described himself as "very quick and durable," and through four years of ice time he developed into a competent, defense-minded defender, becoming a co-captain his senior year[2].

Observers might say that athletes like Brian Molloy and Scottie Pippin grew into their positions, becoming increasingly more valuable contributors with increased size and experience. For others such a progression occurs under different circumstances, with coaches' perceptions and actions playing an important part in the development of a cultural fit.

Coaches' Tactics in Singling Out Some Prospects Who Were Initially Overlooked or Nearly So

John O'Sullivan, a veteran coach, has studied and written about the process of building athletic teams. O'Sullivan contended that a distinction between two approaches lies at the heart of team development in any sport. *Talent selection*, he suggested, involves a choice of prospects whose observable skills and attributes make it likely that they will fit in and immediately contribute to the team's success. In contrast, *talent identification* is an assessment of players' future performance based on an examination of their current skills and attributes, with scouts and/or coaches taking into account such developmental factors as physical growth, coaching effectiveness, and a willingness to train hard, to evaluate whether the prospects in question might be capable of making the necessary improvements to contribute to the team in ways not yet manifested in their play (O'Sullivan 2013). Obviously the second approach is more complicated, with success requiring both acumen and patience—a broader conception of the coaching or scouting role which has the potential of producing invaluable cultural fits.

Clearly the idea of talent identification extends beyond sports. Between 2002 and 2009, researchers published over 100 articles examining job applicants' interviews for a variety of organizations—articles that often addressed the idea of talent identification (Carless and Imber 2007; Macan 2009).

Not that those on the firing line always endorse the latter option. O'Sullivan indicated that when youth coaches are under pressure from parents or club officials to win, they almost invariably go with the option of talent selection, choosing prospects with the traits for short-term success. He wrote, "You naturally select the biggest, strongest and fastest young athletes, and play them extensive minutes. You limit playing time for the kids who are not up to snuff, and tell them they need to work harder, get tougher, etc., if they want to play more. You yell at them because they cannot get to the ball quick enough, or cannot shoot well enough to score. You tell them that this type of pressure is what they will face when they are older, so they better get used to it now." Such responses undoubtedly contribute to the figure we saw earlier indicating that 70 percent of youth athletes quit organized sports by the age of 13 (O'Sullivan 2013).

While pro coaches are often under intense pressure, some of them take the time and make the effort to pursue talent identification. Bill Belichick has been a potent practitioner of that skill as the Patriots' painstaking effort to draft and later develop Tom Brady illustrated—the situation that was reviewed at the beginning of this chapter. In this instance Belichick in his development of Brady as a qb focused on his positive potential and downplayed or even ignored the quite glaring negatives.

As far as Belichick himself is concerned, he appears to be a coach with a superb football mind whose background was ideal not only to propel him into coaching but to prepare him to be adept at talent identification. Steve Belichick, his father, coached around the country, then became a scout for the Navy football team, and eventually became a mentor for his son. Whenever possible, the younger Belichick went with his father on the road, observing the meticulous way he gathered detailed information about prospects.

Back home young Bill would go to coaches' meetings where Rick Forzano, a Navy assistant, would instruct the preteen boy in analyzing film, with Belichick soon providing detailed information about which opposing receivers were running which routes on which downs. "I hate to think what his IQ is," Forzano said. "He looks beyond what's happening." Sociologically it appears that the young future coach had a more detailed perception of the team's organizational totality than his older, more experienced associates.

In 1976 Forzano, who still called the 23-year-old Belichick "Billy," hired him as one of his assistants with the Baltimore Colts. Belichick focused on special teams, but soon his duties also included wide receivers and linebackers. In meetings his contributions were impressive. For instance, an assistant coach would propose an adjustment in the strong safety's assignment, and it would be Belichick who would explain to the assemblage the impact on various other defenders, then indicating why or why not the change should be made (Kilgore 2015). At that point the young man was fast becoming the consummate model for a coach who would readily use talent identification to fit new players into all three of the Patriots' units, helping to produce over time one of the top teams in the league.

The approach can take a while to yield results. Whether the coach in question is Belichick, O'Sullivan, or someone else, the proponents of talent identification are engaged in *delayed gratification*—an ability to resist an immediate reward, recognizing that the benefits will be greater if the individual in question, in this case the coach, restrains the impulse to obtain an immediate positive outcome. Extensive research has featured the concept (Bembenutty and Karabenick 1998; Lickerman 2012; Silverman 2003).

In various coaching settings, talent identification can come into play.

Assessing a Prospect's Performance in One Sport as an Indicator of Potential in Another

Earlier in the chapter, a discussion focused on Jimmy Graham, who transformed from a mediocre basketball player to a fine NFL player. One coach has been particularly adept at engineering such a switch from basketball to football. For years Gil Brandt, a former executive for the Dallas Cowboys, studied the college basketball ranks, contending that between 2 and 3 percent of college basketball players would make fine football prospects. Brandt's discoveries included Pete Gent, a receiver who spent five years in the league, and Cornell Green, who made five Pro Bowls as a cornerback. Frank Haith, Jimmy Graham's coach at Miami, was also a proponent of the same conversion, observing that players' performance in basketball would provide clues about their football potential. Graham, for example, not only had good size, but he led the team in charges drawn, suggesting foot speed, and also in blocks, indicating his jumping ability.

In spite of some successes, players' enthusiasm for going through the process of changing sports has waned. Brandt suggested that one reason the decline has occurred has been that marginal basketball players find it simpler and perhaps more lucrative to transfer their game to Europe than to undertake the long, hard transition to football (Clark 2012).

When assessing the idea of talent identification, some coaches want or even demand that the athletes they choose for their college or pro teams have played multiple sports. They are likely to believe that the breadth of experience provided by playing diverse sports helps competitors develop critical abilities—for instance, to become more effective at decision making and perhaps also more creative. Pete Carroll, USC and later Seattle Seahawks coach, who was emphatic on this point, said, "I hate that kids don't play three sports in high school. I think that they should play year-round and get every bit of it that they can through that experience."

In the same vein, Dom Starsia, the men's lacrosse coach at the University of Virginia, indicated that he had "a trick question" for the boys at his lacrosse camp. "My trick question to young campers is always, 'How do you learn the concepts of team offense in lacrosse or team defense in lacrosse in the off-season, when you're not playing with your team?' The answer is by playing basketball, by playing hockey and by playing soccer and those other team games, because many of those principles are exactly the same. Probably 95 percent [of our players] are multi-sport athletes." It seems clear that when young athletes play multiple sports a talent-identifying coach is more likely to consider that they would develop into players who would fit productively into their team (O'Sullivan 2015).

When employing talent identification, however, most coaches are concentrated on prospects' performances within the sport at hand.

Jolting or Coaxing Players into a Different Style of Play

In these situations coaches are pivotal influences in athletes' development, often enhancing or saving their careers. Courtney Paris, who is 6-feet-4-inches, 250 lbs., had a magnificent four years in college, averaging 19.9 points and 14.8 rebounds and becoming the first four-time Associated Press first-team All-American in women's basketball while setting 20 individual Division I records, including career rebounds and career double-doubles (*ESPN* 2009; WNBA 2009). In 2009 the Sacramento Monarchs drafted her seventh. Was she a surefire superstar in the WNBA? Hardly.

Following college Paris languished for five years in the league, playing for five WNBA teams and starting fewer games overall than in the course of a month in college. She even dropped out of the league for a year, and that's when significant changes started to occur.

In 2013 Paris signed with Mersin in the Turkish Basketball League, where she had done well playing the previous two years during the WNBA offseason. She found, however, that Ceyhun Yıldızoğlu, her new coach, who was also the leader of the national team, was a tough guy, constantly demanding that she commit to a more rigorous set of performance norms. When Paris rebounded free throws, he wanted her also to block out the opponent, and if she got the rebound and didn't block out, he yelled at her. Much of the time Paris felt angry and ill-at-ease. Over time, though, she appreciated that she was developing a new understanding of the game and that her play was distinctly improving. "He challenged me every day," Paris said, "and it was just good for me."

Obviously Yıldızoğlu felt the same way, using his own version of talent identification to assess her cultural fit with pro basketball teams. He had concluded that she was a tall, powerful player with skills that had allowed her to dominate in college but not in the more demanding WNBA, and recognized that she needed to use her size and strength against opponents who were often faster and more agile, honing in on the elements of the game she could readily improve—blocking out, rebounding, and posting up. "Take this season, and use everything you learned," he told Paris shortly before she went home. "Go to the WNBA, and use this" (Carlson 2014).

Which she promptly did. In Paris's subsequent three years in the WNBA, per-game points, rebounds, and minutes played all accelerated, with rebounds and minutes played more than doubling over her previous personal best (*Basketball-Reference.com* 2016; Carlson 2014). Yıldızoğlu, a tough but insightful coach, engaged in first-rate talent identification, resurrecting Paris's career.

Jill Redfern, the Lehigh women's lacrosse head coach, has also been accomplished at talent identification. At a lacrosse camp during Allison LaBeau's junior year of high school, Redfern saw the unheralded player but was impressed, telling her coach that she was promising. "Our coach (Redfern) kind of refers to her as a diamond in the rough," goalie Taylor Tvedt said, "because she was so underrated, and then she came in and immediately filled a top position for our scoring unit." In fact, beginning as a freshman, LaBeau led the team in scoring each year, always improving her numbers (Farmer 2016).

Besides discovering diamonds in the rough, Redfern's talent identification sometimes has involved taking good performers and making them better. For instance, when Redfern was an assistant coach at Lehigh, the team signed Lauren Dykstra, a high scorer and all-around player. "We had a total party. We were really excited," Redfern said. However, Dykstra still needed to develop, and in part because of not using her left hand, she was easy to cover. So the player and the assistant coach worked together for hours each day, gradually improving her left-handed skill. The extra practice paid off. Dykstra ended up as the Patriot Conference leader in scoring and seventh in NCAA Division I history with 253 career goals (Feil 2011).

Talent identification becomes operative when an astute coach can tweak athletes' performance to make competitors like this pair of good college lacrosse players even better. (Source: Aspen Photo / Shutterstock.com)

Lauren Dykstra thrived under the expert, caring tutelage of her coach: That relationship demonstrated talent identification in action. But let's reverse the circumstances, assessing the potential significance of the coaching role in a perverse case where the coach did almost nothing positive and much that was negative to affect a player's success. While high school coaches vary in their style and approach, there appear to be relatively few who are as uninvolved and even malignant as was the upcoming individual, who produced various dysfunctional effects for both the player and the program. Summary 6.1 lists situations involving organized sports where the idea of cultural fit applies and coaches labor to find players who contribute effectively to their teams.

SUMMARY 6.1

Examples in Organized Sports Where the Idea of Cultural Fit Applies

Cultural fit: The probability that a certain job candidate will be able and willing to commit to the beliefs, attitudes, and activities that an organization maintains, thereby making it likely that the prospect in question will relate well with others in the workplace and prove productive on the job.

Two broad conditions:

First, players confronting various restrictive conditions at least initially preventing an effective fit with a team:

- While at first overlooked amid the glut of candidates to make the major leagues in their sports, persevering athletes like Dan Girardi and Curt Warner eventually showing the coaches their prospects were first-rate, with the potential of quality contributions to the team.
- Changing sports used as a key tactic allowing athletes like Jimmy Graham, who shifted from basketball to football, to find a quality opportunity to fit with and contribute to a pro team.
- Switching to defense from offense requiring very different challenges: In the case of J.J. Watt, a steady performance improvement until he attained superstar status with a pro team.
- While some players initially considered too small, too slow, too puny, or simply too ordinary to make a team, a number overcoming the deficiency and eventually becoming good or even elite.

Second, coaches' and scouts' creative discovery and development of players' largely hidden talent:

- Talent identification: Coaches' insight into prospects' ability and the case of Bill Belichick's expert use of it.
- Other instances of talent identification: That athletes in one sport might be highly effective performers in another; that with jolting or coaxing selected athletes under competent tutelage can vastly improve their performance.
- Counterpoint: Excelling at negative coaching: The Peter Low case.

The Impact of Negative Coaching Tactics

Peter Low lived in Elizabethtown in northeastern New York state. He loved sports and had several fine coaches in his preteen years. Then in his sophomore year of high school, the situation changed: Low found himself with a coach who was consistently nonsupportive, sometimes outrightly nasty or degrading. There were outbursts. Once during a team discussion, Low was scratching a rash around the belt line, and suddenly the coach threw the basketball hard, smacking him in the chest.

Invariably, however, Low rewarded the coach and the team with excellent play. He was the squad's leading scorer for three years and either first or second in the league in scoring. The coach, in turn, undermined Low's success, curtailing his play unless the game was close.

Occasionally coaches might be on firm ground limiting a player's scoring. Consider a superficially similar case. His junior year at North Carolina Michael Jordan averaged 19.6 point a game, prompting the well-known witticism that coach Dean Smith was the only individual able to hold him under 20 points a game (Dufresne 2015). In that instance the coach's emphasis appeared to be about Jordan's fit with the team—specifically, the greater importance of effectively coordinated team play than an individual's impressive numbers.

In Low's situation the coach's intention appears to have been much less elevated, seemingly dedicated to making sure the player was minimally credited. "Never did I receive any congratulations for any of my team or league accomplishments," reported Low. He indicated that at times "I was having a real 'hot' night when everything was going in and he'd take me out and I wouldn't see another minute for the second half. Often I'd score over 20 points in the first half and sit the entire second half. However, if he needed my scoring to win a game I'd be in there till that last second."

His senior year the coach told Low that "You'll never play college ball because you can't or don't play defense." Low conceded he was more geared to offense but indicated that he took defense seriously and consistently worked to improve. However, the coach appeared true to his word, doing his best to keep Low out of the college ranks, refusing, even though a number of schools expressed interest in him, to write recommendation letters. Normally that response is a killer for a prospect; high-school athletes are highly dependent on their coaches for assistance reaching the next level, and if the coach is uncooperative, the player has a limited chance to succeed.

Low was equally good in soccer and baseball, but he had the misfortune to have the same coach, whose treatment remained consistently nonsupportive. As a result Low's best bet was Division III Oswego State, where he played three sports, was the basketball team's leading scorer his senior year, twice made the all-tournament team at the state level, finished in the top 20 nationally in Division III field-goal percentage his senior year, was twice the college's athlete of the year, and was inducted into the Oswego State Athletics Hall of Fame[3].

After graduation Low joined a basketball league composed of players from the three NCAA divisions. One day he completed a near-perfect game, hardly missing a shot, scoring 50 points, and going 20 for 20 from the foul line. In the following years, Low found himself pondering what his possibilities might have been. With ordinary support from his high-school coach, could he have played at Division I? Low admitted it would have been a challenge, perhaps requiring him at just 6-feet-2-inches to make the transition from an offense-minded forward to point guard, where he would have needed to become adept at distributing the ball[4].

Peter Low's case demonstrates a distinctly negative example of a prominent issue in this chapter—that sometimes athletes with considerable potential reach a crossroads where coaches' outlook and approach can either impede or promote their progress. At such moments coaches' supportive talent identification can be invaluable —a prized skill that doesn't necessarily provide immediate payback but over time can sometimes produce fine, even breathtaking outcomes.

Conclusion

Once again, consider quarterback hopefuls. Don Shonka, a veteran NFL scout, mentioned Tim Couch, who held a host of quarterbacking records at the University of Kentucky and was the top draft choice in the 1999 draft. "They used to put five garbage cans on the field," Shonka said, "and Couch would stand there and throw … the ball into every one" (Gladwell 2008). But Couch failed in the NFL. Yes, he could throw accurately, but quarterbacks also need to fit effectively with their teams as leaders of a NFL offense.

Shonka emphasized that pro quarterbacks are playing a game that is much more rapid and more complex than the college version. As a case in point, Shonka was watching college film of a player named Chase Daniel, and he praised how he threw the ball accurately in the face of the opposing team's rush and also how quickly and accurately he released the ball. In the pros, however, he would have three or four receivers instead of five; the defenders would be much faster than in college and start the play closer to the ball, leaving Daniel very little time to release it. Additionally unlike in college, pass defenders are almost invariably quick and talented, sometimes prompting the qb to use his eyes to divert them to prevent their intercepting the ball. With the indeterminate influence of this complex of factors, it's often almost impossible to decide before they turn pro whether quarterback prospects in the NFL pressure cooker can fit well with their teams.

At one point Shonka watched the TV screen, where a college player who might become the best in the nation was having a stellar day. "How will that ability translate to the National Football League?" he asked rhetorically. Shonka shook his head, his face went blank, and he said resignedly, "Shoot" (Gladwell 2008). This was simply an inadequate setting to determine if this promising candidate would become an effective cultural fit with a NFL team.

Summary

The idea of cultural fit refers to the probability that a certain job candidate will be able and willing to commit to the beliefs, attitudes, and activities that an organization maintains, and it readily applies to sports programs. The chapter divides into two major sections, with the opening part assessing why in their youth some fine players were unable to advance their sports careers. The situations examined include athletes overlooked in crowded minor-league or college leagues, involved in a sport for which they are ill-suited, assigned to a position where they lack the requisite skills, or deficient in important physical requirements.

The second major section concerns coaches' perceptions of prospects and emphasizes a provocative distinction between talent selection and talent identification, with the latter concept focusing on the utility of locating valuable players for the long haul, individuals whose potential contributions are not currently apparent but might develop under competent tutelage. Coaches suspecting that they have athletes for whom talent identification applies find that they might need to convince the players to alter their style of play in order to develop stellar qualities.

Class Discussion Questions

1. Describe a sports-related situation where the idea of cultural fit applies, providing detail about players' roles in the process. Evaluate whether it is a useful concept.
2. Do you know of either college or professional athletes who were not particularly successful at first but persevered and became either good or excellent contributors to their teams? Describe what happened.
3. Mention athletes who have changed positions within a sport, improving in the process. Are players likely to prompt such moves, or are coaches more likely to be the initiators?
4. Based on either your personal experience or what you have heard or read, are coaches at different levels of play (high school, college, or the pros) more likely to engage in talent identification or talent selection? Does the idea of delayed gratification appear

relevant? Spell out the details of any cases you know where talent identification has occurred.

5. While many coaches are successful, others are not. Discuss both the best and the worst coaches you ever observed, and describe their impact on the team.

Notes

1. The quotation is a recreation, but its content accurately reflects what the player told me. My informant seemed convincing, offering the information in a low-key, unpretentious way and simply suggesting that at that moment his age and experience gave him a decisive advantage over an awkward teen.
2. Brian Molloy gave his permission to use this biographical information.
3. Oswego State University of New York. 2016. "Oswego State Athletics Hall of Fame." http://oswegolakers.com/hof.aspx?hof=21&path=&kiosk=.
4. Peter Low gave his permission to use the preceding material, including the quotations which come verbatim from his emails.

References

Basketball-Reference.com. 2016. "Courtney Paris." www.basketball-reference.com/wnba/players/p/parisco01w.html.

Bembenutty, Héfer, and Stuart A. Karabenick. 1998. "Academic Delay of Gratification." *Learning and Individual Differences* 10: 329–346.

Bender, Bill. 2017. "Kurt Warner's Remarkable Story Binds Two Generations of Hall of Fame QBs." *Sporting News* (August 5). www.sportingnews.com/nfl/news/kurt-warner-nfl-hall-of-fame-story-career-stats-rams-cardinals-qb/1ibrq7ot5ljk31je5un q8mya0h.

Berkes, Peter. 2015. "You Can Make a Pretty Great NFL Team from Players Who Were Two-star Recruits." *SB Nation* (June 22). www.sbnation.com/college-football/2015/6/22/8743525/nfl-two-star-recruits.

Biography.com. 2016a. "Kurt Warner Biography." www.biography.com/people/kurt-warner-519490.

Biography.com. 2016b. "Scottie Pippen Biography." www.biography.com/people/scottie-pippen-21323083.

Biography.com. 2016c. "Tom Brady." www.biography.com/people/tom-brady-259541.

Bouton, Katie. 2015. "Recruiting for Cultural Fit." *Harvard Business Review* (July 17). https://hbr.org/2015/07/recruiting-for-cultural-fit.

Brooks, Larry. 2015. "How Undrafted Reliable Dan Girardi Saved Rangers' Failed Draft." *New York Post* (May 17). http://nypost.com/2015/05/17/how-undrafted-reliable-dan-girardi-saved-rangers-failed-draft/.

Burka, Paul. 1998. "On the Court and Off, He's in a League of His Own." Texas Monthly (September). www.texasmonthly.com/articles/sports-%E2%80%A2-dennis-rodman/.

Carless, Sally A., and Amantha Imber. 2007. "The Influence of Perceived Interviewer and Job and Organizational Characteristics on Applicant Attraction and Job Choice

Intentions: The Role of Applicant Anxiety." *International Journal of Selection and Assessment* 15 (December): 359–371.

Carlson, Jenni. 2014. "How a Season with 'Coach C' Helped Spark Former Oklahoma Star Courtney Paris' Breakout WNBA Season." *NewsOK* (July 4). http://newsok.com/article/4985741.

Clark, Kevin. 2012. "Saints Tight End a Basketball Dud Turned to Football." *Wall Street Journal* (January 12). www.wsj.com/articles/SB10001424052970204124204577154951555262404.

Corbett, Jim. 2012. "J.J. Watt Goes from Pizza Delivery Man to NFL Star." *USA Today* (October 9). www.usatoday.com/story/sports/nfl/texans/2012/10/09/watt-brings-energy-to-undefeated-texans/1623497/.

D'Andrea, Christian. 2017. "Kurt Warner Inducted into the Hall of Fame." *SBNation* (February 4). www.sbnation.com/nfl/2017/2/4/14256280/kurt-warner-pro-football-hall-of-fame-class.

Demirel, Evin. 2013. "The Rise of Scottie Pippin." *Slam* (June 28). www.slamonline.com/nba/the-rise-of-scottie-pippen/#gjV6D2geAT4CeQBL.97.

Dufresne, Chris. 2015. "Dean Smith Dies at 83; North Carolina Coaching Legend." *Los Angeles Times* (February 8). www.latimes.com/local/obituaries/la-me-dean-smith-story-20150208-story.html.

ESPN. 2009. "Two from UConn Named to First Team" (March 31). http://espn.go.com/ncw/news/story?id=4030503.

Farmer, Casey. 2016. "How Allison LaBeau Became Lehigh Women's Lacrosse's Top Scorer." *The Brown and White* (April 11). http://thebrownandwhite.com/2016/04/10/allison-labeau-profile/.

Feil, Justin. 2011. "Dykstra Says Feats Would Be Meaningless Minus Patriot League Title." *Lax.Magazine.com* (April 28). www.laxmagazine.com/college_women/DI/2010-11/news/042811_dykstra_says_feats_would_be_meaningless_without_patriot_league_title.

Friedman, Vicki L. 2017. "Why Volleyball—Not Basketball—Is Winning the Popular Vote." *ESPNW* (February 15). www.espn.com/espnw/sports/article/18659764/why-young-athletes-flocking-volleyball-not-basketball-record-numbers.

Gaines, Cork. 2015. "How the Patriots Pulled Off the Biggest Steal in NFL Draft History and Landed Tom Brady in the 6th Round." *Business Insider* (February 1). www.businessinsider.com/patriots-tom-brady-draft-2015-1.

Gladwell, Malcolm. 2008. "Most Likely to Succeed." *The New Yorker* (December 15). www.newyorker.com/magazine/2008/12/15/most-likely-to-succeed-malcolm-gladwell.

Goodbread, Chase. 2016. "J.J. Watt Has Fun with Negatives from His Draft Scouting Report." *College Football 24/7* (February 4). www.nfl.com/news/story/0ap3000000632276/article/jj-watt-has-fun-with-negatives-from-his-draft-scouting-report.

Kaylor, Jimmie. 2015. "NFL Stars verses Then: How These Stars Looked in College." *Sports Cheat Sheet* (August 22). www.cheatsheet.com/sports/how-were-todays-most-famous-nfl-players-rated-in-college.html/?a=viewall.

Kertscher, Tom. 2016. "Walk-Ons despite the Odds." *On Wisconsin Magazine*. http://onwisconsin.uwalumni.com/features/walk-ons-despite-the-odds/.

Kilgore, Adam. 2015. "All Football, Bill Belichick Leaves His Narrative to His Friends and Enemies." *The Washington Post* (September 9). www.washingtonpost.com/sports/redskins/all-football-bill-belichick-leaves-his-narrative-to-his-friends-and-enemies/2015/09/09/ad68398a-566b-11e5-8bb1-b488d231bba2_story.html.

Koen, Jessie, Ute-Christine Klehe, Annelies E.M. Van Vianen, Jelena Zikic, and Aukje Nauta. 2010. "Job-search Strategies and Reemployment Quality: The Impact of Career Adaptability." *Journal of Vocational Behavior* 62 (August). https://yorkspace.library.yorku.ca/xmlui/bitstream/handle/10315/6306/HRM0033.pdf?sequence=1&origin=publication_detail.

Land of Basketball.com. 2016. "Dennis Rodman." www.landofbasketball.com/nba_players/r/dennis_rodman.htm.

Lickerman, Alex. 2012. "The Power of Delaying Gratification." *Psychology Today* (July 29). www.psychologytoday.com/blog/happiness-in-world/201207/the-power-delaying-gratification.

Macan, Therese. 2009. "The Employment Interview: A Review of Current Studies and Directions for Future Research." *Human Resource Management Review*: 1–16.

Molloy, Brian. 2017. "Personal Commentary." *HockeyDB.com*. 2011. "Brown University All-time Player Roster." www.hockeydb.com/ihdb/stats/display_players.php?tmi=5039.

MSG Presentations. 2017. "Hiring Strategies Followed by Organizations." www.managementstudyguide.com/managing-employee-performance.htm.

NFL.com. 2016. "Scouting Combine: Jimmy Graham" (February 22–29). www.nfl.com/combine/profiles/jimmy-graham?id=497236.

Ohebsion, Rodney. 2016. "Mr. Very Irrelevant." *rodneyohebsian.com*. www.rodneyohebsion.com/kurt-warner.htm.

O'Sullivan, John. 2013. "Our Biggest Mistake: Talent Selection Instead of Talent Identification." *Changing the Game Project* (December 9). http://changingthegameproject.com/our-biggest-mistake-talent-selection-instead-of-talent-identification/.

O'Sullivan, John. 2015. "The Perils of Single-Sport Participation." *Changing the Game Project* (January 25). http://changingthegameproject.com/the-perils-of-single-sport-participation/.

Oswego State University of New York. 2016. "Oswego State Athletics Hall of Fame." http://oswegolakers.com/hof.aspx?hof=21&path=&kiosk=.

Rivals.com. 2007. "JJ Watt." https://n.rivals.com/content/prospects/2007/jj-watt-11356.

Silverman, Irwin. 2003. "Gender Differences in Delay of Gratification: A Meta-Analysis." *Sex Roles* 49 (November): 451–469.

WNBA. 2009. "Shock Signs OU Standout Courtney Paris." www.wnba.com/archive/wnba/shock/shock_signs_oklahoma_sooner_courtney_paris.html.

Zak, Michaels. 2015. "Top 20 Elite Athletes Who Weren't Noticed in High School." *TheSporster* (August 25). www.thesportster.com/entertainment/top-20-elite-athletes-who-werent-noticed-in-high-school/.

7

A New Playbook: The Challenge of Retirement from Professional Sports

Since childhood, pro athletes have survived and thrived in a lengthy sequence of organized sports programs. Retirement, however, is quite a different challenge. George Earl Koonce, Jr. spent nine years playing linebacker for the Green Bay Packers and the Seattle Sea Hawks. After retiring he earned a Ph.D. in sports administration at Marquette University and then took several administrative positions at universities (Borsellino 2015; Getlen 2014; *Pro Football Reference* 2017).

In his paper about NFL players' retirement, Koonce indicated that while involved in the game they had possessed structure in their lives. He wrote, "In college, a player's day is scheduled from morning to night. In the pros, strict guidelines are set for the majority of the day. This structure is essential for success on and off the field. Essentially, a playbook is not just provided for on the field, but for off the field as well." Koonce described a typical day from mini-camp, with the scheduled events beginning at 6:15 a.m. and extending until 7:15 p.m. (Koonce 2013, 319–20).

Then, often suddenly, the playing days are finished, and individuals experience an abrupt change. Koonce explained, "Unfortunately, when the player exits sport, the structure and support does not carry over. This is a time when the player has to take charge and design a playbook for his own life. Essentially, he has to recruit a 'new team' and make decisions regarding how to proceed in this next phase of life" (Koonce 2013, 320).

That's the burning issue—how to proceed with life after sports. Early sociological research on retirement in general emphasized many experts' decided preference for disengagement—withdrawal of elderly job holders from the work world, with such a move proving productive both for a smoothly functioning society and the retirees' healthy aging (Cumming and Henry 1961). Such an outcome, however, received little support from either the general public or retirees (Mabry and Bengston 2005), and it seems particularly inapplicable to ex-athletes, who are much younger than most retirees.

George Koonce's idea of developing a new playbook, in fact, suggests quite the opposite of disengagement. *Engagement* is the establishment of social bonds in the areas of work, family relations, and friendship patterns, with individuals committing to the process to differing extents (Hochshild 1975, 567). For retiring athletes the loss of engagement from their sport and its social world can be painful and perplexing. Gaining a new playbook suggests a type of new engagement that bears at least some resemblance to the life they were forced to forsake.

A study of 27 former professional athletes living in Colorado produced several reasons why they found retirement from sports particularly difficult. For instance, an ex-football player explained, "I think the main thing that most guys—and me included ... I think we want to find something we can approach with the same passion we had in playing football. It's the intensity and passion that it takes to play professional football is absolutely amazing. Probably of anything you miss, it's just that" (Drahota and Eitzen 1998, 275). In business a former pro basketball player often felt completely on his own. In contrast, when competing "... no matter how bad things got, you knew you could look around the locker room and ... that you were going through it with somebody else. *That I miss!*" (Drahota and Eitzen 1998, 275). The nearby Box 7.1 examines the emotional struggle retiring pro athletes often encounter.

As George Koonce indicated, retirement from pro sports requires new playbooks—new roles with a distinct sense of how to produce self-satisfying engagement. It seems probable that positive outcomes are more likely to materialize when ex-athletes find new roles with which they feel comfortable and where they either are already prepared to do the work or can feasibly obtain the appropriate skills and information.

BOX 7.1

Retiring Pro Athletes and the Specter of Depression

Ample testimony suggests that pro athletes often find retirement acutely painful. Robert Laura, a money manager and expert on retirement, interviewed many prominent athletes and was convinced that the psychological aspect of pro athletes' retirement is very important, indicating that its influence on revamping the playbook is indisputable and that it requires at least as much attention as financial matters. Laura suggested that the psychological side emphasizes engagement, which "includes finding ways to replace your work-identity, managing your time and family relationships, and maintaining your mental and physical health" (Laura 2012).

Depression, a state of gloom and withdrawal from previously pursued activities, is both commonplace and destructive, potentially hindering people's ability to function at work and elsewhere (American Psychiatric Association 2017). Athletes often suggest that a prime source of depression is the impossibility of replacement for the public performance of a role that was so exciting and engaging. "There aren't many jobs that you retire from where you get to prove that you are the very best of the best in front of thousands and thousands of people every night," said former NHL all-star Al Iafrate (Laura 2012).

In the retirement setting, many ex-athletes feel disengaged, finding their lives tedious, even distressing, especially if their finances have become precarious. Their self-esteem can plummet, and they are likely to feel that they are letting down family and friends. Tight end Eddie "Boo" Williams, who spent four years with the New Orleans Saints, summed up his feelings. "I felt like I was a big disappointment to people. I felt like I was less than a man because of the things I was doing and how I couldn't really provide for my family like I used to. It was tough feeling like you're 3-foot-nothing when you're 6-foot-5. I felt like I didn't have anybody to turn to [who could] understand the things I was going through. I was at the point that I just wanted to end it all." He nearly did, driving to nearby railroad tracks, lying down, and waiting for a train to end his life. However, two passers-by saved him, and Williams eventually began the demanding but ultimately rewarding task of engaging once more, producing a new playbook (Trotter 2015).

Sources indicate that depression is common among retired professional athletes in a variety of sports (Baillie 1993; Johnson 2016; Nanowski 2017). A sports journalist focused on a list of 20 prominent pro athletes who suffered depression; they came from eight different sports (Harmer 2015). It is uncertain how widespread depression is among ex-NFL players. Former Packers offensive lineman Aaron Taylor said, "It'd be easier to start with which ones do NOT have depression. Observationally, it's a significant percentage. It varies by degree, obviously, but everyone struggles" (Trotter 2015).

> It can be difficult to find evidence of those struggles since the retirees themselves often aren't cooperative. Traditionally pro athletes have taken the allegedly strong, silent route, believing that "'real men' do not need help and acknowledging vulnerable emotions such as sadness, grief or fear indicate[s] weakness" (Johnson 2016). That approach leaves a depression-ridden individual alone, without help, hardly an effective starting point for restoring mental health.
>
> The times, however, are changing. Nowadays a major strategy for protecting ex-pro athletes from depression is to have a plan for life after sports, making essential changes including the location of one or more new occupational roles that, if not as compelling as the former role in pro sports, nonetheless provide a satisfying sense of engagement.
>
> Unlike many people who when leaving a job can find another in the same field, pro athletes are eventually forced to realize that age and injury eliminate the chances to keep playing. Psychologically and economically, they need to make an abrupt switch in work roles. Exit counseling can help, along with group therapy involving peers undergoing the same experience of coming to grips with the necessity to move beyond their identity as athletes and to understand and accept the accompanying grief. Such steps can make a huge difference for avoiding depression and other adverse effects of sports retirement (Goldberg 2012).
>
> NFL Hall of Famer Deion Sanders, whose post-retirement engagement has been energetic, concluded, "It's important to walk away from the game and not have the game walk away from you because when the game walks away from you it can damage you mentally" (Laura 2012).
>
> Boo Williams is well aware of the damage that can occur in players' post-retirement years. Whenever he hears the names of several ex-NFL players whose depression drove them to suicide, he shudders, knowing how close he came to joining them. "Depression is real," he says. "Guys are out there thinking about killing themselves every day. I mean, not too long ago I reached out to one of my friends, a former teammate, just to reach out, just to check on him and see how he was doing. He called me back and told me that God must've made me call him. I asked him why, and the answer was that he was sitting down with a .45 in his lap, contemplating blowing his brains out. That just made me cringe, because I was at that point one time. I know what he was feeling ... And it's just a part of the game that you wish that wasn't there" (Trotter 2015).

Players' Adjustment to Post-retirement Challenges

The problems pro athletes face at the end of careers often go back to their earlier years. As Chapter 3 indicated, officials in top college sports programs often are uncommitted to helping recruits develop educational credentials that will qualify them for the work world. Instead coaches' frequent emphasis is to maintain a 2.0 GPA, keeping athletes eligible, and that is the extent of the interest in their schooling. Writing about a talented basketball player, a journalist asserted, "But no adult, not even, it appears, his own mother, seems to have demonstrated more than a passing interest in his education. As long as he stroked jumpers and took jagged, high-leaping dashes to the hoop, all was fine" (Powell 2016).

Not only are retiring pros often unprepared educationally, but some have serious money problems, which can drastically affect their lives. A study of 2,016 NFL players drafted between 1996 and 2003 found that after 12 years of retirement, about 16 percent had filed for bankruptcy, meaning that they lacked the funds to pay their debts (Bradford 2012; Carlson, Kim, Lusardi, and Camerer 2015, 381–83). That outcome is impressive if not astounding. With such newsworthy topics, exaggerated claims sometimes emerge. Widespread references drawing from claims in a *Sports Illustrated* article indicated that after two years about 78 percent of NFL and after five years 60 percent of NBA players go bankrupt in retirement, but no specific sources are cited to support those numbers (Steinberg 2015; Torre 2009). The authors of the NFL study tersely addressed the discrepancy. They wrote, "The result of our comprehensive research on bankruptcy risk among NFL players is quite different from a widely-cited *Sports Illustrated* article, which reported that 78 percent of former NFL players are bankrupt or under 'financial stress' within two years of retirement ... After two years of retirement, only about 1.9 percent of players in our sample have filed for bankruptcy" (Carlson, Kim, Lusardi, and Camerer 2015, 384).

The *Sports Illustrated* article aside, many reputable journalists indicate that bankruptcy and financial insecurity are quite common among pro sports retirees. Furthermore the NFL study concluded that players who stayed in the game longer and had greater earnings were as often the victims of economic distress as those with fewer years in the league (Carlson, Kim, Lusardi, and Camerer 2015, 382). In addition, celebrity athletes are well represented in the various media stories about retired athletes' financial woes (Osborn 2015).

The following set of threatening factors can come into play for retirees in the leading professional sports, suggesting that both during and after their athletic careers, some of these individuals are trapped in lifestyles that can lead to financial downfall and impede effective engagement in both work and other challenging areas:

- No or inadequate financial counseling. Like most young adults, pro athletes often know little or nothing about such issues as developing budgets and making investments. Competent agents and other advisers urge their clients to choose an established financial adviser. However, many NFL players are approached on campus by unknown individuals offering to help with their finances and then when chosen ask their clients for a power of attorney, allowing them the right to make investments or withdraw money without the players' permission.
- Financial assistance for family and friends. Many athletes find themselves supporting a costly entourage, involving family, extended family, various friends, and others. Antoine Walker, a three-time NBA all star, supposedly provided financial assistance to about 70 people in the course of his 13-year career.
- Divorce. It can require extensive court costs and dissipate funds, often leaving active athletes with no more than half their earnings because of the drain of alimony and child support. *The New York Times*, *Sports Illustrated*, and other sources indicate that between 60 and 80 percent of professional athletes divorce at some point, well above the nation's approximate 50-percent rate. If they have more than one divorce, obviously the drain is much greater.
- Largely unrestrained spending habits. Players often fail to recognize that substantial income is a temporary condition, which injury or release from a team can abruptly end.
- Failure to plan for life after playing sports. Pro athletes often don't take advantage of a lengthy offseason providing the chance to start to obtain key information and contacts for initiating productive engagement in their retirement years (Bradford 2012; Kadlec 2016; Lariviere 2014; Satter 2014; Steinberg 2015).

Some pro athletes escape these pitfalls. Adonal Foyle, who played 13 years in the NBA, scrupulously avoided the dangers listed above. He came from a small Caribbean island, where he was scouted as a teenager and was brought to the US, living with a foster family whom he acknowledged taught him to be smart with money. Drafted by Golden State, he made the rookie minimum for the first three years but then signed a four-year, $16 million contract. Foyle developed a firm outlook on the norms governing his earnings—never considering the money he made as reflective of his personal value and always realizing that each NBA contract could be his last. Foyle was the only member of the team who didn't drive an expensive car, buying a Toyota 4Runner his rookie year because "It was what I could afford." He didn't purchase such items as jewelry and designer clothes, which would invariably depreciate in value. Foyle tried to share his approach, sometimes accosting younger players with the critical need to develop a sound financial plan (Callahan 2015).

While issues involving money can be troublesome, some pro sports retirees have faced more destructive conditions—in particular, NFL players victimized by concussions. As previously noted, the NFL reached a settlement with ex-NFL players, who could establish that their symptoms from CTE and other diseases related to head injuries were the result of league play. The settlement will cover 65 years and will cost the NFL about $1 billion (Belson 2016; Groves 2017; Mihoces and Axon 2015).

With that huge payment in play, a number of companies, most notably Validus in Tampa, Florida, have mobilized to provide care for the ex-NFL pros with CTE and other forms of dementia. Validus has planned to build facilities over five years in or near 33 NFL cities. The luxurious individual live-in units will feature beds and bathrooms to accommodate these large residents and also decorations that will serve to remind them of their days in the game. As a result of the NFL settlement, ex-players who suffer the effects of dementia from head blows will be eligible for the league's 88 Plan, which provides $130,000 a year and should cover Validus's yearly fee (Belson 2016).

In recent years the medical and public attention paid to the impact of concussions on NFL players has increased enormously, with research making a major contribution. For instance, studies have found that concussions are a major source of depression. An investigation of 1,617

Leonard Marshall, who played 12 years in the NFL, appeared in Los Angeles at the premiere of the film Concussion, *which told the story of research linking concussions in the NFL to CTE. Marshall, who has early signs of the disease, will donate his brain to CTE research. (Source: Featureflash Photo Agency / Shutterstock.com)*

retired NFL members indicated that 14.7 percent suffered moderate to severe depression (Schwenk, Gorenflo, Dopp, and Hipple 2007). A more detailed study of 1,044 ex-NFL players revealed that over a nine-year interval respondents with many concussions were much more likely to have suffered depression than their counterparts who had received few such injuries—for instance, a 3 percent likelihood of depression in the "no concussions" category reaching 26.8 percent in the 10+ grouping (Kerr, Marshall, and Harding 2012). Another study of 42 retired NFL players displayed a similar relationship between number of concussions and the presence of depression (Didehbani, Cullum, Mansinghani, Conover, and Hart 2013). Such research can provide a growing body of useful information about the relationship between concussions and depression, strongly suggesting the utility of curtailing these interrelated hazards.

Overall, however, a substantial number of retiring pro athletes are healthy enough to undertake the production of new occupational playbooks.

Successful Post-career Employment

The experts running programs for former pro athletes fully recognize the engagement challenges their clients face, knowing that many of them need to develop a new, focused approach, learning to avoid the set of previously listed habitual pitfalls. Organizations like the Business Management and Entrepreneurial Program, a cooperative venture of the Wharton School of Business and the National Football League, spell out values and norms the ex-pros need to adopt. In the course of six years, about 220 athletes completed the program. Morvarid Taheripour, the director, commented on the participants' commitment. "They are like sponges. Everything we tell them, they can't get enough, honestly," said Taheripour. "Many guys come in and say, 'You know, I want to make a difference and I want to be known for something besides the number on my jersey. I just need to know how'" (Hadavi 2011).

The NHL has had a similar program called "Life after Hockey" for retiring players, but its seminars have not proved useful in assisting players to take a productive next step. Mathieu Schneider, the head of the NHL Players' Association, suggested that until recently the problem had been that with years of disruption in the players' association itself, the retirement issue has received limited attention.

To remedy the situation, the players' association has revised its approach. Officials researched how various sports in other countries prepared players for retirement, and they learned something interesting—that active athletes who became engaged in retirement preparation often ended up improving their level of pro performance. This finding opposed the widespread belief among North American pro athletes that if they did anything besides focusing on their play, then their production would decline. The NHL Players' Association, while low-key about telling its members what they should do, is trying to get an initial group of players interested in retirement preparation and then encouraging those individuals to engage others. When asked whether players had time for such activity, Schneider, who had 20 years of pro hockey experience, said, "Having played as long as I did and knowing players' schedules, there's absolutely time … You're on the road for half the year and that's when you do have down time to put some effort and thought into these kind of programs" (Pack 2015). A carefully planned regimen for active players, in short, might provide a fruitful background for eventual preparation for retirement.

With the support of programs or on their own, former pros can find a number of jobs related to sports available to them. Most require a bachelor's degree and some knowledge of the prospective positions. Such jobs include:

- Public-relations specialists managing the image that a team projects. Individuals performing this job for college or pro teams need to keep following accounts about the team or players, sometimes providing timely damage control if necessary and making all possible efforts to maintain or restore a positive public perception.
- Sports administrators serving from high-school programs to pro leagues. Sports-management bachelor's degree programs are available in many colleges, including online access. Duties are wide-ranging and include fundraising, organizing the various events in which the team engages, including its games, and running the sports facilities, which are large and costly in both big-time college sports and the pros.
- Marketing managers, a position requiring a degree in either marketing or communications. Individuals are employed by either college or pro teams in a front office job as part of a team focusing on media commercials, game giveaways, and advertising. For individuals who completed a degree in either marketing or communi-

cations and have both a yen and a skill for sales, it can be a very satisfying job.
- Sports psychologists, currently highly valued because of the increase in athletes and ex-athletes suffering both physical and psychological disability. The profession generally requires more than a bachelor's degree, turning out to be highly rewarding for former athletes, who have knowledge, including first-hand information, about issues like concussions and retirement that can provide much-needed assistance to active or retiring athletes (Clapp 2015).

An additional occupation is a well-known choice for some retired athletes.
- Broadcasters, who provide play-by-play commentary or supply observations and analysis about teams' tactics and strategy. This is a common choice for popular former athletes, but there is a large supply of candidates, keeping salaries down; while well-known stars can earn up to $5 million dollars a year, lesser names receive much lower pay, averaging about $42,000 a year broadcasting games for colleges, minor-league clubs, or high schools (Gardner 2013; Sports Management Degrees 2016).

Women's participation in sportcasting has steadily increased over time, with WNBA TV teams primarily composed of women, many of whom are former WNBA players. The 2017 *ESPN* schedule of 16 WNBA regular-season games featured three individuals on the broadcasting team, including two women, one of whom served as analyst – the renowned Rebecca Lobo, a long-time TV personality and a Hall of Fame inductee (*WNBA* 2017).

Ex-WNBA players are more likely to participate as reporters or program hosts than analysts (Dybas 2015). A similar trend occurs in broadcasting other sports. When retired fastpitch superstar Jessica Mendoza became an analyst for MLB on national television, she recognized the importance of the step. She said, "If you're going to put me in the booth, make sure it's because I'm good enough to be there." Mendoza realized it was a significant moment. "I think it's important for young girls and for women to see that I'm not just going to open this door and walk through it," she said. "I'm going to keep it open" (de la Cretaz 2016).

While some well-known retiring athletes go into broadcasting, a selected few have additional options.

Celebrities' Opportunities

A very few ex-athletes have access to a privileged set of business connections—for instance, working relations with prominent companies producing highly lucrative deals. In the 1980s and 1990s, Michael Jordan was unprecedentedly successful, collaborating with the sports giant Nike to sell the Jordan Brand which made $2.6 billion in 2014 and brought Jordan $100 million during the year, more than any athlete had ever obtained. Nike provides the largest share of Jordan's earnings, but he also has lucrative sponsorship deals with Gatorade, Haines, Upper Deck, 2K Sports, and Five Star Fragrances that greatly exceed most other sports celebrities' income. With the exploding values of NBA franchises, Jordan's ownership of the Charlotte Hornets along with his other assets has made him a billionaire (Badenhausen 2015).

While no former team-sport athlete is as wealthy as Jordan, ex-NFL star Michael Strahan has been financially successful and popular as a TV personality. Many observers consider Strahan a perfect fit for television, but he indicated that engagement in TV programming has been nerve-racking. "Of course I get jitters," he said. "I think people see you on TV every day and think it's natural and it just happens. Definitely, you become more comfortable — you're not as nervous — but you definitely have bouts of nervousness every day" (Belson 2014).

Like Strahan, Shaquille O'Neal is a regular on TV, part of TNT's multiple Emmy-winning show *Inside the NBA*, which, while dispensing some useful information about the league and its game, always contributes humor. O'Neal, the chief funnyman on the show, chose TNT over an offer from *ESPN* because the format was more enjoyable. He said, "TNT allows you to be yourself and have a good time and joke around" (Boudway 2014).

A similar humorous standard also prevails when O'Neal engages in selling a long line of products. His business partners feel he should be able to present with a wink—whether it's breakfast cereal, video games, skin lotion, men's jewelry, cars, auto insurance, fruit punch, or designer clothes. Since 2012 O'Neal and his associates have held a yearly Shaq Summit, where companies (19 in 2014) come to him to demonstrate how they would use him to help sell their products (Boudway 2014; Groves 2014; Levine 2016). Every time O'Neal meets with a new creative team, he says, "Give me what you want, and I'll Shaq it up." To "Shaq it up" means providing what in O'Neal's estimation the commercial seems to require. It might mean simply a demure smile, which could end up featured on 11 million boxes of Fruity Pebbles (Cacciola 2014). Arguably O'Neal appears to have engaged as effectively in his humor-laden TV and pitchman roles as he did when performing the skills required to be a Hall of Fame center.

Lebron James seems headed for a retirement that makes him a worthy financial rival of his previously mentioned elders. According to his agent Maverick Carter, James's lifetime shoe deal with Nike is worth over $1 billion (Green 2016). Other highly productive endorsement deals have involved McDonald's, Coca-Cola, Kia, and State Farm (*Forbes* 2016).

While ex-players who become head coaches and managers do not enter the Michael Jordan or Shaquille O'Neal income brackets, their transition from playing to coaching/managing can represent an important contribution to their sports.

Ex-pros Still Linked Directly to the Game

In MLB some general patterns about ex-players who become managers and coaches are apparent. About a quarter of the individuals who competed between 1950 and 1965 became either major-league managers or coaches. Compared to other ex-players, those who became coaches or managers tended to stay longer as active players in the major and minor leagues and also had better batting averages. Middle-infielders and catchers have been more likely to become coaches or managers than other players (Singell 1991, 80–81). In fact, one position has been particularly notable in this regard.

In the 80 years extending between 1901 and 1981, 338 men managed major-league baseball teams. Ex-catchers, with a 21.6 percentage of the total, showed the greatest likelihood of becoming managers (Schumann 2016). In modern times many catchers have continued to make the shift, often proving very successful in the transition. In 2012 the managers for all four teams in the League Championship Series were catchers (Ringolsby 2012). Then in the 2014 season, nine managers were catchers. When one member of the group, Mike Matheny of the St. Louis Cardinals, was asked why the transition from catcher to manager was fairly common, he said, "It's just part of the job description for a catcher, where you have to understand what's going on with the pitching, what's going on with certain defenses, what's going on with the status of the team and understanding the game situation, not just my space right here" (Grathoff 2014). In other words, Matheny was suggesting that the perceptions required for and the norms governing a catcher's job required him to address the range of issues, or at least most of those, with which managers needed to grapple, inevitably supplying on-the-job manager training for athletes performing that role. For catchers, it seems safe to say, engagement in many of the concrete realities with which managers needed to deal was already well underway. Such a continuity between a player's and a coach's role also occurs in other sports.

In the NBA, point guards like catchers in MLB are particularly inclined to become head coaches. In 2014, in fact, 15 of the NBA head coaches had been point guards in either college or the pros. Mark Jackson, who had played point guard at both levels and had been a NBA head coach, said, "The ones that really played the position, whether they want to coach or not, they have coached." Jackson added, "The real point guards in this league, to me, are like quarterbacks in the NFL. They're picking and choosing what to do, who to go to, who to stay away from, what reads [are there], how to react by being an extension of the coach on the floor" (Robbins 2014). Like Mike Matheny commenting on catchers' relationship to baseball managers, Jackson was suggesting that point guards have already encountered many of the challenges head coaches are likely to face. In both pro sports, in short, continuity exists between the role requirements of players and managers/coaches.

While some former point guards such as Red Holtzman, Lenny Wilkins, and Larry Brown had fine coaching records, others, including Hall of Fame NBA performers like Bob Cousy, Isaiah Thomas, and Magic Johnson, were clearly unsuccessful (Wade 2013).

Then there is Becky Hammon, the point guard who went undrafted by the WNBA but persevered, developing fine passing and shooting skills that eventually qualified her as one of the top 20 players in the league's history (D'Arcangelo 2016; *Sports Illustrated* 2011). In 2014 the NBA

San Antonio Spurs hired her as an assistant coach. "I very much look forward to the addition of Becky Hammon to our staff," head coach Greg Popovich said in a statement released by the team. "Having observed her working with our team this past season, I'm confident her basketball IQ, work ethic, and interpersonal skills will be a great benefit to the Spurs" (*ESPN* 2014). In 2015 as head coach of the Spurs' team in the NBA summer league, Hammon validated Popovich's confidence by winning the title (Silverstein 2017).

Finally there's a third prominent pro player position that might seem to be a promising source of coaches—NFL quarterbacking. After all, the athletes filling this position are distinctly team leaders who study game film involving both their own offenses and opposing defenses and fill a prominent role in executing the plays that can defeat other teams. Seldom, however, do they pursue coaching. One reason might be that in many cases they don't need to—that their prominence can readily allow them to become TV commentators or, perhaps better still financially, to take advantage of lucrative business connections.

New York Liberty's point guard Becky Hammon (with the ball) had a playing experience effectively preparing her for a coaching career. At the time this photo was taken, however, she had no idea that she would be the first woman to coach in the NBA. (Source: Joyce Boffert / Shutterstock.com)

But what about top quarterbacks who chose to become head coaches? The evidence is decisive, with five Hall of Famers—Sammy Baugh, Bob Waterfield, Norm Van Brocklin, Otto Graham, and Bart Starr—winning fewer than half their NFL games as coaches. In fact, the only quarterback who had a decent pro playing career and went on to become a successful decade-long NFL coach was Tom Flores, who led the Oakland Raiders to two Super Bowl victories (Daly 2011). It might be that the two roles in question draw on distinctly dissimilar attributes—that the combination of leading one's teammates and playing a physically active role in the process requires somewhat different skills from the sideline provision of ideas and incentive. Is it possible that being good at the first might actually make it less likely the player is competent at the second? Possibly ex-quarterbacks might find effective engagement as coaches a frustrating or elusive reality when excluded from taking part in the action.

Compared to the four major leagues, the WNBA is much newer, with fewer opportunities to employ former players. In 2016 only six former WNBA members were either coaches or in other team leadership positions in the league (Favor 2016). However, as the WNBA matures, that number is likely to increase, perhaps substantially, as teams recognize that many of these retirees bring valuable knowledge and experience to the pro game, potentially promoting players' engagement both on and off the field.

Retired WNBA members are now eligible for the NBA Assistant Coaches Program, providing participants an unusual opportunity to learn about the basic content of the role and the functions it performs (*Legendsofbasketball.com* 2016; Zwerling 2016). One participant in the program praised its contribution. "It covers every aspect of coaching, learning how to handle a rotation, learning how to make in-game decisions, game-to-game adjustments. It helps you ... just to manage a team" (Zwerling 2016).

Besides coaching, some ex-WNBA members enter league front offices. In 2017 former star Tamika Catchings took a position with the Indiana Fever as director of player programs and franchise development, a position providing access to members of the Indiana Pacers (NBA), the Indiana Fever (WNBA), and the Fort Wayne Mad Ants (NBAG League). "The thing I ... love the most is the interaction with the players," she said. "Just being able to help them figure out what they want to be good at outside of basketball, and the things that truly interest them." Using Koonce's phrase, Catchings added, "We focus a lot on having a game plan for your life" (Lester 2017).

Meanwhile during that season, the New York Liberty hired former WNBA star Swin Cash to fill a similar position, and elsewhere in the league two other former players took front-office jobs. Commenting on the four hirings, WNBA president Lisa Borders referred to the ex-players' continuing high-quality engagement when she declared, "It is wonderful to see that players who have been so impactful on the game's growth and the league's endurance remain connected to the WNBA as they transition to their next career phase," she said. "The same passion, perseverance, and purpose that fueled their success on the court will serve them well in their front-office roles" (*USA Today* 2017).

Besides coaching and front-office activity, retired players can contribute to their game in countless ways, some of which might be quite unexpected. For instance, in March of 2016, ex-soccer player Brandi Chastain, who scored the winning penalty kick in the World Cup Final in 1999, decided to donate her brain to the CTE Center at Boston University, where pioneer research in the study of concussions and CTE has been taking place. Chastain indicated that while observers sometimes pointed out that she and her renowned teammates had left a legacy for players who followed, she added, "This would be a more substantial legacy—something that could protect and save some kids, and to enhance and lift up soccer in a way that it hasn't before" (Branch 2016, B8).

The interviewer reminded Chastain that she had said that there were probably about a half-dozen occasions when she received possible concussions after heading the ball but continued to play, and given that reality did she ever suffer what might be considered concussion effects? She replied, "There are definitely days when I turn a corner and I'm like, 'Why did I come into this room?'" At that point she would catch herself wondering whether previous concussions were starting to take their toll (Branch 2016, B13).

Brandi Chastain can wonder about the future impact of those probable concussions. The rest of us can also look ahead and speculate about various elusive issues that have run through these chapters. Consider just a few of the more significant ones:

- In the years ahead, what norms will parents endorse when dealing with their children in organized sports? Obviously their choices can make a substantial difference, supporting their children with strategic information, advice, and encouragement or alternatively pushing them to nearly uninterrupted competition and play and accelerating the likelihood of burnout or injury.
- Will family income continue to be a major factor in affecting athletes' progress in their sport, with those better off financially proving distinctly advantaged in coaching and competitive opportunities? Will government's and/or private organizations' contributions significantly alleviate that persistent inequality? If such changes occur, will the percentage of African Americans in MLB once again increase appreciably?
- What about the frequency of injuries—concussions and all the others? At the moment the NFL's protocol for examining players who received a head injury sometimes meets with resistance from teams impatient to get individuals back into the game (*New York Times* 2018). Will the NFL establish new normative guidelines that significantly limit head injuries? Will NHL procedures and outcomes improve?
- Then what about an evaluation of the standards for teams' recruitment, ranging from the peewee variety up to the major leagues? Will the examiners become more accurate in their assessments and, if so, what steps will prove particularly useful? Even at the top professional level, the current evaluations are often deficient, either hyping candidates who prove inadequate at their assigned positions or failing to reveal players who eventually emerge as diamonds in the rough.
- And what about women's team sports? Selected women's college basketball teams are consistently drawing both fans and media coverage much more extensively than several decades ago. Other college sports for women have also become more popular. However, in spite of the WNBA's two-decade existence, no women's professional league has been able to establish what is clearly a lasting presence in

the American sports scene. In the years ahead, it remains to be seen whether that situation changes substantially for the WNBA and/or other women's pro leagues.
- Will the various major leagues be able to develop alone or in partnership more effective work-preparation programs for their retirees? Will (a) selected league's or leagues' guidelines prove so effective that they become the models for the others? Summary 7.1 lists various positive situations that can prove helpful for pros nearing or reaching retirement.

SUMMARY 7.1

Various Situations That Can Assist Retiring Pro Athletes' Transition to New Roles

- Colleges' increased emphasis on providing top athletes more effective educational programs, thus preparing them well for work after sports.
- The development of plans such as the one by the NHL Players' Association to provide guidelines to active players for work and life in general after retirement from the game.
- Ex-pro athletes' participation in programs helping them avoid a variety of financial and personal pitfalls.
- Opportunities for ex-players to enter a number of sports-related jobs.
- Instances generally of celebrity ex-athletes who become successful as TV announcers and in a variety of businesses.
- Players in selected positions developing familiarity with the perceptions and norms that can promote their becoming managers, head coaches, or coaches.

The upcoming discussion shifts the focus from pro to college athletes, recognizing that they too go through an advancement stage to retirement at the end of their sports careers.

Conclusion: A Preliminary Look at College Athletes' Retirement

While this chapter has focused on pro athletes' retirement from elite leagues, most team players never reach such exalted heights. Many retire after college, and preliminary research on the topic is instructive, including an initial investigation involving a comparison group of nonathletes.

Gallup Poll and Purdue University collaborated on a survey that compared athletes and nonathletes for both their careers and their outlooks on life following graduation. The report commissioned by the NCAA involved students who graduated between 1970 and 2014. There were 712 Division I, 206 Division II, and 523 Division III athletes along with 22,813 nonathletes from the same colleges and universities. Athletes displayed a 2 percent higher likelihood of both graduating college in four years and entering graduate programs. Compared to the nonathletes, the athletes were more likely to be employed and also more likely to describe themselves as engaged in the workplace; a significant discrepancy existed between female athletes versus female nonathletes in the workforce — 48 percent for athletes to 41 percent for nonathletes (New 2016).

In addition, the athletes were more likely than the nonathletes to have a distinctly greater sense of well-being — about 8 or 9 percent in the four areas of purposive, social, community, and physical well-being (Busteed and Ray 2016). Linked to well-being, the athletes were more likely to have had what the researchers called "key campus experiences"—for instance, 67 percent to 59 percent among nonathletes indicated that they had professors "who cared about [them] as a person" (New 2016).

In later research it would be interesting to delve into whether participation in college sports influences athletes' sense of well-being, whether those going out for college teams simply possess traits that provide them a stronger sense of well-being than nonathletes, or perhaps both.

While the Gallup report was generally optimistic about college athletes' experience, David Ridpath, a professor of sports administration at Ohio University, criticized it as "incomplete." He added, "Comparing all athletes to the general student population is not really a fair comparison." Ridpath said, "There's a lot of statistical dancing here. The report pulls out ... a lot of positive things, but we also know ... that many Division I football and men's basketball players are not very engaged in the classroom, and that they graduate at lower rates. I think we have to really look at the devil in these details" (New 2016).

Those details, of course, are significant and are discussed in Chapter 3. In light of Ridpath's comments, it seems useful to speculate about broad sets of perceptions college athletes might maintain. Many of the top-level pro prospects, with the support of such agents of socialization as coaches, teammates, and family members, prioritize engagement in their sport, concluding that college attendance is just a means to the end of maximizing preparation for a professional career. In distinct contrast, less prominent athletes with no illusions about pro careers are likely to assume a different point of view, recognizing that sports life after college will hardly provide a career and that their time in college is essential as preparation for some career outside of sports.

Overall, this survey seems to uncover some important, previously unexamined data about the college athletic experience. Hopefully it will encourage further research, perhaps reaching back to younger age groups and starting to assess the impact that earlier sports programs have had on athletes' lives.

Summary

George Koonce, Jr., the former NFL player and college administrator, argued that on retiring from pro sports, athletes need to adopt another playbook, finding a new structure that replaces the previous one—new directions for engagement that can be very challenging for many ex-athletes. With adjustment difficult, the onset of depression is distinctly possible.

In many instances former pro athletes are poorly prepared to face the work world, with money matters a common problem for many of them. An encouraging reality, however, is that some former pros are well organized, following careful plans involving both their choices for work and their budgeting. A distinctly difficult issue some retirees face is the onset of CTE or some other lethal disease caused by concussions; because of the settlement with the NFL, victims can now get substantial payments, with Validus providing comfortable, even luxurious residential facilities.

Both the NFL and the NHL have training programs preparing former pros for the work world, and the NHL players' association has endorsed the idea developed in other countries that retiring athletes can benefit from starting their post-career preparation while still active players.

Various sports-related jobs are available to retired pro athletes. They include public-relations specialists, sports administrators, marketing managers, sports psychologists, and sportscasters. Selected celebrity ex-athletes like Michael Jordan, Michael Strahan, and Shaquille O'Neal have become both hugely popular and very wealthy.

As coaches, managers, and administrators, some ex-pros have stayed close to the game they once played. Those who filled selected positions—catchers and infielders in MLB and point guards in the NBA—have been particularly likely to enter managing or coaching. Few former WNBA players have entered coaching, but their access to the NBA Assistant Coaches Program might enlarge those numbers.

Retired pro athletes sometimes contribute in original ways—for instance, Brandy Chastain's effort to alleviate the lethal effects of concussions. In the text a follow-up discussion takes a somewhat similar tack, addressing some important, often troubling issues that are likely to remain prominent for sports programs in the years ahead.

Class Discussion Questions

1. Is it is more difficult and emotionally taxing to retire from a pro sport than from most other occupations? Compare.
2. If you were involved in a program preparing retiring pro athletes for roles after sports, what is an issue involving engagement that you would emphasize? Provide an example, offering detail about the engagement process.
3. Are there ex-athletes who seem to have made a particularly healthy adjustment to retirement, both for themselves and others close to them? Comment on them, perhaps referring to but not simply focusing on celebrities.
4. Looking at one sport, discuss the relationship between being a player and becoming a successful coach or manager. Does it seem surprising that so many former catchers and point guards become managers and head coaches?
5. Discuss women's retirement from pro sports, bringing in the WNBA but, if possible, offering information about other pro and college leagues. What about the prospect of more Becky Hammons, moving into men's coaching at either the pro or college level?

References

American Psychiatric Association. 2017. "What Is Depression?" www.psychiatry.org/patients-families/depression/what-is-depression.
Baillie, Patrick H.F. 1993. "Understanding Retirement from Sports: Therapeutic Ideas for Helping Athletes in Transition." *The Counseling Psychologist* 21 (July).
Badenhausen, Kurt. 2015. "Michael Jordan Leads the Highest-Paid Retired Athletes 2015." *Forbes* (March 11). www.forbes.com/sites/kurtbadenhausen/2015/03/11/michael-jordan-leads-the-highest-paid-retired-athletes-2015/#2fb117f2155e.
Battochio, Randy C., Robert J. Schinke, Danny L. Battochio, Wayne Halliwell, and Gershon Tenenbaum. 2010. "The Adaptation Process of National Hockey League Players." *Journal of Clinical Sport Psychology* 4: 282–301.
Belson, Ken. 2014. "Strahan Still in Spotlight Ahead of Hall of Fame Induction." *The New York Times* (August 1). www.nytimes.com/2014/08/02/sports/football/into-the-hall-of-fame-with-michael-strahan.html?_r=0.
Belson, Ken. 2016. "Dementia Care, Tailored to N.F.L. Retirees." *The New York Times* (March 23). www.nytimes.com/2016/03/23/sports/dementia-care-tailored-to-nfl-retirees.html.
Borsellino, Drew. 2015. "Former East Carolina Linebacker Creates Software for College Athletes." *Football Matters* (June 30). http://footballmatters.org/former-east-carolina-linebacker-creates-software-for-college-athletes/.
Boudway, Ira. 2014. "Shaq's Still Scoring in Retirement." *Bloomberg Business* (April 24). www.bloomberg.com/bw/articles/2014-04-24/retired-shaquille-oneal-cultivates-fame-and-fortune.
Bradford, Harry. 2012. "NBA Players Now Forced to Put Some Money into Retirement Fund." *Huffington Post* (July 12). www.huffingtonpost.com/2012/07/12/nba-retirement-funds_n_1669312.html.
Branch, John. 2016. "A Star Isn't Done Helping Her Sport." *The New York Times* (March 4): B8+.
Busteed, Brandon, and Julie Ray. 2016. "Former Student Athletes Are Winners in Well-Being." *Gallup-Purdue Index 2015 Report on College Graduates* (February 17). www.gallup.com/poll/189206/former-student-athletes-winners.aspx.
Cacciola, Scott. 2014. "Looming Even Larger Off the Court: Shaquille O'Neal Has His Hands Full as a Pitchman." *The New York Times* (October 8). www.nytimes.com/2014/10/09/sports/basketball/shaquille-oneal-has-his-hands-full-as-a-pitchman.html.
Callahan, Maureen. 2015. "How Pro Athletes Lose Everything." *New York Post* (June 14). http://nypost.com/2015/06/14/how-pro-athletes-lose-everything-buying-cars-jewels-and-pet-tigers/.
Carlson, Kyle, Joshua Kim, Annamaria Lusardi, and Colin F. Camerer. 2015. "Bankruptcy Rates among NFL Players with Short-Lived Income Spikes." *American Economic Review: Papers & Proceedings* 105: 381–385. http://authors.library.caltech.edu/56772/2/aer.p20151038.pdf.
Clapp, Brian. 2015. "6 Sports Careers to Consider after Your Pro-Athlete Dream Falls Short." *Work in Sports.com* (June 15). www.workinsports.com/blog/6-sports-careers-to-consider-after-your-pro-athlete-dream-falls-short/.

Cumming, Elaine, and William E. Henry. 1961. *Growing Old: The Process of Disengagement.* New York: Basic Books.
Daly, Dan. 2011. "It's No Snap Going from Quarterback to Head Coach." *The Washington Times* (November 3). www.washingtontimes.com/news/2011/nov/3/daly-its-no-snap-going-from-qb-to-head-coach-in-nf/?page=all.
D'Arcangelo, Lyndsey. 2016. "For WNBA Undrafted, an Uncertain Road to Follow Hammon." *Excelle Sports* (July 7). www.excellesports.com/news/for-wnba-undrafted-follow-hammon/.
de la Cretaz, Britni. 2016. "*ESPN*'s Jessica Mendoza Just Wants to Call Some Postseason Baseball." *RollingStone* (October 5). www.rollingstone.com/sports/jessica-mendoza-on-being-espn-first-woman-mlb-analyst-w443391.
Didehbani, Nyaz, C. Munro Cullum, Sethesh Mansinghani, Heather Conover, and John Hart, Jr. 2013. "Depressive Symptoms and Concussions in Aging Retired NFL Players." *Archives of Clinical Neuropsychology* 28: 418–424.
Drahota, Jo Anne Tremaine, and Stanley Eitzen. 1998. "The Role Exit of Professional Athletes." *Sociology of Sport* 15: 263–278.
Dybas, Todd. 2015. "The Conversation: The Mystics' Kara Lawson on Being Home, Broadcasting and the WNBA." *The Washington Times* (June 17). www.washingtontimes.com/news/2015/jun/17/conversation-mystics-kara-lawson-broadcasting-wnba/.
Ebaugh, Helen Rose. 1988. *Becoming an Ex: The Process of Role Exit.* Chicago, IL: University of Chicago Press.
ESPN. 2014. "Becky Hammon Hired to Spurs' Staff." (August 5). www.espn.com/nba/story/_/id/11312366/becky-hammon-hired-san-antonio-spurs.
Favor, Sue. 2016. "To Grow the WNBA, Get More Former Players Involved." *Women's Hoops World* (September 10). http://womenshoopsworld.com/2016/09/10/to-grow-the-wnba-get-more-former-players-involved/.
Forbes. 2016. "Lebron James Net Worth." www.therichest.com/celebnetworth/athletes/nba/lebron-james-net-worth/.
Gardner, Eriq. 2013. "Ray Lewis, Shannon Sharpe and the Business of Turning Athletes into Broadcasters." *The Hollywood Reporter* (August 15). www.hollywoodreporter.com/news/ray-lewis-shannon-sharpe-business-604890.
Getlen, Larry. 2014. "How the NFL Leaves Players Broke and Broken." *New York Post* (December 14). http://nypost.com/2014/12/14/how-the-nfl-leaves-players-broken-and-broke/.
Goldberg, Carey. 2012. "When You Lose Your Sport, What Happens to Your Self?" *wbur* (May 11). http://commonhealth.legacy.wbur.org/2012/05/former-athletes-group.
Grathoff, Pete. 2014. "The Rundown: Why Are So Many Managers Former Catchers?" *The Kansas City Star* (June 28). www.kansascity.com/sports/mlb/kansas-city-royals/article640324.html.
Green, Mark Anthony. 2016. "Meet Maverick Carter, the Man Behind Lebron's Billion-Dollar Nike Deal." *GQ* (May 17). www.gq.com/story/lebron-james-nike-deal-bilion-maverick-carter.
Groves, Roger. 2014. "Every Smart Athlete Should Be a Shaq-Tag." *Forbes* (October 11). www.forbes.com/sites/rogergroves/2014/10/11/every-smart-athletes-should-be-a-shaq-tag/#449e6ac15ab8.
Groves, Roger. 2017. "Study That 110 Out Of 111 NFL Former Players Have Brain Disease May Hurt Future Player Lawsuits." *Forbes* (July 26). www.forbes.com/sites/

rogergroves/2017/07/26/study-that-110-out-of-111-nfl-former-players-have-brain-disease-may-hurt-future-player-lawsuits/#6bac01467efd.

Hadavi, Tala. 2011. "Professional Athletes Prepare for Life after Sports." *Voice of America* (March 20). www.voanews.com/content/professional-athletes-prepare-for-life-after-sports-118377659/163130.html.

Harmer, Alfie Potts. 2015. "Top 20 Athletes Who Have Battled Depression." *TheSportster* (August 27). www.thesportster.com/entertainment/top-20-athletes-who-have-battled-depression/.

Hochshild, Arlie Russell. 1975. "Disengagement Theory: A Critique and a Proposal." *American Sociological Review* (October): 553–569.

Johnson II, Bill. 2016. "Beyond the Game: Athletes and Depression." *The Huffington Post* (September 23). www.huffingtonpost.com/bill-johnson-ii/beyond-winning-and-losing-athletes-and-depression_b_8174292.html.

Kadlec, Dan. 2016. "What You Have in Common with Bankrupt Pro Athletes." *Money* (June 10). http://time.com/money/4362102/bankrupt-athletes-lessons-for-you/.

Kerr, Zachary Y., Stephen W. Marshall, and Herndon P. Harding. 2012. "Nine-Year Risk of Depression Diagnosis Increases with Increasing Self-Reported Concussions in Retired Professional Football Players." *The American Journal of Sports Medicine* 40 (August). *Journals.sagepub.com/doi/abs/10.1177/0363546512456193.*

Koonce, Jr., George Earl. 2013. "Role Transition of National Football League Retired Athletes: A Grounded Theory Approach." *Marquette Sports Law Review* 23 (Spring): 249–338.

Lariviere, David. 2014. "Divorce, Not Domestic Violence, Is Biggest Issue at Home for Professional Athletes." *SportsMoney* (August 15). www.forbes.com/sites/davidlariviere/2014/08/15/divorce-not-domestic-violence-is-biggest-issue-at-home-for-professional-athletes/#3b9054222fc1.

Laura, Robert. 2012. "How Star Athletes Deal with Retirement." *Forbes* (May 22). www.forbes.com/sites/robertlaura/2012/05/22/how-star-athletes-deal-with-retirement/#2eb6e81e2a4e.

Legendsofbasketball.com. 2016. "Legends Spotlight: Andrea Stinson." www.legendsofbasketball.com/legends-spotlight-andrea-stinson/.

Lester, Justin. 2017. "Tamika Catchings Feeling Right at Home in New Front Office Role." WNBA (April 20). www.wnba.com/news/tamika-catchings-feeling-right-home-new-front-office-role/.

Levine, Daniel S. 2016. "Shaquille O'Neal's Net Worth: 5 Fast Facts You Need to Know." *heavy* (October 28). http://heavy.com/sports/2016/06/shaquille-o-neal-shaq-lyft-net-worth-nba-basketball/.

Mabry, J. Beth, and Vern Bengston. 2005. "Disengagement Theory," pp. 113–117 in E. Palmore, L. Branch, and D. Harris (eds.), *Encyclopedia of Ageism.* New York: Haworth Press.

Mihoces, Gary, and Rachel Axon. 2015. "Judge Approves Settlement—at Least $900 Million—to NFL Concussion Lawsuits." *USA Today* (April 22). www.usatoday.com/story/sports/nfl/2015/04/22/concussion-related-lawsuits-judge-settlement-nfl/26199011/.

Nanowski, Natalie. 2017. "59% of Former NHLers Studied Prone to Psychiatric Disorders, Research Suggests." *CBCNews* (April 16). www.cbc.ca/news/canada/toronto/nhl-concussions-head-trauma-hockey-study-1.4071584.

New, Jake. 2016. "Athletes' Postcollege Outcomes." *The Wall Street Journal* (February 17). www.insidehighered.com/news/2016/02/17/athletes-are-more-likely-be-find-employment-be-engaged-work-study-suggests.

New York Times. 2018. "NFL, NFLPA to Review How Panthers Handled Hit on QB Newton" (January 8). www.nytimes.com/aponline/2018/01/08/sports/football/ap-fbn-panthers-newton-hit.html?_r=0.

Osborn, Katy. 2015. "10 Insanely Rich Pro Athletes Humbled by Financial Ruin." *Money* (August 13). http://time.com/money/3983997/famous-athletes-bankruptcy/.

Pack, Joe. 2015. "Exiting the Game: How the NHL's New Retirement Program Aims to Help Players in Their Post-Hockey Life." *Vice Sports* (September 8). https://sports.vice.com/ca/article/exiting-the-game-how-the-nhls-new-retirement-program-aims-to-help-players-in-their-post-hockey-life.

Powell, Michael. 2016. "The Tragedy of a Hall of Fame Coach and His Star Recruit." *The New York Times* (March 2). www.nytimes.com/2016/03/06/sports/ncaabasketball/smu-keith-frazier-larry-brown-corruption.html.

Pro Football Reference. 2017. "George Koonce, Jr." www.pro-football-reference.com/players/K/KoonGe20.htm.

Ringolsby, Tracy. 2012. "Former Catchers Excel In Managerial Roles." *MLB.com* (October 14). http://m.mlb.com/news/article/39805144/.

Robbins, Josh. 2014. "Former Point Guards Dominate NBA Head-Coaching Ranks." *Orlando Sentinel* (March 17). http://articles.orlandosentinel.com/2014-03-17/sports/os-nba-head-coach-point-guards-0318-20140317_1_mark-jackson-atlanta-hawks-scott-brooks.

Satter, Marlene. 2014. "High Divorce Rate Pays Havoc on Athletes' Retirement." *BenefitsPro* (August 14). www.benefitspro.com/2014/08/14/high-divorce-rate-plays-havoc-on-athletes-retireme.

Schumann, Richard. 2016. "Playing Background of Major League Managers." *Society for American Baseball Research*. http://research.sabr.org/journals/playing-background-of-major-league-managers.

Schwenk, T.L., D.W. Gorenflo, R.R. Dopp, and E. Hipple. 2007. "Depression and Pain in Retired Football Players." *Medicine and Science in Sports and Exercise* 39 (April): 599–605.

Silverstein, Adam. 2017. "Report: Spurs Assistant Becky Hammon Turns Down Florida Gators Job." *Only Gators* (March 27). www.onlygators.com/03/27/2017/report-spurs-assistant-becky-hammon-turns-down-florida-gators-job/.

Singell, Jr., Larry D. 1991. "Baseball-Specific Human Capital: Why Good but Not Great Players Are More Likely to Coach in the Major Leagues." *Southern Economic Journal* 58: 77–86.

Sports Illustrated. 2011. "WNBA's Top 15 Players of All Time" (July 23). www.si.com/nba/photos/2011/07/23wnbas-top-15-players-of-all-time.

Sports Management Degrees. 2016. "How Much Does a Sports Broadcaster Make?" www.sports-management-degrees.com/faq/how-much-does-a-broadcast-sports-announcer-make/.

Steinberg, Leigh. 2015. "5 Reasons Why 80 Percent of NFL Players Go Broke." *Forbes* (February 9). www.forbes.com/sites/leighsteinberg/2015/02/09/5-reasons-why-80-of-retired-nfl-players-go-broke/#117ca7474e36.

Torre, Pablo S. 2009. "How (and Why) Athletes Go Broke." *Sports Illustrated* (March 23). www.si.com/vault/2009/03/23/105789480/how-and-why-athletes-go-broke.

Trotter, Jim. 2015. "Depression Prevalent in Ex-players." *ESPN* (February 25). www.espn.com/nfl/story/_/page/hotread150225/depression-suicide-raise-issue-mental-health-former-nfl-players.

USA Today. 2017. "Former WNBA Players Getting Front Office Position." (June 6). www.usatoday.com/story/sports/wnba/2017/06/06/former-wnba-players-getting-front-office-positions/102541560/.

Wade, Jared. 2013. "How Former Point Guards Fare as NBA Coaches." *Bleacher Report* (June 20). http://bleacherreport.com/articles/1679465-how-former-point-guards-fare-as-nba-head-coaches.

WNBA. 2017. "ESPN To Broadcast 16 Regular-Season WNBA Games, Entire Post-season" (April 27). www.wnba.com/news/2017-wnba-schedule-espn-broadcast/.

Zwerling, Jared. 2016. "Inside the NBPA's Coaching Program, the Training Spot for Luke Walton and 90 Others." NBPA (June 30). http://nbpa.com/inside-the-nbpas-coaching-program-the-training-spot-for-luke-walton-and-90-others/.

SOCIOLOGICAL CONCEPTS AND IDEAS

Adaptation—A process by which individuals understand the setting in which they are located and learn to perform their role effectively within it

Advancement stage—The stage at which a player moves out of the sports program in which he or she is currently involved

Agents of socialization—Parents, coaches, teachers, siblings, teammates, and other individuals and groups who are an important source of socialization for players

Career—An occupation pursued for a significant number of years and offering prospects for advancement

Cultural fit—A job candidate's ability and willingness to commit to the beliefs, attitudes, and activities that an organization maintains, thereby making it likely that the prospect in question will relate well with others in the workplace and prove productive on the job

Delayed gratification—The ability to resist an immediate reward, recognizing that the benefit will be greater if the individual in question restrains the impulse to obtain an immediate positive result

Dysfunction—A disruptive or destabilizing consequence produced by an individual, group, or situation and affecting a particular group or society

Engagement—The establishment of social bonds in the areas of work, family relations, and friendship patterns, with individuals committing to the process to differing extents

Enrollment/recruitment stage—The opening stage in an organized sports program, with a distinction drawn between enrollment and recruitment

Formal organization—A group possessing clearly stated rules, well defined members' roles, and distinct objectives

History and biography—Mills's reference to sociology involving the interrelationship between history, broadly defined, and biography, namely the individual; a perspective maintained throughout the chapters

Institutional logics—Beliefs about what actions are appropriate and acceptable for an organization's members, with an inevitable focus on actions deemed rewarding for themselves and for the organization

Investment years—According to coaching experts, at age 16 elite athletes reaching the point at which they specialize in one sport, perhaps even a single position in that sport

Niche sports—Professional sports suffering structural vulnerability

Norm—A standard of required or expected behavior

Play (According to George Herbert Mead)—A process in which individuals become attuned to others' roles, learning the rights and obligations involved

Relative age effect—Coaches' preference to recruit and to provide more playing time for slightly older children in a sport, with this early advantage sometimes carried into more advanced programs including the professional ranks

Retention stage—The stage of a sports program in which a player is an active member with motivation, commitment, and agents of socialization affecting his/her effectiveness

Role—The expected behaviors associated with a particular social position

Sampling years—Coaching experts' claim that children aged 6 to 12 in organized sports programs should emphasize having fun

Social class—A large category of people who possess similar levels of income, education, and occupational prestige ranking

Socialization—A lifelong process of becoming a social being, learning the necessary culture content and behavior in the course of relations with people who supply influential guidance about established societal standards

Social reproduction—The process by which people in certain categories, such as social classes, have differing access to the valuable resources that influence the transmission of inequality from one generation to the next

Specializing years—Coaching experts' contention that while at ages 13 to 15 having fun is still important, a growing emphasis exists on effective competition and performance, encouraging both motivation and commitment in programs' retention stage

Sports triangle—Parents, coaches, and athletes together forming interconnections to promote young players' development

Structural vulnerability—A condition where individuals, groups, or larger units like sports leagues face deficiencies in such critical resources as money, productive networks, or strategic information, inhibiting positive outcomes for the participants and the organizations to which they belong

Talent identification—An assessment of players' future performance based on an examination of their current skills and attributes, with scouts and/or coaches taking into account such developmental factors as physical growth, coaching effectiveness, and a willingness to train hard

Talent selection—A choice of prospects whose observable skills and attributes make it likely that they will fit in and immediately contribute to the team's success

The 10,000 hour rule—The claim that 10,000 hours of so-called "deliberate practice" in the preteen years are required to become world-class in any endeavor

The unwinding—A society-wide process starting to reveal itself in mid-20th century America where many of the structures that bound people together—communities, businesses, farms, political organizations, religious groups, colleges, schools, and more—began to decline and sometimes collapse, losing vitality for and control over their members

INDEX

Entries presented in bold are defined in the text and also in the Sociological Ideas and Concepts section at the end of the book.

50–mile rule 156
1994 World Cup 215–16

A
Abbott, Monica 227
adaptation 156, 157, 164, 167, 169, 172, 173, 177, 179, 180–81, 182, 184, 188, 189, 191, 195, 197
advancement stage in sports programs 20–24, 128, 187, 285
agents of socialization 17–19, 24, 35, 42–45, 66, 75, 79, 81, 82, 95, 125–27, 128, 133, 138, 140, 164, 166, 169, 181, 182, 185, 195, 286–87
Alabama football team 114–16, 123
Alou, Felipe 140
Alou, Matty 140
Amateur Athletic Union (AAU) 71, 72–73
American Basketball League 213–14
American Hockey League 112, 137, 138
American League 9

Arena, Bruce 224
Arlotta, John 232
Auriemma, Geno 104–05

B
Balague, Gloria 16–17
Baugh, Sammy 282
Bautista, José 141
Beckham, David 216–17
Belichick, Bill 242, 254–55
Belichick, Steve 254, 260
Belisle, Mitch 89
Berube, Carla 104
Bilas, Jay 154–55
Beane, Billy 177–78
Benedict, David 109
Bennett, Sam 179
Bird, Larry 163
Blass, Steve 195–96
Bledsoe, Drew 243
Boeheim, Jim 121
Borders, Lisa 283

299

Borland, Chris 191
Boston Celtics' racial integration 162–63
Bowen, Bruce 24–26
bowing out: the close of a big-league career 187–194
Bradley, Michael 222
Brady, Tom 50, 82, 242, 243, 244, 254
Branch, Taylor 142–43
Brandt, Gil 255
Braud, Kayla 127
Broshuis, Garrett 132
Brown, Dale 143
Brown, Larry 280
Brown, Mack 169
Brown, Walter 162
Bryant, Kobe 117
Buehrle, Mark 75
burnout in organized sports 13–14, 46–47, 54, 55, 89, 90, 93, 284
buscones 139
Butler, Kristen 228

C

Cabrera, Miguel 184, 189
Calipari, John 118
Cammalieri, Mike 135
Campo Las Palmas 3 Dominican
Canadian Hockey League (CHL) 112, 136,
careers 164; in the major leagues 164–66, 189, 195
Carroll, Pete 256
Carter, Cris 50
Cash, Swin 283
Catchings, Tamika 225, 282–83
Center for the Study of Race and Equity in Education 122
chances of college and high-school athletes reaching the major leagues 165
Chastain, Brandi 283
Chavez, Larry 89–90
Chelios, Chris 188

chronic traumatic encephalopathy (CTE) 190–91, 273
Clifton, Nat "Sweetwater" 162–63
closing out the pro career 187–95
clustering of majors in Division I football 121–22
coaches' influence 19–20, 44–45, 84–88, 94, 125, 126–27, 133, 253–59
college athletes' just treatment 142–43
college baseball 129–31
college hockey 112, 134–36, 138
Collingsworth, Cris 246
commitment in sports programs 16–17, 24, 75, 84, 91, 127, 164–65, 211
community context of teen play 76–78
concussions 49–50, 190–93, 195, 196, 273–75, 283, 284
Conte, Antonio 222–23
Cooper, Chuck 162
Côté, Jean 51, 82, 84–85, 95
Couch, Tim 262
Cousy, Bob 163, 280
Crosby, Sidney 76–77, 173, 245
Cross, Randy 50
Cuddyer, Michael 193–94
cultural fit 244, 246, 250, 253, 257, 259, 262
Curry, Ayesha 197
Curry, Dell 53, 79
Curry, Steph 53, 79, 184, 197

D

Daniel, Chase 262
Danowski, Matt 230
Davies, Peter 190
Davis, Doug 134
Davis, Malcolm 193
Dean, Dizzy 111
DeBoer, Kathy 248
Deines, Kate 229
delayed gratification 255
Delle Donne, Elena 65–66, 89
Dempsey, Clint 222

DePodesta, Paul 178
Dieffenbach, Kristen 93
DiMaggio, Joe 193
disengagement 268
Dominican baseball 138–41
Dominican baseball academies 139–40
Dorsch, Travis 91
draft and related issues 167–78
Dunn, Crystal 230
Dwyer-Shick, Sarah 87
Dye, Tony 188
Dyer, Don 252
Dykstra, Lauren 258–59
dysfunction 46, 83, 89, 90, 120, 121, 123

E

early sports specialization, 38, 49, 51–55, 56, 65, 84, 85, 89–90, 93, 95
Eichel, Jack 135–36
Eisenhower, Dwight D. 36, 39, 57
elite teen athletes 88–89, 94
Elmendorf, Kyle 85–86
Elmore, Sean 89
Emmert, Mark 122–23
engagement 268, 269, 270, 272, 275–76, 280, 282, 283, 287
English college sports 3
enrollment/recruitment stage in sports programs 12–13, 23, 25, 40–42, 88, 106, 107, 114, 115, 121, 131, 135, 156, 173, 179, 244
Esiason, Boomer 190
ex-pros as coaches and managers 279–82
ex-pros' successful post-career employment 275–83

F

Fair, Ray C. 90
fastpitch softball: guidance and instruction in pitching and hitting 126–27
fighting in hockey 112–13, 137, 192
Finocchio, Dave 197

first encounters with big-time pro sports 178–181
First-Year Players' Draft 168
Fisk, Carlton 182
Fleener, Coby 116
Flood, Curt 157
Flores, Tom 282
Football Ball Subdivision (FBS) 108, 114–17
formal organizations 2–3, 67, 71, 105, 113
Forzano, Rick 254
Foyle, Adonal 272–73
Fultz, Markelle 92

G

Gallup Poll and Purdue University survey on athletes and nonathletes 286
Garagiola, Joe 167
Garnett, Kevin 117, 155
Gates, Antonio 248
Gehrig, Lou 129–30
Geller, Marshall 213
Gent, Pete 255
Girardi, Dan 245, 259
Gladwell, Malcolm 38, 53
Glanville, Doug 178–79, 183
Glasnow, Tyler 131–32
Gmelch, George 132
Golden State Warriors 184–85, 189, 195
Gonzalez, Tony 248
Graham, Jimmy 247–48, 255, 259
Graham, Otto 282
Granderson, Curtis 130–31, 163–64
Green, Christine 11
Green, Cornell 255
Greene, Joe 196
Gretzky, Wayne 173
Grier, Chris 170
growth of big-time college sports 106–10

H

Hagerman, Bonnie 142
Haith, Frank 255
Hamm, Brian 184

Hamm, Mia 52, 218, 242
Hammon, Becky 280–81
Harbaugh, Jim 107
Harlem Globe Trotters 162
Hayhurst, Dirk 133
Heath, Tobin 229
Henry, Thierry 217
Hermann, Julie 109
Herren, Chris 171–72
historical growth of high-school sports 67–74
history and biography 211
history of minor-league hockey 112–13
history of minor-league baseball 110–12
Holtzman, Red 280
Howard, Desmond 143
Howard, Dwight 155
Howe, Gordie 188
Hriniak, Walt 182
Huma, Ramogi 166
Hurdle, Clint 131

I

Iafrate, Al 269
IMG Academy 7–8, 11
injuries 46, 47–50, 52, 54, 55, 56, 90–91, 93, 190–91, 193, 284
institutional logics 105–06, 108, 109, 110, 111, 112, 113, 115, 116, 120, 121, 123, 124, 125–26, 129, 136, 137, 139, 159, 211
investment years 51, 84–85, 88, 94

J

Jackson, Mark 280
Jagger, Mick 215
James, Bill 111–12, 177
James, Lebron 26, 117, 154–55; 173, 186–87, 242, 279
Jay Z 155
Jean Côté's three roughly age-related stages in the development of young athletes; sampling years 51, 84; specializing years 84; investment years 84

Johnson, Magic 280
Jones, Chipper 183
Jones, Cobi 216
Jordan, Marcus 79
Jordan, Michael 79, 252, 260, 278

K

Kaminsky, Frank 172
Keane, Robby 217
Kellor, Frances A. 69–70
Kempf, Cheri 217
Kennedy, John 37, 39
Kenny, Bonny 65–66
Kerr, Steve 79
King, Martin Luther, Jr. 160
Kiraly, Karch 220
Kissinger, Henry 215
Klinsmann, Jurgen 222–24
Koonce, Jr., George Earl 267–68, 283
Krzyzewski, Mike 118
Kurkjian, Tim 187

L

LaBeau, Allison 257–58
Landis, Kenesaw Mountain 9
Lalas, Alexi 216, 223
Lasorda, Tommy 175
Laura, Robert 269
Ledo, Ricky 171
Lee, Spike 155
Leslie, Lisa 213
Licht, Jason 243
Lindsey, John 134
Little League baseball 7, 35–36, 39, 72
Lloyd, Earl 162
Lobo, Rebecca 104–05, 213, 277
Low, Peter 260–61

M

Maddon, Joe 52, 132
major juniors (in hockey) 112, 134, 136, 138
Major-league athletes' type of birth location 77–78

INDEX

Major League Baseball (MLB) 8–9, 72, 156–58, 159–60
Major-league draft 167–78, 188
Major League Lacrosse 219, 230–31
Major League Soccer (MLS) 9, 216–17, 220–23, 231, 232
Mantle, Mickey 167
Marichal, Juan 140
Martinez, Pedro 140
Matheny, Mike 280
Mathis, Robert 190
Mays, Willie 167
McCaig, Rob 136
McCoughtry, Angel 226
McDavid, Connor 173
Mead, George Herbert 185
Mendoza, Jessica 277
Messersmith, Andy 157
Messier, Mark 185–86
Mikan, George 162
Mills, C. Wright IX, 2
minor-league baseball 110–12, 130–34, 137–41
minor-league hockey 112–13, 134–38
MLB Hall of Fame inductees 181–82
Molloy, Brian 252–53
Mondesí, Raúl 140
Montador, Steve 192
Moore, Maya 224
motivation in sports programs 14–15, 24, 84
Motley, Marion 161
Muhammad, Shabazz 171
muscular Christians 5, 35, 39

N

National Basketball Association (NBA) 159, 161–63, 213–14
National Football League's (NFL) 160–61
National Hockey League (NHL) 158–59
National Lacrosse League (NLL) 219

National League 8–9, 156
National Pro Fastpitch (NPF) 210, 217–18, 226–28, 231
National Women's Soccer League (NWSL) 211, 218–19, 228–30, 231
NBA Assistant Coaches Program 282
NBA Draft Combine 170–71, 176
NBA Gatorade (G) League 113
NBA players with NBA fathers 2
NBA draft effectiveness 170–172
NCAA investigation of big-time college recruiting violations 122–23
NCAA v. Board of Regents of the University of Oklahoma 1–2, 107
Nelson, Jordy 250
Newman, Terence 183–84
NFL players' concussion settlement with the league 191–92, 273
NFL Scouting Combine 170
NHL Players' Association 275–76
niche sports 9, 210–11, 216, 218, 220, 228, 229, 230, 231, 232
norms 42, 43, 54, 55, 56, 70, 85–86, 94, 105, 117, 120, 132, 257, 273, 275, 280, 284, 285
North American Soccer League (NASL) 214–15

O

Obama, Barack 37
Ohio State's national championship football team and early specialization in sports 95
on-base average 178
O'Neal, Shaquille 278–79
one-and-done basketball 117–20, 123, 134
Original Six 158, 159
Orr, Bobby 158
Ortiz, David 140, 141
Osterman, Cat 226
O'Sullivan, John 1; 253
Ovechkin, Alex 245

P

Packer, George 2
Pannell, Rob 231
Parents' income affects children's enrollment in organized sports 40, 78, 80–81
parents' influence on children's sports programs 18–19, 28, 35, 42–44
Paris, Courtney 256–57
Patton, Amber 210–11
Pelé 214–215
Petersen, Chris 169
Phoenix, Wynter 133
Piazza, Mike 175–76
Pippin, Scottie 251–52
play 185, 189, 195
playing time 41, 45, 55, 56
Popovich, Greg 281
Pop Warner football 7, 35, 39
Portland Thorns 229
Positive Coaching Alliance 46–47
President's Council on Youth Fitness 36–39, 57
pro athletes' birth cities 77–78
pro athletes' post-retirement depression 269–70, 273–275
pro athletes' post-retirement divorce 272
pro athletes' post-retirement employment 275–85
pro athletes' post-retirement financial problems 271–72, 285
pro players abroad 219–20, 221–24, 225–26, 227–28, 230
pro team leaders 185–86
Pujols, Albert 140
Puritans' outlook on sports 5, 11

Q

quarterbacks' importance in the NFL 186
Quinn, Brady 180

R

Rabil, Paul 230–31
Racial integration of major leagues 159–62
Ramos, Tab 216
Rampone, Christie 219
Rashad, Ahmad 155
Redfern, Jill 257–58
Redford, Robert 215
Rehbein, Dick 243
relative age effect 174–75
Reichardt, Rick 167–68
retention stage in sports programs 13–20, 23, 42, 51, 75, 78, 84–85, 88, 89, 121, 135, 156, 164–65, 178, 179, 181, 184, 188–89
retired college athletes' post-retirement careers 285–86
Reyna, Claudio 216
Rice, Condoleezza 123
Rice, Glen, Jr. 170–71
Ricketts, Keilani 227
Rickey, Branch 110, 160
Riddle, Ryan 180
Ridpath, David 286
Riley, Pat 26, 172
Rivals.com 169–70, 188
Robinson, Jackie 110, 160
Rockne, Knute 107
Rodgers, Aaron 250
Rodman, Dennis 251
roles 3–4, 25, 51, 66, 67–68, 71, 87, 88, 91, 93, 105, 128, 184, 185, 186, 187, 247, 248, 249, 268, 269, 270, 279, 280, 282, 285
Roosevelt, Theodore 5
Rose, Pete 189
Russell, Bill 163, 194
Ryan, Bo 118

S

Saban, Nick 114–16, 143
sabermetrics 177–78, 188
sampling years 51, 84, 88
Sanders, Deion 270
services ranking high-school athletes in basketball and football 73

shifting from offense to defense or vice versa in different sports 250
Schmidt, Brett 230
Schneider, Mathieu 275, 276
shoe and apparel companies 72–73, 92, 94, 119, 123
Shonka, Don 262
siblings' influence, 18, 81–82, 94
Siebold, Max 127
Silver, Adam 118–19
Slaughter, Enos 111
Smith, Dean 260
Snow, Michelle 226
Soccer, a tough sell in the US 215
social class 2, 78, 80, 94
socialization 17, 35, 52, 195
social reproduction 79, 94
Solo, Hope 211
specializing years 84, 88, 94
sportscasters who are retired pro athletes 277–78
sport journalists' changing role 195–97
sports triangles 18, 24, 42–45
stacked pro football players 161
Staal, Marc 245
Stanford football team's strength program 116–17
Starr, Bart 282
Starsia, Dom 256
Steinfeld, Jake 219
Strahan, Michael 278
structural vulnerability 210–11, 213, 214, 215, 217, 218, 220, 222, 224, 227, 228, 231, 232
survival in the majors 181–87
Swoopes, Sheryl 213

T
Taheripour, Morvarid 275
talent identification 253, 254, 255, 256, 257, 258–59, 260, 262
talent selection 253
Taurasi, Diana 225, 232

Taylor, Aaron 269
teammates' influence 83
technology and pro athletes' skill development 183–84, 189
Telfair, Sebastian 155
Temple University study of major infractions in Division I college sports 121, 123, 124
the reserve clause 156–57, 167
the 10,000 hour rule 38–39, 53–54, 55
The unwinding 2, 77
Thomas, Isaiah 280
Tierney, Trevor 127–28
Title IX 10, 11, 105, 125, 142
Travel teams 18, 52, 54, 55, 65, 71–73, 74, 80, 84, 91–93, 94, 160
Turley, Shannon 116–17

U
underbelly of big-time sports 120–23
United Women's Lacrosse League (UWLL) 219
University of Connecticut women's basketball team 104–05, 124
University of Florida study of summer tournament play 92–93, 94
Urschel, John 191
US male soccer pros' role 221–24
US men's national soccer team 211, 221–24
US women's national soccer team 81–82, 211–212, 232
US Women's National Volleyball Team 220

V
Van Brocklin 282
VanDerveer, Tara 185
Ventura, Yordano 196
Villarreal, Natalie 227
Virgil, Ozzie 138
Visek, Amanda J. 14
volleyball 73–74, 248

W

Walker, Antoine 272
Warner, Curt 245–46, 259
Waterfield, Bob 282
Washington, Kenny 161
Watt, J.J. 248–50, 259
White, Byron Raymond "Whizzer" 1
White, Micaya 248
Wilkins, Lenny 280
Wilkinson, Bud 37
Williams, Boo 269, 270
Williams, Michael 115–16
women coaches 87–88, 125
women ex-pro athletes in sportscasting 277
Women's National Basketball Association (WNBA) 9–10, 212–14, 224–26, 231, 232, 282
Women's Professional League 218, 228
Women's pro volleyball 219–20
Women's United Soccer Association (WUSA) 218
Wynalda, Eric 216

Y

Yıldızoğlu, Ceyhun 257
young athletes' injuries 47–50
young people's physical conditioning over time 56–47